Asymmetric Dependence in Finance

Asymmetric Dependence in Finance

Diversification, Correlation and Portfolio Management in Market Downturns

EDITED BY

JAMIE ALCOCK
STEPHEN SATCHELL

WILEY

This edition first published 2018

© 2018 John Wiley & Sons Ltd

Registered office
John Wiley & Sons Ltd, The Atrium, Southern Gate, Chichester, West Sussex, PO19 8SQ, United Kingdom

For details of our global editorial offices, for customer services and for information about how to apply for permission to reuse the copyright material in this book please see our website at www.wiley.com.

Library of Congress Cataloging-in-Publication Data

Names: Alcock, Jamie, 1971– author. | Satchell, S. (Stephen) author.
Title: Asymmetric dependence in finance : diversification, correlation and
    portfolio management in market downturns / Jamie Alcock, Stephen Satchell.
Description: Hoboken : Wiley, 2018. | Series: Wiley finance | Includes
    bibliographical references and index. |
Identifiers: LCCN 2017039367 (print) | LCCN 2017058043 (ebook) |
    ISBN 9781119289029 (epub) | ISBN 9781119289012 (hardback) |
    ISBN 9781119289005 (ePDF) | ISBN 9781119288992 (e-bk)
Subjects: LCSH: Portfolio management. | BISAC: BUSINESS & ECONOMICS / Finance.
Classification: LCC HG4529.5 (ebook) | LCC HG4529.5 .A43 2018 (print) |
    DDC 332.6—dc23
LC record available at https://lccn.loc.gov/2017039367

Cover Design: Wiley
Cover Image: © thanosquest / Shutterstock

Set in 9/11pt, SabonLTStd by SPi Global, Chennai, India.

Printed and bound by CPI Group (UK) Ltd, Croydon, CR0 4YY

10 9 8 7 6 5 4 3 2 1

To the memory of John Knight

Contents

About the Editors

Dr Jamie Alcock is Associate Professor of Finance at the University of Sydney Business School. He has previously held appointments at the University of Cambridge, Downing College Cambridge and the University of Queensland. He was awarded his PhD by the University of Queensland in 2005. Dr Alcock's research interests include asset pricing, corporate finance and real estate finance. Dr Alcock has published over 40 refereed research articles and reports in high-quality international journals. The quality of Dr Alcock's research has been recognized through multiple international research prizes, including most recently the EPRA Best Paper prize at the 2016 European Real Estate Society conference.

Stephen Satchell is a Life Fellow at Trinity College Cambridge and a Professor of Finance at the University of Sydney. He is the Emeritus Reader in Financial Econometrics at the University of Cambridge and an Honorary Member of the Institute of Actuaries. He specializes in finance and econometrics, on which subjects he has written at least 200 papers. He is an academic advisor and consultant to a wide range of financial institutions covering such areas as actuarial valuation, asset management, risk management and strategy design. Satchell's expertise embraces econometrics, finance, risk measurement and utility theory from both theoretical and empirical viewpoints. Much of his research is motivated by practical issues and his investment work includes style rotation, tactical asset allocation and the properties of trading rules, simulation of option prices and forecasting exchange rates.

Dr Satchell was an Academic Advisor to JP Morgan Asset Management, the Governor of the Bank of Greece and for a year in the Prime Minister's department in London.

Introduction

Asymmetric dependence (hereafter, AD) is usually thought of as a cross-sectional phenomenon. Andrew Patton describes AD as 'stock returns appear to be more highly correlated during market downturns than during market upturns' (Patton, 2004).[1] Thus, at a point in time when the market return is increasing, we might expect to find the correlation between any two stocks to be, on average, lower than the correlation between those same two stocks when the market return is negative. However, the term can also have a time-series interpretation. Thus, it may be that the impact of the current US market on the future UK market may be quantitatively different from the impact of the current UK market on the future US market. This is also a notion of AD that occurs through time. Whilst most of this book addresses the former notion of AD, time-series AD is explored in Chapters 4 and 7.

Readers may think that discussion of AD commenced during the Global Financial Crisis (GFC) of 2007–2009, however scholars have been exploring this topic in finance since the early 1990s. Mathematical statisticians have investigated asymmetric asymptotic tail dependence for much longer. The evidence thus far has found that the cross-sectional correlation between stock returns has generally been much higher during downturns than during upturns. This phenomenon has been observed at the stock and the index level, both within countries and across countries. Whilst less analysis of time-series AD with relation to market states has been carried out, it is highly likely that the results for time-series AD will depend upon the frequency of data observation and the conditioning information set, *inter alia*.

The ideas behind the measurement of AD depend upon computing correlations over subsets of the range of possible values that returns can take. Assuming that the original data comes from a constant correlation distribution, once we truncate the range of values, the conditional correlation will change. This is the idea behind one of the key tools of analysis, the exceedance correlation. To understand the power of this technique, readers should consult Panels A and B on p. 454 of Ang and Chen (2002).[2] The distributional assumptions for the data generating process now become critical. It can be shown that, as we move further into the tails, the exceedance correlation for a multivariate normal distribution tends to zero. Intuitively, this means that multivariate normally distributed random variables approach independence in the tails. Empirical plots in the analysis of AD tend to suggest that, in the lower tail at least, the near independence phenomenon does not occur. Thus we are led to consider other distributions than normality, an approach addressed throughout this book.

The most obvious impact of AD in financial returns is its effect on risk diversification. To understand this, we look at quantitative fund managers whose behaviour is described as follows. They typically use mean-variance analysis to model the trade-off between return and risk. The risk (variance) of a portfolio will depend upon the variances and correlations of the stocks in the portfolio. Optimal investments are chosen based on these numbers. One feature of such mean-variance strategies

---

[1]Patton, A. (2004). On the out-of-sample importance of skewness and asymmetric dependence for asset allocation. *Journal of Financial Econometrics*, 2(1), 130–168.

[2]Ang, A. and Chen, J. (2002). Asymmetric correlations of equity portfolios. *Journal of Financial Economics*, 63(3), 443–494.

is that one often ends up investing in a small number of funds and all other risks are diversified away as idiosyncratic correlations will average out. However, if these correlations tend to one then the averaging process will not eliminate idiosyncratic risks, diversification fails and the optimal positions chosen are no longer optimal. Said another way, risk will be underestimated and hedging strategies will no longer be effective.

The example above is just one case where AD will affect financial decision making. To the extent that AD influences the optimal portfolios of investors, it will clearly also affect the allocation of capital within the broader market and hence the cost of that capital to corporate entities. An understanding of AD as a financial phenomenon is not only important to financial risk managers but also to other senior executives in organizations. Solutions for managing AD are scarce, however Chapter 5 provides some answers to these problems.

This book looks at explanations for the ubiquitous nature of AD. One explanation that is attractive to economists is that AD derives from the preferences (utility functions) of individual market agents. Whilst quadratic preferences typically lead to relatively symmetric behaviour, theories such as loss aversion or disappointment aversion give expected utilities that have built-in asymmetries with respect to future wealth. These preferences and their implications are discussed in Chapter 1. Such structures lead to the pricing of AD, and coupled with suitable dynamic processes for prices will generate AD that, theoretically at least, could be observed in financial markets. Chapter 3 explores the pricing of AD within the US equities market. These chapters discuss non-linearity in utility as a potential source of AD. Another approach that will give similar outcomes is to model the dynamic price processes in non-linear terms. Such an approach is carried out in Chapters 2 and 4.

It is understood that the origins of AD may well have a basis in individual and collective utility. This idea is investigated in Chapter 1, where Jamie Alcock and Anthony Hatherley explore the AD preferences of disappointment-averse investors and how these preferences filter into asset pricing. One of the advantages of the utility approach is that it can be used to define gain and loss measures. The authors develop a new metric to capture AD based upon disappointment aversion and they show how it is able to capture AD in an economic and statistically meaningful manner. They also show that this measure is better able to capture AD than commonly used competing methods. The theory developed in this chapter is subsequently utilized in various ways in Chapters 3 and 9.

One explanation of AD is based on notions of non-linear random variables. Stephen Satchell and Oliver Williams use this framework in Chapter 2 to build a model of a market where an option and a share are both traded, and investors combine these instruments into portfolios. This will lead to AD on future prices. The innovation in this chapter is to use mean-variance preferences that add a certain amount of tractability. This model is then used to assess the factors that determine the size of the commodity trading advisor (CTA) market. This question is of some importance, as CTA returns seem to have declined as the volume of funds invested in them has increased. The above provides another explanation of the occurrence of AD.

In Chapter 3, Jamie Alcock and Anthony Hatherley investigate the pricing of AD. Using a metric developed in Chapter 1, they demonstrate that AD is significantly priced in the market and has a market price approximately 50% of the market price of β risk. In particular, lower-tail dependence has displayed a mostly constant price of 26% of the market risk premium throughout 1989–2015. In contrast, the discount associated with upper-tail dependence has nearly tripled in this time. This changed, however, during the GFC of 2007–2009. These changes through time suggest that both systematic risk and AD should be managed in order to reduce the return impact of market downturns. These findings have substantial implications for the cost of capital, investor expectations, portfolio management and performance assessment.

Chapter 4, by Salman Ahmed, Nandini Srivastava, John Knight and Stephen Satchell, addresses the role of volatility and AD therein and its implications for volatility forecasting. The authors use a novel methodology to deal with the issue that volatility cannot be observed at discrete frequencies. They review the literature and find the most convincing model that they assume to be the true model; this is an EGARCH(1,2) model. They then generate data from this true model to assess which of two commonly used models give better forecasts; a GARCH or stochastic volatility (SV) model. Interestingly, because the SV model captures AD whilst a GARCH model does not, it seems better able to forecast in most instances.

Whilst previous chapters have not directly addressed the question of how a risk manager could manage AD, Chapter 5 by Anthony Hatherley does precisely this. He demonstrates how an investor can hedge upper-tail dependence and lower-tail dependence risk by buying and selling multi-underlying derivatives that are sensitive to implied correlation skew. He also proposes a long–short equity derivative strategy involving corridor variance swaps that provides exposure to aggregate implied AD that is consistent with the adjusted *J*-statistic proposed in Chapter 1. This strategy provides a more direct hedge against the drivers of AD, in contrast to the current practice of simply hedging the effects of AD with volatility derivatives.

In Chapter 6, Mark Lundin and Stephen Satchell use orthant probability-based correlation as a portfolio construction technique. The ideas involved here have a direct link to AD because measures used in this chapter based on orthant probabilities can be thought of as correlations, as discussed earlier. The authors derive some new test results relevant to these problems, which may have wider applications. A *t*-value for orthant correlations is derived so that a *t*-test can be conducted and *p*-values inferred from Student's *t*-distribution. Orthant conditional correlations in the presence of imposed skewness and kurtosis and fixed linear correlations are shown. They conclude with a demonstration that this dependence measure also carries potentially profitable return information.

From our earlier empirical discussion, we know that multivariate normality is not a distributional assumption that leads to the known empirical results of AD. Chapter 7, by Sharon Lee and Geoffrey McLachlan, assumes different distributions to model AD more in line with empirical findings. They consider the application of multivariate non-normal mixture models for modelling the joint distribution of the log returns in a portfolio. Formulas are then derived for some commonly used risk measures, including probability of shortfall (PS), Value-at-Risk (VaR), expected shortfall (ES) and tail-conditional expectation (TCE), based on these models. Their focus is on skew normal and skew *t*-component distributions. These families of distributions are generalizations of the normal distribution and *t*-distribution, respectively, with additional parameters to accommodate skewness and/or heavy tails, rendering them suitable for handling the asymmetric distributional shape of financial data. This approach is demonstrated on a real example of a portfolio of Australian stock returns and the performances of these models are compared to the traditional normal mixture model.

Following on from Chapter 7, multivariate normality cannot be justified by empirical considerations. It does have the advantage that the first two moments define all the higher moments thereby controlling, to some extent, the dimensionality of the problem. By contrast, the uncontrolled use of extra parameters rapidly leads to dimensionality issues. Artem Prokhorov, Stanislav Anatolyev and Renat Khabibullin address this issue in Chapter 8 using a sequential procedure where the joint patterns of asymmetry and dependence are unrestricted, yet the method does not suffer from the curse of dimensionality encountered in non-parametric estimation. They construct a flexible multivariate distribution using tightly parameterized lower-dimensional distributions coupled by a bivariate copula. This effectively replaces a high-dimensional parameter space with many simple estimations of few parameters. They provide theoretical motivation for this estimator as a pseudo-MLE with known asymptotic properties. In an asymmetric GARCH-type application with regional stock indices, the procedure provides an excellent fit when dimensionality is moderate. When dimensionality is high, this procedure remains operational when the conventional method fails.

Previous chapters have discussed the importance of AD in risk management but little has been said about whether AD can be forecasted. In Chapter 9, Jamie Alcock and Petra Andrlikova investigate the question of whether AD characteristics of stock returns are persistent or forecastable and whether AD could be used to forecast future returns. The authors examine the differences between the upper-tail and lower-tail AD and analyse both characteristics independently. Methods involved use ARIMA models to try to understand the patterns and cyclical behaviour of the autocorrelations with a possible extension to the family of GARCH models. They also use out-of-sample empirical asset pricing techniques to explore the AD predictability of stock returns. Broadly, they find that AD does not predict future AD but does predict future returns.

As previous chapters have demonstrated, copulas are a valuable tool in capturing AD, which in turn can be used to construct portfolios. Ba Chu and Stephen Satchell apply these ideas in Chapter 10 by using a copula they call the most entropic canonical copula (MECC). In an empirical study, they focus on an application of the MECC theory to a 'style investing' problem for an investor with a constant relative risk aversion (CRRA) utility function allocating wealth between the Russell 1000 'growth' and 'value' indices. They use the MECC to model the dependence between the indices' returns for their investment strategies. They find the gains from using the MECC are economically and statistically significant, in cases either with or without short-sales constraints.

In the context of managing downside correlations, Jamie Alcock, Timothy Brailsford, Robert Faff and Rand Low examine in Chapter 11 the use of multi-dimensional elliptical and asymmetric copula models to forecast returns for portfolios with 3–12 constituents. They consider the efficient frontiers produced by each model and focus on comparing two methods for incorporating scalable AD structures across asset returns using the Archimedean Clayton copula in an out-of-sample, long-run multi-period setting. For portfolios of higher dimensions, modelling asymmetries within the marginals and the dependence structure with the Clayton canonical vine copula (CVC) consistently produces the highest-ranked outcomes across a range of statistical and economic metrics when compared to other models incorporating elliptical or symmetric dependence structures. Accordingly, the authors conclude that CVC copulas are 'worth it' when managing larger portfolios.

Whilst we have addressed many issues relating to AD, there are too many to comprehensively address in one book. As an example of a topic that is not covered in this book, one might consider the relationship between AD and the time horizon of investment returns. A number of authors have argued that returns over very short horizons should have diffusion-like characteristics and therefore behave like Brownian motion, and hence be normally distributed. Other investigators have invoked time-series central limit theorems to argue that long-horizon returns, being the sum of many short-horizon returns, should approach normality. Since the absence of normality seems a likely requirement for AD, it may well be that AD only occurs over some investment horizons and not others.

CHAPTER 1

Disappointment Aversion, Asset Pricing and Measuring Asymmetric Dependence

Jamie Alcock[a] **and Anthony Hatherley**

[a]The University of Sydney Business School

Abstract

We develop a measure of asymmetric dependence (AD) that is consistent with investors who are averse to disappointment in the utility framework proposed by Skiadas (1997). Using a Skiadas-consistent utility function, we show that disappointment aversion implies that asymmetric joint return distributions impact investor utility. From an asset pricing perspective, we demonstrate that the consequence of these preferences for the realization of a given state results in a pricing kernel adjustment reflecting the degree to which these preferences represent a departure from expected utility behaviour. Consequently, we argue that capturing economically meaningful AD requires a metric that captures the relative differences in the shape of the dependence in the upper and lower tail. Such a metric is better able to capture AD than commonly used competing methods.

1.1 INTRODUCTION

The economic significance of measuring asymmetric dependence (AD), and its associated risk premium, can be motivated by considering a utility-based framework for AD. An incremental AD risk premium is consistent with a marginal investor who derives (dis-)utility from non-diversifiable, asymmetric characteristics of the joint return distribution. The effect of these characteristics on investor utility is captured by the framework developed by Skiadas (1997). In this model, agents rank the preferences of an act in a given state depending on the state itself (state-dependence) as well as the payoffs in other states (non-separability). The agent perceives potentially subjective consequences, such as disappointment and elation, when choosing an act, $b \in B = \{ \dots , b, c, \dots \}$, in the event that $E \in \Omega = \{ \dots , E, F, \dots \}$ is observed,[1] where B represents the set of acts that may be chosen on the set of states, $S = \{ \dots , s, \dots \}$, and Ω represents all possible resolutions of uncertainty and corresponds to the set of events that defines a σ-field on the universal event S.

---

[1]For example, the event E might represent a major market drawdown.

Within this context, (weak) disappointment is defined as:

$$(b = c \text{ on } E \text{ and } c \geq^{\Omega} = b) \Longrightarrow b \geq^{E} c,$$

where the statement '$b \geq^{E} c$' has the interpretation that, ex ante, the agent regards the consequences of act b on event E as no less desirable than the consequences of act c on the same event (Skiadas, 1997, p. 350). That is, if acts b and c have the same payoff on E, and the consequences of act b are generally no more desirable than the consequences of act c, then the consequence of having chosen b conditional on E occurring is considered to be no less desirable than having chosen c when the agent associates a feeling of elation with b and disappointment with c conditional upon the occurrence of E.

For example, consider two stocks, X and Y, that have identical βs, equal average returns and the same level of dependence in the lower tail. Further, suppose Y displays dependence in the upper tail that is equal in absolute magnitude to the level of dependence in the lower tail, but X has no dependence in the upper tail. In this example, Y is symmetric (but not necessarily elliptical), whereas X is asymmetric, displaying lower-tail asymmetric dependence (LTAD). Within the context of the Capital Asset Pricing Model (CAPM), the expected return associated with an exposure to systematic risk should be the same for X and Y because they have the same β. However, in addition to this, a rational, non-satiable investor who accounts for relative differences in upside and downside risk should prefer Y over X because, conditional on a market downturn event, Y is less likely to suffer losses compared with X. Similarly, a downside-risk-averse investor will also prefer Y over X. These preferences should imply higher returns for assets that display LTAD and lower returns for assets that display upper-tail asymmetric dependence (UTAD), independent of the returns demanded for β.

Now, let the event E represent a major market drawdown and assume that AD is not priced by the market. In the general framework of Skiadas, an investor may prefer Y over X because Y is more likely to recover the initial loss associated with the market drawdown in the event that the market subsequently recovers. Disappointment aversion manifests itself in an additional source of ex-ante risk premium over and above the premium associated with ordinary beta risk because an investor will display greater disappointment having not invested in a stock with compensating characteristics given the drawdown event (that is, holding X instead of Y).[2]

With regard to preferences in the event that E occurs, a disappointment-averse investor will prefer Y over X because the relative level of lower-tail dependence to upper-tail dependence is greater in X than in Y.[3] More generally, this investor prefers an asset displaying joint normality with the market

---

[2]An additional risk premium may be required in order to hold either X or Y relative to what the CAPM might dictate. The consequence of holding either X or Y in the event that E occurs is that the investor experiences greater disappointment; losses are larger than what the market is prepared to compensate for because of the greater-than-expected dependence in both the upper and lower tail. This would amount to a risk premium for excess kurtosis. We do not consider this explicitly here.

[3]We note that a preference for stocks with favourable characteristics during adverse market conditions is consistent with investment decisions made following the marginal conditional stochastic dominance (MCSD) framework developed by Shalit and Yitzhaki (1994). In this framework, expected-utility-maximizing investors have the ability to increase the risk exposure to one asset at the expense of another if the marginal utility change is positive. Shalit and Yitzhaki (1994) show that for a given portfolio, asset X stochastically dominates asset Y if the expected payoff from X conditional on returns less than some level, r, is greater than the equivalent payoff from Y, for all levels of r. Further conditions on the utility function and conditions for general Nth-order MCSD are provided by Denuit et al. (2014).

compared with *either* X or Y as the risk-adjusted loss given event E is lower. A risk premium is required to entice a disappointment-averse investor to invest in either X or Y, and this premium will be greater for X than for Y.

Ang *et al.* (2006) employ a similar rationale based upon Gul's (1991) disappointment-averse utility framework to decompose the standard CRRA utility function into upside and downside utility, which is then proxied by upside and downside βs. In contrast to a Skiadas agent that is endowed with a family of conditional preference relations (one for each event), Gul agents are assumed to be characterized by a single unconditional (Savage) preference relation (Grant *et al.*, 2001). A Skiadis-consistent AD metric conditions on multiple market states, rather than a single condition such as that implied by downside or upside β.

The impact of AD on the utility of an investor who is disappointment-averse in the Skiadas sense is identified using the disappointment-averse utility function proposed by Grant, Kajii and Polak (GKP). Define an outcome $x \in \mathcal{X} = \{ \dots, x, y, z, \dots \}$ such that $b(s) = x$, that is, an act b on state s results in outcome x. A disappointment-averse utility function that is consistent with Skiadas preferences is given by

$$V^E_{\alpha,\beta_u}(b) = \int_{s \in E} v_{\alpha,\beta_u}(b(s), V_{\beta_u}(b)) \mu ds, \tag{1.1}$$

with

$$v_{\alpha,\beta_u}(x, w) = \alpha \varphi(x, w) + (1 - \alpha)w$$

and

$$\varphi_{\beta_u}(x, w) = (x - w)\left(1 + \mathbb{I}_{x<w}\beta_u\right), \tag{1.2}$$

where $\beta_u > -1$ is a disappointment-aversion parameter and $\mathbb{I}$ is an indicator function taking value 1 if the condition in the subscript is true, zero otherwise. The GKP utility function is consistent with Skiadas disappointment[4] if $\beta_u > \frac{1}{\alpha} - 2 > 0$. The variable $V_{\beta_u}(b)$ solves

$$\int_S \varphi_{\beta_u}\left(b(s), V_{\beta_u}\right) \mu ds = 0, \tag{1.3}$$

and can be interpreted as a certainty-equivalent outcome for act b, representing the unconditional preference relation $\succeq_{\beta_u}$ over the universal event S. Therefore, for all states s in event E, an agent assigns utility for outcomes $b(s) = x \geq V_{\beta_u}$ and conversely assigns dis-utility to disappointing outcomes $b(s) = x < V_{\beta_u}$, where the dis-utility is scaled by $1 + \beta_u$. The preference, $V^E_{\alpha,\beta_u}(b)$, is then given by a weighted sum of the utility associated with event E, given by the disappointment-averse utility function, $\varphi_{\beta_u}(x, w)$, and the utility associated with the universal event S, given by the certainty equivalent, w.

The influence of AD on the utility of disappointment-averse investors can be explored using a simulation study. We repeatedly estimate Equation (1.1) using simulated LTAD data and multivariate normal data, where both data sets are mean-variance equivalent by construction. We simulate LTAD using a Clayton copula with a copula parameter of 1, where the asset marginals are assumed to be standard normal. A corresponding symmetric, multivariate normal distribution (MVN) is generated using the same underlying random numbers used to generate the AD data, in conjunction with the sample covariance matrix produced by the Clayton copula data. In this way, we ensure the mean-variance equivalence of the two simulated samples. The mean and variance–covariance matrices of the simulated samples have

---

[4]Equation (1.1) is also consistent with Gul's representation of disappointment aversion if $\beta_u > 0$. If, in addition, $\alpha > 1/(2 + \beta_u)$, then the conditional preference relation is consistent with Skiadas disappointment (Grant *et al.*, 2001).

the following L^1- and L^2-norms: $||\mu_{AD} - \mu_{MVN}||_1 < 0.0001$ and $||\Sigma_{AD} - \Sigma_{MVN}||_2 < 0.01$. The certainty equivalent is generated using 50,000 realizations of the Clayton sample and the corresponding MVN sample for a given set of utility parameters, (α, β_u). Given the certainty-equivalent values, we estimate Equation (1.1) 20,000 times, where the realizations of the outcome, x, are re-sampled with each iteration using a sample size of 5,000. The certainty equivalent is computed using market realizations in conjunction with Equation (1.3).

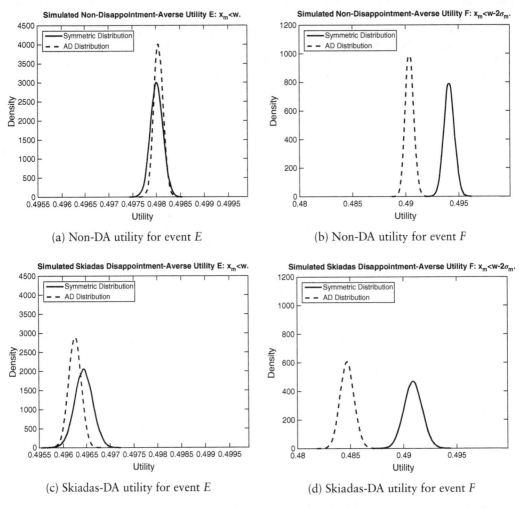

(a) Non-DA utility for event E

(b) Non-DA utility for event F

(c) Skiadas-DA utility for event E

(d) Skiadas-DA utility for event F

FIGURE 1.1   Simulated densities of GKP utility functions calculated when returns are symmetrically distributed (MVN) and asymmetrically distributed. Non-disappointment-averse utility is described by the GKP utility function (1.1) with $\alpha = 0.5$ and $\beta = 0$. Skiadas disappointment-averse utility is described with $\alpha = 0.5$ and $\beta = 1$. Each of these two utility functions are calculated for both AD and symmetric distributions for two different conditioning events, E and F. The event E is the event that the market return is less than the certainty-equivalent market return, w_m, and event F is the event that the market return is lower than the certainty-equivalent market return, w_m, less two market return standard deviations.

We consider two sets of utility parameters: disappointment aversion, given by $\alpha = 0.5$ and $\beta_u = 0.5$, and no disappointment aversion, given by $\alpha = 0.5$ and $\beta_u = 0$.[5] We define two events: E, the event that the market return is less than the certainty-equivalent market return, w_m, and F, the event that the market return is lower than the certainty-equivalent market return, w_m, less two market return standard deviations. The density of Equation (1.1) for event E is given in Figure 1.1(a) and (c). If an investor is not disappointment-averse, then their utility is similar regardless of the return distribution for event E. The utility of a disappointment-averse investor drops for both AD and symmetric distributions, with lower utility for the AD distribution than the symmetric distribution.

Further into the lower tail, the realizations of the AD distribution are much further away from the certainty equivalent than those of the symmetric distribution. Therefore, the utility of event F is less than that for event E. In addition, the utility of the disappointment-averse investor is lower for the AD distribution than for the symmetric distribution (Figure 1.1(b) and (d)). That is, as the level of tail dependence that defines our event, F, becomes even more pronounced, an investor displaying aversion to disappointing outcomes will experience lower net utility compared with an investor whose preferences are defined over an event spanning a much wider range of market realizations (event E, for example). Furthermore, the characteristics of the joint return distribution will ultimately dictate the value of the certainty equivalent, which in turn impacts the overall level of utility via the weighting $(1 - \alpha)w$. Therefore, to capture economically meaningful AD requires a metric that captures the relative differences in the shape of the dependence in the upper and lower tail.

1.2   FROM SKIADAS PREFERENCES TO ASSET PRICES

The implication of Skiadas-style preferences is that the ranking of the preferences of an act in a given state depends on the state itself (state-dependence) as well as on the payoffs at other states (non-separability). Following Skiadas (1997), disappointment aversion therefore uniquely satisfies

$$u(b) = A[f(b, u(b))], \qquad b \in B, \tag{1.4}$$

where u is an unconditional utility, f is non-increasing in its last argument representing the conditional utility given some fixed partition, $\mathcal{F}$, and $A : L \to \mathbb{R}$ is an increasing mapping where L is the set of all random variables. Hence, the subjective consequences that define the conditional utility function associated with the outcome of a random lottery are captured by the aggregator function, A.

Skiadas (1997) shows that for arbitrary probability, $\mathbb{P}$, the pair $(U, \mathbb{P})$ admits an additive representation if, for every event D,

$$b \geq^D c \Leftrightarrow \int_D U(b)d\mathbb{P} \geq \int_D U(c)d\mathbb{P}, \quad b, c \in B,$$

if U is of the form $U : \Omega \times B \to \mathbb{R}$.

Under certain conditions, the aggregate consequence of these preferences for the realization of a given state results in a pricing kernel adjustment, reflecting the degree to which these preferences represent a departure from expected utility behaviour. To consider the Skiadas preferences in an asset-pricing

---

[5] We retain $\alpha = 0.5$, meaning that although the agent does not display either Skiadas (1997) or Gul (1991) disappointment aversion conditional on E, the net utility continues to be a weighted average of the local utility and the certainty equivalent. This implies that if all returns are equal to the asset's certainty equivalent, then $x - w$ in the expression for φ is zero. Therefore, $\alpha\varphi = 0$, but $(1 - \alpha)w$ is non-zero, so the agent continues to generate some utility in this instance.

framework, we draw upon the insights of Kraus and Sagi (2006) and the derivations therein. Let $F = (F_1, \dots, F_T)$ be a sequence of sigma algebras over T periods, such that $F_1 = \{\Omega, \emptyset\}, F_t \subseteq F_{t+1}$ and F_T contain all subsets of Ω.

Unique partitions of Ω, denoted A_t, are assumed to generate each of the F_t filtrations. Elements of F_t are referred to as date-t events, while arbitrary atoms of the date-t partition, $a_t \in A_t$, are referred to as date-t macro states, where $a_{t+1} \in A_{t+1} \implies a_{t+1} \subseteq a_t$ for one and only one $a_t \in A_t$. State prices are computed by maximizing the expected utility over all future $t + 1$ macro states, a_{t+1} for a given pair of date-t consumption, c_t and date $t + 1$ realization of wealth, w^i_{t+1}. The expected utility is given by

$$\sum_{a_{t+1} \subseteq a_t} \pi(a_{t+1}|a_t) U^{g^i_t}_t(c_t, w^i_{t+1}, a_{t+1}) = u_{g^i}(c_t) + \beta \sum_{a_{t+1} \subseteq a_t} \pi(a_{t+1}|a_t) \varphi^{g^i_t}_t(V^{g^i_1 \star}_{t+1}, \dots, V^{g^i_n \star}_{t+1}), \qquad (1.5)$$

where $0 < \beta < 1$ is a constant, $\pi(a_{t+1}|a_t)$ is the conditional probability of realizing macro state a_{t+1} given current macro state a_t, $U_t(c_t, w^i_{t+1}, a_{t+1})$ is the contribution of (c_t, w^i_{t+1}) to the agent's utility in state a_{t+1}, $u(c_t)$ is the time-independent utility of date-t consumption, g^i_t is the agent's current preference state and V^*_{t+1} is the indirect utility function for date $t + 1$ realization of wealth, given by

$$V^\star_{t+1}(w^i_t, a_{t+1}) \equiv \max_{(c_t, \tilde{w}^i_{t+1}) \in B(w^i_t)} \sum_{a_{t+1} \subseteq a_t} \pi(a_{t+1}|a_t) U_t(c_t, w^i_{t+1}, a_{t+1}),$$

where $B(w^i_t)$ is the agent's budget set. The aggregator, φ_t, accounts for the date $t + 1$ preference states, $g'_1, \dots, g'_n$, conditional on attaining macro state a_{t+1}. When the aggregator, φ_t, is chosen to be consistent with agents displaying hyperbolic absolute risk aversion,[6] the system of time $(t + 1)$ state-prices can be derived from the solution to the agent's maximum utility optimization problem:

$$\phi(a_{t+1}|a_t) = \pi(a_{t+1}|a_t) \tilde{M}_{t+1}$$

$$= \pi(a_{t+1}|a_t) \beta \left(\frac{\tilde{C}_{t+1}}{C_t} \right)^{-\gamma} \left(\frac{\tilde{R}^R_{t+1}}{R^R_t} \right)^{\gamma} \left[1 - \frac{\tilde{\delta}_{t+1}}{\tilde{Q}_{t+1} + 1} \right]^{-\gamma}. \qquad (1.6)$$

Here, $\tilde{M}_{t+1}$ is the state-price deflator, C_t is aggregate market consumption, R^R_t is a measure of aggregate relative risk aversion, $\tilde{C}_{t+1}$ and $\tilde{R}^R_{t+1}$ are random variables reflecting aggregate consumption and risk aversion at time $t + 1$ conditional upon information at date t, γ and β are constants, and $\tilde{Q}_{t+1}$ is a function of the aggregate variables as well as a wealth-consumption ratio. The variable $\tilde{\delta}_{t+1} \equiv \delta(a_{t+1}|a_t)$ is a state-dependent function representing the aggregate departure from expected utility behaviour. With $\tilde{\delta}_{t+1} = 0$, $\tilde{M}_{t+1}$ reduces to the Lucas (1978) model under certain simplifying assumptions on the relation between aggregate risk aversion and aggregate consumption.

If, in Equation (1.6), we set $\delta(a_{t+1}|a_t) = f(g'_1, \dots, g'_n)$, where f is defined in Equation (1.4), we see that deviations from expected utility depend on the collective incremental experiences associated with state a_{t+1} being realized. This observation has several implications for measuring AD, in that any measure of AD will need to suppose that two incremental characteristics matter for asset pricing. First, it must measure AD over and above the level of dependence that is consistent with ordinary beta. This supposes that an incremental risk premium may be required to hold an asset that displays LTAD with the market beyond what would typically be expected if the assets were jointly normal. The consequence of holding a tail-dependent asset is that the investor experiences a sense of disappointment that losses are larger than what the market is prepared to compensate for. Second, any measure of

---

[6] Chosen by Kraus and Sagi (2006) for tractability.

AD must incorporate differences in tail dependence across the upper and lower tail. This is consistent with an investor preferring UTAD to LTAD, as a stock with UTAD is more likely to recover the initial loss associated with market drawdowns in the event that the market subsequently bounces. The consequence of the investor holding a LTAD asset can therefore be expected to elicit a sense of disappointment that they did not invest in a stock with compensating characteristics (i.e., UTAD) given the drawdown event.

1.3 CONSISTENTLY MEASURING ASYMMETRIC DEPENDENCE

To measure the relevant characteristics embodied within Skiadas's framework of preferences, we propose a metric that captures the asymmetry of dependence in the upper and lower tail, across a range of market events, over and above the level of dependence that is consistent with ordinary beta. We measure AD using an adjusted version of the J statistic, originally proposed by Hong *et al.* (2007). J^{Adj} is a non-parametric and β-invariant statistic that measures AD using conditional correlations across opposing sample exceedances. Several alternative metrics have been used to assess non-linearities in the dependence between asset returns, including extreme value theory (Poon *et al.*, 2004), higher-order moments (Harvey and Siddique, 2000), downside beta (Ang *et al.*, 2006), copula function parameters (Genest *et al.*, 2009; Low *et al.*, 2013) and the J statistic itself. However, many of these metrics have difficulty capturing the level and price of AD in asset return distributions independently of other price-sensitive factors such as the CAPM beta.

To illustrate, we concoct an approximate AD distribution by simulating $N = 25,000$ pairs of random variables (x, y) where $x_i \sim N(\mu_S, \sigma_S)$ and $y_i = \beta x_i + \epsilon_i$, where $\epsilon_i \sim N(0, (x_i + \mu_S)^\alpha)$, with $\mu_S = 0.25$ and $\sigma_S = 0.15$. When $\alpha = 0$, no AD is present and (x, y) are bivariate normal with linear dependence equal to β. Higher LTAD is proxied by increasing $\alpha > 0$, and higher UTAD is proxied by decreasing $\alpha < 0$. A sample of $N = 500$ simulated data points is given in Figure 1.2.

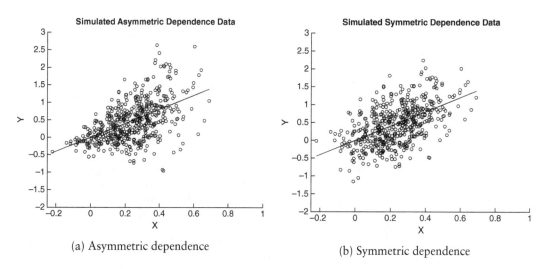

(a) Asymmetric dependence (b) Symmetric dependence

FIGURE 1.2 Scatter plot of simulated bivariate data with asymmetric dependence (a) and symmetric dependence (b) that is used to test different downside-risk metrics. The $N = 500$ sample is a random draw of bivariate data (x, y) where $x_i \sim N(\mu_S, \sigma_S)$ and $y_i = \beta x_i + \epsilon_i$, where $\epsilon_i \sim N(0, (x_i + \mu_S)^\alpha)$, with $\mu_S = 0.25$, $\sigma_S = 0.15$ and $\beta = 2.0$. In (a), $\alpha = 2$ so the sample displays LTAD. In (b), $\alpha = 0$ so no AD is present and (x, y) are bivariate normal with linear dependence equal to β. Higher LTAD is proxied by increasing $\alpha > 0$, and higher UTAD is proxied by decreasing $\alpha < 0$.

Ordinary least-squares estimates of the CAPM beta and the downside beta, and IFM estimates[7] of the Clayton copula parameter of LTAD, are provided in Figure 1.3 for various combinations of α and β.

The CAPM beta and the downside beta are largely insensitive to AD and their estimates of linear dependence are not confounded by the presence of AD.[8] The Clayton copula parameter is unable to uniquely identify either the presence or level of AD or of linear dependence. This seems to be due to the fact that the Clayton copula parameter attempts to fit both dimensions of dependence with a single parameter. As a result, the copula measure of AD is sensitive to the value of linear dependence and to the value of α. Almost all Archimedean copulae, including multi-parameter copulae, will similarly be unable to determine AD separately from linear dependence, unless one parameter is especially dedicated to estimating linear dependence. To the best of our knowledge, a copula with these characteristics is yet to be described in the literature.

Further, downside and upside βs are also likely to be confounded with the CAPM β, so that any risk premium empirically associated with downside β, upside β, or even the difference in upside and downside β, is likely to reflect both the compensation for systematic risk and asymmetries in upside and downside risk. Ang *et al.* (2006) are careful to avoid this confounding by ensuring that the CAPM β and the upside/downside βs are not included in the same cross-sectional regression.

1.3.1 The Adjusted *J* Statistic

The *J* statistic of Hong *et al.* (2007) is able to identify AD and allows the use of critical values to establish a hypothesis test on the presence of AD. We introduce the β-invariant adjusted *J* statistic, in order to establish the AD premium separately from the CAPM β premium while retaining the integrity of the dependence structure. We obtain β-invariance by unitizing β for each data set before a modified version of the *J* statistic is computed. In particular, given $\{R_{it}, R_{mt}\}_{t=1}^{T}$ (Figure 1.4(a)), we first let $\hat{R}_{it} = R_{it} - \beta R_{mt}$ (Figure 1.4(b)), where R_{it} and R_{mt} are the continuously compounded return on the ith asset and the market, respectively, and $\beta_{\hat{R}_{it}, R_{mt}} = \text{cov}(R_{it}, R_{mt})/\sigma_{R_{mt}}^2$. This initial transformation sets $\beta_{\hat{R}_{it}, R_{mt}} = 0$, making it possible to standardize the data without contaminating the linear relation between the variables (Figure 1.4(c)).[9] Standardization yields R_{mt}^S and $\hat{R}_{it}^S$ and ensures that the standard deviation of the market model residuals, a measure of idiosyncratic risk, is identical for all data sets.[10] We then re-transform the data to have $\hat{\beta}_{\hat{R}_{it}, R_{mt}} = 1$ by letting $\tilde{R}_{mt} = R_{mt}^S$ and $\tilde{R}_{it} = \hat{R}_{it}^S + R_{mt}^S$ (Figure 1.4(d)). Therefore, all data display the same β after these transformations,[11] forcing the output of J^{Adj} to be invariant to the overall level of linear dependence, as well as being independent of idiosyncratic risk.

---

[7] For full details of the inference function for margins (IFM) method of estimating copula parameters, see Joe (1997).

[8] The unadjusted *J* statistic of Hong *et al.* (2007) is similar to the difference between upside and downside beta, $\beta^+ - \beta^-$, if only one exceedance ($\delta = 0$) is used. The notable difference is that the *J* statistic determines the squared differences in correlations, whereas the upside/downside βs scale the unsquared differences by market semi-variance. The adjustment of the *J* statistic, described in Section 1.3.1, removes the influence of β altogether.

[9] We are careful to avoid look-ahead bias by ensuring that at time t, only historical data up to time t is employed to estimate the $\beta_{\hat{R}_{it}, R_{mt}}$ used to standardize the data.

[10] From the market model, the total variance of a stock's returns can be written as $\sigma_T^2 = \beta^2 \sigma_M^2 + \sigma_\epsilon^2$, where σ_M^2 is the market's variance and σ_ϵ^2 is the variance of the idiosyncratic component of returns. Since we set $\beta = 0$, $\sigma_T^2 = \sigma_\epsilon^2$. Hence, standardizing at this point is equivalent to dividing out the idiosyncratic component of transformed returns.

[11] At this point, $\tilde{R}_{mt} \sim N(0, 1)$ whereas $\tilde{R}_{it} \sim N(0, \sqrt{2})$ assuming marginal distributions are normal. This holds for all stocks.

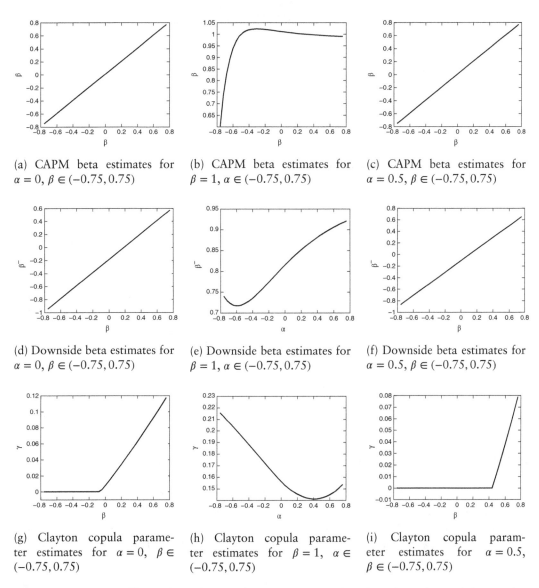

(a) CAPM beta estimates for $\alpha = 0$, $\beta \in (-0.75, 0.75)$

(b) CAPM beta estimates for $\beta = 1$, $\alpha \in (-0.75, 0.75)$

(c) CAPM beta estimates for $\alpha = 0.5$, $\beta \in (-0.75, 0.75)$

(d) Downside beta estimates for $\alpha = 0$, $\beta \in (-0.75, 0.75)$

(e) Downside beta estimates for $\beta = 1$, $\alpha \in (-0.75, 0.75)$

(f) Downside beta estimates for $\alpha = 0.5$, $\beta \in (-0.75, 0.75)$

(g) Clayton copula parameter estimates for $\alpha = 0$, $\beta \in (-0.75, 0.75)$

(h) Clayton copula parameter estimates for $\beta = 1$, $\alpha \in (-0.75, 0.75)$

(i) Clayton copula parameter estimates for $\alpha = 0.5$, $\beta \in (-0.75, 0.75)$

FIGURE 1.3 Estimates of linear dependence and AD. We estimate the CAPM beta, downside beta and the Clayton copula parameter using $N = 10{,}000$ simulated pairs of data (x, y), where $y_i = \beta x_i + \epsilon_i$, with $x_i \sim N(0.25, 0.15)$ and $\epsilon_i \sim N(0, (x_i + 0.25)^\alpha)$. Higher levels of linear dependence are incorporated with higher values of β and higher levels of LTAD are incorporated with higher levels of α. Figure parts (a), (d) and (g) provide estimates for varying levels of linear dependence but with no AD ($\alpha = 0$). Figure parts (b), (e) and (h) provide estimates for varying degrees of AD with constant linear dependence ($\beta = 1$). Figure parts (c), (f) and (i) provide estimates for varying degrees of linear dependence with constant AD ($\alpha = 0.5$).

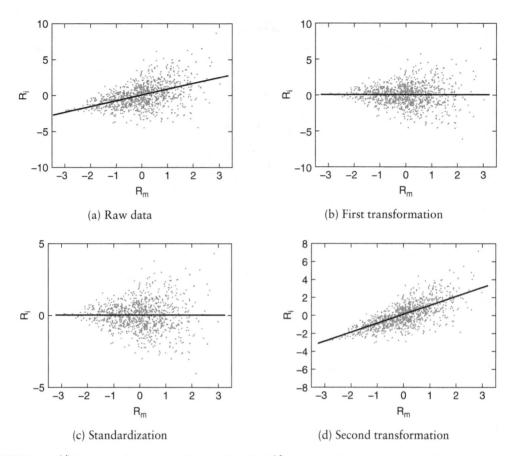

(a) Raw data

(b) First transformation

(c) Standardization

(d) Second transformation

FIGURE 1.4 J^{Adj} data transformations. To calculate the J^{Adj} statistic with a random sample, $\{R_{it}, R_{mt}\}_{t=1}^{T}$, as in (a), we let $\hat{R}_{it} = R_{it} - \beta R_{mt}$ where R_{it} is the continuously compounded return on the ith asset, R_{mt} is the continuously compounded return on the market and $\beta = \text{cov}(R_{it}, R_{mt})/\sigma_{R_{mt}}^2$. This transformation forces $\beta_{\hat{R}_{it}, R_{mt}} = 0$, as in (b). We standardize the transformed data, yielding R_{mt}^S and $\hat{R}_{it}^S$ in (c). Finally, we re-transform the data to have $\hat{\beta} = 1$ by letting $\tilde{R}_{mt} = R_{mt}^S$ and $\tilde{R}_{it} = \hat{R}_{it}^S + R_{mt}^S$ in (d). The solid line through the middle of each plot is given to illustrate how the linear trend changes with each transformation.

J^{Adj} is given by

$$J^{Adj} = [\text{sign}([\tilde{\rho}^+ - \tilde{\rho}^-]\mathbf{1})]T(\tilde{\rho}^+ - \tilde{\rho}^-)'\tilde{\Omega}^{-1}(\tilde{\rho}^+ - \tilde{\rho}^-), \qquad (1.7)$$

for $\tilde{\rho}^+ = \{\tilde{\rho}^+(\delta_1), \tilde{\rho}^+(\delta_2), \dots, \tilde{\rho}^+(\delta_N)\}$ and $\tilde{\rho}^- = \{\tilde{\rho}^-(\delta_1), \tilde{\rho}^-(\delta_2), \dots, \tilde{\rho}^-(\delta_N)\}$, where $\mathbf{1}$ is an $N \times 1$ vector of ones, $\hat{\Omega}$ is an estimate of the variance–covariance matrix (Hong $et\ al.$, 2007) for the difference vector $(\tilde{\rho}^+ - \tilde{\rho}^-)$ and

$$\tilde{\rho}^+(\delta) = \text{corr}\left(\tilde{R}_{mt}, \tilde{R}_{it} | \tilde{R}_{mt} > \delta, \tilde{R}_{it} > \delta\right), \qquad (1.8)$$

$$\tilde{\rho}^-(\delta) = \text{corr}\left(\tilde{R}_{mt}, \tilde{R}_{it} | \tilde{R}_{mt} < -\delta, \tilde{R}_{it} < -\delta\right). \qquad (1.9)$$

The null hypothesis for the significance of the adjusted J statistic is that dependence is symmetric across the joint distribution, that is: $\rho^+(\delta_i) = \rho^-(\delta_i)$, $i = 1, \ldots, N$. Under the null, $|J^{Adj}| \sim \chi^2_N$ following Hong *et al.* (2007).[12] Where dependence is symmetric across upper and lower tails, J^{Adj} will be near zero. Conversely, any strong asymmetries in dependence between upper and lower tails will result in a significant, non-zero J^{Adj}. A positive (negative) J^{Adj} is indicative of UTAD (LTAD), over and above the tail dependence implied by ordinary β.

We demonstrate the suitability of the adjusted J statistic in capturing LTAD and UTAD, as well as the β-invariance of J^{Adj} in Figure 1.5, estimated using the same simulations as above. In its own right,

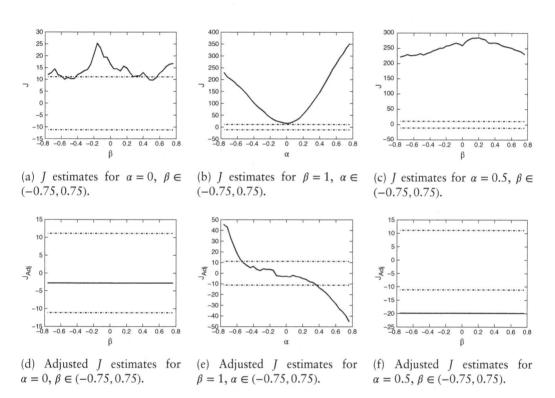

(a) J estimates for $\alpha = 0$, $\beta \in (-0.75, 0.75)$.

(b) J estimates for $\beta = 1$, $\alpha \in (-0.75, 0.75)$.

(c) J estimates for $\alpha = 0.5$, $\beta \in (-0.75, 0.75)$.

(d) Adjusted J estimates for $\alpha = 0$, $\beta \in (-0.75, 0.75)$.

(e) Adjusted J estimates for $\beta = 1$, $\alpha \in (-0.75, 0.75)$.

(f) Adjusted J estimates for $\alpha = 0.5$, $\beta \in (-0.75, 0.75)$.

FIGURE 1.5 Estimates of linear dependence and AD. We estimate the J statistic (Hong *et al.*, 2007) and the adjusted J statistic using $N = 10,000$ simulated pairs of data (x, y), where $y_i = \beta x_i + \epsilon_i$, with $x_i \sim N(0.25, 0.15)$ and $\epsilon_i \sim N(0, (x_i + 0.25)^\alpha)$. Higher levels of linear dependence are incorporated with higher values of β and higher levels of LTAD are incorporated with higher levels of α. Figure parts (a) and (d) provide estimates for varying levels of linear dependence but with no AD ($\alpha = 0$). Figure parts (b) and (e) provide estimates for varying degrees of AD with constant linear dependence ($\beta = 1$). Figure parts (c) and (f) provide estimates for varying degrees of linear dependence with constant AD ($\alpha = 0.5$).

---

[12]The transformations described represent (non-singular) affine transformations that may ultimately be expressed as linear transformations (Webster, 1995). Birkhoff and Lane (1997) show that a non-singular linear transformation of the space, V, is an isomorphism of the vector space, V, to itself. The assumptions used by Hong *et al.* (2007) to derive an asymptotic distribution for the J statistic therefore hold for the transformed returns $\{\tilde{R}_{1t}, \tilde{R}_{2t}\}$. $|J^{Adj}| \sim \chi^2_N$ then follows the proof described in Hong *et al.* (2007).

J^{Adj} captures both LTAD and UTAD between a stock and the market. To isolate upside and downside risk for the purposes of our regression analysis, we compute

$$J^{Adj}+ = J^{Adj}\mathbb{I}_{J^{Adj}>0},$$ (1.10)

$$J^{Adj}- = J^{Adj}\mathbb{I}_{J^{Adj}<0}.$$ (1.11)

We capture a family of conditional preferences, consistent with those of the Skiadas agent, by employing a range of exceedances in the calculation of J^{Adj}. Adjusting J to be β-invariant enables identification of the price paid by disappointment-averse agents in addition to the ordinary β risk premium. $J^{Adj}-$ and $J^{Adj}+$ capture disappointment and elation premia distinctly.

Further, as a non-parametric measure of AD, the J^{Adj} statistic facilitates the separation of the actual price of tail dependence from the effect of non-normal marginal return characteristics. J^{Adj} is also consistent with the work of Stapleton and Subrahmanyam (1983) and Kwon (1985), who suggest a means of deriving a linear relation between β and expected return without the need for multivariate normal assumptions. J^{Adj} is also consistent with the evidence that correlations tend to be larger in the lower tail of the joint return distribution compared with the upper tail (Longin and Solnik, 2001; Ang and Chen, 2002). LTAD exists provided that dependence in the lower tail exceeds dependence in the upper tail. Normality in the opposite tail is not required by this definition, which precludes parametric alternatives such as the H statistic (Ang and Chen, 2002) for the purposes of our investigation.

Another advantage of transforming the data in the way described above is that the standard deviation of market model residuals is forced to be the same across data sets. Controlling for the effects of idiosyncratic risk is important given (and despite) the debate over whether idiosyncratic risk is relevant in an asset-pricing context (Goyal and Santa-Clara, 2003; Bali *et al.*, 2005). It is sometimes argued that idiosyncratic risk should be priced whenever investors fail to hold sufficiently diversified portfolios (Merton, 1987; Campbell *et al.*, 2001; Fu, 2009). However, when tail risk is characterized by dependence that increases during down markets, the ability to diversify will be affected and the ability to protect the portfolio from risk will be reduced. Hence, downside risk may be mistakenly identified as idiosyncratic risk. Where this occurs, we expect idiosyncratic risk to increase as downside risk increases. Standardizing market model residuals allows us to distinguish between downside risk and other firm-specific risks.

Note that because tail risk is estimated by analysing the difference in correlation beyond N exceedances, the occurrence of net AD may be contingent upon a relatively small number of positive or negative joint returns. As a result, any measure of AD will suffer from a high likelihood of Type II errors, making it difficult to detect AD unless large data sets are utilized. Consequently, we present conservative estimates of AD between equity returns and the market.

1.4 SUMMARY

Skiadas (1997) offers an alternative framework to the standard von Neumann–Morgenstern expected utility theory, in which subjective consequences (disappointment, elation, regret, etc.) are incorporated indirectly through the properties of the decision maker's preferences rather than through explicit inclusion among the formal primitives.

Individuals with Skiadas preferences are endowed with a family of conditional preference relations, one for each event (Grant *et al.*, 2001). Preferences are state-dependent, as in the Gul (1991) framework, and because consequences are treated implicitly through the agent's preference relations, preferences can be regarded as 'non-separable' in that the ranking of an act given an event may depend on subjective consequences of these acts outside the event.

We demonstrate that AD influences the utility of disappointment-averse investors and establish the conditions under which this implies a market price for LTAD and UTAD. Using a comprehensive set of simulations, we demonstrate that many of the commonly employed risk metrics are unable to adequately capture the salient distributional characteristics of AD. We further propose a β-invariance metric to capture AD consistent with Skiadas preferences and demonstrate its suitability using simulated AD data sets.

REFERENCES

Ang, A. and Chen, J. (2002). Asymmetric correlations of equity portfolios. *Journal of Financial Economics*, 63(3), 443–494.

Ang, A., Chen, J. and Xing, Y. (2006). Downside risk. *Review of Financial Studies*, 19(4), 1191–1239.

Bali, T., Cakici, N., Yan, X. and Zhang, Z. (2005). Does idiosyncratic risk really matter? *Journal of Finance*, 60(2), 905–929.

Birkhoff, G. and Lane, M. (1997). *A Survey of Modern Algebra*. Macmillan, New York.

Campbell, J., Lettau, M., Malkiel, B. and Xu, Y. (2001). Have individual stocks become more volatile? An empirical exploration of idiosyncratic risk. *Journal of Finance*, 56(1), 1–43.

Denuit, M., Huang, R., Tzeng, L. and Wang, W. (2014). Almost marginal conditional stochastic dominance. *Journal of Banking and Finance*, 41(1), 57–66.

Fu, F. (2009). Idiosyncratic risk and the cross-section of expected stock returns. *Journal of Financial Economics*, 91(1), 24–37.

Genest, C., Gendron, M. and Boureau-Brien, M. (2009). The advent of copulas in finance. *European Journal of Finance*, 15(7&8), 609–618.

Goyal, A. and Santa-Clara, P. (2003). Idiosyncratic risk matters! *Journal of Finance*, 58(3), 975–1007.

Grant, S., Kajii, A. and Polak, B. (2001). Different notations of disappointment aversion. *Economics Letters*, 70(2), 203–208.

Gul, F. (1991). A theory of disappointment aversion. *Econometrica*, 59(3), 667–686.

Harvey, C. and Siddique, A. (2000). Conditional skewness in asset pricing tests. *Journal of Finance*, 55(3), 1263–1295.

Hong, Y., Tu, J. and Zhou, G. (2007). Asymmetries in stock returns: statistical tests and economic evaluation. *Review of Financial Studies*, 20(5), 1547–1581.

Joe, H. (1997). *Multivariate Models and Dependence Concepts*. Monographs on Statistics and Applied Probability. Chapman & Hall, London.

Kraus, A. and Sagi, J. (2006). Asset pricing with unforeseen contingencies. *Journal of Financial Economics*, 82(2), 417–453.

Kwon, Y. (1985). Derivation of the capital asset pricing model without normality or quadratic preference: a note. *Journal of Finance*, 40(5), 1505–1509.

Longin, F. and Solnik, B. (2001). Extreme correlation of international equity markets. *Journal of Finance*, 56(2), 649–676.

Low, R., Alcock, J., Brailsford, T. and Faff, R. (2013). Canonical vine copulas in the context of modern portfolio management: are they worth it? *Journal of Banking and Finance*, 37(8), 3085–3099.

Lucas, R. (1978). Asset prices in an exchange economy. *Econometrica*, 46(6), 1429–1445.

Merton, R. (1987). Presidential address: a simple model of capital market equilibrium with incomplete information. *Journal of Finance*, 42, 483–510.

Poon, S., Rockinger, M. and Tawn, J. (2004). Extreme value dependence in financial markets: diagnostics, models, and financial implications. *Review of Financial Studies*, 17(2), 581–610.

Shalit, H. and Yitzhaki, S. (1994). Marginal conditional stochastic dominance. *Management Science*, 40(5), 670–684.

Skiadas, C. (1997). Conditioning and aggregation of preferences. *Econometrica*, 65(2), 347–367.

Stapleton, R. and Subrahmanyam, M. (1983). The market model and capital asset pricing theory: a note. *Journal of Finance*, 38(5), 1637–1642.

Webster, R. (1995). *Convexity*. Oxford University Press, New York.

FURTHER READING

Ang, A. and Bekaert, G. (2002). International asset allocation with regime shifts. *Society for Financial Studies*, 15(4), 1137–1187.

Ang, A., Hodrick, R., Xing, Y. and Zhang, X. (2006). The cross-section of volatility and expected returns. *Journal of Finance*, 61(1), 259–299.

Bali, T., Demirtas, O. and Levy, H. (2009). Is there an intertemporal relation between downside risk and expected returns? *Journal of Financial and Quantitative Analysis*, 44(4), 883–909.

Bali, T., Cakici, N. and Whitelaw, R. (2011). Maxing out: stocks as lotteries and the cross-section of expected returns. *Journal of Financial Economics*, 99(2), 427–446.

Bekaert, G., Hodrick, R. and Marshall, D. (1997). The implications of first-order risk aversion for asset market risk premiums. *Journal of Monetary Economics*, 40(1), 3–39.

Bekaert, G. and Wu, G. (2000). Asymmetric volatility and risk in equity markets. *Review of Financial Studies*, 13(1), 1–42.

Benartzi, S. and Thaler, R. (1995). Myopic loss aversion and the equity premium puzzle. *Quarterly Journal of Economics*, 110(1), 73–92.

Bhansali, V. (2008). Tail risk management. *Journal of Portfolio Management*, 34(4), 68–75.

Black, F., Jensen, M. and Scholes, M. (1972). The capital asset pricing model: some empirical tests, in M. Jensen (ed.), *Studies in the Theory of Capital Markets*. Praeger, New York.

Blume, M. (1975). Betas and their regression tendencies. *Journal of Finance*, 30(3), 785–795.

Bollerslev, T., Engle, R. and Wooldridge, J. (1988). A capital asset pricing model with time-varying covariances. *Journal of Political Economy*, 96(1), 116–131.

Bollerslev, T. and Todorov, V. (2009). Tails, fears and risk premia. *Journal of Finance*, 66(6), 2165–2211.

Bos, T. and Newbold, P. (1984). An empirical investigation of the possibility of stochastic systematic risk in the market model. *Journal of Business*, 57(1), 35–41.

Boudoukh, J., Richardson, M. and Smith, T. (1993). Is the ex-ante risk premium always positive? *Journal of Financial Economics*, 34(3), 387–408.

Butler, K. and Joaquin, D. (2002). Are the gains from international portfolio diversification exaggerated? The influence of downside risk in bear markets. *Journal of International Money and Finance*, 21(7), 981–1011.

Campbell, R., Koedijk, K. and Kofman, P. (2002). Increased correlation in bear markets. *Financial Analysts Journal*, 58(1), 87–94.

Cappiello, L., Gerard, B., Kadareja, A. and Manganelli, S. (2014). Measuring comovements by regression quantiles. *Journal of Financial Econometrics*, 12(4), 645–678.

Cont, R. (2001). Empirical properties of asset returns: stylized facts and statistical issues. *Quantitative Finance*, 1(2), 223–236.

Diamond, E. and Rajan, R. (2009). The credit crisis: conjectures about causes and remedies. *American Economic Review: Papers & Proceedings*, 99(2), 606–610.

Dimson, E., Marsh, P. and Staunton, M. (2003). Global evidence on the equity risk premium. *Journal of Applied Corporate Finance*, 15(4), 27–38.

Eleswarapu, V. and Thompson, R. (2007). Testing for negative expected market return premia. *Journal of Banking and Finance*, 31(6), 1755–1770.

Erb, C., Harvey, C. and Viskanta, T. (1994). Forecasting international equity correlations. *Financial Analysts Journal*, 50(6), 32–45.

Fabozzi, F. and Francis, J. (1978). Beta as a random coefficient. *Journal of Financial and Quantitative Analysis*, 13(1), 101–116.

Fama, E. (1996). Multifactor portfolio efficiency and multifactor asset pricing. *Journal of Financial and Quantitative Finance*, 31(4), 441–465.

Fama, E. and Macbeth, J. (1973). Risk, return and equilibrium: empirical tests. *Journal of Political Economy*, 81(3), 607–636.

Fama, E. and French, K. (1992). The cross-section of expected stock returns. *Journal of Finance*, 48(2), 427–465.

Ferson, W. and Harvey, C. (1991). The variation of economic risk premiums. *Journal of Political Economy*, 99(2), 385–415.

Ferson, W. and Harvey, C. (1993). The risk and predictability of international equity returns. *Review of Financial Studies*, 6(3), 527–566.

Ferson, W. and Korajczyk, C. (1995). Do arbitrage pricing models explain the predictability of stock returns? *Journal of Business*, 68(3), 309–349.

Fielding, D. and Stracca, L. (2007). Myopic loss aversion, disappointment aversion, and the equity premium puzzle. *Journal of Economic Behaviour and Organization*, 64(2), 250–268.

Gibbons, M.R. (1982). Multivariate tests of financial models. *Journal of Financial Economics*, 10(1), 3–27.

Hartmann, P., Straetmans, S. and De Vries, C. (2004). Asset market linkages in crisis periods. *Review of Economics and Statistics*, 86(1), 313–326.

Harvey, C., Liu, Y. and Zhu, H. (2015). ... and the cross-section of expected returns. NBER Working Paper 20592.

Karni, E. (1987). State-dependent preferences, in J. Eatwell, M. Milgate and P. Newman (eds), *The New Palgrave: A Dictionary of Economics*. Palgrave Macmillan, New York.

Khandani, A. and Lo, A. (2007). What happened to the quants in August 2007? *Journal of Investment Management*, 5(4), 5–54.

Kim, D. (1995). The errors in the variables problem in the cross-section of expected stock returns. *Journal of Finance*, 50(5), 1605–1634.

Kullmann, L., Kertesz, L., Toyli, J., Kaski, K. and Kanot, A. (2000). Breakdown of scaling and convergence to Gaussian distribution in stock market data. *International Journal of Theoretical and Applied Finance*, 3(3), 371–372.

Lewellen, J. and Nagel, S. (2006). The conditional CAPM does not explain asset-pricing anomalies. *Journal of Financial Economics*, 82(2), 289–314.

Li, F. (2014). Identifying asymmetric comovements of international stock market returns. *Journal of Financial Econometrics*, 12(3), 507–543.

Lo, A. and Mackinlay, A. (1990). An econometric analysis of nonsynchronous trading. *Journal of Econometrics*, 45(1&2), 181–211.

Mackinlay, A. (1995). Multifactor models do not explain deviations from the CAPM. *Journal of Financial Economics*, 38(1), 3–28.

Newey, W. and West, K. (1987). A simple, positive semi-definite, heteroskedasticity and autocorrelation consistent covariance matrix. *Econometrica*, 55(3), 703–708.

Newey, W. and West, K. (1994). Lag selection in covariance matrix estimation. *Review of Financial Studies*, 61(4), 631–653.

Pastor, L. and Stambaugh, R. (2001). The equity premium and structural breaks. *Journal of Finance*, 56(4), 1207–1239.

Pastor, L. and Stambaugh, R. (2003). Liquidity risk and expected stock returns. *Journal of Political Economy*, 111(3), 642–685.

Patton, A. (2004). On the out-of-sample importance of skewness and asymmetric dependence for asset allocation. *Journal of Financial Econometrics*, 2(1), 130–168.

Pedersen, C. and Hwang, S. (2007). Does downside Beta matter in asset pricing? *Applied Financial Economics*, 17(12), 961–978.

Post, T. and Van Vliet, P. (2006). Downside risk and asset pricing. *Journal of Banking and Finance*, 30(3), 823–849.

Rajan, R. (2006). Has finance made the world riskier. *European Financial Management*, 12(4), 499–533.

Ramchand, L. and Susmel, R. (1998). Volatility and cross correlation across major stock markets. *Journal of Empirical Finance*, 5(4), 397–416.

Roll, R. and Ross, S. (1994). On the cross-sectional relation between expected returns and betas. *Journal of Finance*, 49(1), 101–121.

Ross, S. (1978). Mutual fund separation in financial theory – the separating distributions. *Journal of Economic Theory*, 17(2), 254–286.

Routledge, B. and Zin, S. (2010). Generalized disappointment aversion and asset prices. *Journal of Finance*, 65(4), 1303–1332.

Savage, L. (1954). *The Foundations of Statistics*. Dover Publications, New York.

Shanken, J. (1987). Multivariate proxies and asset pricing relations: living with the roll critique. *Journal of Financial Economics*, 18(1), 91–110.

Sharpe, W. (1977). The capital asset pricing model: a 'multi-beta' interpretation, in H. Levy and M. Sarnat (eds), *Financial Decision Making Under Uncertainty*. Academic Press, New York.

Siegel, J. (1992). The equity premium: stock and bond returns since 1802. *Financial Analysts Journal*, 48(1), 28–38.

Skiadas, C. (1996). Subjective probability under additive aggregation of conditional preferences. *Journal of Economic Theory*, 76(2), 242–271.

CHAPTER 2

The Size of the CTA Market and the Role of Asymmetric Dependence

Stephen Satchell[a] and Oliver Williams[b]

[a]Discipline of Finance, Sydney University and Trinity College, Cambridge
[b]Kings College, Cambridge and Scalpel Research

Abstract

The purpose of this chapter is to provide a model of a market where asymmetric dependence (AD) arises in equilibrium; that is we wish, intuitively, to endogenize AD. To this end we choose a model where options and shares are both traded. Previous work by Detemple and Selden (1991) addresses this problem using quadratic utility but requires very constrained differences in opinion between investors to generate tractable results. Instead we use mean-variance heuristics to present results which are tractable under a number of reasonable assumptions. As an example application we formulate a stylized model to assess the factors that determine the size of the Commodity Trading Advisor (CTA) market, i.e. total assets under management (AUM) invested in such funds. We show that AD plays a prominent role in the analysis, characterizing the relationship between returns from the active CTA strategy and a passive risky asset holding, and we provide simple empirical illustrations.

2.1 INTRODUCTION

The purpose of this chapter is to provide a model of a market where asymmetric dependence (AD) arises in equilibrium; that is we wish, intuitively, to endogenize AD. We choose a model where options and shares are both traded. Previous work by Detemple and Selden (1991) addresses this problem using quadratic utility but requires very constrained differences in opinion between investors to generate tractable results. Instead we use mean-variance heuristics to present results which are tractable under a number of reasonable assumptions. Our work also differs from that of Detemple and Selden in that we assume disagreements about the volatility of the equity market, as opposed to equity distributions differing by mean-preserving spreads, and we allow asset prices to be continuous, rather than discrete over a state-space. These distinctions make our approach more amenable to empirical work.

As an example application within this setting we formulate a stylized model to assess the factors that determine the size of the Commodity Trading Advisor (CTA) market, i.e. total assets under management (AUM) invested in such funds. We will show that AD plays a prominent role in the analysis, characterizing the relationship between returns from the active CTA strategy and a passive risky asset holding.

Option positions (either long or short) might be held in investment portfolios for various reasons. A long-only manager with a suitably broad mandate might execute option strategies as portfolio overlays with the aim of constructing a specific payoff pattern in single stocks or indices. Similarly, the strategy of covered call writing is well known and analysed in numerous theoretical and empirical papers (including Board *et al.* (2000), Rendleman (2001), Hill *et al.* (2006) and McIntyre and Jackson (2007)). However, in many cases options arise in portfolios embedded in other products, for example a convertible bond can be decomposed into a combination of a corporate bond and a long call option on the company's stock, and a callable bond can be viewed as a long bond position plus a short call option on the bond itself (which is the issuer's right to repay the debt early).[1] According to Merton's (1974) model of capital structure, a long position in a corporate bond is itself a short put option on the assets of the company, and related models can be applied to various credit derivative structures.

At a further level of abstraction there are certain dynamic trading strategies which can be shown to have similar payoff characteristics to option portfolios. For example, in this chapter our particular area of interest is trend-following. This is widely recognized to be a principal strategy for CTAs and it is claimed by Fung and Hsieh (2001) that many of the strategies followed have characteristics similar to look-back straddles. In our framework, which corresponds to a two-period world, this is the same as a plain vanilla straddle.

We think this problem is interesting on both theoretical and practical grounds. Since the payoff of an option depends asymmetrically on the future price of the underlying asset, normality in asset returns will not lead to normality in option returns, which makes optimal portfolio rules more elaborate than conventional mean-variance analysis. From a practical perspective the traditionally opaque nature of derivatives markets has continued to be a source of concern to some practitioners and, particularly, regulators. Whilst underlying assets will typically have observable prices, and (in some cases) may be considered primitive securities, uncertainty about the pricing, supply and demand for derivatives has frequently played a prominent roll in systemic financial crises. In this chapter we consider one approach to estimating the potential size of these markets.

We assume that there are three assets: a stock, a call option and cash with a rate of return r which is exogenous. There is no current consumption. The investors are endowed with initial wealth, which can be invested in any of the three assets, which are held until the next period. Our assumption of mean-variance heuristics instead of expected utility functions is both mathematically convenient and also much more realistic in that the vast majority of investment is done by institutions rather than individuals, and institutional utility functions seem very challenging to define. Mean variance quite naturally captures the trade-off between risk and return and also reflects the very widespread use of quadratic optimizers among institutional funds and hedge funds. We shall refer to these entities as *institutions* in what follows.

The link here between our model and AD can be grasped intuitively if we imagine that one variable (the option payoff) is a linear-transformed censored version of the other (the stock price). As we move the point at which the variable is censored (the exercise price), the correlation between the two variables will change; this creates AD. We explain this example in Section 2.2. Whilst we recognize that in a multi-asset equity market the problem will be much more complex, the simple two-variable setting draws attention to several essential features which we conjecture would also apply in a multivariate context.

This chapter is organized as follows: in Section 2.2 we describe the structure of our model market, in Section 2.3 we compute expressions for the relevant moments of the option (without making any distributional assumptions) and in Section 2.4 we apply these moment formulas to various example distributions: uniform, normal, scale gamma and Pareto. Section 2.5 defines heterogeneity between investors in our model and derives expressions for CTA market size, which we compare with real-world data in Section 2.6. Section 2.7 concludes.

---

[1]Particularly important examples of callable bonds are mortgage-backed securities in the USA and Denmark.

2.2 MARKET MODEL

2.2.1 Equilibrium Prices and Portfolios

There are m institutions investing in this market; in the important case where $m = 2$, one is a trend-follower who, broadly speaking, can be thought of as highly risk-tolerant and prepared to buy volatility whilst the second is more risk-averse and wants to sell volatility. Both institutions have mean-variance utilities in period 1 wealth and institution i has wealth W_{0i} in time 0. Both hold subjective views about the mean and covariances of the two stochastic assets whose current prices are p_1 and p_2. The equity asset is held in fixed supply equal to S, whilst the options market has an overall net supply of 0. Institution i has beliefs about means and covariance matrices of future prices summarized by μ_i and Ω_i, respectively. Institutions have strictly positive risk tolerances ϕ_i.

Wealth in period 1 is given by

$$W_{1i} = W_{0i}(1+r) + \sum_{j=1}^{2} n_{ij}(P_j - (1+r)p_j),$$

where n_{ij} is the number of units of asset j demanded by institution i and P_j is the future price of asset j.

Let N_i be the vector of demands of institution i, then

$$\mathbb{E}(W_{1i}) = W_{0i}(1+r) + \sum_{j=1}^{2} n_{ij}(\mu_{ij} - (1+r)p_j)$$

$$= W_{0i}(1+r) + N_i'(\mu_i - (1+r)P).$$

Here P is the vector of prices. Furthermore,

$$\text{Var}(W_{1i}) = N_i'\Omega_i N_i.$$

Thus, the optimal demands are

$$N_i = \phi_i \Omega_i^{-1}(\mu_i - (1+r)P)$$

and it follows that, in equilibrium, for $m = 2$:

$$N_1 + N_2 = \begin{pmatrix} S \\ 0 \end{pmatrix}.$$

Solving and substituting:

$$P = \frac{(\phi_1\Omega_1^{-1} + \phi_2\Omega_2^{-1})^{-1}(\phi_1\Omega_1^{-1}\mu_1 + \phi_2\Omega_2^{-1}\mu_2) - (\phi_1\Omega_1^{-1} + \phi_2\Omega_2^{-1})^{-1}\begin{pmatrix} S \\ 0 \end{pmatrix}}{1+r}. \tag{2.1}$$

We can investigate the size of the CTA market by looking at

$$n_{12} + n_{22} = 0.$$

The magnitude of n_{12} in terms of the *size* of the position (or $p_2 n_{12}$ in *money* terms) can now be calculated and we can see what the main determinants are.

Using the above equations:

$$N_1 = \phi_1\Omega_1^{-1}\left(\mu_1 - (\phi_1\Omega_1^{-1} + \phi_2\Omega_2^{-1})^{-1}(\phi_1\Omega_1^{-1}\mu_1 + \phi_2\Omega_2^{-1}\mu_2) + (\phi_1\Omega_1^{-1} + \phi_2\Omega_2^{-1})^{-1}\begin{pmatrix}S\\0\end{pmatrix}\right).$$

We shall make a strategic simplification: both institutions agree on their volatility and correlation forecasts. This implies that $\Omega_1 = \Omega_2 = \Omega = \begin{pmatrix}\sigma_{11} & \sigma_{12}\\\sigma_{12} & \sigma_{22}\end{pmatrix}$; in which case,

$$N_1 = \phi_1\Omega^{-1}\left((\phi_1 + \phi_2)^{-1}\phi_2(\mu_1 - \mu_2) + (\phi_1 + \phi_2)^{-1}\Omega\begin{pmatrix}S\\0\end{pmatrix}\right)$$

and

$$n_{12} = \phi_1\phi_2(\phi_1 + \phi_2)^{-1}(\omega_{21}(\mu_{11} - \mu_{21}) + \omega_{22}(\mu_{12} - \mu_{22})),$$

where ω_{21} is an element of Ω^{-1}.

Now, if the option is a call option, then ω_{21} will be negative (we shall return to this point) whilst ω_{22} is positive from positive definiteness. Thus, n_{12} will be positive if $\mu_{11} - \mu_{21}$ is negative and $\mu_{12} - \mu_{22}$ is positive. Such an investor expects that the stock is likely to pay out less and the option to pay out more (compared with the other investor). Interestingly, such a belief is a statement about expectiles, or partial moments.

The investor who is long in calls will hold a straddle, since put–call parity, which will hold in this economy, tells us that the straddle $= 2P_2 - P_1 + k$ if we set time-zero bond prices at 1. Thus we see a long position in calls, short in equity.

To compute the size of the derivatives market under our volatility assumptions, we revisit Equation (2.1) which simplifies to

$$P = \frac{\phi_1\mu_1 + \phi_2\mu_2 - \Omega\begin{pmatrix}S\\0\end{pmatrix}}{(\phi_1 + \phi_2)(1 + r)}.$$

Therefore, the market size in value terms will be

$$p_2 n_{12} = \frac{\phi_1\mu_{12} + \phi_2\mu_{22} - \sigma_{12}S}{(1 + r)(\phi_1 + \phi_2)^2}\phi_1\phi_2(\omega_{21}(\mu_{11} - \mu_{21}) + \omega_{22}(\mu_{12} - \mu_{22})). \tag{2.2}$$

It is clear that the sign and magnitude of the covariance between stock and option will be an important influence on this market size. In fact, when we introduce a more constrained form of heterogeneity in Section 2.5 we will see that two key parameters of interest will be $\beta_{12} \equiv \frac{\sigma_{12}}{\sigma_{22}}$ and $\rho_{12} \equiv \mathrm{Cor}(P_1, P_2)$, and we will consider these also in the sections which follow.

2.3   COMPUTATION OF MOMENTS

2.3.1   Option and Stock

We now obtain expressions for the first and second moments of the option and stock, making no assumptions about the specific underlying price distribution.

Let P_1 be the random future price of the stock with density function pdf(s) and cumulative distribution function $F(s)$. The rth option moment with exercise price k is

$$\mathbb{E}(P_2^r) = \int_k^\infty (s - k)^r \text{pdf}(s)ds.$$

In particular,

$$\mathbb{E}(P_2) = \int_k^\infty s\,\text{pdf}(s)ds - k \int_k^\infty \text{pdf}(s)ds.$$

Define $\mu_{r,k}$ to be the rth partial (upper) moment of P_1:

$$\mu_{r,k} = \int_k^\infty s^r \text{pdf}(s)ds,$$

then

$$\mathbb{E}(P_2) = \mu_{1,k} - k(1 - F(k)) \tag{2.3}$$

and

$$\mathbb{E}(P_2^2) = \int_k^\infty (s^2 - 2ks + k^2)\text{pdf}(s)ds$$

$$= \mu_{2,k} - 2k\mu_{1,k} + k^2(1 - F(k)).$$

Hence,

$$\text{Var}(P_2) = \mu_{2,k} - \mu_{1,k}^2 + k^2(1 - F(k))F(k) - 2k\mu_{1,k} + 2\mu_{1,k}(1 - F(k))k$$

$$= \mu_{2,k} - \mu_{1,k}^2 + k^2(1 - F(k))F(k) - 2\mu_{1,k}F(k)k \tag{2.4}$$

and

$$\mathbb{E}(P_1 P_2) = \int_k^\infty (s - k)s\,\text{pdf}(s)ds$$

$$= \mu_{2,k} - k\mu_{1,k}. \tag{2.5}$$

Therefore,

$$\text{Cov}(P_1, P_2) = \mu_{2,k} - k\mu_{1,k} - \mu\mu_{1,k} + \mu k(1 - F(k)) \tag{2.6}$$

with $\mu \equiv \mathbb{E}(P_1)$. This covariance expression is an important component of the analysis which follows later in this chapter, and combined with $\text{Var}(P_2)$ and $\text{Var}(P_1) \equiv \sigma^2$ gives us the necessary moments for mean-variance analysis.

Note that we do not need an exogenously specified correlation parameter in the model, since the option payout at time 1 is a deterministic function of the contemporaneous stock price and we can write covariance as a function of moments (and partial moments), strike and probability. The correlation between the option price and the stock can be found as follows:

$$\rho_{12} = \mathrm{Cor}(P_1, P_2) = \frac{\mu_{2,k} - k\mu_{1,k} - \mu\mu_{1,k} + \mu k(1 - F(k))}{\sigma\sqrt{\mathrm{Var}(P_2)}}$$

$$= \frac{\mu_{2,k} - k\mu_{1,k} - \mu\mu_{1,k} + \mu k(1 - F(k))}{\sigma\sqrt{\mu_{2,k} - \mu_{1,k}^2 + k^2(1 - F(k))F(k) - 2\mu_{1,k}F(k)k}}. \tag{2.7}$$

In expression (2.7) we see endogenized AD in action. Changing the option strike k clearly impacts the correlation and, as we will shortly see, the relationship between k and ρ_{12} is somewhat non-intuitive.

In anticipation of Section 2.5 we also consider β_{12}. For a general distribution this can be found using Equations (2.4) and (2.6):

$$\beta_{12} = \frac{\mathrm{Cov}(P_1, P_2)}{\mathrm{Var}(P_2)}$$

$$= \frac{\mu_{2,k} - k\mu_{1,k} - \mu\mu_{1,k} + \mu k(1 - F(k))}{\mu_{2,k} - \mu_{1,k}^2 + k^2(1 - F(k))F(k) - 2\mu_{1,k}F(k)k}. \tag{2.8}$$

2.3.2 Comparison with Black–Scholes Delta

Our model is set in a two-period world, where the prices of the stock and option are determined in equilibrium by the relative demands of institutions arising from their subjective forecasts. Within this setting it is impossible for the market to be completed by dynamic trading of the available securities, and so we should expect no relationship between the option price in our model and the price which would be computed by risk-neutral valuation.

Nevertheless, since practitioners generally have well-developed intuition for the behaviour of option prices in the Black–Scholes economy, we briefly consider how β_{12} relates to conventional option Greeks.

We denote the time-t prices of hypothetical stock and call options by p_{1t} and p_{2t}, respectively, arbitrarily set the time-to-expiry equal to 1 and then apply the standard Black–Scholes formula to obtain

$$p_{2t} = p_{1t}N(d_{1t}) - k\exp(-r)N(d_{2t}), \tag{2.9}$$

where d_{1t} and d_{2t} have their usual definitions, p_{1t} follows log-normal Brownian motion, r is the riskless rate and $N(\cdot)$ is the standardized normal distribution.

Applying Ito calculus we see that

$$dp_2 = N(d_{1t})dp_1 + O(dt)$$

so that

$$\mathrm{Cov}_t(p_{2t+1}, p_{1t+1}) = N(d_{1t})\mathrm{var}_t(dp_{1t+1})$$
$$\mathrm{Var}_t(p_{2t+1}) = N(d_{1t})^2\mathrm{var}_t(dp_{1t+1})$$

and hence

$$\beta_{12} = \frac{1}{N(d_{1t})}, \tag{2.10}$$

which is unambiguously greater than 1. We note that β_{12} is a conditional beta and could loosely be thought of as the reciprocal of the option's Black–Scholes delta.

Finally we verify that the limits of Equation (2.8) are plausible for extreme values of the option strike:

$$\lim_{k \to 0} \beta_{12} = \lim_{k \to 0} \frac{\mu_{2,k} - k\mu_{1,k} - \mu\mu_{1,k} + \mu k(1 - F(k))}{\mu_{2,k} - \mu_{1,k}^2 + k^2(1 - F(k))F(k) - 2\mu_{1,k}F(k)k}$$

$$= \frac{\mu_{2,k} - \mu\mu_{1,k}}{\mu_{2,k} - \mu_{1,k}^2}$$

$$= 1 \tag{2.11}$$

and

$$\lim_{k \to \infty} \beta_{12} = \lim_{k \to \infty} \frac{\mu_{2,k} - k\mu_{1,k} - \mu\mu_{1,k} + \mu k(1 - F(k))}{\mu_{2,k} - \mu_{1,k}^2 + k^2(1 - F(k))F(k) - 2\mu_{1,k}F(k)k}$$

$$= \frac{0 - 0 - 0}{0 - 0 - 0}$$

$$= \infty. \tag{2.12}$$

2.3.3　The Sign of ω_{21}

As we have already mentioned, an interesting question is whether the sign of ω_{21} is positive or negative. If we use the expression for a 2×2 determinant,

$$\text{sign}(\omega_{21}) = -\text{sign}(\text{Cov}(P_1, P_2)).$$

A simple condition that guarantees positivity of $\text{Cov}(P_1, P_2)$ is that the covariance is decreasing in k, since $\lim_{k \to \infty} \text{Cov}(P_1, P_2) = 0$ and we show this by means of the proposition below.

Lemma 2.3.1

$$\frac{\partial \text{Cov}(P_1, P_2)}{\partial k} > 0 \ \text{ or } < 0$$

if the mean of the price distribution $(\mu \equiv \mathbb{E}(P_1))$ *is greater than, or less than,* $\dfrac{\mu_{1,k}}{1 - F(k)}$, *respectively.*

Proof: From Equation (2.6) we have

$$\sigma_{12} = \text{Cov}(P_1, P_2) = \mu_{2,k} - k\mu_{1,k} - \mu_{1,k}\mu + \mu k(1 - F(k)).$$

Using Leibnitz's rule to differentiate with respect to k:

$$\frac{\partial \sigma_{12}}{\partial k} = -k^2 \text{pdf}(k) - \mu_{1,k} + k^2 \text{pdf}(k) + k \text{pdf}(k)\mu + \mu(1 - F(k)) - \mu k \text{pdf}(k)$$

$$= \left(\mu - \frac{\mu_{1,k}}{1 - F(k)} \right)(1 - F(k))$$

and the result follows immediately, since $F(k) \leq 1$ by definition of the cumulative distribution function. ∎

Proposition 2.3.1 *If P_1 is almost surely non-negative, then $\mu < \dfrac{\mu_{1,k}}{1 - F(k)}$ for $k > 0$.*

Proof: Feller (1966) and Muldowney *et al.* (2012) show that for any almost surely non-negative random variable X, $\mathbb{E}[X] = \int_0^\infty \mathbb{P}[X > z]dz$. Therefore,

$$\frac{\mu_{1,k}}{1 - F(k)} = \mathbb{E}[P_1 | P_1 > k]$$

$$= \int_0^\infty \mathbb{P}[P_1 > z | P_1 > k]dz$$

$$= \int_0^\infty \frac{\mathbb{P}[P_1 > z \cap P_1 > k]}{1 - \mathbb{P}[P_1 < k]}dz$$

$$= \int_k^\infty \frac{\mathbb{P}[P_1 > z]}{1 - \mathbb{P}[P_1 < k]}dz + \int_0^k \frac{\mathbb{P}[P_1 > k]}{1 - \mathbb{P}[P_1 < k]}dz$$

$$= \int_k^\infty \frac{1 - \mathbb{P}[P_1 < z]}{1 - \mathbb{P}[P_1 < k]}dz + k.$$

Now, using Leibnitz's rule we find

$$\frac{\partial}{\partial k}\left[\frac{\mu_{1,k}}{1 - F(k)}\right] = \frac{f(k)}{1 - F(k)} \int_k^\infty \frac{1 - F[z]}{1 - F[k]}dz + 1 - \frac{1 - F(k)}{1 - F(k)}$$

$$= \frac{f(k)}{1 - F(k)} \int_k^\infty \frac{1 - F[z]}{1 - F[k]}dz$$

$$> 0$$

and since $\mu = \dfrac{\mu_{1,0}}{1 - F(0)}$ it follows that

$$\frac{\mu_{1,k}}{1 - F(k)} > \mu.$$ ∎

Hence, by Proposition 2.3.1 and Lemma 2.3.1 it follows that if P_1 is almost surely non-negative then

$$\frac{\partial \text{Cov}(P_1, P_2)}{\partial k} < 0$$

and so we establish that $\text{Cov}(P_1, P_2) > 0$ and $\omega_{21} < 0$.

2.4　EXAMPLE DISTRIBUTIONS

We now consider several special cases of price distributions. For uniform, scale gamma and Pareto distributions we can obtain tractable expressions for the various partial moments up to order two (and hence for β_{12} and ρ_{12}). We also consider the case of the normal distribution where we find an exact result for a particular case, and use simulation methods for more general analysis.

2.4.1   Uniform Prices

As an introductory example we consider the case where the future price has a uniform distribution. This will highlight a key theme of our results with minimal complexity.

Suppose

$$P_1 \sim \text{Uniform}[0, 1]$$

with $0 < k < 1$. Then

$$F(k) = k$$

$$\mu_{1,k} = \frac{1}{2}(1 - k^2)$$

$$\mu_{2,k} = \frac{1}{3}(1 - k^3)$$

$$\mu = \frac{1}{2}$$

$$\text{Var}(P_1) = \frac{1}{12}$$

$$\mathbb{E}(P_2) = \frac{1}{2}(1 - k)^2$$

$$\text{Var}(P_2) = \mu_{2,k} - \mu_{1,k}^2 + k^2(1 - F(k))F(k) - 2\mu_{1,k}F(k)k$$

$$= \frac{1}{3}(1 - k^3) - \frac{1}{4}(1 - k^2)^2 - k^2(1 - k)$$

$$= \frac{1}{12}(1 - k)^3(1 + 3k)$$

$$\sigma_{12} = \mu_{2,k} - k\mu_{1,k} - \mu\mu_{1,k} + \mu k(1 - F(k))$$

$$= \frac{1}{3}(1 - k^3) - \frac{k}{2}(1 - k^2) - \frac{1}{4}(1 - k^2) + \frac{1}{2}k(1 - k)$$

$$= \frac{1}{3} - \frac{1}{3}k^3 - \frac{k}{2} + \frac{k^3}{2} - \frac{1}{4} + \frac{1}{4}k^2 + \frac{1}{2}k - \frac{1}{2}k^2$$

$$= \frac{1}{6}k^3 - \frac{1}{4}k^2 + \frac{1}{12}$$

$$= \frac{1}{12}(k - 1)^2(1 + 2k)$$

$$> 0 \quad \text{for all} \quad 0 < k < 1.$$

Hence

$$\text{Cor}(P_1, P_2) = \frac{(k - 1)^2(1 + 2k)}{\sqrt{(1 - k)^3(1 + 3k)}}$$

and

$$\beta_{12} = \frac{(k - 1)^2(1 + 2k)}{(1 - k)^3(1 + 3k)}.$$

By repeated applications of L'Hôpital's rule it can be shown that

$$\lim_{k \to 0} \text{Cor}(P_1, P_2) = 1$$

and

$$\lim_{k \to 1} \mathrm{Cor}(P_1, P_2) = 0.$$

Plots of ρ_{12} and β_{12} appear in Figure 2.1. It is immediately striking that the correlation decays very slowly from 1.0 as the strike k is increased towards 1.0 – indeed, when the strike is set at the mean future price ($k = 0.5$), the correlation is approximately 0.9. Although we lack strong prior intuition for the magnitude of this correlation, this relationship seems somewhat surprising and is a characteristic which we will see repeated for the cases of all the other distributions we consider in this section.

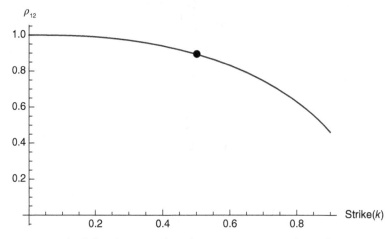

(a) ρ_{12} versus option strike k for the case of Uniform [0,1] prices with $0 < k < 0.9$. The black dot is plotted where strike k equals mean stock price $\mu = 0.5$

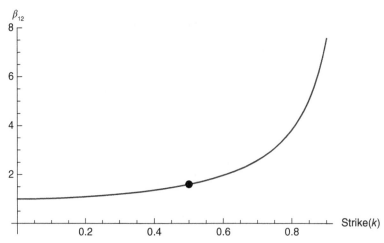

(b) β_{12} versus option strike k for the case of Uniform [0,1] prices with $0 < k < 0.9$. The black dot is plotted where strike k equals mean stock price $\mu = 0.5$

FIGURE 2.1   Correlation and beta for uniform distribution.

2.4.2 Symmetric Distributions with $k = \mu$

Suppose we restrict ourselves to the case where the future price P_1 is a positive random variable from a symmetric distribution and the option strike $k = \mu$, i.e. the option is struck at the mean of the future price distribution and therefore we note that $F(k) = F(\mu) = \frac{1}{2}$.

In this case the expression (2.8) for β_{12} simplifies as follows:

$$\beta_{12} = \frac{\mu_{2,k} - k\mu_{1,k} - \mu\mu_{1,k} + \mu k(1 - F(k))}{\mu_{2,k} - \mu_{1,k}^2 + k^2(1 - F(k))F(k) - 2\mu_{1,k}F(k)k}$$

$$= \frac{\mu_{2k} - 2\mu\mu_{1k} + \frac{1}{2}\mu^2}{\mu_{2k} - \mu_{1k}^2 + \frac{1}{4}\mu^2 - \mu\mu_{1k}}$$

$$= 1 + \frac{\mu_{1k}^2 - \mu\mu_{1k} + \frac{1}{4}\mu^2}{\mu_{2k} - \mu_{1k}^2 + \frac{1}{4}\mu^2 - \mu\mu_{1k}}$$

$$= 1 + \frac{\left(\mu_{1k} - \frac{1}{2}\mu\right)^2}{\mathrm{Var}(P_2)}$$

$$= 1 + \frac{(\mathbb{E}[P_2])^2}{\mathrm{Var}(P_2)}$$

$$= 1 + \frac{(\mathbb{E}[P_2])^2}{\mathbb{E}(P_2^2) - (\mathbb{E}[P_2])^2} \tag{2.13}$$

$$= \frac{\mathbb{E}[P_2^2]}{\mathbb{E}(P_2^2) - (\mathbb{E}[P_2])^2}$$

$$= \frac{1}{1 - \dfrac{(\mathbb{E}[P_2])^2}{\mathbb{E}[P_2^2]}}. \tag{2.14}$$

Now since the option strike $k = \mu$ and the price distribution is symmetric, it follows that the probability of the option payout (P_2) being zero will be $\frac{1}{2}$ (this will happen in all states of the world when $P_1 < k = \mu$). Suppose we denote by θ the ratio of the median of P_2 relative to its mean, i.e.

$$\theta = \frac{\mathrm{median}[P_2]}{\mathbb{E}[P_2]}.$$

The Paley–Zygmund inequality states that if $P_2 \geq 0$ with finite variance then for $0 \leq \theta \leq 1$,

$$\mathrm{Prob}(P_2 > \theta \mathbb{E}(P_2)) \geq (1 - \theta)^2 \frac{(\mathbb{E}[P_2])^2}{\mathbb{E}[P_2^2]}$$

which, using our definition of θ, can be re arranged as

$$\frac{\text{Prob}(P_2 > \text{median}(P_2))}{(1 - \theta)^2} \geq \frac{(\mathbb{E}[P_2])^2}{\mathbb{E}[P_2^2]}$$

$$\frac{1}{2(1 - \theta)^2} \geq \frac{(\mathbb{E}[P_2])^2}{\mathbb{E}[P_2^2]}$$

and applying this to Equation (2.14) above gives

$$\beta_{12} \leq \frac{1}{1 - \dfrac{1}{2(1 - \theta)^2}}$$

$$\leq \frac{2(1 - \theta)^2}{2(1 - \theta)^2 - 1} \equiv \beta_{12}^{\max}.$$

Now for $\theta = 0$ we have

$$\beta_{12}^{\max} = 2$$

and also from Equation 2.13 we know that $\beta_{12} \geq 1$. Hence for symmetric distributions with $k = \mu$ we can improve our bounds on β_{12} and declare that

$$1 \leq \beta_{12} \leq 2 \tag{2.15}$$

irrespective of the specific distribution involved.

In Section 2.3.2 we presented expression (2.10) which – in a contrived example – related β_{12} to the reciprocal of the Black–Scholes delta (for intuitive explanation purposes rather than any mathematical relationship). Following that allusion a little further, for the case of an option with strike $k = \mu$ one might expect a value of β_{12} in the neighbourhood of $\frac{1}{0.5} = 2$, but the second inequality in (2.15) in fact makes 2 the upper limit.

2.4.3 Normal Distribution

2.4.3.1 Where Strike Equals Mean: $k = \mu$ Suppose $P_1 \sim N(\mu, \sigma^2)$ and we define the future option payoff $P_2 = \max[0, P_1 - k] = \max[0, P_1 - \mu]$. To compute $\text{Cor}(P_1, P_2)$ it is convenient to consider instead the transformed variables $Q_1 = \frac{P_1 - \mu}{\sigma}$ and $Q_2 = \frac{P_2}{\sigma}$ so that $Q_1 \sim N(0, 1)$ and $Q_2 = \max[0, Q_1]$. Clearly $\text{Cor}(Q_1, Q_2) = \text{Cor}(P_1, P_2)$, since these are linear transformations. Now Q_1 is a standard normal and Q_2 is a standard normal left-censored at 0. Therefore, $Q_1^2 \sim \chi_1^2$ and $\mathbb{E}[Q_1^2] = 1$. Furthermore, $Q_2^2 | Q_2 > 0 \sim \chi_1^2$ (in other words, given a positive option payoff, the distribution of Q_2^2 will be chi-squared with one degree of freedom, as it is simply the distribution of a squared standard normal). Since $\mathbb{P}[Q_2 > 0] = \frac{1}{2}$ it follows that $\mathbb{E}[Q_2^2] = \frac{1}{2}$.

We also note the following helpful result:

$$\mathbb{E}[Q_2] = \frac{1}{\sqrt{2\pi}} \int_0^\infty x e^{-\frac{1}{2}x^2} dx$$

$$= -\frac{1}{\sqrt{2\pi}} \left[e^{-\frac{1}{2}x^2} \right]_0^\infty dx$$

$$= \frac{1}{\sqrt{2\pi}}.$$

We can now write:

$$\mathrm{Cor}(P_1, P_2) = \mathrm{Cor}(Q_1, Q_2) = \frac{\mathbb{E}[Q_1 Q_2] - \mathbb{E}[Q_1]\mathbb{E}[Q_2]}{\sqrt{\mathrm{Var}(Q_1)\mathrm{Var}(Q_2)}}$$

$$= \frac{\mathbb{E}[Q_1 Q_2]}{\mathrm{SD}(Q_2)}$$

$$= \frac{\frac{1}{2}\mathbb{E}[Q_1 Q_2 | Q_1 > 0] + \frac{1}{2}\mathbb{E}[Q_1 Q_2 | Q_1 < 0]}{\sqrt{\mathbb{E}[Q_2^2] - (\mathbb{E}[Q_2])^2}}$$

$$= \frac{\frac{1}{2}\mathbb{E}[Q_1 Q_2 | Q_1 > 0]}{\sqrt{\mathbb{E}[Q_2^2] - (\mathbb{E}[Q_2])^2}}$$

$$= \frac{\frac{1}{2}\mathbb{E}[Q_1^2]}{\sqrt{\mathbb{E}[Q_2^2] - (\mathbb{E}[Q_2])^2}}$$

$$= \frac{\dfrac{1}{2}}{\sqrt{\dfrac{1}{2} - \dfrac{1}{2\pi}}}$$

$$= \frac{\dfrac{1}{2}}{\sqrt{\dfrac{\pi - 1}{2\pi}}}$$

$$= \sqrt{\frac{\pi}{2(\pi - 1)}}$$

$$\approx 0.856 \text{ to 3 d.p.}$$

Furthermore,

$$\beta_{12} = \frac{\mathbb{E}[Q_1 Q_2] - \mathbb{E}[Q_1]\mathbb{E}[Q_2]}{\mathrm{Var}[Q_2]}$$

$$= \frac{\dfrac{1}{2}}{\dfrac{\pi - 1}{2\pi}}$$

$$= \frac{\pi}{\pi - 1}$$

$$\approx 1.467 \text{ to 3 d.p.}$$

and

$$\beta_{21} = \frac{E[Q_1 Q_2] - E[Q_1]E[Q_2]}{Var[Q_1]}$$

$$= \frac{1}{2}.$$

In this case we see that the beta of the option with respect to the stock (β_{21}) is $\frac{1}{2}$, which is arguably more consistent with intuition from Black–Scholes. Bearing in mind that the variance of Q_1 is 1, this emphasizes that the very high correlation value is influenced by the relatively low variance of the option payoff Q_2 (which is well below 1) rather than the covariance value *per se*.

Our result here contributes to the literature on correlation attenuation, as studied by Muthén (1990) in the case of censored bivariate normal distributions. Muthén provides various general formulas for the computation of correlations in the presence of censoring, and presents numerical results which show that correlations such as ours will remain high and decline at a relatively slow pace even as the amount of censoring is increased quite significantly (corresponding in our model to an increase in the option strike price). Our example above has the merit of an exact analytical solution, albeit for a single special case.

2.4.3.2 General Normal Distributions To develop some intuition for more general cases, in Figure 2.2 we generate several sets of 500,000 independent and identically distributed (i.i.d.) simulated prices and compute associated values of β_{12} and ρ_{12}, applying Equations (2.6), (2.7) and (2.8). We plot the relevant parameter value against strike price for various different choices of σ^2 (the variance of P_1).

In Figure 2.2 it is clear that when the strike $k = \mu = 100$ we find that ρ_{12} and β_{12} do not depend on σ^2. This is precisely the situation which we describe above, and indeed simulated values of ρ_{12}

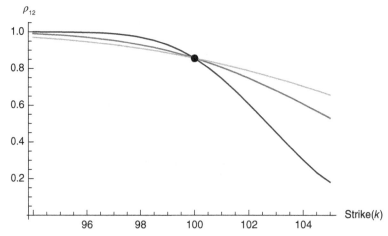

(a) Correlation ρ_{12} versus strike k for $P_1 \sim N(100, \sigma^2)$ and $\sigma \in \{2, 4, 6\}$ (lowest to highest curves, respectively)

FIGURE 2.2 Simulated correlation and beta between stock and option when future price has a normal distribution.

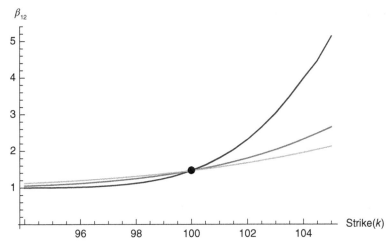

(b) Beta β_{12} versus strike k for $P_1 \sim N(100, \sigma^2)$ and $\sigma \in \{2, 4, 6\}$ (highest to lowest curves, respectively)

FIGURE 2.2 (*Continued*)

and β_{12} approximately equal the theoretical values which we calculated in that case (0.856 and 1.467, respectively).

2.4.4 Scale Gamma

Denote $\mathrm{pdf}_{X'}(s) = \frac{s^{a-1}\exp(-s)}{\Gamma(a)}$. We shall assume a is a positive integer, in which case for X':

$$F_{X'}(k) = 1 - \sum_{i=0}^{a-1} \frac{1}{i!} k^i \exp(-k)$$

and introducing a scale factor so that $X = \lambda X'$ ($\lambda > 0$):

$$F_X(k) = 1 - \sum_{i=0}^{a-1} \frac{1}{i!} \frac{k^i}{\lambda^i} \exp\left(-\frac{k}{\lambda}\right)$$

and

$$1 - F_X(k) = \sum_{i=0}^{a-1} \frac{1}{i!} \frac{k^i}{\lambda^i} \exp\left(-\frac{k}{\lambda}\right).$$

It follows directly from above that the partial mth moment of X' is

$$\int_k^\infty \frac{s^{m+a-1}\exp(-s)}{\Gamma(a)} ds$$

$$= \frac{\Gamma(m+a)}{\Gamma(a)} \int_k^\infty \frac{s^{m+a-1}\exp(-s)}{\Gamma(m+a)} ds$$

$$= \frac{\Gamma(m+a)}{\Gamma(a)} \left(\sum_{i=0}^{m+a-1} \frac{1}{i!} k^i \exp(-k)\right). \tag{2.16}$$

More generally, we can compute the partial moment of X (the scaled random variable) by integration:

$$\mu_{m,k} = \int_k^\infty \frac{s^{m+a-1}e^{-\frac{s}{\lambda}}}{\Gamma(a)\lambda^a}\,ds$$

$$= \frac{1}{\Gamma(a)\lambda^a}\int_{\frac{k}{\lambda}}^\infty (q\lambda)^{m+a-1}e^{-q}\frac{ds}{dq}\,dq \qquad \text{where } q = \frac{s}{\lambda}$$

$$= \frac{\lambda^{m+a}}{\Gamma(a)\lambda^a}\int_{\frac{k}{\lambda}}^\infty q^{m+a-1}e^{-q}\,dq$$

$$= \frac{\lambda^m}{\Gamma(a)}\Gamma\left(m+a,\frac{k}{\lambda}\right) \tag{2.17}$$

where $\Gamma(\cdot,\cdot)$ is the incomplete gamma function, which is the value of the integral by definition. It can be shown that Equation (2.16) is a power-series expansion of the more general expression (2.17) when $\lambda = 1$.

Furthermore, since $\Gamma(m+a,0) = \Gamma(m+a)$ we have

$$\mu_m = \lambda^m\frac{\Gamma(m+a)}{\Gamma(a)}$$

so that

$$\mu = \mu_1 = a\lambda$$

$$\mu_2 = (a+1)a\lambda^2$$

$$\sigma^2 = a\lambda^2$$

$$\mu_{1,k} = \lambda\frac{\Gamma\left(a+1,\frac{k}{\lambda}\right)}{\Gamma(a)}$$

$$\mu_{2,k} = \lambda^2\frac{\Gamma\left(a+2,\frac{k}{\lambda}\right)}{\Gamma(a)}.$$

These parameters can now be substituted into the various expressions in Section 2.3 to compute stock and option moments as required.

In Figure 2.3 we plot values of β_{12} and ρ_{12} which we can obtain analytically without resorting to simulation. For cases where option strike k equals mean μ, we find correlation values of at least 0.9 and β_{12} between 1.0 and 1.5, which echoes our findings for the case of the uniform and normal distributions.

2.4.5 Pareto

The Pareto distribution for prices receives theoretical support based on a number of arguments. The most pertinent is based on a sequence of papers by Reed, who considers the distribution of log-normal Brownian motion whose killing time is exponentially distributed. Reed and Jorgensen (2004) show that if the previous variable is a return, then the price is distributed as double Pareto-lognormal and has power-law behaviour in the tails. A similar distribution but with less obvious financial interpretations is the log-hyperbolic distribution (Barndorff-Nielsen, 1977).

Accordingly, we assume $\text{pdf}(s) = cs^{-(1+a)}$ where $\delta < s$, $c = a\delta^a$ and all three constants are assumed positive. So that the relevant moments exist, we assume $\alpha \geq 3$.

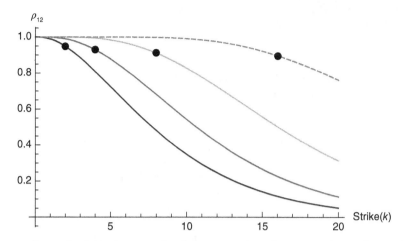

(a) ρ_{12} versus option strike k for the case of scale gamma prices. Curves are drawn for $\lambda = 2$ and shape parameters $a \in \{1, 2, 4, 8\}$ (lowest to highest curves, respectively) corresponding to the price means $\{2, 4, 8, 16\}$ and variances $\{4, 8, 16, 32\}$. For each curve black dots are plotted where strike k equals mean stock price μ

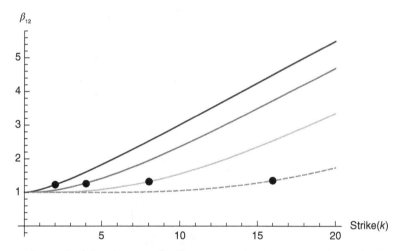

(b) β_{12} versus option strike k for the case of scale gamma prices. Curves are drawn for $\lambda = 2$ and shape parameters $a \in \{1, 2, 4, 8\}$ (highest to lowest curves, respectively) corresponding to the price means $\{2, 4, 8, 16\}$ and variances $\{4, 8, 16, 32\}$. For each curve black dots are plotted where strike k equals mean stock price μ

FIGURE 2.3   Correlation and beta for scale gamma distribution.

Firstly we note that

$$\mathbb{E}(P_1^r) = c \int_\delta^\infty s^{r-1-\alpha} ds = c \left[\frac{s^{r-\alpha}}{r-\alpha} \right]_\delta^\infty = c \frac{\delta^{r-\alpha}}{\alpha - r} = \frac{\alpha \delta^r}{\alpha - r},$$

$$\mu_{r,k} = c \int_k^\infty s^{r-1-\alpha} ds = c \left[\frac{s^{r-\alpha}}{r-\alpha} \right]_k^\infty = c \frac{k^{r-\alpha}}{\alpha - r}$$

and

$$\text{Prob}(P_1 > k) = \left(\frac{\delta}{k}\right)^{\alpha}.$$

We proceed to compute moments below. Although the algebra lacks the elegance of the scale gamma example, we nonetheless obtain closed-form expressions.

$$\mathbb{E}(P_2) = \mathbb{E}([P_1 - k]^+) = c \int_k^{\infty} s^{-\alpha} ds - ck \int_k^{\infty} s^{-1-\alpha} ds$$

$$= c \left[\frac{s^{1-\alpha}}{1-\alpha}\right]_k^{\infty} - k\left(\frac{\delta}{k}\right)^{\alpha}$$

$$= c\frac{k^{1-\alpha}}{\alpha - 1} - k^{1-\alpha}\delta^{\alpha}$$

$$= \alpha\delta^{\alpha}\frac{k^{1-\alpha}}{\alpha - 1} - k^{1-\alpha}\delta^{\alpha}$$

$$= \delta^{\alpha}k^{1-\alpha}\frac{1}{\alpha - 1}$$

$$= \frac{\delta^{\alpha}}{(\alpha - 1)k^{\alpha-1}}$$

and

$$\mathbb{E}(P_1 P_2) = \int_k^{\infty}(s^2 - ks)\text{pdf}(s)ds$$

$$= c\frac{k^{2-\alpha}}{\alpha - 2} - \frac{c}{(\alpha - 1)k^{\alpha-2}}$$

$$= c\frac{k^{2-\alpha}}{\alpha - 2} - c\frac{k^{2-\alpha}}{\alpha - 1}$$

$$= ck^{2-\alpha}\left(\frac{1}{\alpha - 2} - \frac{1}{\alpha - 1}\right)$$

$$= ck^{2-\alpha}\left(\frac{\alpha - 1 - \alpha + 2}{(\alpha - 2)(\alpha - 1)}\right)$$

$$= k^{2-\alpha}\left(\frac{\alpha\delta^{\alpha}}{(\alpha - 1)(\alpha - 2)}\right).$$

Therefore,

$$\text{Cov}(P_1, P_2) = \mathbb{E}(P_1 P_2) - \mathbb{E}(P_1)\mathbb{E}(P_2)$$

$$= k^{2-\alpha}\left(\frac{\alpha\delta^{\alpha}}{(\alpha - 1)(\alpha - 2)}\right) - \frac{\alpha\delta}{(\alpha - 1)}\frac{\delta^{\alpha}}{(\alpha - 1)k^{\alpha-1}}$$

$$= \alpha\delta^{\alpha}k^{1-\alpha}\left(\frac{k(\alpha - 1) - \delta(\alpha - 2)}{(\alpha - 1)^2(\alpha - 2)}\right).$$

Furthermore,

$$Var(P_1) = \sigma^2 = \mathbb{E}(P_1^2) - (\mathbb{E}(P_1))^2$$

$$= \frac{\alpha\delta^2}{(\alpha - 2)} - \frac{\alpha^2\delta^2}{(\alpha - 1)^2}$$

$$= \frac{\alpha\delta^2}{(\alpha - 2)(\alpha - 1)^2},$$

$$\mathbb{E}(P_2^2) = \int_k^\infty (s - k)^2 pdf(s)ds$$

$$= c\int_k^\infty (s - k)^2 s^{-(1+\alpha)}ds$$

$$= c\int_k^\infty (s^2 - 2sk + k^2)s^{-(1+\alpha)}ds$$

$$= c\int_k^\infty s^{1-\alpha} - 2ks^{-\alpha} + k^2 s^{-(1+\alpha)}ds$$

$$= c\left[\frac{s^{2-\alpha}}{2 - \alpha} - 2k\frac{s^{1-\alpha}}{1 - \alpha} - k^2\frac{s^{-\alpha}}{\alpha}\right]_k^\infty$$

$$= c\left[-\frac{k^{2-\alpha}}{2 - \alpha} + 2k\frac{k^{1-\alpha}}{1 - \alpha} + k^2\frac{k^{-\alpha}}{\alpha}\right]$$

$$= c\left[\frac{(1 - \alpha)(2 - \alpha)k^{2-\alpha} + 2(2 - \alpha)\alpha k^{2-\alpha} - \alpha(1 - \alpha)k^{2-\alpha}}{\alpha(1 - \alpha)(2 - \alpha)}\right]$$

$$= c\left[\frac{k^{2-\alpha}(2 - 3\alpha + \alpha^2 + 4\alpha - 2\alpha^2 - \alpha + \alpha^2)}{\alpha(1 - \alpha)(2 - \alpha)}\right]$$

$$= c\left[\frac{2k^{2-\alpha}}{\alpha(1 - \alpha)(2 - \alpha)}\right]$$

$$= \frac{2\delta^\alpha k^{2-\alpha}}{(1 - \alpha)(2 - \alpha)}$$

and

$$Var(P_2) = \mathbb{E}(P_2^2) - (\mathbb{E}(P_2))^2$$

$$= \frac{2\delta^\alpha k^{2-\alpha}}{(1 - \alpha)(2 - \alpha)} - \left(\frac{\delta^\alpha}{(\alpha - 1)k^{\alpha-1}}\right)^2$$

$$= \frac{2\delta^\alpha k^{2-\alpha}}{(1 - \alpha)(2 - \alpha)} - \frac{\delta^{2\alpha}}{(\alpha - 1)^2 k^{2\alpha-2}}$$

$$= \frac{2\delta^\alpha k^\alpha(\alpha - 1) - (\alpha - 2)\delta^{2\alpha}}{(\alpha - 1)^2(\alpha - 2)k^{2\alpha-2}}$$

$$= \frac{2\delta^\alpha k^\alpha(\alpha - 1) - (\alpha - 2)\delta^{2\alpha}}{(\alpha - 1)^2(\alpha - 2)k^{2\alpha-2}}$$

$$= \frac{\delta^\alpha k^{2-2\alpha}(2(\alpha - 1)k^\alpha - \delta^\alpha(\alpha - 2))}{(\alpha - 1)^2(\alpha - 2)}.$$

Therefore,

$$\beta_{12} = \frac{\text{Cov}(P_1, P_2)}{\text{Var}(P_2)}$$

$$= \frac{\alpha \delta^\alpha k^{1-\alpha}(k(\alpha-1) - \delta(\alpha-2))}{\delta^\alpha k^{2-2\alpha}(2(\alpha-1)k^\alpha - \delta^\alpha(\alpha-2))}$$

$$= \alpha k^{\alpha-1} \frac{k(\alpha-1) - \delta(\alpha-2)}{2k^\alpha(\alpha-1) - \delta^\alpha(\alpha-2)}$$

and

$$\rho_{12} = \frac{\text{Cov}(P_1, P_2)}{\sqrt{\text{Var}(P_1)\text{Var}(P_2)}}$$

$$= \frac{\alpha \delta^\alpha k^{1-\alpha}(k(\alpha-1) - \delta(\alpha-2))}{\sqrt{\alpha \delta^2 \delta^\alpha k^{2-2\alpha}(2(\alpha-1)k^\alpha - \delta^\alpha(\alpha-2))}}.$$

As usual we plot examples of ρ_{12} and β_{12} in Figure 2.4 and recognize the now familiar pattern of high correlations and β_{12} values slightly above 1 when the option strike is set at the mean of the price distribution.

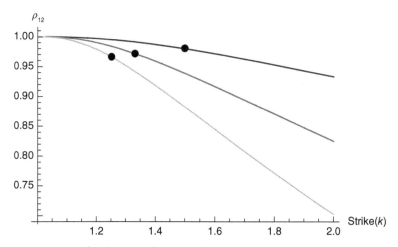

(a) ρ_{12} versus option strike k for the case of Pareto prices. Curves are drawn for $\delta = 1$ and shape parameters $\alpha \in \{3, 4, 5\}$ (highest to lowest curves, respectively) corresponding to the price means $\left\{\frac{3}{2}, \frac{4}{3}, \frac{5}{4}\right\}$ and variances $\left\{\frac{3}{4}, \frac{4}{18}, \frac{5}{48}\right\}$. For each curve black dots are plotted where strike k equals mean stock price μ

FIGURE 2.4   Correlation and beta for Pareto distribution.

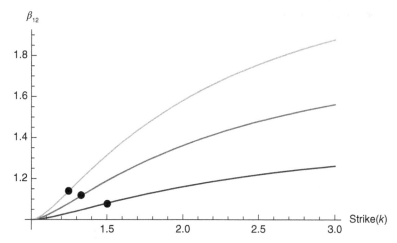

(b) β_{12} versus option strike k for the case of Pareto prices. Curves are drawn for $\delta = 1$ and shape parameters $\alpha \in \{3, 4, 5\}$ (lowest to highest curves, respectively) corresponding to the price means $\left\{\frac{3}{2}, \frac{4}{3}, \frac{5}{4}\right\}$ and variances $\left\{\frac{3}{4}, \frac{4}{18}, \frac{5}{48}\right\}$. For each curve black dots are plotted where strike k equals mean stock price μ

FIGURE 2.4 (*Continued*)

2.5 HETEROGENEITY AND CTA MARKET SIZE

2.5.1 Institutional Demands

We now proceed to impose a specific form of heterogeneity onto the beliefs of investors, and use this to investigate the size of the derivative market. Throughout this section we continue to apply the mean-variance framework introduced in Section 2.2, however the alternative examples of specific distributions presented in Section 2.4 provide general guidance as to plausible parameter values, especially for correlation and beta which we will discuss further later in this section.

Suppose the managers of *Institution 1* believe that stocks are priced as in this model but the managers of *Institution 2* think there is an additional independent noise $(0, d^2)$. They both agree on means. In common with Detemple and Selden (1991), we assume that they agree on the option price. Viewing the option as a simplified abstraction of a CTA fund, we could loosely think of this as a situation where *Institution 2* holds a long equity portfolio combined with a CTA investment as a diversifier against market shocks, to which they accord a greater probability than *Institution 1*.[2]

Expressed symbolically:

$$\Omega_2 = \Omega_1 + \begin{pmatrix} d^2 & 0 \\ 0 & 0 \end{pmatrix}$$

---

[2]Historically, CTAs have tended to perform strongly amidst equity market crises in a number of well-known cases, e.g. sharp falls in September 2008 as well as the prolonged weakness in 2015–16. Hurst *et al.* (2013) discuss the performance of time-series momentum strategies in equity bear markets.

and a matrix inversion lemma gives

$$\Omega_2^{-1} = \Omega_1^{-1} - \frac{\Omega_1^{-1} \begin{pmatrix} d^2 & 0 \\ 0 & 0 \end{pmatrix} \Omega_1^{-1}}{1 + d^2 \omega_{11}}$$

where we define

$$\Omega_1^{-1} = \begin{pmatrix} \omega_{11} & \omega_{12} \\ \omega_{12} & \omega_{22} \end{pmatrix}.$$

For the *Institution 1* demand:

$$\begin{pmatrix} n_{11} \\ n_{12} \end{pmatrix} = \phi_1 \Omega_1^{-1} (\phi_1 \Omega_1^{-1} + \phi_2 \Omega_2^{-1})^{-1} \begin{pmatrix} S \\ 0 \end{pmatrix}$$

$$= \phi_1 \Omega_1^{-1} \Omega_1 \left[\phi_1 I_2 + \phi_2 I_2 - \phi_2 \frac{\Omega_1^{-1} \begin{pmatrix} d^2 & 0 \\ 0 & 0 \end{pmatrix}}{1 + d^2 \omega_{11}} \right]^{-1} \begin{pmatrix} S \\ 0 \end{pmatrix}$$

$$= \phi_1 \left[(\phi_1 + \phi_2) I_2 - \phi_2 \frac{\begin{pmatrix} \omega_{11} d^2 & 0 \\ \omega_{21} d^2 & 0 \end{pmatrix}}{1 + d^2 \omega_{11}} \right]^{-1} \begin{pmatrix} S \\ 0 \end{pmatrix}$$

$$= \phi_1 \begin{pmatrix} \phi_1 + \phi_2 - \phi_2 \dfrac{\omega_{11} d^2}{1 + d^2 \omega_{11}} & 0 \\ -\dfrac{\phi_2 \omega_{21} d^2}{1 + d^2 \omega_{11}} & \phi_1 + \phi_2 \end{pmatrix}^{-1} \begin{pmatrix} S \\ 0 \end{pmatrix}$$

$$= \phi_1 \begin{pmatrix} \dfrac{\phi_1 + \phi_2 + \phi_1 \omega_{11} d^2}{1 + d^2 \omega_{11}} & 0 \\ -\dfrac{\phi_2 \omega_{21} d^2}{1 + d^2 \omega_{11}} & \phi_1 + \phi_2 \end{pmatrix}^{-1} \begin{pmatrix} S \\ 0 \end{pmatrix}$$

$$= \frac{\phi_1}{\det(\cdot)} \begin{pmatrix} \phi_1 + \phi_2 & 0 \\ \dfrac{\phi_2 \omega_{21} d^2}{1 + d^2 \omega_{11}} & \dfrac{\phi_1 + \phi_2 + \phi_1 \omega_{11} d^2}{1 + d^2 \omega_{11}} \end{pmatrix} \begin{pmatrix} S \\ 0 \end{pmatrix}.$$

Therefore,

$$n_{11} = \frac{\phi_1 (1 + d^2 \omega_{11})}{\phi_1 + \phi_2 + \phi_1 \omega_{11} d^2} S = \frac{\phi_1 (1 + d^2 \omega_{11})}{\phi_2 + \phi_1 (1 + \omega_{11} d^2)} S > 0$$

and

$$n_{12} = \frac{\phi_1}{\phi_1 + \phi_2} \frac{\phi_2 \omega_{21} d^2}{\phi_2 + \phi_1 (1 + \omega_{11} d^2)} S$$

so that $\text{sign}(n_{12}) = \text{sign}(\omega_{21})$.

Hence, *Institution 1* will hold a strictly positive quantity of the stock and a *short* position in the option, assuming $\omega_{21} < 0$ as we have proved in Section 2.3.

For the *Institution 2* demand:

$$\begin{pmatrix} n_{21} \\ n_{22} \end{pmatrix} = \phi_2 \Omega_2^{-1} (\phi_1 \Omega_1^{-1} + \phi_2 \Omega_2^{-1})^{-1} \begin{pmatrix} S \\ 0 \end{pmatrix}.$$

Repeating the approach:

$$\Omega_1 = \Omega_2 - \begin{pmatrix} d^2 & 0 \\ 0 & 0 \end{pmatrix}$$

$$\Omega_1^{-1} = \Omega_2^{-1} + \frac{\Omega_2^{-1} \begin{pmatrix} d^2 & 0 \\ 0 & 0 \end{pmatrix} \Omega_2^{-1}}{1 - d^2 \omega_{11}^{(2)}}$$

so

$$\begin{pmatrix} n_{21} \\ n_{22} \end{pmatrix} = \phi_2 \left[(\phi_1 + \phi_2) I_2 + \phi_1 \frac{\Omega_2^{-1} \begin{pmatrix} d^2 & 0 \\ 0 & 0 \end{pmatrix}}{1 - d^2 \omega_{11}^{(2)}} \right]^{-1} \begin{pmatrix} S \\ 0 \end{pmatrix}$$

with

$$\Omega_2^{-1} = \frac{\begin{pmatrix} \sigma_{22} & -\sigma_{12} \\ -\sigma_{21} & \sigma_{11} + d^2 \end{pmatrix}}{\det(\Omega_1) + d^2 \sigma_{22}} \equiv \begin{pmatrix} \omega_{11}^{(2)} & \omega_{12}^{(2)} \\ \omega_{12}^{(2)} & \omega_{22}^{(2)} \end{pmatrix}$$

$$\omega_{11}^{(2)} = \frac{\sigma_{22}}{\det(\Omega_1) + d^2 \sigma_{22}} = \frac{\omega_{11}}{1 + d^2 \omega_{11}}$$

$$\omega_{21}^{(2)} = \frac{-\sigma_{21}}{\det(\Omega_1) + d^2 \sigma_{22}} = \frac{\omega_{21}}{1 + d^2 \omega_{11}}$$

$$\omega_{22}^{(2)} = \frac{\sigma_{11} + d^2}{\det(\Omega_1) + d^2 \sigma_{22}}$$

and

$$1 - d^2 \omega_{11}^{(2)} = 1 - \frac{d^2 \omega_{11}}{1 + d^2 \omega_{11}} = \frac{1}{1 + d^2 \omega_{11}}.$$

Let

$$\theta = \frac{1}{1 + d^2 \omega_{11}}$$

$$1 - \theta = \frac{d^2 \omega_{11}}{1 + d^2 \omega_{11}}$$

then

$$\begin{pmatrix} n_{21} \\ n_{22} \end{pmatrix} = \phi_2 \left(\left(\begin{matrix} \phi_1 + \phi_2 & 0 \\ 0 & \phi_1 + \phi_2 \end{matrix} \right) + \phi_1 \frac{\begin{pmatrix} \theta \omega_{11} d^2 & 0 \\ \theta \omega_{21} d^2 & 0 \end{pmatrix}}{1 - d^2 \omega_{11}^{(2)}} \right)^{-1} \begin{pmatrix} S \\ 0 \end{pmatrix}$$

$$= \phi_2 \left(\begin{matrix} \phi_1 + \phi_2 + \phi_1 \frac{\theta \omega_{11} d^2}{\theta} & 0 \\ \phi_1 \frac{\theta \omega_{21} d^2}{\theta} & \phi_1 + \phi_2 \end{matrix} \right)^{-1} \begin{pmatrix} S \\ 0 \end{pmatrix}$$

$$= \phi_2 \left(\begin{matrix} \phi_1 (1 + d^2 \omega_{11}) + \phi_2 & 0 \\ \phi_1 \omega_{21} d^2 & \phi_1 + \phi_2 \end{matrix} \right)^{-1} \begin{pmatrix} S \\ 0 \end{pmatrix}$$

$$= \frac{\phi_2}{\det(\cdot)} \left(\begin{matrix} \phi_1 + \phi_2 & 0 \\ -\phi_1 \omega_{21} d^2 & \phi_1 (1 + d^2 \omega_{11}) + \phi_2 \end{matrix} \right) \begin{pmatrix} S \\ 0 \end{pmatrix}.$$

Hence demands are given by

$$n_{21} = \frac{\phi_2 S}{\phi_1 (1 + d^2 \omega_{11}) + \phi_2}$$

$$n_{22} = -\frac{\phi_2}{\phi_1 + \phi_2} \frac{\phi_1 \omega_{21} d^2}{\phi_1 (1 + d^2 \omega_{11}) + \phi_2} S.$$

We see that *Institution 2* will hold whatever amount of the stock is not held by *Institution 1* and will take a *long* position in the option, i.e. $n_{11} + n_{21} = S$ and $n_{12} + n_{22} = 0$.

Therefore it follows that

$$\text{Size of option market} = \left| \frac{\phi_1 \phi_2 \omega_{12} d^2 S}{(\phi_1 + \phi_2)(\phi_1 + \phi_2 + \phi_1 \omega_{11} d^2)} \right|$$

$$= \left| \frac{\phi_1 \phi_2 \sigma_{12} d^2 S}{\det(\Omega_1)(\phi_1 + \phi_2)(\phi_1 (1 + \omega_{11} d^2) + \phi_2)} \right|. \tag{2.18}$$

2.5.2   Size of the Option Market

We now consider the possible maximum value which the size of the option market can reach, based on expression (2.18):

$$\text{Size of option market} = \left| \frac{\phi_1 \phi_2 \omega_{12} d^2 S}{(\phi_1 + \phi_2)(\phi_1 + \phi_2 + \phi_1 \omega_{11} d^2)} \right|$$

$$= \left| \frac{\phi_1 \phi_2 a}{(\phi_1 + \phi_2)^2 + \phi_1 (\phi_1 + \phi_2) b} \right|,$$

where we define $a = \omega_{12} d^2 S$ and $b = \omega_{11} d^2$ to keep the algebra tidy. Taking logs we obtain

$$\ln(\text{Size}) = \ln a + \ln(\phi_1 \phi_2) - \ln(\phi_1 + \phi_2) - \ln(\phi_1 + \phi_2 + \phi_1 b).$$

We now find values of ϕ_1 and ϕ_2 which maximize this expression. First we hold ϕ_2 constant and differentiate with respect to ϕ_1:

$$\frac{1}{\phi_1} - \frac{1}{\phi_1 + \phi_2} - \frac{1+b}{\phi_2 + \phi_1(1+b)} = 0$$

$$(\phi_1 + \phi_2)(\phi_2 + \phi_1(1+b)) - \phi_1(\phi_2 + \phi_1(1+b)) - (1+b)\phi_1(\phi_1 + \phi_2) = 0$$

$$\phi_1\phi_2(2+b) + \phi_2^2 + \phi_1^2(1+b) - \phi_1\phi_2 - \phi_1^2(1+b) - \phi_1^2(1+b) - \phi_1\phi_2(1+b) = 0$$

$$-\phi_1^2(1+b) + \phi_2^2 = 0.$$

Therefore, when

$$\phi_1 = \frac{\phi_2}{\sqrt{1+b}}, \tag{2.19}$$

the size of the option market is maximized.

We next note that the size expression (2.18) is homogeneous of degree zero in ϕ_1 and ϕ_2. Therefore we can normalize the risk tolerances by setting $\phi_1 + \phi_2 = 1$, i.e. $\phi_1 \to \phi = \frac{1}{1+\sqrt{1+b}}$ and $\phi_2 \to 1 - \phi$. This gives

$$\text{Size of option market} = \left| \frac{\phi(1-\phi)\omega_{12}d^2 S}{1 + \phi\omega_{11}d^2} \right| \tag{2.20}$$

$$= \left| \frac{\phi(1-\phi)a}{1 + b\phi} \right|. \tag{2.21}$$

We now optimize over ϕ. Once again we start by taking logs:

$$\ln(\text{Size}) = \ln\phi + \ln(1-\phi) + \ln a - \ln(1+\phi b).$$

Differentiating to obtain first-order optimality conditions:

$$\frac{1}{\phi} - \frac{1}{1-\phi} - \frac{b}{1+\phi b} = 0$$

$$(1-\phi)(1+\phi b) - \phi(1+\phi b) - b\phi(1-\phi) = 0$$

$$1 - \phi + \phi b - \phi^2 b - \phi - \phi^2 b - b\phi + b\phi^2 = 0$$

$$1 - 2\phi - \phi^2 b = 0.$$

Hence we find that market size will be maximized when

$$\phi = \phi^* = \frac{-2 + \sqrt{4 + 4b}}{2b}$$

$$= \frac{-1 + \sqrt{1+b}}{b}.$$

Evidently ϕ^* is decreasing in b (recalling our definition of $b = \omega_{11}d^2 > 0$, the b parameter is increasing in the incremental variance believed by *Institution 2*). Furthermore, by L'Hôpital's rule, $\lim_{b \to 0} \phi^* = \frac{1}{2}$, i.e. as the perceived incremental variance d^2 becomes negligible, the market size is maximized when both institutions have approximately equal risk tolerance (since $\phi = \phi_1$ and $\phi_1 + \phi_2 = 1$ by definition). This is consistent with condition (2.19).

Expressed informally, market size will be maximized when *Institution 2* is sufficiently risk-tolerant to take a large position in options and their demand is satisfied by a commensurately risk-tolerant *Institution 1*. If *Institution 2* was to increase its risk tolerance beyond this point, then *ceteris paribus* the size of option trading would decrease because their trading partner would not have enough risk appetite to satisfy additional demand.

By substituting ϕ^* into (2.20) we find the maximum market size

$$
\text{Max.Size} = \left| \frac{(1 - \phi^*)\phi^* \omega_{12} d^2 S}{1 + \phi^* \omega_{11} d^2} \right|
$$

$$
= \left| \frac{\dfrac{-1 + \sqrt{1+b}}{b} \dfrac{b + 1 - \sqrt{1+b}}{b} a}{1 + b\phi^*} \right|
$$

$$
= \left| \frac{\dfrac{-(b+1) + (1+b)^{\frac{3}{2}} + \sqrt{1+b} - (1+b)}{b^2} a}{\sqrt{1+b}} \right|
$$

$$
= \left| \frac{\dfrac{\sqrt{1+b}((1+b) - 2\sqrt{1+b} + 1)}{b^2} a}{\sqrt{1+b}} \right|
$$

$$
= \left| \frac{(\sqrt{1 + \omega_{11}d^2} - 1)^2 \omega_{12} d^2 S}{\omega_{11}^2 d^4} \right|
$$

$$
= \left| \frac{(1 + \omega_{11}d^2 - 2\sqrt{1 + \omega_{11}d^2} + 1)\omega_{12}d^2 S}{\omega_{11}^2 d^4} \right|. \tag{2.22}
$$

We now consider two approximations of expression (2.22).

2.5.2.1 'Small' Incremental Variance d^2

For 'small' d^2 we consider a second-order Taylor approximation, valid for $d^2 \omega_{11} < 1 \Leftrightarrow \frac{d^2}{\sigma_{11}} < (1 - \rho_{12}^2)$ where ρ_{12} is the correlation between the price of the stock (asset 1) and the option payoff (asset 2). Recall that the ratio $\frac{d^2}{\sigma_{11}}$ is the *incremental* stock price variance perceived by *Institution 2* relative to the variance perceived by *Institution 1*, e.g. a value of 1 would mean that *Institution 2* believes the stock price has twice as much variance as *Institution 1*.

$$\text{Max.Size} = \left| \frac{(1 + \omega_{11}d^2 - 2\sqrt{1 + \omega_{11}d^2} + 1)\omega_{12}d^2 S}{\omega_{11}^2 d^4} \right|$$

$$\approx \left| \frac{(1 + \omega_{11}d^2 - 2\left(1 + \frac{1}{2}\omega_{11}d^2 - \frac{1}{8}\omega_{11}^2 d^4\right) + 1)\omega_{12}d^2 S}{\omega_{11}^2 d^4} \right|$$

$$= \left| \frac{\frac{1}{4}\omega_{11}^2 d^4 \omega_{12}d^2 S}{\omega_{11}^2 d^4} \right|$$

$$= \left| \frac{1}{4} \frac{\omega_{12}d^2 S}{\det \Omega} \right|$$

$$= \left| \frac{1}{4} \frac{\sigma_{12}d^2 S}{\sigma_{11}\sigma_{22}(1 - \rho_{12}^2)} \right|$$

$$= \left| \frac{1}{4} \frac{d^2}{\sigma_{11}} \frac{\beta_{12}}{1 - \rho_{12}^2} S \right|, \tag{2.23}$$

where β_{12} is the beta of the stock price (asset 1) with respect to the option price (asset 2). This highlights the importance of β_{12}, which we have computed in previous sections for various distributions.

Referring to Equation (2.23), suppose we assume that $\frac{1}{4}\frac{\beta_{12}}{1-\rho_{12}^2} \approx 1$ (which is feasible given plausible assumptions about the option strike as shown by our various examples in Section 2.4), then the maximum size of the market for the option will be driven by $\frac{d^2}{\sigma_{11}}$. If, for instance, *Institution 2* estimates 25% more variance in the stock price than *Institution 1*, then this would lead to a maximum option market size approximately one-quarter the size of the stock market.

2.5.2.2 'Large' Incremental Variance d^2 For 'large' d^2 we consider the limit of market size as $d \to \infty$. In this situation it is easily seen that $n_{11} \to S$ and $n_{21} \to 0$, i.e. the stock itself is entirely held by *Institution 1* who believes it to have a finite variance. In contrast, *Institution 2* will hold none of the stock, but a large long position in the option instead (where they have finite variance). Recall that both investors agree on the mean return of each asset.

$$\lim_{d \to \infty} \text{Max.Size} = \left| \frac{\omega_{12}}{\omega_{11}} S \right|$$

$$= \left| \frac{\sigma_{12}}{\sigma_{22}} S \right|$$

$$= |\beta_{12}S|. \tag{2.24}$$

2.6 EMPIRICAL EXAMPLES

We now make a tentative step in the direction of empirical analysis by considering whether we can usefully compare actual market size information with the 'small' d^2 approximation (2.23). If we assume values of parameters β_{12} and ρ_{12} then we can invert Equation (2.23) to obtain an expression for the incremental variance $\frac{d^2}{\sigma_{11}}$ perceived by *Institution 2* in terms of maximum market size. However (almost surely) the *maximum* market size will not be a value which is observed in practice, so estimates of this variance ratio will be biased downwards (potentially by a large magnitude) and we proceed with this in mind.

At this point we focus on the key role which AD plays in Equation (2.23). Both β_{12} and ρ_{12} are non-linear functions of the option strike, as we have demonstrated earlier in this chapter, and therefore the option strike assumption has a significant impact on the size calculation. Although it is common among practitioners to refer to the CTA strategy as having 'option-like' characteristics, this is often a qualitative observation, without reference to any particular strike price or time to expiry. In a formal econometric model this would clearly pose an identification problem (assuming the parameters of the price distribution are given), however for the purposes of the embryonic analysis in this section we will proceed with the expeditious (and relatively innocuous) assumption that $\frac{1}{4}\frac{\beta_{12}}{1-\rho_{12}^2} \approx 1$.

As regards market data: ideally we would like to choose a collection of assets, and for each one compute the ratio between the observed size of CTA trading and the total size of the underlying asset market. This is a challenging task, since neither the numerator nor the denominator are directly observable for any assets commonly traded. Nevertheless, whilst we reserve more rigorous empirical analysis for a separate paper, we make some informal preliminary comments here.

Since CTAs tend to use derivatives for trading, we can obtain some indication of the magnitude of their positions in specific futures markets from the Commitments of Traders report published weekly by the U.S. Commodity Futures Trading Commission (CFTC). This provides the net position in futures held by so-called 'non-commercial' traders, which are commonly considered to be speculators. Although this data is limited to futures exchanges in the USA, in many products this constitutes the vast majority of global trading volume. Naturally not all 'non-commercial' traders are CTAs, so we recognize and highlight that these data points should be considered merely a crude estimate.

Our model is not readily applicable to consumable commodities, e.g. energy and agricultural products, since it is particularly hard to quantify the amount held for investible (as opposed to industrial) purposes, therefore we omit these from our analysis. For example purposes we have instead chosen the investment markets for gold and silver. Although these are not equity investments, they have the appeal that a very large proportion of available supply is already believed to have been produced (mined), so the supply side can be considered relatively fixed, and credible estimates of investible market size are available from industry trade bodies.

Table 2.1 contains our example data. In the final column we present computed ratios which can be compared with the factor which multiplies S in Equation (2.23). We reiterate that under the assumption that $\frac{1}{4}\frac{\beta_{12}}{1-\rho_{12}^2} \approx 1$, these ratios are comparable with the $\frac{d^2}{\sigma_{11}}$ factor in Equation (2.23).

Approaching the same question from a different direction, we could compare the size of the AUM in CTAs with total global investible wealth (most of which is invested in the traditional asset markets which underlie the futures traded by CTAs). According to BCG (2015), global private financial wealth

TABLE 2.1   Estimated market size data: futures positions are the largest absolute position size (long or short) in the weekly CFTC Commitments of Traders report during 2010 (gold is 304,564 lots, equivalent to 30,456,400 troy ounces; silver is 66,066 lots or 330,330,000 troy ounces); gold market size estimate is from World Gold Council (WGC, 2010) and silver from Thomson Reuters (GFMS, 2011)

Commodity	I: Underlying market size (tonnes)	II: Futures position (tonnes)	Ratio II/I
Gold	60,400	947	1.6%
Silver	59,000	10,274	17.4%

stood at USD 156 trillion in 2014. In comparison, BarclayHedge[3] estimated 2015Q2 AUM in CTAs at USD 328bn, a fraction of approximately 0.2%.

Clearly these various estimates are consistent with a very wide range of incremental variances perceived by hypothetical *Institution 2*. As discussed, several assumptions are involved when interpreting the data relative to investors' views, and these suggest interesting avenues for further research.

2.7 CONCLUSIONS

In this chapter we have presented a model where AD arises endogenously, rather than being a feature of exogenously imposed probability distributions. Although we devised this structure with a particular purpose in mind (estimating the size of the CTA market), it is clear that similar instances of endogenous AD arise naturally in many common circumstances. The essence of our example was that dependency could be significantly affected by adjusting a model parameter with ostensibly no connection to a probability distribution (the option strike), and that the nature of this effect was not immediately intuitive: both non-linear and with a surprising magnitude.

Although these AD effects are far from hidden, their subtleties may not be uppermost in the mind of a model builder or user. The main output of our model (market size) is driven by the behaviour of agents who apply mean-variance optimization despite the fact that their portfolio choices are non-normal. Their decision is highly sensitive to the correlation between underlying asset and derivative, and we have shown that this is exactly where the effects of 'option-strike' AD are acute: the correlation is sensitive to the option strike assumption but the value itself is hard to interpret intuitively, for instance we have shown that it tends to lie close to 1 under plausible conditions (an effect which is related to correlation attenuation as studied in the regression literature).

We deliberately cast our model in a mean-variance setting due to its ubiquity among practitioners, therefore understanding the nature and effects of AD in this context seems important, notwithstanding the fact that there are alternative frameworks for portfolio choice which may be more closely suited to options markets. An interesting area for further study would be to consider the effects of 'option-strike' AD in those cases.

From a structural perspective, we differ from Detemple and Selden (1991) in that: (i) their framework is state-space, (ii) ours is more amenable to econometric estimation, (iii) our mean-variance rule is more practical and (iv) their second-moment heterogeneity is tail risk whereas we have additive noise. This has enabled us to highlight the effects of AD more vividly and seems a versatile formulation for further work on related themes.

Reflecting on our empirical results, it is clear that there are certain obstacles on the road to achieving the ambition of market size estimation (such as econometric identification challenges). Nevertheless, an important step towards resolving such issues is to establish a well-founded model and we have made some progress in that direction, paying particular attention to the intriguing role of AD.

REFERENCES

Barndorff-Nielsen, O. (1977). Exponentially decreasing distributions for the logarithm of particle size. *Proceedings of the Royal Society, Series A*, 353, 401–419.

BCG (2015). *Global Wealth 2015: Winning the Growth Game*. Boston Consulting Group, Boston, MA.

Board, J., Sutcliffe, C. and Patrinos, E. (2000). The performance of covered calls. *European Journal of Finance*, 6, 1–17.

---

[3]http://www.barclayhedge.com/research/indices/cta/Money_Under_Management.html

Detemple, J. and Selden, L. (1991). A general equilibrium analysis of option and stock market interactions. *International Economic Review*, 32(2), 279–303.

Feller, W. (1966). *An Introduction to Probability Theory and its Applications*, Vol. 2. John Wiley & Sons, New York.

Fung, W. and Hsieh, D. (2001). The risk in hedge fund strategies: theory and evidence from trend followers. *Review of Financial Studies*, 14, 313–341.

GFMS (2011). *The Silver Investment Market – An Update*. Thomson Reuters GFMS.

Hill, J., Balasubramanian, V., Gregory, K. and Tierens, I. (2006). Finding alpha via covered index writing. *Financial Analysts Journal*, 62(5), 29–46.

Hurst, B., Ooi, Y. and Pedersen, L. (2013). Demystifying managed futures. *Journal of Investment Management*, 11(3), 42–58.

McIntyre, M. and Jackson, D. (2007). Great in practice, not in theory: an empirical examination of covered call writing. *Journal of Derivatives and Hedge Funds*, 13, 66–79.

Merton, R. (1974). On the pricing of corporate debt: the risk structure of interest rates. *Journal of Finance*, 29, 449–470.

Muldowney, P., Ostaszewski, K. and Wojdowski, W. (2012). The Darth Vader rule. *Tatra Mountains Mathematical Publications*, 52, 53–63.

Muthén, B. (1990). Moments of the censored and truncated bivariate normal distribution. *British Journal of Mathematical and Statistical Psychology*, 43, 131–143.

Reed, W. and Jorgensen, M. (2004). The double Pareto–lognormal distribution – a new parametric model for size distributions. *Communications in Statistics – Theory and Methods*, 33, 1733–1753.

Rendleman, R. (2001). Covered call writing from an expected utility perspective. *Journal of Derivatives*, 8(3), 63–75.

WGC (2011). *Liquidity in the Global Gold Market*. World Gold Council, London.

CHAPTER 3

The Price of Asymmetric Dependence

Jamie Alcock[a] and Anthony Hatherley

[a]The University of Sydney Business School

Abstract

We examine the price of asymmetric dependence (AD) in the cross-section of US equities. Using a β-invariant AD metric – the adjusted J statistic – we demonstrate that the return premium for AD is approximately 47% of the premium for β. The premium for lower-tail AD is equivalent to 26% of the market risk premium and has been relatively constant through time. The discount associated with upper-tail AD is 29% of the market risk premium and has been increasing markedly in recent years. Our findings have substantial implications for the cost of capital, investor expectations, portfolio management and performance assessment.

3.1   INTRODUCTION

It seems self-evident that for any characteristic, such as asymmetric dependence (AD), to be priced then at least three conditions must hold: (i) the characteristic must exist, (ii) investors must hold a preference for the characteristic and (iii) the characteristic must be neither diversifiable nor otherwise manageable at no cost. In the case of AD, its existence is well established in the literature, as are investor preferences for AD. The price of AD then provides useful information on the cost of managing AD. Furthermore, if the upside and downside risk associated with AD attracts a premium independent of the premium demanded for β, then it also has significant implications for the firm's cost-of-capital and capital budgeting decisions, the performance measurement of fund managers and the structure of executive remuneration contracts.

Asymmetric dependence describes the characteristic of the joint return distribution whereby the dependence between a stock and the market during market downturns differs from that observed during market upturns (Patton, 2004). Lower-tail asymmetric dependence (LTAD) refers to the situation where dependence in the lower tail is higher than that in the upper tail, and upper-tail asymmetric dependence (UTAD) refers to the opposite situation. We expect that an investor with state-dependent preferences will demand a return premium to invest in assets with higher state-dependent correlations in the LTAD and accept a discount in return for the potential utility gains associated with UTAD.

We identify the existence and nature of an AD premium by employing the adjusted J statistic described in Chapter 1. We control separately for adjusted-J and β in a regression on returns in order to assess the relative size of the AD risk premia and the market risk premia over time. We find that upper-tail (lower-tail) AD requires a significant discount (premium) that is robust to controlling for commonly cited return covariates. We find that the price of AD is approximately 50% of the price of beta risk. We also find that the price of UTAD has nearly tripled in recent years.

Several authors have explored the pricing of downside risk. Bali *et al.* (2009) use Value-at-Risk (VaR) and expected shortfall (ES) to demonstrate a significant relation between downside risk and the returns of the NYSE/AMEX/NASDAQ value-weighted index. Similarly, Post and van Vliet (2006) use a stochastic dominance framework to show that downside risk is important in explaining the high return of small, value and winner stocks, and Ang *et al.* (2006a) find that downside β requires a premium of approximately 6% per annum.

To date, it has been difficult to identify whether cross-sectional variation in traditional tail-risk metrics, such as upside and downside β and VaR, is due to variation in the overall relation between stock returns and the market, or to variation in the sensitivity of stock returns to extreme market movements. The risk caused by upper-, and lower-tail co-movements and the ability to differentiate these risks from ordinary co-movements is likely to have important implications for asset allocation decisions.[1] For example, an increase in Capital Asset Pricing Model (CAPM) β will also be reflected by an increase in both upside and downside β. In this instance, any downside-risk hedge utilising changes in downside β is likely to be confounded as the full β risk is an aggregate of the upside and downside β risk. In general, the hedging demands of investors will differ for exposure to stocks that fall disproportionately with market downturns, relative to upturns (an increase in LTAD), in contrast to stocks that are symmetric in their response to market movements (an increase in systematic risk).

To highlight the importance of considering the systematic risk premium separate from the premia demanded for AD, consider two assets, X and Y, that have identical βs, equal average returns and the same level of dependence in the lower tail. Further, suppose that Y displays dependence in the upper tail that is equal in absolute magnitude to the level of dependence in the lower tail, but X has no dependence in the upper tail. In this example, Y is symmetric (but not necessarily elliptical), whereas X is asymmetric displaying LTAD (see Figure 3.1). The expected return associated with an exposure to systematic risk should be the same for X and Y because they have the same β. In addition, a rational, non-satiable investor who accounts for relative differences in upside and downside risk should prefer Y over X because, conditional on a market downturn event, Y is less likely to suffer losses compared with X. Similarly, a downside-risk-averse investor will also prefer Y over X. These preferences should imply higher returns for assets that display LTAD and lower returns for assets that display UTAD, independent of the returns demanded for β. To the best of our knowledge, the relative magnitude of the premia demanded for dependence-driven tail risk and ordinary market risk has yet to be established.[2]

Our main contribution is two fold. Our first contribution lies in measuring AD over and above the tail dependence implied by β using the adjusted J statistic (Alcock and Hatherley, 2016). We do not dispute the existence of a downside-risk premium. Rather, we extend the economic framework upon

---

[1] A significant reduction in portfolio value can occur with moderate market declines if dependence is state-dependent, particularly if there is a tendency for dependence amongst assets to increase more during bear market periods relative to bull market periods. Dependence of this nature has been established between international equity indices and amongst subsets of the US equity market (Erb *et al.*, 1994; Ramchand and Susmel, 1998; Longin and Solnik, 2001; Ang and Bekaert, 2002; Ang and Chen, 2002; Butler and Joaquin, 2002; Campbell *et al.*, 2002; Hartmann *et al.*, 2004; Patton, 2004; Hong *et al.*, 2007; Cappiello *et al.*, 2014; Li, 2014), suggesting that state dependence is non-diversifiable.

[2] Pedersen and Hwang (2007) show that the CAPM can be used to explain 50–80% of the returns of UK equities, while downside β explains only 15–25%. The authors therefore rule out the general applicability of downside β in explaining UK equity return variation on the basis of the proportion of equities explained by the CAPM and the lower partial moment asset pricing framework. They do not quantify the relative magnitude of the compensation for systematic and downside risk, however.

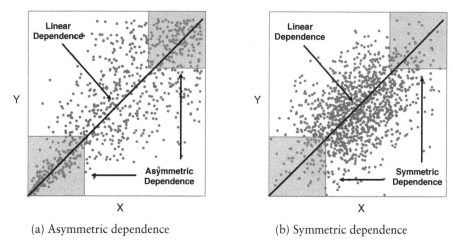

(a) Asymmetric dependence   (b) Symmetric dependence

FIGURE 3.1 Linear vs. asymmetric dependence. Scatter plot of simulated bivariate data with asymmetric dependence (a) and symmetric dependence (b). The dependence between X and Y may be described by a linear component and a higher-order component, reflecting differences in dependence across the joint return distribution. A joint distribution that displays larger dependence in one tail compared with the opposite tail is said to display asymmetric dependence. In the case of (a), the dependence in the lower tail is higher than that of the upper tail, which is characteristic of LTAD in particular.

which the premium is built in the literature. Identifying AD risk separately from β risk enables us to clearly determine the premia of AD risk. We find that the magnitude of the associated downside-risk premium is approximately 26% of the magnitude of the premium for traditional β. Similarly, we find that UTAD demands a discount, and represents 29% of the premium demanded for β. These results qualitatively hold in both in-sample and predictive regressions and when controlling for book-to-market ratio, size, past return, idiosyncratic risk, coskewness and cokurtosis. These results are also robust to alternative data-length specifications and volatility.

Our second contribution involves an analysis of how the AD premia have changed over time relative to the premium for systematic risk. We find that the premium required for LTAD has been relatively constant at 1.32% p.a. of excess return (per unit of standard deviation) between 1989 and 2015, whereas the size of the discount for UTAD has nearly tripled throughout this time. Changes in the UTAD premium occur as a result of changes in the preference for stocks that display UTAD with the market. In addition, the 2007–2009 financial crisis appears to be as much a systematic risk story as it is an AD story, implying that the risks associated with both linear dependence and higher-order dependence should be managed to reduce the portfolio impact of future market crashes.

Our results therefore build on previous work by Ang *et al.* (2006a), showing that both linear dependence and higher-order dependence are important in the cross-section. These results imply that important price information is contained within the relative magnitude of upside and downside risk, as well as within the overall relation between asset returns.

3.2 THE ASYMMETRIC DEPENDENCE RISK PREMIUM

3.2.1 Empirical Design

Our methodology broadly follows Ang *et al.* (2006a), to build on the existing evidence of a downside-risk premium in the cross-section. We analyse the in-sample relation between systematic risk,

AD and returns, controlling for a range of factors including size, book-to-market ratio, past 12-month excess return, idiosyncratic risk, coskewness and cokurtosis.[3] A particular factor is a relevant risk attribute if highly adverse factor changes coincide with higher returns, consistent with the concept of a contemporaneous risk–return relation (Black *et al.*, 1972; Gibbons, 1982). In addition, we also explore the AD premia using a more traditional Fama and MacBeth (1973) approach, where we first estimate risk measures based on past data and then regress current returns on these measures. This robustness test is used to ensure that our findings do not suffer from any forward-looking bias.

We use exceedances $\delta = \{0, 0.2, 0.4, 0.6, 0.8, 1\}$ in order to calculate the adjusted J measure of AD. Following Hong *et al.* (2007), we employ the Bartlett kernel for the estimation of the variance–covariance matrix, $\hat{\Omega}$. We first measure risk premia using an in-sample asset pricing procedure where cross-sectional regressions are computed every month rolling forward using a 12-month window to estimate the relevant factors. We measure statistical significance using Newey and West (1987) adjusted t-statistics to control for overlapping data using the Newey and West (1994) automatic lag selection method to determine the lag length.[4] The use of short, rolling window risk factor estimates may be better positioned to account for the evidence of time variation in systematic risk (Blume, 1975; Fabozzi and Francis, 1978; Bos and Newbold, 1984; Bollerslev *et al.*, 1988; Ferson and Harvey, 1991, 1993; Ferson and Korajczyk, 1995) and any potential time variation in tail dependence relative to a static model. Further, estimates based on short windows are thought to have higher power in an environment where risk factors may be time-varying. We test the robustness of our results to alternative window lengths in Section 3.2.2.

3.2.2 Data

Our data collection method attempts to follow Ang *et al.* (2006a) in order to generate comparable results. We use data from the CRSP database, collected through Wharton Research Data Services (WRDS). Using the daily stock file, we collect share code, permno, price, holding period return, and number of shares outstanding between 01 January 1963 and 31 December 2015. For our main analysis, we only include data for stocks with exchange code (exchcd) equal to 1 (NYSE data).

We use all unique permnos to obtain book value data using the CRSP/COMPUSTAT merged database. We collect 'Common/Ordinary Equity – Total' (CEQ) data, restricting our attention to link types 'LC' and 'LU'. Stocks with multiple company names for a given permno are excluded. The risk-free rate is proxied by the 1-month T-bill rate, collected from the Kenneth R. French Data Library.[5] The market portfolio is proxied by the CRSP value-weighted return of all NYSE, AMEX and NASDAQ stocks.

We calculate the relevant variables for a given month, t, for those stocks with data for months $t - 12$ to $t + 12$, and for those stocks that have a sharecode of 10 or 11 for that period. Holding period returns, r_h, are converted to continuously compounded returns, r_c, by setting $r_c = \log(1 + r_h)$.

Market capitalizations are computed as the absolute value of the product of share price and total shares outstanding.[6] We use book values from the previous year whenever the month at time t is less than 6, and current-year book values whenever the month at time t is greater than or equal to 6. The book-to-market ratio is then computed using the current market cap at time t. Any stock with missing book-value data is assigned a BM ratio of zero.

---

[3]An in-sample methodology attempts to avoid the errors-in-variables problem (Kim, 1995) that occurs when relating risk factors estimated using past data with returns in a future period using the two-pass methodology. This facilitates the performance of cross-sectional regression for individual securities rather than for portfolio groupings.

[4]Although the theoretical number of lags required to account for the use of overlapping data is 11, the Newey and West (1994) automatic lag selection method produces an optimal lag length of 14 given the length of data we consider.

[5]We thank Ken French for making this data available.

[6]CRSP assigns a negative sign to price in the event that closing price is not available for a given trading day. The bid/ask average is instead reported on that day.

We compute excess daily returns, using the risk-free rate at a given month, divided by the number of days for that month. Regular β, upside and downside β, realized volatility, coskewness and cokurtosis are then computed according to Equations (B-7) to (B-9) of Ang *et al.* (2006a).

At a given month, t, the average of the next 12 excess monthly returns is regressed against combinations of CAPM β, upside and downside β, idiosyncratic risk, coskewness, cokurtosis and J^{Adj} estimated using the next 12 months of daily excess return data, and size, book-to-market ratio and average past 12-monthly excess return, all computed as at time t. We measure idiosyncratic risk as the standard deviation of market model residuals. We substitute this measure for realized return volatility used by Ang *et al.* (2006a) because we explicitly involve ordinary β in our regression methodology. Including β and realized return volatility, measured as the standard deviation of realized excess returns, would induce multicollinearity into our analysis and therefore bias our results. We proxy the market portfolio with the CRSP value-weighted return of all NYSE, AMEX and NASDAQ stocks and the risk-free rate with the 1-month T-bill rate. All regressors are winsorized at the 1% and 99% level at each month to control for outliers and inefficient factor estimates.

We use daily data to estimate risk factors primarily to ensure we have sufficient observations to accurately measure upside and downside risk, estimated using J^{Adj}. Although risk-factor estimates computed using daily data over short periods are likely to be noisy compared with estimates computed with lower frequency data over longer periods, subsequent tests of the significance of factor risk premia will have reasonable power because they are estimated using a long time series of estimates (Lewellen and Nagel, 2006).

To minimize the possibility of non-synchronous trading associated with the use of daily data, we restrict our attention to stocks listed on the NYSE between January 1963 and December 2015. The sample size at each month is depicted in Figure 3.2.

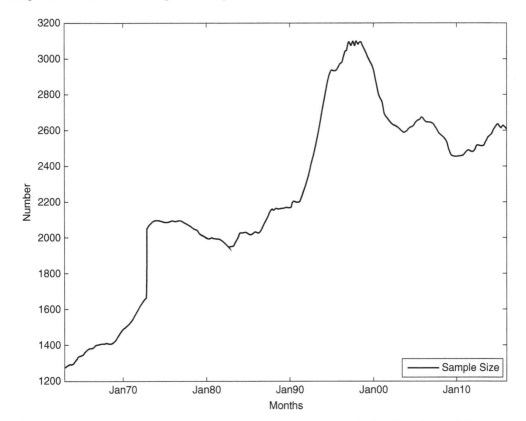

FIGURE 3.2 Our monthly sample size. We restrict our attention to stocks listed on the NYSE between January 1963 and December 2015.

3.2.3 Factor Correlations

Table 3.1 highlights the difficulty of measuring separate premia for AD and ordinary market risk using upside or downside β. Computing the correlation between risk factors for our entire sample, we find that upside and downside β are both highly correlated with ordinary β, implying that upside/downside β cannot be included in the same regression as ordinary β due to multicollinearity.

Consistent with our construction, J^{Adj} and β have low correlation (0.043). This indicates that AD, be it LTAD or UTAD, exists independent of systematic risk and has implications for risk management and portfolio construction. For example, two portfolios with equal βs will likely display varying degrees of market risk given the existence of AD. Significant tail dependence may therefore have contributed to the losses experienced by equity-market-neutral hedge funds during August 2007 (Khandani and Lo, 2007). We investigate whether this hypothesis is evident for our sample.

The orthogonality between β and J^{Adj} may also affect particular aspects of asset pricing. In particular, a zero-β portfolio may not necessarily be a risk-free portfolio due to the existence of AD. Black *et al.* (1972) found that portfolios with zero covariance with the market display average returns that significantly exceed the risk-free rate. This is consistent with the existence of tail risk, which could cause the market risk of the zero-β portfolio to be significantly different from zero.

We find that β and return are positively correlated, as are β^- and return. However, the correlation with β^- is larger in magnitude, consistent with a market aversion to downside risk.

TABLE 3.1 This table presents the correlation between each factor. We restrict our attention to stocks listed on the NYSE between January 1963 and December 2015. At each month, t, we estimate β, β^-, β^+, idiosyncratic risk ('Idio'), coskewness ('Cosk'), cokurtosis ('Cokurt') and J^{Adj} estimated using the next 12 months of daily excess return data, and natural logarithm of size ('Size'), book-to-market ratio ('BM') and the average past 12-monthly excess return ('Past Ret') computed as at time t. Returns ('Ret') are estimated as the average of the next 12-monthly excess return. We proxy the market portfolio with the CRSP value-weighted return of all NYSE, AMEX and NASDAQ stocks and the risk-free rate with the 1-month T-bill rate. All factors are winsorized at the 1% and 99% level at each month

	β	β^-	β^+	Log-size	BM	Past Ret	Idio	Cosk	Cokurt	J^{Adj}
β	1	0.807	0.830	0.137	0.028	0.108	0.260	0.017	0.243	0.048
β^-		1	0.562	0.028	0.024	0.110	0.282	−0.146	0.198	−0.083
β^+			1	0.162	0.022	0.081	0.157	0.169	0.259	0.192
Log-size				1	−0.223	0.061	−0.384	−0.075	0.201	0.068
BM					1	−0.146	0.086	0.055	−0.039	0.012
Past ret						1	−0.128	−0.104	0.063	−0.021
Idio							1	0.063	−0.059	−0.042
Cosk								1	−0.676	0.345
Cokurt									1	0.046
J^{Adj}										1

3.2.4 Distribution of J^{Adj}

We depict the distribution of AD, as measured by J^{Adj}, for all firms in our sample between 1963 and 2015 following the methodology described in the previous section. A histogram of all J^{Adj} observations reveals that the distribution of J^{Adj} is (asymmetrically) bi-modal with 67.33% of J^{Adj} observations less than zero and the remaining 32.67% of observations greater than zero.

For comparison, we include the distribution of the J^{Adj} computed using simulated multivariate normal data, parameterized at each month (Figure 3.3(b)). The size of each sample is chosen to match the number of days in each 12-month period. The distribution is (symmetrically) bi-modal with a statistically insignificant average of −0.004. Comparison with Figure 3.3(a) suggests that AD is more characteristic of actual returns data than that suggested under multivariate normality.

There are likely to be a number of reasons for the observation that LTAD occurs more often than UTAD. One possibility is offered by Bekaert and Wu (2000), who effectively suggest that AD may be driven by the asymmetric effect of news on the conditional covariance between stock and market returns. They argue that asymmetric volatility at the firm level is a direct result of asymmetric covariance with the market. The negative price reaction caused by volatility feedback offsets the initial price increase associated with good news and amplifies the negative price reaction associated with bad news. In order to explain asymmetric volatility for individual stock returns, an asymmetric response in the covariance between stock returns and the market is required, because changes in firm-specific volatility can be theoretically diversified away. Our results are consistent with Bekaert and Wu's finding that the dependence is affected more by jointly negative shocks to firm-level and market-level returns compared with jointly positive shocks.

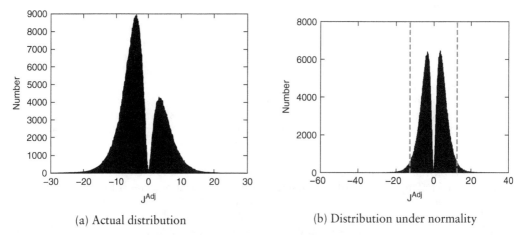

(a) Actual distribution   (b) Distribution under normality

FIGURE 3.3 Actual and hypothetical distribution of the J^{Adj}. We focus on stocks listed on the NYSE between January 1963 and December 2015. At a given month, t, we estimate J^{Adj} using the next 12 months of daily excess return data. We proxy the market portfolio with the CRSP value-weighted return of all NYSE, AMEX and NASDAQ stocks and the risk-free rate with the 1-month T-bill rate. The histogram of all J^{Adj} observations is presented in (a). We include the distribution of the J^{Adj}, computed using simulated multivariate normal data, parameterized at each month in (b). The size of each sample is chosen to match the number of days in each 12-month period. The vertical lines represent 95% cutoffs following a χ_6^2 distribution. A positive (negative) J^{Adj} is indicative of excess upside (downside) risk over and above the tail risk implied by ordinary β.

3.2.5 Conditional Dependence Patterns

In light of the correlation among factors and between factors and returns observed, it is important to ensure that the relation between J^{Adj} and return does not simply reflect a relation between return and some unidentified latent risk. We therefore investigate the interplay between dependence and return by analysing patterns in the in-sample relation between realized average return and realized risk (Table 3.2).

After controlling for β, we find a positive relation between LTAD and returns regardless of the level of β (Panel A). The average return and the spread between the 1st and the 10th J^{Adj} decile are also seen to increase with β. This suggests that higher returns associated with high LTAD exist irrespective of β, however, compensation for differences in AD between groups becomes larger as β risk increases. This could imply that an increase in systematic risk coincides with an increase in downside risk when systematic risk is high, and less so when systematic risk is low. Further, if a larger return spread is assumed to provide an indication of the strength of the relation between risk and return, then J^{Adj} is more capable than β^- to capture the AD risk not captured by β.

We informally test whether the observed relation between J^{Adj} and return indirectly reflects the relation between return and size or coskewness risk in Panels B and C, respectively. We continue to find a monotonic relation between J^{Adj} and return, despite controlling for these factors. Further, the return spread and average across J^{Adj} deciles for each characteristic decile are comparable in magnitude to the return spread associated with size and coskewness. This provides additional evidence that the relation between J^{Adj} and return is not a reflection of compensation for variation in coskewness or size. The existence of an AD premium measured using J^{Adj} is therefore distinct from the risk premia demanded for these factors.

3.2.6 In-Sample Regression Results

We first explore the in-sample relationships for data (Ang et al., 2006a) between 1963 and 2015 using contemporaneous returns. Regressions I and II in Table 3.3 Panel A indicate that this method is able to generate results comparable with those presented by Ang et al. (2006a). For example, we find that β, β^- and β^+ are significantly related to returns. The sensitivity for downside β implies an increase in returns of 7.6% p.a. per unit of β^- and a discount for upside β of 1.8% p.a. per unit of β^+, suggesting that upside and downside risk are priced asymmetrically. A one-unit increase in ordinary β is associated with a 10.6% p.a. increase in returns. The magnitude of this market risk premium estimate differs from traditional market risk premium estimates (Siegel, 1992; Pastor and Stambaugh, 2001; Dimson et al., 2003) due to the use of equally weighted regressions. Our coefficient for β in Table 3.4 is similar to the coefficient reported by Ang et al. (2006a) when computed on an average factor loading basis.

To assess the relative importance of systematic risk and AD risk in the cross-section, we regress returns on β and J^{Adj} in regression III, controlling for the standard set of factor risks. We find that both systematic risk and AD are significantly priced.[7] Consistent with expectations, the negative coefficient of the J^{Adj} factor loading implies that stocks with LTAD ($J^{Adj} < 0$) demand a premium and stocks with UTAD ($J^{Adj} > 0$) demand a discount. Based purely on factor loadings, a one-standard-deviation increase in β equates to a 5.20% p.a. increase in average returns, similar to the coefficient of β in regression I, whilst a one-standard-deviation increase (decrease) in J^{Adj} equates to a 2.11% p.a. decrease (increase) in average returns. The magnitude of the J^{Adj} risk premium, computed for a one-standard-deviation increase in J^{Adj}, is 46.75% of the magnitude of the β risk premium computed for a one-standard-deviation increase in β. This highlights the importance of accounting for the effect of changes in both systematic risk and AD on expected returns.

In its own right, J^{Adj} captures both LTAD and UTAD between a stock and the market. To isolate upside and downside risk for the purposes of our regression analysis, we compute

$$J^{Adj}+ = J^{Adj}\mathbb{1}_{J^{Adj}>0} \tag{3.1}$$

$$J^{Adj}- = J^{Adj}\mathbb{1}_{J^{Adj}<0}. \tag{3.2}$$

---

[7]The t-statistics of these coefficients are well above the Harvey et al. (2015) significance hurdle of 3.0.

TABLE 3.2 For a given month, we first sort stocks into β deciles and then into J^{Adj} deciles within each characteristic decile in Panel A. In Panels B and C, we first sort stocks into size or coskewness deciles, respectively, and then into J^{Adj} deciles within each characteristic decile. Dependence ranges from low (group 1) to high (group 10), which implies that J^{Adj}_1 consists of stocks with high downside risk and J^{Adj}_{10} consists of stocks with high upside potential. We record and report the equal-weighted average 12-monthly excess return for all stocks within each group, expressed as an effective annual rate of return. We restrict our attention to stocks listed on the NYSE between January 1963 and December 2015. We proxy the market portfolio with the CRSP value-weighted return of all NYSE, AMEX and NASDAQ stocks and the risk-free rate with the 1-month T-bill rate. We provide the spread ('Diff') for each row and column, given by the return associated with the high-risk group, less the return associated with the low-risk group. We also include the average return ('Avg') for each row and column

	β_1	β_2	β_3	β_4	β_5	β_6	β_7	β_8	β_9	β_{10}	Diff	Avg
β-1	0.085	0.067	0.081	0.067	0.068	0.051	0.070	0.068	0.061	0.118	0.033	0.078
β-2	0.079	0.073	0.072	0.067	0.069	0.064	0.045	0.037	0.002	0.052	-0.028	0.071
β-3	0.091	0.083	0.076	0.077	0.075	0.055	0.056	0.077	0.033	0.150	0.059	0.077
β-4	0.090	0.092	0.087	0.086	0.078	0.064	0.073	0.075	0.050	0.047	-0.043	0.081
β-5	0.098	0.106	0.091	0.097	0.089	0.089	0.076	0.076	0.099	0.077	-0.021	0.090
β-6	0.116	0.124	0.103	0.099	0.105	0.105	0.107	0.095	0.089	0.095	-0.020	0.103
β-7	0.126	0.118	0.109	0.117	0.115	0.117	0.111	0.107	0.097	0.117	-0.009	0.111
β-8	0.151	0.131	0.177	0.137	0.128	0.124	0.120	0.127	0.125	0.117	-0.034	0.126
β-9	0.131	0.139	0.220	0.162	0.169	0.143	0.143	0.148	0.147	0.144	0.013	0.147
β-10	-0.054	0.155	0.211	0.213	0.176	0.201	0.193	0.203	0.201	0.243	0.296	0.224
Diff	0.138	-0.088	-0.130	-0.147	-0.108	-0.150	-0.123	-0.136	-0.140	-0.125		
Avg	0.086	0.082	0.087	0.091	0.096	0.100	0.108	0.122	0.137	0.196		

(Continued)

TABLE 3.2 (Continued)

Panel A: β/J^{Adj} sorted portfolios

	β_1	β_2	β_3	β_4	β_5	β_6	β_7	β_8	β_9	β_{10}	Diff	Avg
J^{Adj}_1	0.138	0.129	0.135	0.140	0.147	0.150	0.161	0.177	0.220	0.325	0.186	0.172
J^{Adj}_2	0.118	0.102	0.117	0.124	0.130	0.144	0.157	0.166	0.175	0.272	0.154	0.149
J^{Adj}_3	0.105	0.098	0.109	0.118	0.118	0.120	0.138	0.147	0.174	0.259	0.154	0.138
J^{Adj}_4	0.102	0.101	0.106	0.106	0.116	0.121	0.133	0.150	0.165	0.236	0.134	0.133
J^{Adj}_5	0.098	0.094	0.093	0.107	0.114	0.109	0.119	0.138	0.149	0.211	0.113	0.122
J^{Adj}_6	0.080	0.089	0.085	0.092	0.101	0.103	0.111	0.120	0.149	0.197	0.117	0.112
J^{Adj}_7	0.075	0.075	0.079	0.086	0.086	0.097	0.089	0.112	0.128	0.160	0.085	0.098
J^{Adj}_8	0.059	0.057	0.063	0.062	0.069	0.070	0.080	0.090	0.102	0.134	0.075	0.078
J^{Adj}_9	0.046	0.043	0.048	0.052	0.049	0.055	0.064	0.081	0.075	0.104	0.058	0.062
J^{Adj}_{10}	0.039	0.028	0.030	0.027	0.032	0.038	0.039	0.048	0.050	0.086	0.048	0.042
Diff	0.099	0.101	0.106	0.113	0.115	0.112	0.122	0.129	0.170	0.238		
Avg	0.086	0.082	0.087	0.091	0.096	0.100	0.108	0.122	0.137	0.196		

Panel B: $Size/J^{Adj}$ sorted portfolios

	M_1	M_2	M_3	M_4	M_5	M_6	M_7	M_8	M_9	M_{10}	Diff	Avg
J^{Adj}_1	0.292	0.209	0.177	0.162	0.166	0.134	0.129	0.143	0.130	0.122	0.170	0.172
J^{Adj}_2	0.240	0.185	0.159	0.146	0.141	0.125	0.116	0.121	0.123	0.109	0.130	0.149
J^{Adj}_3	0.214	0.159	0.154	0.133	0.142	0.125	0.112	0.110	0.111	0.098	0.116	0.138
J^{Adj}_4	0.206	0.172	0.146	0.119	0.135	0.119	0.114	0.114	0.101	0.097	0.109	0.133
J^{Adj}_5	0.184	0.144	0.136	0.117	0.130	0.115	0.106	0.107	0.095	0.083	0.102	0.122
J^{Adj}_6	0.179	0.128	0.125	0.118	0.118	0.109	0.100	0.096	0.085	0.069	0.110	0.112
J^{Adj}_7	0.141	0.113	0.111	0.107	0.095	0.096	0.091	0.089	0.073	0.071	0.069	0.098
J^{Adj}_8	0.106	0.087	0.087	0.087	0.087	0.075	0.072	0.072	0.066	0.056	0.050	0.078
J^{Adj}_9	0.092	0.059	0.071	0.058	0.067	0.067	0.060	0.055	0.050	0.049	0.043	0.062
J^{Adj}_{10}	0.061	0.056	0.044	0.028	0.037	0.036	0.044	0.040	0.042	0.043	0.018	0.042
Diff	0.231	0.153	0.133	0.134	0.129	0.098	0.084	0.104	0.088	0.079		
Avg	0.180	0.136	0.123	0.108	0.111	0.099	0.094	0.093	0.084	0.074		

Panel C: Coskewness/J^{Adi} sorted portfolios

	C_1	C_2	C_3	C_4	C_5	C_6	C_7	C_8	C_9	C_{10}	Diff	Avg
J_1^{Adi}	0.199	0.205	0.182	0.155	0.145	0.149	0.148	0.152	0.138	0.145	0.054	0.172
J_2^{Adi}	0.168	0.168	0.157	0.147	0.142	0.136	0.139	0.127	0.114	0.147	0.021	0.149
J_3^{Adi}	0.158	0.156	0.147	0.138	0.136	0.130	0.122	0.116	0.105	0.125	0.033	0.138
J_4^{Adi}	0.161	0.168	0.144	0.150	0.133	0.121	0.114	0.107	0.082	0.096	0.065	0.133
J_5^{Adi}	0.148	0.157	0.153	0.137	0.122	0.116	0.104	0.087	0.095	0.066	0.082	0.122
J_6^{Adi}	0.155	0.149	0.144	0.132	0.119	0.109	0.099	0.082	0.074	0.057	0.098	0.112
J_7^{Adi}	0.130	0.128	0.128	0.116	0.118	0.098	0.097	0.076	0.064	0.057	0.073	0.098
J_8^{Adi}	0.121	0.100	0.104	0.099	0.079	0.079	0.070	0.070	0.060	0.059	0.062	0.078
J_9^{Adi}	0.059	0.073	0.075	0.078	0.072	0.073	0.064	0.069	0.049	0.042	0.017	0.062
J_{10}^{Adi}	0.044	0.054	0.050	0.050	0.053	0.048	0.046	0.049	0.039	0.028	0.015	0.042
Diff	0.155	0.151	0.132	0.105	0.093	0.101	0.102	0.103	0.100	0.117		
Avg	0.156	0.152	0.139	0.126	0.114	0.105	0.096	0.086	0.070	0.059		

TABLE 3.3 We measure risk premia using the in-sample (Ang et al., 2006a) regressions where cross-sectional regressions are computed every month rolling forward. At a given month, t, the average of the next 12 excess monthly returns is regressed against β, β^-, β^+, idiosyncratic risk ('Idio'), coskewness ('Cosk'), cokurtosis ('Cokurt') and f^{Adj}, estimated using the next 12 months of daily excess return data, and size ('Log-size'), book-to-market ratio ('BM') and the average past 12-monthly excess return ('Past Ret'), computed as at time t. We proxy the market portfolio with the CRSP value-weighted return of all NYSE, AMEX and NASDAQ stocks and the risk-free rate with the 1-month T-bill rate. All regressors are winsorized at the 1% and 99% level at each month. We restrict our attention to stocks listed on the NYSE between January 1963 and December 2015. Statistical significance is determined using Newey and West (1987) adjusted t-statistics, given in parentheses, to control for overlapping data using the Newey and West (1994) automatic lag selection method to determine the lag length. The mean and standard deviation (in parentheses) for each variable are provided in the last column. All coefficients are reported as effective annual rates

Equally weighted

	I	II	III	IV	V	Mean/Std
Int	0.351	0.041	0.337	0.337	0.309	
	[5.125]	[2.393]	[5.088]	[5.076]	[4.970]	
β	0.083		0.077	0.077		0.889
	[3.574]		[3.409]	[3.403]		(0.507)
β^-		0.080			0.079	0.952
		[4.818]			[4.511]	(0.596)
β^+		−0.024			−0.024	0.841
		[2.894]			[2.225]	(0.638)
Log-size	−0.023		−0.023	−0.023	−0.020	13.233
	[5.234]		[5.227]	[5.243]	[5.057]	(1.892)
BM	−0.044		−0.043	−0.043	−0.042	0.631
	[4.224]		[4.221]	[4.220]	[4.152]	(0.520)

Value weighted

	I	II	III	IV	V	Mean/Std
Int	0.356	0.040	0.342	0.343	0.314	
	[5.095]	[2.362]	[5.056]	[5.047]	[4.929]	
β	0.082		0.076	0.077		0.899
	[3.496]		[3.338]	[3.333]		(0.498)
β^-	0.000	0.079			0.080	0.954
	[0.000]	[4.753]			[4.478]	(0.590)
β^+	0.000	−0.025			−0.024	0.856
	[0.000]	[2.886]			[2.192]	(0.632)
Log-size	−0.023		−0.022	−0.023	−0.020	13.504
	[5.191]		[5.185]	[5.200]	[4.999]	(0.501)
BM	−0.045		−0.045	−0.045	−0.043	0.614
	[4.210]		[4.203]	[4.201]	[4.133]	(1.890)

Past Ret	−0.023 [0.161]	0.002 [0.017]	0.002 [0.017]	0.013 [0.095]	0.009 (0.030)	−0.004 [0.024]	0.022 [0.157]	0.023 [0.157]	0.034 [0.241]	0.009 (0.029)
Idio	−1.355 [1.310]	−1.372 [1.336]	−1.380 [1.346]	−1.297 [1.265]	0.021 (0.010)	−1.584 [1.504]	−1.601 [1.532]	−1.611 [1.544]	−1.526 [1.463]	0.020 (0.010)
Cosk	−0.198 [5.090]	−0.096 [3.255]	−0.094 [3.223]	0.116 [2.926]	−0.103 (0.295)	−0.196 [5.073]	−0.096 [3.260]	−0.094 [3.226]	0.116 [2.978]	−0.107 (0.297)
Cokurt	0.013 [1.929]	0.018 [2.780]	0.018 [2.756]	0.028 [3.635]	2.097 (2.495)	0.012 [1.843]	0.018 [2.642]	0.018 [2.604]	0.026 [3.439]	2.169 (2.504)
J^{Adj}	0.000 [5.906]	−0.005 [5.906]	−0.005 [5.906]		−2.345 (6.037)		−0.005 [5.888]	−0.005 [5.526]		−2.286 (7.499)
J^{Adj-}		−0.005 [5.595]	−0.006 [5.799]		−5.738 (3.354)		−0.005 [5.526]	−0.006 [5.758]		−5.709 (3.345)
J^{Adj+}		−0.005 [3.446]	−0.006 [3.438]		5.298 (2.971)		−0.005 [3.502]	−0.006 [3.504]		5.293 (2.972)

TABLE 3.4 This table presents out-of-sample (Fama and MacBeth, 1973) regression results where the averages of the next 1 month, 3 months, 6 months and 12 months of monthly excess returns are regressed upon past risk factors. At a given month, t, the average of the next excess monthly returns is regressed against β, β^-, β^+, idiosyncratic risk ('Idio'), coskewness ('Cosk'), cokurtosis ('Cokurt'), J^{Adj-} and J^{Adj+}, estimated using the past 12 months of daily excess return data. We also include the average past 12-monthly excess return ('Past Ret'). The relevant book-to-market ratio ('BM') at time t for a given stock is computed using the last available (most recent) book value entry. Size ('Log-size') is computed at the same date that the book-to-market ratio is computed. We proxy the market portfolio with the CRSP value-weighted return of all NYSE, AMEX and NASDAQ stocks and the risk-free rate with the 1-month T-bill rate. We restrict our attention to stocks listed on the NYSE between January 1963 and December 2015. Statistical significance is determined using Newey and West (1987) adjusted t-statistics, given in parentheses, to control for overlapping data using the Newey and West (1994) automatic lag selection method to determine the lag length. The mean and standard deviation (in parentheses) for each variable are also provided. All coefficients are reported as effective annual rates

	III				V				Mean (std)
	1m	3m	6m	12m	1m	3m	6m	12m	
Int	0.170	0.182	0.178	0.179	0.177	0.192	0.189	0.189	
	[4.248]	[3.829]	[3.564]	[3.568]	[4.545]	[3.933]	[3.686]	[3.614]	
β	−0.026	−0.033	−0.036	−0.034					0.889
	[1.197]	[2.003]	[2.187]	[2.200]					(0.507)
β^-	0.000	0.000	0.000	0.000	0.001	−0.014	−0.018	−0.022	0.952
	[0.000]	[0.000]	[0.000]	[0.000]	[0.080]	[1.126]	[1.560]	[2.219]	(0.597)
β^+	0.000	0.000	0.000	0.000	−0.022	−0.013	−0.014	−0.010	0.841
	[0.000]	[0.000]	[0.000]	[0.000]	[1.416]	[1.402]	[1.711]	[1.464]	(0.638)
Log-size	−0.012	−0.013	−0.013	−0.013	−0.012	−0.014	−0.014	−0.013	13.230
	[4.293]	[4.049]	[3.802]	[3.735]	[4.371]	[4.059]	[3.904]	[3.781]	(0.001)
BM	11.413	0.014	0.011	0.007	11.194	0.014	0.011	0.007	0.001
	[1.630]	[1.834]	[1.493]	[0.925]	[1.532]	[1.800]	[1.522]	[0.946]	(1.892)

	(1)	(2)	(3)	(4)	(5)	(6)	(7)	(8)	(9)
Past Ret	0.887	1.009	0.818	0.400	0.899	1.022	0.838	0.417	0.009
	[4.192]	[4.146]	[3.513]	[2.409]	[4.152]	[4.112]	[3.595]	[2.486]	(0.029)
Idio	1.508	2.282	2.809	3.166	0.991	1.869	2.479	2.983	0.021
	[2.073]	[3.099]	[3.490]	[3.932]	[1.275]	[2.245]	[2.833]	[3.302]	(0.010)
Cosk	0.186	0.073	0.050	0.030	0.266	0.076	0.042	0.009	−0.103
	[4.132]	[2.961]	[2.474]	[1.773]	[5.262]	[2.173]	[1.327]	[0.352]	(0.295)
Cokurt	0.026	0.026	0.022	0.019	0.014	0.019	0.015	0.015	2.097
	[2.953]	[3.341]	[2.972]	[2.796]	[1.462]	[2.214]	[1.938]	[1.980]	(2.497)
J^{Adj}	−0.008	−0.002	−0.001	−0.001					−2.340
	[15.442]	[5.667]	[3.491]	[2.825]					(6.038)
J^{Adj}_-					−0.008	−0.003	−0.001	−0.001	−5.738
					[10.351]	[4.206]	[2.745]	[1.668]	(3.354)
J^{Adj}_+					−0.012	−0.004	0.000	0.000	5.298
					[5.158]	[2.703]	[0.450]	[0.178]	(2.971)

We regress returns on $J^{Adj}+$ and $J^{Adj}-$ to isolate the premia demanded for upside and downside risk. After accounting for scale, we find that the premium demanded for LTAD, given by $J^{Adj}-$, is 25.50% of the β risk premium, whereas UTAD, given by $J^{Adj}+$, is 28.76% of the β risk premium. There is no evidence for a significant difference between the premia for UTAD and LTAD in the in-sample full-sample regressions.

Replacing β with β^+ and β^- (ignoring the potential multicollinearity issue) in regression V yields little change in our results. The significance of β^- and β^+ indicates that censored measures of linear dependence are priced in the cross-section, where in particular, downside measures are more heavily priced than upside measures. The significance of $J^{Adj}-$ and $J^{Adj}+$ continues to indicate that UTAD and LTAD demand a price in the cross-section.

Our results suggest that higher-order dependence (in the form of UTAD and LTAD) is important in explaining the variation in returns, implying that the CAPM ignores a significant characteristic of the joint return distribution. Investors are not only concerned with the overall level of linear dependence between stock returns and the market, they are also concerned with the symmetry of the joint return distribution around β.

A significant positive (negative) relation between lower (upper) tail dependence and return is consistent with existing evidence of a preference towards stocks that display upside risk. Given the way we measure AD, our results imply that investors may display relative disappointment aversion consistent with Skiadas's (1997) preference framework. That is, investors display conditional preference relations for all possible joint outcomes of security and market returns.

If expected returns can be written as a linear function of k factors, then k-fund separation can be used to span the mean-variance efficient frontier (Ross, 1978; Fama, 1996). This implies that a mean-variance-efficient portfolio defined by linear dependence is unlikely to be efficient with respect to an efficient portfolio spanned by both linear and asymmetric dependence. This suggests that the risk of a well-diversified portfolio will reflect both the average covariance and the average tail dependence between the assets.

Using deep out-of-the-money index options, Bollerslev and Todorov (2009) show that compensation for investor fear towards low-probability, highly catastrophic events accounts for a substantial fraction of the equity risk premium in the US market. Bali *et al.* (2011) find a negative relation between maximum daily returns over the previous month and expected stock returns. When applied to individual equities, the risk premium for downside risk is likely to depend on the magnitude of the relation between the stock's returns and the aggregate market. Our results suggest that there need only be a tendency for stocks to display higher dependence during market downturns, relative to upturns, for a tail dependence risk premium to arise. This is a weaker condition than the requirement for a low-probability, highly catastrophic market crash. Of course, what would otherwise be a market decline can quickly precipitate a potential market crash in the presence of levered positions in tail risk. In particular, Diamond and Rajan (2009) and Rajan (2006) describe an incentive for managers to load up on 'hidden' downside risk in the form of tail risk and report the compensation as reward for α. This may partly explain the excessive risks taken by managers prior to the 2007–2009 financial crisis.

3.2.7   Out-of-Sample Regressions

Consistent with previous downside-risk pricing research (Ang *et al.*, 2006a), we have shown that LTAD (UTAD) is related to higher (lower) returns in-sample. To ensure that our findings are robust to any forward-looking bias, we also determine whether past estimates of AD affect future returns. That is, we employ an out-of-sample (Fama–MacBeth) approach and analyse the relation between past dependence, estimated using the previous 12 months of daily excess returns data, and the average next-month excess return.

We do not find significant coefficients for β^-, β^+ or β. However, we do observe significant coefficients associated with J^{Adj} (Table 3.4). The (significant) premium demanded for J^{Adj}, adjusted for scale, is a substantial 289.08% of the (insignificant) predictive premium demanded for β, providing additional support in favour of an AD premium relative to the market risk premium. The scaled predictive premium for LTAD is 180.26% of that for β, and 243.91% for UTAD. Hence, our key finding that AD is priced in the market is robust to any forward-looking bias.

Ang *et al.* (2006a) investigate the role played by volatility in measuring the relation between past upside and downside β and future return. They argue on the one hand that high return volatility could lead to less accurate β^- estimates, thereby reducing the ability to predict future β^-. Alternatively, they suggest a confounding relation between β^- and stock volatility, which is compounded by the possibility that stocks with very high volatility have extremely low returns, as demonstrated by Ang *et al.* (2006b). The remedy for this problem is to consider the relation between past dependence and future return, excluding the most volatile stocks.

We investigate the role of volatility on our predictive results following Ang *et al.* (2006a) by measuring volatility as the standard deviation of excess daily returns estimated over the past 12 months (Table 3.5). Excluding the top quintile of volatile stocks each month causes the coefficient of β to become insignificant, suggesting that volatility plays an important role in the β predicability of future returns. The coefficients of J^{Adj}, $J^{Adj}+$ and $J^{Adj}-$ are all significant. Excluding the top decile and the top 5%-tile of volatile stocks only serves to reinforce our key findings. Hence, AD is more influential than linear dependence in forecasting the returns of the least volatile stocks. Across the entire sample, the importance of tail dependence continues to represent only a fraction of the importance associated with linear dependence in explaining equity return variation.

3.2.8 Time-Varying Risk

One feature of the Skiadas (1997) framework that is not shared by alternative models of disappointment aversion (e.g., Gul, 1991) is that preference orders do not necessarily hold in the instance that the event D is expected to occur with certainty. Therefore, in the situation where a market drawdown occurs and an asset is revealed to possess LTAD with the market, a Skiadas agent may be less disappointed were another drawdown to occur a short time later. This is because the downside-dependent behaviour of the asset, contingent upon a market drawdown, is now a known characteristic of the joint return distribution. As a consequence, we may observe a premium for LTAD during normal market conditions but this premium may change subsequent to the occurence of a major market crash.

From a practical perspective, recent market events[8] have revealed significant information about the conditional distribution of many assets. Consequently, tail-risk management has been of increasing concern amongst practitioners in recent years (Bhansali, 2008). The development of a superior tail-risk management product therefore represents a potentially important and lucrative enterprise as the economy recovers and proceeds into subsequent boom–bust cycles. In the absence of a zero-cost tail-risk hedge, investors must identify whether such products are justified in light of what historically drives market crashes, and the likelihood of these drivers being associated with future market failures. Products that manage changes in linear dependence are likely to look very different from products that manage changes in AD. However, products that target increases in systematic risk when crashes are driven by changes in AD (and vice versa) may not adequately protect portfolios during market crashes. To identify the extent that investors should be concerned with this problem, we examine the relative importance of systematic risk (changes in linear dependence) and AD (changes in higher-order dependence) over time.

The increasing concern for tail-risk management is likely to reflect an increase in the sensitivity of individual securities to market movements, or an increase in aversion to risk, or some combination of the two. To capture potential changes in aversion to risk, we re-estimate model IV of Table 3.3 using the Ang *et al.* (2006a) in-sample regression at each month t between January 1989 and December 2015 (Table 3.6). The factor premium at time t is then given by the median of all regression coefficients

---

[8]For example, the Asian financial crisis (1996), the collapse of the dotcom bubble (2001), the global financial crisis of 2007/8 and the Eurozone crises (2010).

TABLE 3.5 We measure risk premia using in-sample (Ang et al., 2006a) regressions where cross-sectional regressions are computed every month rolling forward. We provide regression results using all available observations, as well as a series of regressions excluding the top quintile, top decile and top vigintile of volatile stocks, where volatility is measured as the standard deviation of the past 12 months of daily excess returns. We proxy the market portfolio with the CRSP value-weighted return of all NYSE, AMEX and NASDAQ stocks and the risk-free rate with the 1-month T-bill rate. All regressors are winsorized at the 1% and 99% level at each month. We restrict our attention to stocks listed on the NYSE between January 1963 and December 2015. With the exception of the non-overlapping data regression, statistical significance is determined using Newey and West (1987) adjusted t-statistics, given in parentheses, to control for overlapping data using the Newey and West (1994) automatic lag selection method to determine the lag length. All coefficients are reported as effective annual rates

	All			Excluding Top Quintile			Excluding Top Decile			Excluding Top Vigintile		
	I	IV	Mean/Std	I	IV	Mean/Std	I	IV	Mean/Std	I	IV	Mean/Std
Int	0.188	0.168		0.186	0.168		0.186	0.168		0.186	0.168	
	[4.542]	[4.194]		[4.373]	[4.037]		[4.153]	[3.826]		[4.152]	[3.825]	
β	-0.016	-0.026	0.889	-0.016	-0.025	0.898	-0.016	-0.025	0.898	-0.016	-0.025	0.898
	[0.765]	[1.212]	(0.507)	[0.745]	[1.167]	(0.496)	[0.774]	[1.229]	(0.496)	[0.780]	[1.235]	(0.496)
Log-size	-0.012	-0.012	13.230	-0.012	-0.011	13.506	-0.012	-0.011	13.506	-0.012	-0.011	13.506
	[4.273]	[4.303]	(0.001)	[4.021]	[4.040]	(0.000)	[3.795]	[3.725]	(0.495)	[3.796]	[3.726]	(0.495)
BM	12.569	11.530	0.001	12.716	11.581	0.001	0.013	0.011	0.613	0.013	0.011	0.613
	[1.704]	[1.648]	(1.892)	[1.639]	[1.534]	(1.887)	[1.600]	[1.489]	(1.887)	[1.597]	[1.485]	(1.887)

Past Ret	1.021 [4.676]	0.882 [4.172]	0.009 (0.029)	1.029 [4.538]	0.891 [4.028]	0.008 (0.029)	1.027 [4.175]	0.889 [3.703]	0.008 (0.029)	1.027 [4.175]	0.889 [3.703]	0.008 (0.029)
Idio	1.563 [2.131]	1.518 [2.086]	0.021 (0.010)	1.428 [1.936]	1.377 [1.843]	0.020 (0.010)	1.432 [1.912]	1.381 [1.841]	0.020 (0.010)	1.438 [1.919]	1.387 [1.848]	0.020 (0.010)
Cosk	0.025 [0.564]	0.189 [4.193]	−0.103 (0.295)	0.028 [0.619]	0.188 [3.970]	−0.106 (0.298)	0.028 [0.624]	0.188 [3.699]	−0.106 (0.298)	0.028 [0.622]	0.188 [3.697]	−0.106 (0.298)
Cokurt	0.017 [1.970]	0.027 [3.018]	2.097 (2.497)	0.017 [1.981]	0.026 [2.910]	2.170 (2.511)	0.017 [2.006]	0.026 [2.931]	2.170 (2.511)	0.017 [2.013]	0.027 [2.937]	2.170 (2.511)
J^{Adj}_{-}		−0.009 [12.698]	−5.738 (3.354)		−0.008 [11.088]	−5.705 (3.341)		−0.008 [8.189]	−5.705 (3.341)		−0.008 [8.189]	−5.705 (3.341)
J^{Adj}_{+}		−0.0120 [5.732]	5.298 (2.971)		−0.0119 [5.297]	5.293 (2.972)		−0.0118 [4.132]	5.293 (2.972)		−0.0118 [4.133]	5.293 (2.972)

TABLE 3.6 We measure risk premia using in-sample (Ang et al., 2006a) regressions where cross-sectional regressions are computed every month rolling forward. Risk factors are estimated each month rolling forward and are calculated using 60, 24 and 6 months' worth of daily data, 5 and 3 years' worth of weekly data and 5 years' worth of fortnightly data. We also include value-weighted regression results and non-overlapping data regression results. We proxy the market portfolio with the CRSP value-weighted return of all NYSE, AMEX and NASDAQ stocks and the risk-free rate with the 1-month T-bill rate. All regressors are winsorized at the 1% and 99% level at each month. We restrict our attention to stocks listed on the NYSE between January 1963 and December 2015. With the exception of the non-overlapping data regression, statistical significance is determined using Newey and West (1987) adjusted t-statistics, given in parentheses, to control for overlapping data using the Newey and West (1994) automatic lag selection method to determine the lag length. All coefficients are reported as effective annual rates. Note that for the value-weighted regressions, we calculate the value-weighted mean and value-weighted standard deviation of each risk factor at each month and report the time-series average value-weighted mean and the time-series average value-weighted standard deviation

	Fort 5 yr		Week 5yr		Week 3yr		Daily 24m		Daily 6m			
	I	IV	I	IV	I	IV	I	IV	I	IV	VW	non OL
Int	−0.059	−0.061	0.091	0.089	−0.047	−0.052	0.085	0.079	0.197	0.186	0.343	0.011
	[0.659]	[0.706]	[3.149]	[3.106]	[1.652]	[1.776]	[2.438]	[2.261]	[4.022]	[3.870]	[5.047]	[3.077]
β	0.149	0.147	0.044	0.044	0.037	0.035	0.014	0.011	0.020	0.015	0.077	0.005
	[3.266]	[3.243]	[3.523]	[3.519]	[2.581]	[2.476]	[0.666]	[0.517]	[1.557]	[1.184]	[3.333]	[2.754]
Log-size	−0.003	−0.003	−0.010	−0.010	−0.001	−0.001	−0.003	−0.003	−0.012	−0.011	−0.023	−0.001
	[0.642]	[0.652]	[4.366]	[4.359]	[0.633]	[0.668]	[1.764]	[1.746]	[3.686]	[3.654]	[5.200]	[2.839]
BM	−0.173	−0.173	−0.046	−0.046	−0.034	−0.034	−0.035	−0.036	−0.039	−0.039	−0.045	−0.003
	[4.656]	[4.657]	[4.831]	[4.833]	[4.029]	[4.045]	[3.647]	[3.710]	[4.010]	[3.995]	[4.201]	[3.176]
Past Ret	−0.275	−0.269	−0.652	−0.631	0.135	0.168	0.223	0.189	0.206	0.227	0.023	0.018
	[1.847]	[1.808]	[2.089]	[2.027]	[0.349]	[0.433]	[1.478]	[1.277]	[1.357]	[1.488]	[0.157]	[1.118]
Idio	12.431	12.371	3.994	3.969	4.605	4.579	2.087	1.957	1.708	1.741	−1.611	−0.003
	[5.465]	[5.469]	[5.480]	[5.469]	[5.430]	[5.425]	[1.978]	[1.860]	[2.076]	[2.126]	[1.544]	[0.032]
Cosk	−0.068	−0.016	−0.042	−0.030	−0.052	−0.024	−0.182	−0.093	−0.080	−0.006	−0.094	−0.010
	[1.378]	[0.329]	[2.377]	[1.776]	[2.867]	[1.396]	[4.268]	[2.661]	[4.583]	[0.431]	[3.226]	[2.507]

	(1)	(2)	(3)	(4)	(5)	(6)	(7)	(8)	(9)	(10)	(11)	(12)
Cokurt	0.015	0.019	0.011	0.012	0.009	0.013	0.005	0.008	0.011	0.016	0.018	0.001
	[0.874]	[1.118]	[2.363]	[2.562]	[1.526]	[1.995]	[0.661]	[1.076]	[2.387]	[3.363]	[2.604]	[0.706]
J^{Adj}_-		−0.003		−0.001		−0.002		−0.004		−0.005		0.000
		[3.310]		[2.435]		[4.197]		[5.079]		[5.985]	[5.526]	[5.196]
J^{Adj}_+	−0.0055		−0.0005		−0.0005		−0.0009		−0.0048	−0.0037	−0.0054	−0.0005
	[2.878]		[1.616]		[2.618]		[3.452]		[4.574]	[3.502]	[4.614]

	Fort 5 yr		Week 5yr		Week 3yr		Daily 24m		Daily 6m		VW		non OL	
	mean	(std)	mean	(std)	mean	(std)	mean	(std)	mean	(std)	mean	(std)	mean	(std)
β	1.013	(0.519)	0.965	(0.470)	0.972	(0.515)	0.890	(0.473)	0.884	(0.556)	0.899	(0.498)	0.891	(0.513)
β^-	1.037	(0.679)	1.014	(0.546)	1.027	(0.693)	0.950	(0.525)	0.947	(0.738)	0.954	(0.590)	0.957	(0.609)
β^+	0.989	(0.771)	0.936	(0.627)	0.931	(0.748)	0.847	(0.565)	0.833	(0.779)	0.856	(0.632)	0.842	(0.644)
Log-size	13.763	(1.651)	13.249	(1.858)	13.698	(1.691)	13.882	(0.508)	13.233	(1.892)	13.504	(0.501)	13.669	(1.627)
BM	0.638	(0.485)	0.643	(0.489)	0.637	(0.513)	0.619	(1.637)	0.631	(0.520)	0.614	(1.890)	0.629	(0.524)
Past Ret	0.033	(0.063)	0.004	(0.008)	0.004	(0.007)	0.009	(0.029)	0.009	(0.030)	0.009	(0.029)	0.008	(0.031)
Idio	0.063	(0.029)	0.046	(0.021)	0.045	(0.022)	0.021	(0.010)	0.020	(0.011)	0.020	(0.010)	0.021	(0.010)
Cosk	−0.128	(0.327)	−0.119	(0.279)	−0.106	(0.301)	−0.134	(0.385)	−0.083	(0.278)	−0.107	(0.297)	−0.099	(0.285)
Cokurt	2.212	(1.200)	2.333	(1.560)	1.854	(1.244)	2.949	(4.866)	1.632	(1.431)	2.169	(2.504)	2.051	(2.382)
J^{Adj}	−2.927	(6.612)	−2.974	(5.677)	−2.832	(7.301)	−2.613	(8.139)	−2.129	(7.022)	−2.286	(7.499)	−2.495	(5.956)
J^{Adj}_-	−6.408	(4.124)	−5.724	(3.369)	−6.873	(4.470)	−5.733	(3.425)	−6.408	(3.972)	−5.709	(3.345)	−5.736	(3.336)
J^{Adj}_+	5.286	(3.271)	4.952	(2.790)	5.945	(3.631)	5.229	(2.930)	5.942	(3.589)	5.293	(2.972)	5.248	(2.929)

associated with that factor up to and including time t. We have chosen to compute the factor premium using medians because we are interested in the trend in risk premium over time rather than an accurate portrayal of the compensation for risk. Short-term, non-permanent increases in regression coefficients are likely to result in permanent changes in risk premium estimates computed using averages over all historical coefficient estimates. Changes in the median regression coefficient are therefore more likely to reflect permanent trend changes rather than short-term trend changes. Similarly, we capture changes in the factor loadings by computing the median of a given factor at time t using all observations up to and including t.

An inspection of the average loading for β, $J^{Adj}-$ and $J^{Adj}+$ indicates that the heightened concern for tail-risk management is unlikely to be a result of changes in stock sensitivity to market movements (Figure 3.4(a)). To highlight this point, we observe that the median loading on $J^{Adj}-$ between 2007 and 2009 appears no greater than the median loading immediately prior to, or after, this,[9] indicating that

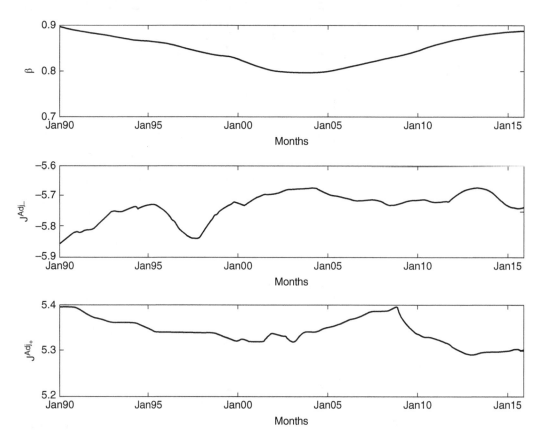

FIGURE 3.4   This figure depicts the median factor loading for β, $J^{Adj}-$ and $J^{Adj}+$ at a given month, t, between January 1989 and December 2015 using the next 12 months of daily excess returns. We proxy the market portfolio with the CRSP value-weighted return of all NYSE, AMEX and NASDAQ stocks and the risk-free rate with the 1-month T-bill rate. The estimate is calculated using all historical data up to, and including, time t.

---

[9]This observation holds after scaling by the standard deviation of $J^{Adj}-$ at each month.

sensitivity to market crashes did not alter significantly, relative to historical sensitivity, in response to the financial crisis. Similarly, there was an increase in systematic risk (β) between 2007 and 2009; however, the magnitude of this increase does not differ significantly from the level of increase that began in 2001 and has continued through to the end of our sample period.

A plot of the factor sensitivity of β (per unit of factor loading) highlights the change in the price of systematic risk corresponding to the run up in prices during the 1990s (Figure 3.5). Despite the use of medians in our estimation of risk premia, the magnitude of this sensitivity subsequently remains at this heightened level with only a slight decrease from 2001 onwards. This implies that the run up in prices during the 1990s had more of an effect on the reward for systematic risk than the market turmoil

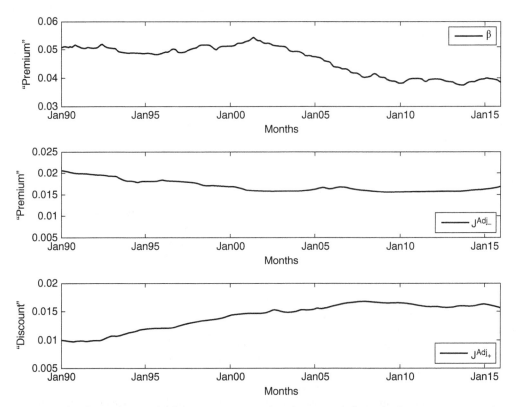

FIGURE 3.5   This figure depicts the factor sensitivity using the Fama and MacBeth (1973) asset-pricing procedure where cross-sectional regressions are computed every month rolling forward. At a given month, t, the average of the next 12 excess monthly returns is regressed against β, idiosyncratic risk, coskewness, cokurtosis, $J^{Adj}-$ and $J^{Adj}+$ estimated using the next 12 months of daily excess return data, and size ('Log-size'), book-to-market ratio ('BM') and the average past 12-monthly excess return ('Past Ret'), computed as at time t. We proxy the market portfolio with the CRSP value-weighted return of all NYSE, AMEX and NASDAQ stocks and the risk-free rate with the 1-month T-bill rate. All regressors are winsorized at the 1% and 99% level at each month. We restrict our attention to stocks listed on the NYSE between January 1963 and December 2015. The 'Premium' for β and for $J^{Adj}-$ and the 'Discount' for $J^{Adj}+$ between January 1989 and December 2015 is given by the time-series median factor sensitivity using all historical sensitivity estimates up to, and including, time t.

of 2007–2009. Combined with the slight increase in β loading over this time, the net effect is a slight increase in the β risk premium during the financial crisis.

Interestingly, the positive premium demanded for LTAD has remained relatively constant between 1989 and 2009, suggesting that LTAD has been priced in equities for a long period of time. The discount for upside potential, on the other hand, increased markedly between 1990 and 2007 and plateaued from 2007 onwards. Taken together, this implies that the market became more downside-risk-averse overall, but more as a result of increased demand for stocks displaying sensitivity to market upturns rather than as a result of an increased aversion to stocks with downturn sensitivity. In the context of Skiadas's downside-risk framework, where disappointment is judged with respect to outcomes that could have occurred, this implies that a stock with constant downside market sensitivity will demand an increasing risk premium over time due to the increasing importance of stocks that generate elating outcomes.

On the basis of changes in risk premia, the 2007–2009 financial crises appear to be as much a systematic risk story as a tail risk story, implying that the risks associated with both linear dependence and higher-order dependence should be managed to insulate a portfolio from future market crashes. For many investors, techniques to manage changes in systematic risk are likely to already be in place, particularly through the ability to tactically allocate funds between assets on the basis of changes in overall fundamentals. A value-accreting tail-risk-management product should therefore target changes in tail dependence over and above the tail dependence implied by β. Further, such products should account for changes in the relative aversion to upside and downside market movements.

3.3 CONCLUSION

The aim of this chapter is to characterize the AD premium relative to the market risk premium. This investigation is motivated by the need to identify whether the effect of an apparent tail event on returns reflects compensation for changes in tail dependence (symmetry) or compensation for changes in systematic risk (linear dependence). To measure AD, we employ a linear (β) dependence-invariant metric, based on the J statistic originally proposed by Hong et al. (2007).

We find that the magnitude of the premium associated with AD is a substantial fraction of the premium associated with β, highlighting the importance of accounting for the effect of changes in both systematic risk and tail dependence on returns. Both the prevalence and price of UTAD have been increasing in recent years, indicating that investors are valuing UTAD more, while the returns of more firms are exhibiting this characteristic. The premium demanded for LTAD has remained relatively constant over a long period of time. As a result, the market environment in large cap equities between 2007 and 2009 can be explained in part by changes in systematic risk, but also by changes in the importance of stocks that display UTAD with the market.

These results have important practical implications, particularly for future endeavours to manage tail risk. Buyers and sellers of tail-risk protection both need to carefully consider the likely magnitude of systematic risk changes relative to changes in AD. A strategy that hedges the risk associated with changes in linear dependence may be significantly different from the strategy an investor might otherwise put in place to manage changes in tail dependence. By analysing the magnitude of the sensitivity of returns to AD, relative to the sensitivity of returns to systematic risk, investors may be able to assess whether systematic risk hedges are sufficient to mitigate the potential losses associated with tail dependence.

Our results also have significant implications for a firm's cost of capital and the associated capital-raising decisions. The existence of AD between the firm's returns and those of the market will induce a corresponding discount (UTAD) or premium (LTAD). Failing to recognize the influence of AD on the cost of capital is likely to render public capital offerings either underpriced or undersubscribed. Similarly, capital managers who recognize the value of AD are likely to be able to generate measurable alpha by exploiting the associated premium. However, this alpha is not without risk. To identify whether this alpha is 'genuine', suitable AD-sensitive performance measures need to be identified and utilized. Our results also suggest that such measures are unlikely to be based upon copula parameters, β or downside β.

REFERENCES

Alcock, J. and Hatherley, A. (2017). Characterizing the price of asymmetric dependence. *Review of Finance*, 21(4), 1701–1737.

Ang, A. and Bekaert, G. (2002). International asset allocation with regime shifts. *Society for Financial Studies*, 15(4), 1137–1187.

Ang, A. and Chen, J. (2002). Asymmetric correlations of equity portfolios. *Journal of Financial Economics*, 63(3), 443–494.

Ang, A., Chen, J. and Xing, Y. (2006a). Downside risk. *Review of Financial Studies*, 19(4), 1191–1239.

Ang, A., Hodrick, R., Xing, Y. and Zhang, X. (2006b). The cross-section of volatility and expected returns. *Journal of Finance*, 61(1), 259–299.

Bali, T., Demirtas, O. and Levy, H. (2009). Is there an intertemporal relation between downside risk and expected returns? *Journal of Financial and Quantitative Analysis*, 44(4), 883–909.

Bali, T., Cakici, N. and Whitelaw, R. (2011). Maxing out: stocks as lotteries and the cross-section of expected returns. *Journal of Financial Economics*, 99(2), 427–446.

Bekaert, G. and Wu, G. (2000). Asymmetric volatility and risk in equity markets. *Review of Financial Studies*, 13(1), 1–42.

Bhansali, V. (2008). Tail risk management. *Journal of Portfolio Management*, 34(4), 68–75.

Black, F., Jensen, M. and Scholes, M. (1972). The capital asset pricing model: some empirical tests, in M. Jensen (ed.), *Studies in the Theory of Capital Markets*. Praeger, New York.

Blume, M. (1975). Betas and their regression tendencies. *Journal of Finance*, 30(3), 785–795.

Bollerslev, T., Engle, R. and Wooldridge, J. (1988). A capital asset pricing model with time-varying covariances. *Journal of Political Economy*, 96(1), 116–131.

Bollerslev, T. and Todorov, V. (2009). Tails, fears and risk premia. *Journal of Finance*, 66(6), 2165–2211.

Bos, T. and Newbold, P. (1984). An empirical investigation of the possibility of stochastic systematic risk in the market model. *Journal of Business*, 57(1), 35–41.

Butler, K. and Joaquin, D. (2002). Are the gains from international portfolio diversification exaggerated? The influence of downside risk in bear markets. *Journal of International Money and Finance*, 21(7), 981–1011.

Campbell, R., Koedijk, K. and Kofman, P. (2002). Increased correlation in bear markets. *Financial Analysts Journal*, 58(1), 87–94.

Diamond, E. and Rajan, R. (2009). The credit crisis: conjectures about causes and remedies. *American Economic Review: Papers & Proceedings*, 99(2), 606–610.

Dimson, E., Marsh, P. and Staunton, M. (2003). Global evidence on the equity risk premium. *Journal of Applied Corporate Finance*, 15(4), 27–38.

Erb, C., Harvey, C. and Viskanta, T. (1994). Forecasting international equity correlations. *Financial Analysts Journal*, 50(6), 32–45.

Fabozzi, F. and Francis, J. (1978). Beta as a random coefficient. *Journal of Financial and Quantitative Analysis*, 13(1), 101–116.

Fama, E. (1996). Multifactor portfolio efficiency and multifactor asset pricing. *Journal of Financial and Quantitative Finance*, 31(4), 441–465.

Fama, E. and MacBeth, J. (1973). Risk, return and equilibrium: empirical tests. *Journal of Political Economy*, 81(3), 607–636.

Ferson, W. and Harvey, C. (1991). The variation of economic risk premiums. *Journal of Political Economy*, 99(2), 385–415.

Ferson, W. and Harvey, C. (1993). The risk and predictability of international equity returns. *Review of Financial Studies*, 6(3), 527–566.

Ferson, W. and Korajczyk, R. (1995). Do arbitrage pricing models explain the predictability of stock returns? *Journal of Business*, 68(3), 309–349.

Gibbons, M.R. (1982). Multivariate tests of financial models. *Journal of Financial Economics*, 10(1), 3–27.

Gul, F. (1991). A theory of disappointment aversion. *Econometrica*, 59(3), 667–686.

Hartmann, P., Straetmans, S. and De Vries, C. (2004). Asset market linkages in crisis periods. *Review of Economics and Statistics*, 86(1), 313–326.

Harvey, C., Liu, Y. and Zhu, H. (2015). … and the cross-section of expected returns. NBER Working Paper 20592.

Hong, Y., Tu, J. and Zhou, G. (2007). Asymmetries in stock returns: statistical tests and economic evaluation. *Review of Financial Studies*, 20(5), 1547–1581.

Khandani, A. and Lo, A. (2007). What happened to the quants in August 2007? *Journal of Investment Management*, 5(4), 5–54.

Kim, D. (1995). The errors in the variables problem in the cross-section of expected stock returns. *Journal of Finance*, 50(5), 1605–1634.

Lewellen, J. and Nagel, S. (2006). The conditional CAPM does not explain asset-pricing anomalies. *Journal of Financial Economics*, 82(2), 289–314.

Li, F. (2014). Identifying asymmetric comovements of international stock market returns. *Journal of Financial Econometrics*, 12(3), 507–543.

Longin, F. and Solnik, B. (2001). Extreme correlation of international equity markets. *Journal of Finance*, 56(2), 649–676.

Newey, W. and West, K. (1987). A simple, positive semi-definite, hetcroskedasticity and autocorrelation consistent covariance matrix. *Econometrica*, 55(3), 703–708.

Newey, W. and West, K. (1994). Lag selection in covariance matrix estimation. *Review of Financial Studies*, 61(4), 631–653.

Pastor, L. and Stambaugh, R. (2001). The equity premium and structural breaks. *Journal of Finance*, 56(4), 1207–1239.

Patton, A. (2004). On the out-of-sample importance of skewness and asymmetric dependence for asset allocation. *Journal of Financial Econometrics*, 2(1), 130–168.

Pedersen, C. and Hwang, S. (2007). Does downside Beta matter in asset pricing? *Applied Financial Economics*, 17(12), 961–978.

Post, T. and Van Vliet, P. (2006). Downside risk and asset pricing. *Journal of Banking and Finance*, 30(3), 823–849.

Rajan, R. (2006). Has finance made the world riskier. *European Financial Management*, 12(4), 499–533.

Ramchand, L. and Susmel, R. (1998). Volatility and cross correlation across major stock markets. *Journal of Empirical Finance*, 5(4), 397–416.

Ross, S. (1978). Mutual fund separation in financial theory – the separating distributions. *Journal of Economic Theory*, 17(2), 254–286.

Siegel, J. (1992). The equity premium: stock and bond returns since 1802. *Financial Analysts Journal*, 48(1), 28–38.

FURTHER READING

Bali, T., Cakici, N., Yan, X. and Zhang, Z. (2005). Does idiosyncratic risk really matter? *Journal of Finance*, 60(2), 905–929.

Bekaert, G., Hodrick, R. and Marshall, D. (1997). The implications of first-order risk aversion for asset market risk premiums. *Journal of Monetary Economics*, 40(1), 3–39.

Benartzi, S. and Thaler, R. (1995). Myopic loss aversion and the equity premium puzzle. *Quarterly Journal of Economics*, 110(1), 73–92.

Birkhoff, G. and Lane, M. (1997). *A Survey of Modern Algebra*. Macmillan, New York.

Boudoukh, J., Richardson, M. and Smith, T. (1993). Is the ex ante risk premium always positive? *Journal of Financial Economics*, 34(3), 387–408.

Cappiello, L., Gerard, B., Kadareja, A. and Manganelli, S. (2014). Measuring comovements by regression quantiles. *Journal of Financial Econometrics*, 12(4), 645–678.

Campbell, J., Lettau, M., Malkiel, B. and Xu, Y. (2001). Have individual stocks become more volatile? An empirical exploration of idiosyncratic risk. *Journal of Finance*, 56(1), 1–43.

Cont, R. (2001). Empirical properties of asset returns: stylized facts and statistical issues. *Quantitative Finance*, 1(2), 223–236.

Denuit, M., Huang, R., Tzeng, L. and Wang, W. (2014). Almost marginal conditional stochastic dominance. *Journal of Banking and Finance*, 41(1), 57–66.

Eleswarapu, V. and Thompson, R. (2007). Testing for negative expected market return premia. *Journal of Banking and Finance*, 31(6), 1755–1770.

Fama, E. and French, K. (1992). The cross-section of expected stock returns. *Journal of Finance*, 48(2), 427–465.

Fielding, D. and Stracca, L. (2007). Myopic loss aversion, disappointment aversion, and the equity premium puzzle. *Journal of Economic Behaviour and Organization*, 64(2), 250–268.

Fu, F. (2009). Idiosyncratic risk and the cross-section of expected stock returns. *Journal of Financial Economics*, 91(1), 24–37.

Genest, C., Gendron, M. and Boureau-Brien, M. (2009). The advent of copulas in finance. *European Journal of Finance*, 15(7&8), 609–618.

Goyal, A. and Santa-Clara, P. (2003). Idiosyncratic risk matters! *Journal of Finance*, 58(3), 975–1007.

Grant, S., Kajii, A. and Polak, B. (2001). Different notations of disappointment aversion. *Economics Letters*, 70(2), 203–208.

Harvey, C. and Siddique, A. (2000). Conditional skewness in asset pricing tests. *Journal of Finance*, 55(3), 1263–1295.

Joe, H. (1997). *Multivariate Models and Dependence Concepts*. Monographs on Statistics and Applied Probability. Chapman & Hall, London.

Karni, E. (1987). State-dependent preferences, in J. Eatwell, M. Milgate and P. Newman (eds), *The New Palgrave: A Dictionary of Economics*. Palgrave Macmillan, New York.

Kraus, A. and Sagi, J. (2006). Asset pricing with unforeseen contingencies. *Journal of Financial Economics*, 82(2), 417–453.

Kullmann, L., Kertesz, L., Toyli, J., Kaski, K. and Kanot, A. (2000). Breakdown of scaling and convergence to Gaussian distribution in stock market data. *International Journal of Theoretical and Applied Finance*, 3(3), 371–372.

Kwon, Y. (1985). Derivation of the capital asset pricing model without normality or quadratic preference: a note. *Journal of Finance*, 40(5), 1505–1509.

Lo, A. and Mackinlay, A. (1990). An econometric analysis of nonsynchronous trading. *Journal of Econometrics*, 45(1&2), 181–211.

Low, R., Alcock, J., Brailsford, T. and Faff, R. (2015). Canonical vine copulas in the context of modern portfolio management: are they worth it? *Journal of Banking and Finance*, 37(8), 3085–3099.

Lucas, R. (1978). Asset prices in an exchange economy. *Econometrica*, 46(6), 1429–1445.

Mackinlay, A. (1995). Multifactor models do not explain deviations from the CAPM. *Journal of Financial Economics*, 38(1), 3–28.

Merton, R. (1987). Presidential address: a simple model of capital market equilibrium with incomplete information. *Journal of Finance*, 42, 483–510.

Pastor, L. and Stambaugh, R. (2003). Liquidity risk and expected stock returns. *Journal of Political Economy*, 111(3), 642–685.

Poon, S., Rockinger, M. and Tawn, J. (2004). Extreme value dependence in financial markets: diagnostics, models, and financial implications. *Review of Financial Studies*, 17(2), 581–610.

Roll, R. and Ross, S. (1994). On the cross-sectional relation between expected returns and betas. *Journal of Finance*, 49(1), 101–121.

Routledge, B. and Zin, S. (2010). Generalized disappointment aversion and asset prices. *Journal of Finance*, 65(4), 1303–1332.

Savage, L. (1954). *The Foundations of Statistics*. Dover Publications, New York.

Shalit, H. and Yitzhaki, S. (1994). Marginal conditional stochastic dominance. *Management Science*, 40(5), 670–684.

Shanken, J. (1987). Multivariate proxies and asset pricing relations: living with the roll critique. *Journal of Financial Economics*, 18(1), 91–110.

Sharpe, W. (1977). The capital asset pricing model: a 'multi-beta' interpretation, in H. Levy and M. Sarnat (eds), *Financial Decision Making Under Uncertainty*. Academic Press, New York.

Skiadas, C. (1996). Subjective probability under additive aggregation of conditional preferences. *Journal of Economic Theory*, 76(2), 242–271.

Skiadas, C. (1997). Conditioning and aggregation of preferences. *Econometrica*, 65(2), 347–367.

Stapleton, R. and Subrahmanyam, M. (1983). The market model and capital asset pricing theory: a note. *Journal of Finance*, 38(5), 1637–1642.

Webster, R. (1995). *Convexity*. Oxford University Press, New York.

CHAPTER 4

Misspecification in an Asymmetrically Dependent World: Implications for Volatility Forecasting[1]

Salman Ahmed[a], Nandini Srivastava[a] and Stephen Satchell[b]

[a]Christ's College, Cambridge University
[b]Discipline of Finance, Sydney University and Trinity College, Cambridge

Abstract
In this chapter we assess the relative abilities of GARCH and stochastic volatility (SV) models to forecast volatility in a world where the true volatility data exhibit asymmetric dependence (AD). To avoid problems of data dependence, we shall assume that we know the true model and use artificially generated data to assess the competing models' forecasting abilities. Specifically, we initially assume that the true model is EGARCH(1,2). Our analysis confirms the superiority of the SV model under the normal distribution assumption. However, using t-distributed shocks, the results vary and appear to depend on the value of β, which we believe is related to the behaviour of the relevant volatility models when β is close to 1. We also find that, based on conventional measures of forecast accuracy such as the mean square error, SV forecasts are very exposed to outliers relative to GARCH. This is partially a consequence of the need to exponentiate the SV forecasts (since SV is a model of log-volatility). We show how the presence of non-normality maps onto the time-series structure. We show that exponentiation under some circumstances leads to non-existence of population moments.

4.1 INTRODUCTION

Applied economists are often uncertain as to which of the common volatility models is better to use, especially in the context of forecasting. In this chapter we add to the literature by assessing the relative abilities of GARCH and stochastic volatility (SV) models to forecast volatility. To avoid problems of data dependence, we shall assume that we know the true model and use artificially generated data to assess the competing models' forecasting abilities. This has the advantage that volatility is observable

---

[1]We would like to record our thanks to and admiration for Professor John Knight, who was an author in an earlier version of this chapter but who is, sadly, no longer with us.

from the point of view of the simulator. Thus, we can avoid using variations of realized volatility, which is difficult to calculate in cases where the data are generated by processes with jumps and other irregularities.

We shall initially assume that the true model is EGARCH(1,2) based on convincing empirical work by Pagan and Schwert (1990). This also recognizes the importance of AD in financial data. We extend their analysis to an up-to-date data set. Their analysis was on the US equity market. We also apply it to US 10-year bonds. The difficulty with any simulation is that, by adroit choice of the true model, we can tilt the simulation to favour our preferred method. We would argue that we have fixed the true model to be different from both alternative models, which the econometrician assumes are GARCH(1,1) and SV(1,1). Both the true model and the SV(1,1) model are log-volatility models, which may confer an advantage on SV. SV possesses two sources of noise whilst GARCH has only one, which may also favour SV. However, EGARCH(1,2) has only one source of noise, so it is possible that this could help GARCH. Neither assumed model has the more complex asymmetric lag structure of EGARCH(1,2).

In Section 4.2 we present a literature survey and in Section 4.3 we describe the models and analyse their statistical attributes. In Section 4.4 we provide context by considering and analysing equity and bond return data and the relevant markets to motivate our choice of 'true' parameter values. This involves an inspection of the economic history of US financial macroeconomics. Turning to Section 4.5, we discuss the various metrics used to assess the forecasting abilities of the two competing models. In Section 4.6 we outline in detail the exact simulation method deployed and present our results with analysis. Section 4.7 concludes.

4.2 LITERATURE SURVEY

Research activity focused on constructing, analysing and evaluating non-linear time-series models of variance and covariance has increased significantly over the last two decades. The importance of variance in both theory and application is paramount. For instance, variance is the only unknown variable that drives the pricing of contingent assets, such as the European and American options which are often used by market participants for both hedging and speculation purposes.[2] In essence, the options value volatility of the return of the underlying security rather than its mean. Moreover, the volatility of the return of risky securities plays an important role in the calibration of various risk management frameworks, such as those based on the Value-at-Risk (VaR) methodology.[3] Here, the objective of the risk management exercise is to estimate the ex-ante risk profile of a portfolio of risky assets, where the consolidated tracking error or absolute volatility[4] is the key variable of interest.

Given the forward-looking nature of both option pricing/trading and risk management exercises, it is imperative to model the dynamics of variance, especially as financial time series (such as equity, foreign

---

[2]Trading of option contracts in modern financial markets encompasses a broad range of underlying securities (both financial and real). See BIS Semi-Annual Report (2014) for more details. Moreover, exchanges such as the CME group which facilitate trading of listed-option contracts predominantly offer European- or American-type products.

[3]The usage of VaR as a risk-assessment metric really took off during the late-1990s, when JP Morgan released estimates of variance and covariance of various securities and asset classes. Given its intuitive appeal, over the last decade, VaR has become the established measure of market risk exposure in the global financial industry.

[4]Ex-ante absolute volatility is the target risk assessment variable for absolute return strategies, such as global macro, equity long/short, etc. and is important for financial institutions, such as banks and insurance companies, which have a regulatory duty to measure the market risk embedded in their balance sheets.

exchange and fixed income returns) rarely exhibit constant variance.[5] Focusing on additional empirical stylized facts exhibited by volatility of key financial time series, studies such as Shephard (1996) note the presence of heavy tails (reflected in very large standardized fourth moments) and clustering[6] (periods of large moves tend to be followed by periods of similar characteristics), which is linked to the strong autocorrelation characteristic displayed by squared returns at extended lags.[7]

Indeed, the existence of the above stylized attributes in the behaviour of volatility (with respect to time) can create serious issues with the usage of simple specifications, such as random walk and historical moving averages (including exponentially weighted) as reliable volatility forecasting mechanisms.

Again, as noted by Shephard (1996), there are various variance modelling methodologies, which attempt to explicitly account for stylized characteristics displayed by the behaviour of variance of financial and economic time series. Following Cox (1981), these methodologies can be conceptually divided into either belonging to observation-driven or parameter-driven categories.

In the observation-driven category, the autoregressive conditional heteroscedasticity (ARCH) model developed by Engle (1982) dominates the field. Specifically, the ARCH model allows the variance of the return process to be a linear function of lagged squared returns. Not surprisingly, ARCH-type models have attracted significant attention in recent years, especially given their similarity with moving-average-type models used for capturing changing means.

An important extension of the ARCH framework is the Generalized ARCH model (or GARCH),[8] which models the variance of the underling return process to be a linear function of both lagged squared observations and variance. The GARCH (1,1) model (see Section 4.3 for the exact specification) has had tremendous success in empirical work and, as discussed by Shephard (1996), is usually considered as the benchmark model by many econometricians.

In terms of further important extensions of the ARCH framework, the EGARCH model developed by Nelson (1991) has also had a significant impact on the preferred method of modelling and forecasting of financial time series volatility. Specifically, the EGARCH specification (see Section 4.3 for details on the exact specification) allows the variance process to respond to asymmetric shocks to the underlying stochastic series. The ability to let the variance process respond differently to a rise or fall in financial time series (such as equity returns) is very handy. For instance, as noted first by researchers such as Black (1976), Schwert (1989a,b) and Sentana (1991), equity return volatility tends to be significantly higher during periods of negative returns compared with periods when the relative price changes are positive.[9]

Focusing on the fundamental drivers of this important asymmetry, the leverage skew argument discussed by Geske and Johnson (1984), whereby a firm's value can be seen as the net present value of future income plus assets minus liabilities, can explain part of the irregularity seen in the behaviour of equity returns volatility during periods of rising and falling stock prices. These various components have different volatilities and can lead to leverage-related skew.

Moreover, as noted by Schwert (1989b), firms operating in high-fixed-cost environments can also lead to an operational leverage effect, as sensitivity of near-term earnings to business-cycle gyrations increases during recession periods, as final sales fall and the cost base responds with a lag. Furthermore, in asset markets, such as equities, it is significantly more important to hold downward protection, given the systematic long held by long-term investors such as pension funds and insurance companies, coupled with the inability of certain types of investors to undertake outright short positions (such as retail investors).

---

[5] For example, see Taylor (1986).
[6] First studied by Mandelbrot (1963).
[7] This feature is visible in the correlogram of squared returns of financial time series, such as equity returns.
[8] Usually attributed to Bollerslev (1986), but developed simultaneously by Taylor (1986).
[9] Commonly referred to as the 'leverage effect'.

Lastly, regulatory and risk-management frameworks can exacerbate volatility during negative return periods, which force position liquidation as certain thresholds are hit (for example, forced portfolio shifts on the back of changes in ratings of underlying securities). For instance, Gande and Parsley (2004) showed the asymmetric impact of sovereign rating changes on the size and direction of equity capital flows in 85 countries using the 1996–2002 sample period. Their empirical study found that rating downgrades led to significantly higher capital outflows, while the response to upgrades was more muted. In addition, they also reported that a lower level of corruption decreased the response, whereby countries with less corruption experienced smaller outflows around rating downgrade actions.

In the asset-management space, which essentially embeds a principal–agent setup, the tendency to use VaR mechanisms to transparently manage market exposure risk can increase volatility in falling markets and attenuate it during rising markets. For example, Basak and Shapiro (2001), using a utility-maximizing framework, showed that investors using a VaR method to manage market exposures tend to take larger risk positions and, as a result, incur heavier losses when markets turn against them.

In the foreign exchange (FX) markets, clear fundamental drivers of this type of asymmetry often exist in emerging markets, in the form of a stronger tendency of the relevant authorities to intervene,[10] viewing the FX rate as a policy tool. Likewise, in interest-rate markets, central bank actions and communication can also lead to an asymmetry of response in certain directions.

Turning to the parameter-driven variance modelling category, state-space models allow the variance to be a function of some unobserved or latent component. The SV model (see Section 4.3 for an exact specification of the SV model) is an example of such a state-space setup, usage of which in econometrics is usually associated with the work of Harvey (1989). Specifically, the SV technique fits a model to the variance of the series of interest, by treating it as an unobserved random variable which follows a stochastic process. To ensure that the variance is always positive, a stochastic process is set up for the logarithm of variance. Despite the difficulty in estimating an exact likelihood function, the key attraction of the SV model lies in its connection with the Orstein–Uhlenbeck diffusion process used in finance theory. Indeed, Dassios (1992), using Edgeworth expansions, has shown that the volatility formulation depicted in the SV model is a better approximation to the continuous-time Ornstein–Ulhenbeck process observed at discrete intervals than the EGARCH model is.

In the options pricing literature, recently, increased attention has been directed at examining the implications of non-linear volatility models on option prices. Duan (1995) developed the option pricing framework using ARCH in an equilibrium setting, which was further augmented by Kallsen and Taqqu (1995) in an arbitrage-free, continuous-time setting. In terms of evaluation of the ARCH-based framework, studies such as those of Satchell and Timmermann (1993) and Amin and Ng (1993) found that a GARCH-based option pricing model produced a better fit to market prices than the Black–Scholes model. Although GARCH-type models do a good job of depicting FX dynamics, as noted above, the presence of 'volatility skew' in the equity space requires additional assessment. Here, studies such as that of Schmidt (1996) extended the option pricing framework further to incorporate EGARCH effects in the volatility process. Furthermore, a SV process has also been deployed to improve the option pricing framework, with studies such as that of Heston (1993) providing a neat closed-form solution for options with SV.

As discussed above, given the central role of volatility calibration in option pricing/trading and risk-management systems, evaluating the forecasting ability of various volatility models is also an important area of research. Poon and Granger (2003) provide a summary of 93 research papers, which focus on the forecasting performance of various volatility methodologies. Conclusions based on the comparison exercises carried out in the different studies vary, and also depend on the nature of the asset class studied, coupled with the exact forecasting evaluation metric(s) used. All in all, as Poon and Granger (2003) noted, given the complexity of the issues involved and the importance of

---

[10]The Chinese Yuan is a good example of a heavily managed currency with frequent central bank-induced changes in the exact mechanics of the managed float.

the volatility measure, volatility forecasting continues to remain a specialist subject area, attracting vigorous research focus.

4.3 MODEL SPECIFICATIONS

We first describe our true model, the EGARCH (1,2) model:

$$x_t = \sigma_t \varepsilon_t, \tag{4.1}$$

$$\ln(\sigma_t^2) = a + \beta \, \ln(\sigma_{t-1}^2) + \sum_{k=1}^{2} \alpha_k \left[\lambda \varepsilon_{t-k} + \delta(|\varepsilon_{t-k}| - E(|\varepsilon_{t-k}|)) \right]. \tag{4.2}$$

Essentially, the $\delta(\cdot)$ function in Equation (4.2) allows both the size and the sign of its argument to affect its value. Given the addition of $\delta(\cdot)$ in the variance term, when $\varepsilon_{t-k} > 0$, $d\sigma_t/d\varepsilon_{t-k} = \sum_{k=1}^{2} \alpha_k[\lambda + \delta]$, while the derivative is $\sum_{k=1}^{2} \alpha_k[\lambda - \delta]$ when $\varepsilon_{t-k} < 0$.

The explicit ability of the model to incorporate an asymmetric response of variance to the sign of the underlying stochastic disturbance is very useful. As discussed in detail in Section 4.2, this irregularity observed in volatility's behaviour is an important empirical stylized fact of several asset markets and is driven by a number of fundamental and behavioural factors.

In terms of statistical properties, if ε_{t-1} is independent and identically distributed (i.i.d.), then $\delta(\cdot)$ is also i.i.d. Equation (4.2) also has a constant mean and variance. In addition, ε_t is uncorrelated with $(|\varepsilon_t| - E|\varepsilon_t|)$, given the symmetry of ε_t. As a result, it is clear to see that Equation (4.2) is an autoregression and σ_t is stationary as long as $|\beta| < 1$ (this condition allows asymptotic normality to be achieved as well).

We now examine returns which are modelled via SV, considering both popular specifications. These specifications only differ in the way the return is correlated with the latent volatility, which is itself a stochastic process.

Model A. Contemporaneous correlation

$$x_t = \sigma_t \varepsilon_t, \tag{4.3}$$

$$\ln(\sigma_t^2) = \alpha + \beta \ln(\sigma_{t-1}^2) + v_t, \tag{4.4}$$

where

$$\begin{pmatrix} \varepsilon_t \\ v_t \end{pmatrix} \sim \text{i.i.d.} \, N \left(\begin{pmatrix} 0 \\ 0 \end{pmatrix}, \begin{pmatrix} \sigma_1^2 & \rho\sigma_1\sigma_2 \\ \rho\sigma_1\sigma_2 & \sigma_2^2 \end{pmatrix} \right). \tag{4.5}$$

Model B. Lagged inter-temporal correlation. Here we merely replace Equation (4.4) with the below and leave Equations (4.3) and (4.5) unchanged:

$$\ln(\sigma_{t+1}^2) = \alpha + \beta \ln(\sigma_t^2) + v_t. \tag{4.6}$$

We notice immediately that for Model B, ε_t and σ_t are independent irrespective of the value of ρ, given that ε_t and v_t are i.i.d. In what follows, we use Model B.

In this chapter, we consider the case where $\rho = 0$, so that in either model ε_t and σ_t are independent. Considering now Model B, the dynamic properties of the SV model become clearer after using a log-transformation on x_t^2:

$$\ln x_t^2 = \ln \sigma_t^2 + \ln \varepsilon_t^2. \tag{4.7}$$

From Equations (4.6) and (4.7), we notice that $\ln(x_{t+1}^2)$ is given as the sum of two components: AR(1) and white noise. Consequently, its autocorrelation function is equivalent to that of ARMA(1,1).

In fact, the precise form of ARMA(1,1) in terms of Equations (4.6) and (4.7) is given by:

$$\ln(x_{t+1}^2) = \alpha + \beta \ln(x_t^2) + v_t + \ln(\varepsilon_{t+1}^2) - \beta \ln(\varepsilon_t^2). \tag{4.8}$$

We now examine this equation under different distributional assumptions on the two errors v_t and ε_t. In particular, we show how distributional assumptions feed into the ARMA structure.

Theorem 4.3.1 *Assume $v_t : i.i.d.(0, \sigma_v^2)$, $\varepsilon_t : i.i.d.(0, 1)$ and the mean and variance of $\ln(\varepsilon_t^2)$ are given by μ and δ^2, where $\mu = K'(0)$ and $\delta^2 = K''(0)$, where $K^i(s)$ is the cumulant generating function of $\ln(\varepsilon_t^2)$. Using the above notation, the ARMA(1,1) representation of Equation (4.8) is*

$$\ln(x_{t+1}^2) = \alpha + K'(0)(1 - \beta) + \beta \ln(x_t^2) + w_{t+1} - q w_t, \tag{4.9}$$

where w_t and w_{t+1} are white noise processes with zero mean and variance equal to

$$d^2 = \frac{\sigma_v^2 + (1 + \beta^2)K''(0) + (\sigma_v^4 + (1 - \beta^2)^2(K''(0))^2 + 2\sigma_v^2(1 + \beta^2)K''(0))^{0.5}}{2}$$

and

$$q = \frac{2\,\beta K''(0)}{\sigma_v^2 + (1 + \beta^2)K''(0) + (\sigma_v^4 + (1 - \beta^2)^2(K''(0))^2 + 2\sigma_v^2(1 + \beta^2)K''(0))^{0.5}}$$

Proof: See Appendix 4.B.   ∎

In the following corollaries, we specialize the result of Theorem 4.3.1 for particular distributions of v_t and ε_t. Their proofs are also to be found in Appendix 4.B.

Corollary 4.1 *When v_t and ε_t are both normally distributed but independent, $\varepsilon_t^2 : \chi_{(1)}^2$ and consequently $\ln(\varepsilon_t^2) : (-1.27, 4.93)$. The result in Theorem 4.3.1 holds with $\mu = -1.27$ and $\delta^2 = 4.93$. The above results verify the assertions of Harvey et al. (1994).*

Corollary 4.2 *When v_t and ε_t have independent t-distributions with n and m degrees of freedom, respectively, we need to scale them to ensure their variances are σ_v^2 and 1. The results in Theorem 4.3.1 now hold with $\mu = \ln(m - 2) + \psi\left(\frac{1}{2}\right) - \psi\left(\frac{m}{2}\right)$ and $\delta^2 = \psi'\left(\frac{1}{2}\right) + \psi'\left(\frac{m}{2}\right)$ where $\psi(\cdot)$ and $\psi'(\cdot)$ are the digamma and trigamma functions, respectively.*

It is worth investigating how q changes with $\delta^2 = K''(0)$. We see that an increase will lead to an increase in q. This supports the idea that the more non-normality in the underlying process, the more autocorrelation in the derived dynamic process. Of course, these remarks are predicated by a number of implicit assumptions, namely that q is less than one and that an increase in δ^2 is an increase in non-normality. We also note that an increase in δ^2 leads to an increase in d.

For the case of normality, we discuss how we would forecast volatility. Whilst we can recover our original parameters from this structure as the three parameters are identified from a forecasting perspective, we need only consider the conditional mean one period ahead of $\ln(x_{t+1}^2)$, which under normality is given by:

$$\alpha - 1.27(1 - \beta) + \beta \ln(x_t^2) - q\hat{z}_t. \tag{4.10}$$

Since our model is ARMA(1,1); there are appropriate formulas for k-period-ahead forecasts. To recover our forecast of $\ln(\sigma_{t+k}^2)$ we simply add 1.27 to our original forecasts; finally we exponentiate our answer to convert our forecast to a volatility forecast (there is an issue as to whether we bias-adjust, which we do not address here).

If the ε_t and v_t terms are allowed to be correlated with each other via ρ, then, similar to the EGARCH model, the SV model also allows asymmetric response of variance to the sign of the innovation in the underlying series of interest (see Harvey and Shephard, 1996). In fact, a negative correlation coefficient between v_t and ε_t generates the 'leverage effect'.

More generally, $\ln(\sigma_t)$ can follow any stationary ARMA process, in which case x_t is also stationary and its properties depend on the dynamic properties of $\ln(\sigma_t)$. Alternatively, $\ln(\sigma_t)$ can also be allowed to follow a random walk process:

$$\ln(\sigma_{t+1}^2) = \alpha + \ln(\sigma_t^2) + v_t, v_t \sim \text{NID}(0, s_v^2). \tag{4.11}$$

In the above case, $\log x_t^2$ has two components: random walk and white noise. This specification is very similar to the Integrated GARCH (IGARCH)[11] model, as both models share the same best linear unbiased predictor (Harvey *et al.*, 1994). However, the crucial difference between the two is that the variance in the random-walk SV model is an unobserved component, whereas in the IGARCH model it is exactly known.

Model C. We contrast the SV(1,1) model with the GARCH(1,1) model which, in our current notation, is given by

$$\sigma_t^2 = \alpha + \beta \varepsilon_{t-1}^2 \sigma_{t-1}^2 + \delta \sigma_{t-1}^2. \tag{4.12}$$

As noted in Section 4.1, the GARCH model is an important extension of the ARCH modelling methodology, which includes moving average terms in the variance process. The main advantage of the GARCH formulation compared with ARCH lies in its ability to capture serial correlation in ε_t^2 terms with a smaller number of parameters.

It is important to note that in the GARCH model, the response of conditional variance to underlying innovations depends on the latter's size and not its sign (unlike in the EGARCH formulation).

4.3.1 Existence of Moments

The issue of the existence of moments turns out to be highly relevant when forecasting fat-tailed distributions. We show in this subsection exactly why this is important in the context of our problem. Considering log-volatility processes generally:

$$r_t = \vartheta + u_t, \tag{4.13}$$

$$n(\sigma_t^2) = a + \beta \ln(\sigma_{t-1}^2) + V_t, \tag{4.14}$$

say, so $|\beta| < 1$.

$\ln(\sigma_t^2) = \frac{a}{1-\beta} + \sum_{j=0}^{\infty} \beta^j V_{t-j}$ is a representation of the steady-state distribution of $\ln(\sigma_t^2)$. This case covers both EGARCH(1,1) and SV(1) models. It also covers EGARCH (1,2) models as used by Pagan and Schwert (1990):

$$\ln(\sigma_t^2) = a + \beta \ln(\sigma_{t-1}^2) + \sum_{k=1}^{2} \alpha_k \left[\lambda \varepsilon_{t-k} + \delta(|\varepsilon_{t-k}| - E(|\varepsilon_{t-k}|)) \right], \tag{4.15}$$

where $\varepsilon_t = \frac{u_t}{\sigma_t}$ and u_t is the error in the returns equation and $E(u_t^2/F_t) = \sigma_t^2$.

---

[11] For further details on this model, see Nelson (1990).

The calculations that we present below will follow for these models, once we compute the moving average representation of the process. We shall present details.

Using the independence of V_{t-j},

$$\sigma_t^2 = \exp\left(\frac{a}{1-\beta}\right), \exp\left(\sum_{j=0}^{\infty} \beta^j V_{t-j}\right) \tag{4.16}$$

$$= \exp\left(\frac{a}{1-\beta}\right) \prod_{j=0}^{\infty} \exp(\beta^j V_{t-j}) \tag{4.17}$$

and hence

$$E(\sigma_t^{2s}) = \exp\left(\frac{sa}{1-\beta}\right) \prod_{j=0}^{\infty} E(\exp(s\beta^j V_{t-j})). \tag{4.18}$$

Now, if the moment generating function (mgf) of V_t exists, then $M_V(s\beta^j) = E\left(\exp(s\beta^j V_{t-j})\right)$ exists with possibly some restrictions on s and β.

Therefore:

$$E(\sigma_t^{2s}) = \exp\left(\frac{sa}{1-\beta}\right) \prod_{j=0}^{\infty} M_V(s\beta^j). \tag{4.19}$$

We now consider EGARCH(1,2) under normality and derive $E(\sigma_t^{2s})$ for that case.

Here,

$$V_t = \sum_{k=1}^{2} \alpha_k (\lambda \epsilon_{t-k} + \delta(|\epsilon_{t-k}| - E(|\epsilon_{t-k}|))).$$

Under normality, the existence of the mgf implies the existence of moments of all orders for both the SV model and the EGARCH model. In particular, for EGARCH, we need expressions for half-normal mgfs, i.e. if $V \sim N(0, \sigma_v^2)$.

$$M_v^+(t) = E(\exp(tV)/V > 0) \tag{4.20}$$

$$= 2 \exp\left(\frac{\sigma_v^2 t^2}{2}\right)(1 - \Phi(= \sigma_v^2 t)) \tag{4.21}$$

and $M_v^-(t) = 2\exp\left(\frac{\sigma_v^2 t^2}{2}\right)(1 - \Phi(\sigma_v t))$. Using such calculations, we arrive at the formula below (see Appendix 4.C).

Theorem 4.3.2 *For EGARCH(1,2), the sth moment of SV, where*

$$\gamma_1 = \alpha_1, \ \gamma_2 = (\alpha_1\beta + \alpha_2)$$

$$\gamma_j = (\alpha_1\beta + \alpha_2)\beta^{j-2}, \ j \geq 3$$

is given by

$$E(\sigma_t^{2s}) = \exp\left(\frac{sa}{1-\beta}\right) \exp\left(\frac{-s\delta\sqrt{2/\pi}(\alpha_1 + \alpha_2)}{1-\beta}\right) \prod_{j=0}^{\infty} \left[\sum_{k=1}^{2} \exp\left(\frac{b_k^2\gamma_j^2}{2}\right)\Phi(b_k\gamma_j)\right]. \tag{4.22}$$

However, for the mgf to exist and be finite, all moments of V_t must be finite and if V_t does not have finite moments of all orders, $E(\sigma_t^{2s})$ will not be finite. This has implications for using mean square error (MSE) and similar measures to evaluate forecasting accuracy. In such a case, as, for example, the EGARCH model having t-distributed errors, we may need to use a different criterion for assessing forecast accuracy.

4.4 ESTIMATING 'TRUE' PARAMETER VALUES

In this section, we use certain financial series of interest to extract parameter values for the true model, namely EGARCH(1,2), which are then used in the forecast quality assessment exercise carried out in Section 4.6. Given their unmatched importance in global asset markets, we focus on S&P 500 (the key US equity market benchmark) and US 10yr bond market returns.

We have included bond market data in our analysis as well, given the scant attention paid to this asset class in the volatility forecasting literature, where the main focus has traditionally been on equity and FX universes. For bond returns, we have used zero-coupon 10yr bond yield and converted it into price to generate returns[12] using:

$$y_t = \left[\left(\frac{F}{PV} \right)^{1/n} \right] - 1, \tag{4.23}$$

where y_t is the zero-coupon bond yield, F is the face value of the bond, PV is the present value or the current price and $n = $ number of periods.

4.4.1 US Equity Returns

First, focusing on data sources, we have used Global Financial Data and Bloomberg databases[13] to extract S&P 500 and US 10yr bond yield data since September 1791. The relevance of using pre-war data in analysing current asset price dynamics has increased in the post-2007/8 crisis world. For instance, high-profile asset managers such as Pacific Investment Management Company (PIMCO) have characterized the post-crisis world as 'the new normal', whereby advanced economies such as that of the USA are likely to experience lower-trend economic growth for an extended period of time. Put another way, PIMCO's main contention is that historical analysis carried out using post-war economic and market data is losing relevance, given structural shifts in the global economy seen over the last six years. Given this backdrop, a key objective of our empirical analysis is to highlight and discuss any shift (compared with recent and long-term historical data) in model parameters that is visible in post-2007/8 crisis data.

Starting with S&P 500 monthly returns, we fitted both EGARCH(1,1) and EGARCH(1,2) and compared the log-likelihood statistic of the two competing models in order to ascertain the appropriate specification. The resultant log-likelihood goodness-of-fit ratio test statistic yielded clear preference for the EGARCH(1,2) model.[14]

---

[12]We also take account of carry in bond return calculations.

[13]See Appendix 4.A for additional details on underlying data sources.

[14]Modelling exercises show a log-likelihood of 5199.4 for EGARCH(1,2) vs. 5191.9 for EGARCH(1,1) using the September 1791–May 2014 sample period under the normal distribution assumption. Performing the log-likelihood ratio test yielded a statistic of 15.0 vs. 5% critical value of 5.991 for a chi-square 2 distribution.

TABLE 4.1 S&P 500 returns – normal distribution specification, EGARCH(1,2)

Period	δ_1	δ_2	λ_1	λ_2	β	Log-Likelihood	AIC
September 1791–May 2014	**0.25**	−0.01	**−0.13**	0.1	**0.98**	5199.4	−3.88
	3.2	−0.17	−2.4	1.95	101.4		
January 1834–December 1925	**0.38**	**−0.11**	−0.08	0.02	**0.92**	2104.8	−3.8
	4.04	−1.2	−2.4	0.4	22.9		
January 1925–December 1939	−0.23	**0.67**	**−0.32**	0.24	**0.96**	215.5	−2.32
	−1.5	3.6	−3.0	2.0	44.9		
September 1791–December 1949	**0.39**	−0.17	−0.04	0.01	**0.98**	3821.3	−4.0
	3.7	−1.6	−2.3	0.73	133.2		
January 1950–May 2014	−0.03	**0.25**	**−0.33**	**0.26**	**0.90**	1407.4	−3.6
	−0.32	2.8	−4.4	2.7	20.5		
January 2000 to Dec 2007	−0.44	0.2	−0.06	−0.27	**0.88**	191.6	−3.8
	2.1	1.0	−0.6	−2.5	31.2		
January 2008 to May 2014	−0.28	0.09	**−0.7**	0.5	**0.95**	138.6	−3.4
	−1.2	0.38	4.6	3.2	45.1		

*Bold entries display coefficients that are significant at 5% level.
Note: Using HAC Adjustment for hypothesis testing.

Focusing on the full sample period results (September 1791–May 2014) shown in Tables 4.1 and 4.2, a number of salient points come through:

1. First, we find evidence of a t-distribution in the error process with degrees-of-freedom of around 6 and a p-value of 0.0%. This result confirms the presence of a fat tail in the error process.
2. There is also clear evidence of 'leverage effects' in the volatility process, with positive shocks associated with a coefficient of 0.20 vs. 0.26 for negative shocks using the t-distribution specification and 0.21 vs. 0.27, respectively, for the normal distribution specification. Put simply, the results confirm that negative shocks have a stronger impact on equity return volatility compared with positive return shocks. This highlights the usefulness of using the EGARCH methodology when modelling the equity market volatility process.
3. Finally, there is evidence of high autocorrelation in the volatility process of equity returns with an estimated beta parameter of 0.98. However, a standard Wald restriction test rejected the $\beta = 1$ null hypothesis for both normal and t-distribution specifications at 5% level of significance.

Turning to the various subsample-period results, we first focus on the January 1834 to December 1925 sample, which is the period studied by Pagan and Schwert (1990). The magnitude and sign of leverage effects estimates are similar to Pagan and Schwert's (1990) findings, though the size of the beta parameter was ascertained to be higher.

Comparing the t-distribution specification's estimation results of the pre- to post-war period, the fall in size of the beta parameter (from 0.98 to 0.89) is quite striking. The numerous episodes of deep

TABLE 4.2   S&P 500 – *t*-distribution specification, EGARCH(1,2)

Period	δ_1	δ_2	λ_1	λ_2	β	Log-Likelihood	T dist D.o.F	AIC
September 1791–May 2014	**0.23**	0.00	**−0.15**	**0.12**	**0.98**	5276.8	6.2	−3.94
	4.7	0.0	−4.3	3.7	242.9			
January 1834–December 1925	**0.37**	−0.09	−0.07	0.01	**0.90**	2120.8	8.0	−3.8
	5.0	−1.1	−1.5	0.23	27.9			
January 1925–December 1939	−0.14	**0.53**	**−0.35**	**0.26**	**0.96**	216.0	10.6	−2.31
	−0.75	2.6	−3.1	2.5	35.90			
September 1791–December 1949	**0.34**	**−0.12**	−0.07	0.05	**0.98**	3894.4	5.1	−4.1
	5.7	−2.1	−2.0	1.30	257.1			
January 1950–May 2014	−0.03	**0.25**	**−0.29**	0.2	**0.89**	1414.6	11.6	−3.6
	−0.3	2.3	−4.9	2.9	20.0			
January 2000 to Dec 2007	−0.4	0.33	−0.07	−0.24	**0.88**	190.3	311.1	−3.8
	−1.06	1.0	−0.32	−0.93	18.8			
January 2008 to May 2014	−0.31	0.2	**−0.66**	0.45	**0.94**	137.1	257.8	−3.35
	−0.6	0.4	−2.2	1.9	27.1			

*Bold entries display coefficients that are significant at 5% level.

equity market corrections captured during the pre-war period (especially the presence of the Great Depression period in the sample) may explain this finding. Indeed, comparing the pre- (2000/2007) with the post-Great Recession period (2008/2014) yields a similar pattern. For instance, using the 2000/2007 period, the β parameter is estimated to be 0.88 compared with 0.94 for the subsequent January 2008–May 2014 sample.

Focusing on the volatility dynamics observed during the Great Depression period (January 1925–December 1939), the beta parameter is estimated as 0.96,[15] with the standard Wald statistic failing to reject the $\beta = 1$ null hypothesis, resulting in a *p*-value of 14.5%. This result is in-line with observations made by Pagan and Schwert (1990), who noted that the stationarity property of the volatility process seems to be rejected by the data during the Great Depression period.

Looking at more recent data, unlike the Great Depression period, we found evidence that the volatility process remained stationary during January 2008 to May 2014 but, as noted above, we did find a sharp rise in the degree of autocorrelation in the volatility process compared with the pre-crisis period.

Studying the size and sign of leverage effects using the pre- and post-Great Recession period data also generates a number of interesting observations. First, the leverage effect parameters (λ and δ) were

---

[15]Using the *t*-distribution specification. The same conclusion holds for the normal-distribution specification as well.

ascertained to be statistically insignificant using the pre-Great Recession period. Second, in terms of magnitude, it appears that a positive return shock had a negative impact on volatility (coefficient of −0.38), while a negative return shock was associated with a coefficient of +0.24, suggesting an increase in volatility. Shifting to the January 2008–May 2014 period, the coefficient associated with a positive shock was ascertained to be −0.32, while it was estimated as +0.10 for negative return shocks (although it is worth noting that only λ_1 was determined to be statistically significant at the 5% level).

Taking into account the statistical significance of the parameters, it appears that leverage effects were missing during the pre-crisis period (all coefficients are statistically insignificant), while they were estimated as −0.66 (λ_1) for positive shocks and +0.66 for negative shocks during the January 2008–May 2014 period.

Comparing the above results with both the full-sample- and post-war-sample-based estimates, it is interesting to note that the impact of positive return shocks on equity return volatility appears to have shifted in its sign. Specifically, the empirical exercise shows that positive return shocks are no longer associated with an increase in volatility (and may actually be consistent with a reduction in volatility) using recent data. An additional noticeable attribute of the sample period since the start of the 21st century is the absence of fat tails in the error process.

In our view, these attributes appear to be connected with the emergence of major boom–bust-type cycles in the price of equities in a number of advanced economies (including the USA) since the 1980s (Borio *et al.*, 1994). The main property of asset markets (in our case equities) experiencing boom–bust cycles is that they undergo periods of sustained gains (thus creating a 'bubble') and subsequent price corrections. The sustained and steady nature of the returns experienced during the boom phase of the cycle can explain the reduction or lack of response of volatility to positive shocks. Furthermore, the relative lack of absence of very sharp corrections (such as the October 1987 crash in the more recent sample period) can explain the absence of t-distribution-type effects in the error process. For instance, Table 4.3 shows the estimated kurtosis of squared returns (as a proxy for unconditional variance) for the various sample periods studied. Here, what is clear is the relative decrease in the magnitude of kurtosis visible in the more recent periods, which corroborates the evidence of lack of fat tails found in the volatility process.

'Stability is destabilizing'. These three words succinctly convey a view first put forward by Hyman Minsky (1975, 1982, 1986). The basic thesis of this idea is that institutional support provided to back-stop and stabilize asset price discovery mechanisms in the aftermath of a crisis can change behaviour in such a manner that supports creation of future speculative bubbles. We think the attribute of the volatility process, whereby it falls in response to positive shocks, is an empirical manifestation of this thesis. For instance, if the Sharpe ratio of the equity holdings (aided by both the magnitude of the return and the reduction in volatility) starts to rise sharply during bull market periods, then it can potentially create a view reinforcement mechanism which then attracts additional demand for the risky asset. Indeed, the resultant self-enforced view-based flow can then contribute to a bubble creation (defined as a situation where the valuation of the asset class in question starts to show a de-link with underlying fundamentals) and its eventual correction.

TABLE 4.3   Kurtosis of squared equity returns

September 1791–May 2014	175.7
January 1950–May 2014	108.3
January 2000–December 2007	8.9
January 2008–May 2014	29.9

4.4.2 US 10yr Bond Returns

Tables 4.4 and 4.5 show the parameter estimates of fitting an EGARCH(1,2) model to US 10yr bond returns data. As noted above, bond returns were calculated using the 10yr zero-coupon bond yield data available from Global Financial Data and Bloomberg. Similar to the case of equities, data availability means we are able to run the regression from September 1791 to May 2014 using monthly data.

Focusing on the model parameter estimates, diagnostic tests show evidence of better goodness-of-fit for the EGARCH(1,2) specification compared with EGARCH(1,1) (the EGARCH(1,1) results are available upon request). Here, like in the equities case, the goodness-of-fit is assessed on the basis of the log-likelihood ratio statistic, which is appropriate in this setting, given the nested nature of the two competing models of interest.

Analysing the EGARCH(1,2) fitted model parameters, three key points come through on the basis of the exercise carried out using the September 1791–May 2014 sample period (or the full sample):

1. The t-distribution error process version of the EGARCH(1,2) estimation leads to a better in-sample model fit (assessed using the minimum Akaike information criterion) and the degrees-of-freedom of the underlying t-distribution is ascertained to be around 3, thus indicating the presence of fat tails in the error process.
2. Second, there is evidence of leverage effects in the bond market as well, with negative return shocks (or an increase in yields) yielding a coefficient of 0.19 vs. 0.03 for positive return shocks using the normal error distribution specification and 0.24 vs. 0.14 for the t-distributed error specification.
3. The β parameter is estimated to be around 0.99 for both normal and t-distributed specifications, indicating evidence of high autocorrelation in the bond market volatility process. However, standard Wald-statistic-based hypothesis testing shows that the null hypothesis of $\beta = 1$ restriction has a p-value of 0.0%, thus rejecting it at the 5% level of significance.

TABLE 4.4 US 10yr bond returns – normal distribution specification, EGARCH (1,2)

Period	δ_1	δ_2	λ_1	λ_2	β	Log-Likelihood	AIC
September 1791–May 2014	0.55	−0.44	−0.37	0.29	0.99	8169.0	−6.1
	4.8	−3.8	−3.6	2.9	447.3		
January 1834–December 1925	0.6	−0.44	−0.6	0.52	1.00	3810.3	−6.9
	3.9	−2.6	−4.6	3.9	286.4		
September 1791–December 1949	0.57	−0.45	−0.49	0.4	0.99	6352.9	−6.7
	4.81	−3.9	−4.3	3.60	396.0		
January 1950–May 2014	0.34	−0.06	−0.003	−0.07	0.98	1857.6	−4.8
	3.4	−0.6	−0.05	−1.1	144.1		
January 2000 to Dec 2007	−0.37	0.13	**0.22**	**0.46**	−0.21	220.8	−4.45
	−1.9	0.5	2.0	2.41	−0.7		
January 2008 to May 2014	0.09	**−0.58**	0.22	0.31	**0.63**	173.3	−4.32
	0.28	−1.96	1.1	1.2	3.4		

*Bold entries display coefficients that are significant at 5% level or lower.

TABLE 4.5 US 10yr bond returns – t-distribution specification, EGARCH (1,2)

Period	δ_1	δ_2	λ_1	λ_2	β	Log-Likelihood	T dist D.o.F	AIC
September 1791–May 2014	**0.42**	**−0.23**	**−0.12**	0.07	**0.99**	8659.4	3.1	−6.47
	8.4	−4.8	−3.3	2.0	636.1			
January 1834–December 1925	**0.46**	**−0.27**	−0.06	0.01	**0.99**	4204.8	2.4	−7.6
	4.2	−2.97	−0.96	0.16	317.7			
September 1791–December 1949	**0.45**	**−0.23**	**−0.17**	**0.12**	**0.99**	6822.8	2.6	−7.2
	6.2	−3.6	−3.2	2.50	345.9			
January 1950–May 2014	**0.33**	−0.07	0.03	**−0.1**	**0.99**	1874.1	7.0	−4.8
	4.04	−0.8	0.5	−1.9	154.8			
January 2000–December 2007	−0.36	0.14	0.22	**0.46**	−0.20	220.8	340.8	−4.4
	−1.1	0.35	0.84	2.89	−0.44			
January 2008–May 2014	0.11	**−0.56**	0.22	0.3	**0.63**	173.4	27.9	−4.3
	0.31	−1.9	1.03	1.05	3.2			

*Bold entries display coefficients that are significant at 5% level or lower.

Turning to the various subsample estimation results, it is interesting to note that during the pre-Great Financial Crisis period (2000–2007), the beta parameter was found to be statistically insignificant for both the normal and t-distribution specifications (unlike both the full- and post-war-period sample-based estimates), while evidence of leverage effects was also found to be statistically weak. In addition, there was no statistical evidence supporting a t-distribution error process during this period (the t-distribution's degrees-of-freedom was ascertained to be 341 with a p-value of 99%).

The absence of autocorrelation in the volatility process during the 2000–2007 period is quite striking. In our view, this attribute of the bond market volatility process can be explained by the 'global savings glut' dynamic and the relatively steady nature of the Federal Reserve's monetary policy witnessed over this period.

The global savings glut hypothesis was explained in considerable detail by former Federal Reserve chairman Ben Bernanke in a speech he delivered in 2005.[16] In his remarks, Bernanke (2005) postulated that a significant increase in the flow of international savings had been finding its way into US debt markets during that period, thus creating a fundamental de-link between domestic US macro fundamentals and the yield curve (the flipside of this dynamic was the large current account deficit being run by the US economy over this period). Bernanke (2005) pointed to two important drivers behind this important development: an enhanced saving motive in rich countries with aging populations and an increase in desired savings by developing countries as they switched from net user to net supplier of funds to international capital markets in the aftermath of the Asian crisis and Russian default during the late-1990s.

---

[16]The full text of the speech is available at the Federal Reserve website: http://www.federalreserve.gov/boarddocs/speeches/2005/200503102/

In our view, the impact of this structural increase in desired level of international savings can explain the shift in the nature of the bond market volatility that manifested itself via absence of high autocorrelation in the volatility process. Put another way, we think that the significant increase in structural flow into the US debt markets witnessed during this period had a stabilizing effect on bond return dynamics, thus reducing the persistence of exogenous shocks.

In addition, during this period, we think that the steady nature of the Federal Reserve's policy decisions also played a price-stabilizing role as policy uncertainty fell. Looking back, the central bank ran an incredibly steady hiking cycle (compared with historical experience) as the economy started to turn around in 2004. Indeed, the Fed hiked the funds rate by 25 bp per meeting almost continuously over the 2004–2006 period and the base rate reached 5.25% in mid-2006 from a low of 1% in mid-2004. Indeed, in the post-crisis literature, the highly predictable nature of Fed policy during this period has been identified as one of the drivers behind the formation of the US housing bubble (e.g., see Obstfeld and Rogoff, 2009).

Overall, we think that a combination of these two factors (i.e., a structural increase in global savings flow to US debt markets and an extremely steady, and hence largely predictable, Fed policy path) can explain the neutralization of the high-autocorrelation attribute of bond market volatility with shocks to the returns process showing significantly reduced persistence during this period compared with historical experience.

Shifting to the post-December 2007 period estimation, empirical results show evidence of an increase in the magnitude of beta (although it is still assessed to be below the 0.99 level estimated using both the full- and post-war-sample periods) to 0.63, while evidence of the presence of leverage effects still comes out as statistically weak. That said, in terms of magnitude and direction of the estimated asymmetric effects, it appears that a positive return shock is still driving an increase in volatility (coefficient of 0.04), while a negative return shock now appears to be consistent with a reduction in volatility (coefficient of −1.02).

This 'odd' leverage effect behaviour appears to be capturing numerous episodes of sharp falls in bond yields (generating positive returns), witnessed over the 2008/9 and 2011/12 periods, as key central banks led by the Federal Reserve embarked on a series of unconventional monetary policies (mainly in the form of outright purchases of government bonds) in an effort to provide stimulus to their respective economies in the aftermath of the bursting of the US housing bubble. As noted by prominent central bankers such as former Fed chairman Ben Bernanke himself, the unconventional monetary policy framework adopted (with the zero bound hit in short rates) by key central banks such as the Federal Reserve and the Bank of England as the economic crisis hit in 2008/9 was designed to work through the 'portfolio rebalance effect' (e.g., see Bernanke and Reinhart, 2004). Specifically, the central bank's suppression of risk-free real interest rates on the back of outright asset purchases was designed to force investors to buy risky assets. Looking back, this shift in future asset return expectations on the back of the above-noted policy moves appears to have happened suddenly, which led to episodes of a sharp fall in nominal bond yields as the easing action (in the case of late 2008) or the communication of easing intention (in the case of quantitative easing phase 2 done in late 2010) was transmitted by central bank officials to market participants. All in all, the rapid fall in aggregate real demand and the accompanying monetary/fiscal policy response was the key bond-market-return-shaping force during this period. The reaction to these developments was also visible in the sharp fall in bond yields as lower inflation/growth dynamics and consequently an easier monetary policy path were priced in by the market.

Focusing on the increase in the magnitude of the β parameter visible in the post-December 2007 period estimation results (compared with the 2000–2007 sample period), it appears that the bond return volatility process started to 'normalize' towards historical average, as evidenced by the re-emergence of higher autocorrelation in the volatility process.

4.5 EVALUATING FORECASTING PERFORMANCE

A number of subjective decisions along various dimensions have to be made in forecasting volatility and the evaluation of the model's forecast. As noted in Section 4.2, Poon and Granger (2003) provide a nice summary of forecasting-related decisions and the problem's different dimensions using information gleaned from more than 90 papers. Specifically, the two most important dimensions of the forecast assessment exercise are the proxy used for realized volatility (which is a latent variable) and the treatment of the data set with either an in-sample/out-of-sample bifurcation or the use of a rolling scheme, under which the model parameter estimates are updated with each additional observation. As discussed in detail in Section 4.6, in this study, we use the in/out sample data division on each iteration of the true model's simulation (using the EGARCH(1,2) specification depicted in Equations (4.1) and (4.2)) to provide the relevant data points on which we then apply various forecast evaluation techniques. Here, we use the true model's underlying volatility as the benchmark to assess the quality of forecasts.

The nature of different metrics used to compare forecasting ability needs to be guided by a combination of statistical considerations and the required application of the forecast. For instance, in the options space (specifically, to guide trading decisions), the forecaster may prefer to take into account the asymmetry of the forecast error and therefore penalize over- or under-prediction.

The ability to assess/penalize under-prediction is useful within the context of risk-management systems as well, where the forecaster can have an incentive or preference (driven by regulation) to apply a heavier penalty to under-prediction. This is especially true in the post-2008/9 crisis world, which has seen a number of new financial-sector-focused regulations come into effect (e.g., Dodd–Frank and Basel III). These new regulation regimes embed a shift towards using more conservative risk-assessment methodologies in the banking sector. Indeed, this change in preference towards using more conservative methodologies has been driven by the severity of the recession (in terms of the loss of output and sharp rise in unemployment seen globally) and the important role played by the global financial sector in amplifying the original US housing-centric shock.[17] Moreover, this important change in the regulatory landscape was further strengthened in 2011/12 as the European debt crisis situation came to the fore, leading to the emergence of severe funding pressures on key European financial institutions.[18]

However, despite the context-specific appeal of studying asymmetric prediction error, analysis of symmetric forecast errors (same weight to under- and over-prediction) is a more appropriate benchmark for assessing overall goodness-of-fit and allows relevant comparison with other studies in this research area.

Focusing on symmetric prediction error assessment, the two widely used forecast evaluation metrics (MSE and root mean square error, RMSE) are deployed in this study. In addition, we also use mean absolute error (MAE) in order to undertake a comprehensive assessment of the forecast ability of the two models.

The exact specifications of the above forecast evaluation statistics are given below:

$$\text{MEAN} = \frac{1}{n} \sum_{t=1}^{n} \left(h_t - \overline{h}_t \right), \tag{4.24}$$

$$\text{RMSE} = \sqrt{\frac{1}{n} \sum_{t=1}^{n} (h_t - \overline{h}_t)^2}, \tag{4.25}$$

---

[17] For example, see Aiyar (2012), who explores how the funding market shock to globalized banks was transmitted to the real economy via reduced domestic credit supply.

[18] For example, see Neri and Ropele (2013), who carried out an analysis on the macroeconomic effects of the European sovereign debt crisis.

$$\text{MAE} = \frac{1}{n} \sum_{t=1}^{n} abs\left(h_t - \overline{h}_t \right), \tag{4.26}$$

where h_t is the true volatility, $\overline{h}_t$ is the relevant model's forecast generated by minimizing the MSE forecast function and n is the total number of forecasts assessed.

Turning to asymmetric forecasting error evaluation metrics, we use the mean mixed error-under (MME-U) and mean mixed error-over (MME-O) statistics to assess the tendency to under- or over-predict true volatility:

$$\text{MME-U} = \frac{1}{n} \left(\sum_{t=1}^{k} abs\left(h_t - \overline{h}_t \right)^{0.5} + \sum_{t=1}^{l} abs\left(h_t - \overline{h}_t \right)^{0.5} \right), \tag{4.27}$$

$$\text{MME-O} = \frac{1}{n} \left(\sum_{t=1}^{l} abs\left(h_t - \overline{h}_t \right)^{0.5} + \sum_{t=1}^{k} abs\left(h_t - \overline{h}_t \right)^{0.5} \right), \tag{4.28}$$

where $k + l = n$ and k is the number of under-predictions and l is the number of over-predictions, respectively.

4.6   SIMULATION METHOD AND RESULTS

In this section, we outline the method of simulation used in our study. We deploy our agreed true model (i.e., EGARCH(1,2) calibrated using the parameters estimated in Section 4.4). These empirical estimations are an extension of Pagan and Schwert (1990). We then use a random generator to generate a time series by assuming that the estimated parameters are true parameters. In the first instance, it will be normal and hence all moments will exist. We also experiment with a *t*-distribution specification with 5, 10 and 50 degrees-of-freedom in order to compare the results.

In terms of the specific mechanics, and assuming our initial estimates satisfy stationarity conditions, we let the true model run for 10,000 periods, so that the resultant time series is stationary. We then used the 9850th observation as the first observation of the sample set to be used. The above exercise generates a true return and volatility series which should not suffer from initial value problems.

Specifically, we took the 9850th to the 9949th observation as the sample set ($T = 100$) to estimate the SV(1,1) and GARCH(1,1) models. Next, we used the estimated models to forecast the next 20 periods, which were then stored in order to estimate their absolute and relative forecasting accuracy using the various forecasting assessment metrics discussed in Section 4.5.

The entire exercise was repeated 100 times (Figure 4.1), where we kept the 'true' model intact but took a new 'true' sample of 100 observations followed by re-estimation of the SV and GARCH models in each iteration. The point of the procedure is that true volatilities are observable, which is not the case with historical volatility, thus allowing us to compare forecasts with true underlying volatility.

4.6.1   Results

The results of the simulation exercise are shown in Tables 4.6 to 4.9, which tabulate the various forecast assessment metrics estimated using various distribution and β assumptions. The quantities shown in these tables are Monte-Carlo averages and standard deviations based on 100 replications (as noted above) for a 20-period forecast length for each set.

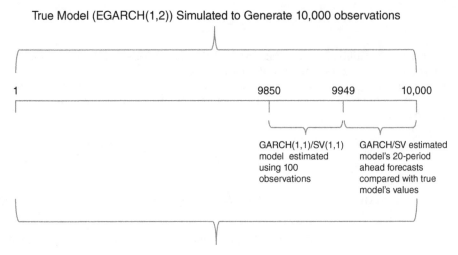

FIGURE 4.1   Simulation schematic
Notes:
1. For illustrative purposes only. Not drawn to scale.
2. Entire exercise repeated 100 times.

TABLE 4.6(a)   GARCH forecast error results: $\beta = 0.98$

	Normal	$t(5)$	$t(10)$	$t(50)$
Mean				
average	−2.49	−3.15	−1.87	−1.68
stdev	0.61	1.14	0.58	0.34
t-stat	−4.08	−2.76	−3.22	−4.96
MAE				
average	2.69	3.43	2.20	1.89
stdev	0.60	1.13	0.57	0.33
t-stat	4.46	3.03	3.86	5.79
RMSE				
average	6.60	11.81	6.10	3.77
stdev	1.47	2.99	1.45	0.69
t-stat	4.49	3.95	4.21	5.47
MME-U				
average	1.15	1.21	1.00	1.02
stdev	0.12	0.14	0.11	0.09
t-stat	9.82	8.56	8.83	11.22
MME-O				
average	2.72	3.46	2.24	1.94
stdev	0.60	1.13	0.57	0.32
t-stat	4.53	3.06	3.94	5.99

TABLE 4.6(b)   SV forecast error results: $\beta = 0.98$

	Normal	$t(5)$	$t(10)$	$t(50)$
Mean				
average	−0.53	−2.20	−0.98	−0.77
stdev	0.18	0.86	0.22	0.26
t-stat	−2.96	−2.54	−4.49	−2.91
MAE				
average	0.91	2.50	1.38	1.16
stdev	0.16	0.86	0.19	0.25
t-stat	5.57	2.92	7.09	4.63
RMSE				
average	1.82	8.86	2.37	2.74
stdev	0.43	2.66	0.44	0.70
t-stat	4.22	3.33	5.37	3.89
MME-U				
average	0.72	1.12	0.96	0.79
stdev	0.06	0.12	0.08	0.07
t-stat	11.40	9.58	12.24	10.99
MME-O				
average	0.97	2.51	1.40	1.22
stdev	0.16	0.86	0.19	0.25
t-stat	6.10	2.94	7.39	4.92

TABLE 4.7(a)   GARCH forecast error results: $\beta = 0.90$

	Normal	$t(5)$	$t(10)$	$t(50)$
Mean				
average	−0.19	−0.46	−0.18	−0.15
stdev	0.03	0.05	0.04	0.04
t-stat	−6.14	−8.87	−5.23	−3.97
MAE				
average	0.29	0.57	0.32	0.32
stdev	0.02	0.04	0.02	0.03
t-stat	14.18	14.29	13.60	12.35
RMSE				
average	0.36	0.69	0.40	0.41
stdev	0.04	0.12	0.05	0.06
t-stat	8.53	5.82	7.43	7.18
MME-U				
average	0.46	0.70	0.47	0.47
stdev	0.02	0.03	0.02	0.03
t-stat	19.89	21.31	19.35	18.22
MME-O				
average	0.34	0.58	0.37	0.37
stdev	0.02	0.03	0.02	0.03
t-stat	16.05	17.07	15.78	14.57

TABLE 4.7(b)   SV forecast error results: $\beta = 0.90$

	Normal	$t(5)$	$t(10)$	$t(50)$
Mean				
average	0.00	−0.43	−0.28	−0.06
stdev	0.03	0.05	0.03	0.04
t-stat	0.08	−9.05	−8.50	−1.59
MAE				
average	0.22	0.54	0.37	0.28
stdev	0.02	0.03	0.02	0.02
t-stat	12.02	15.89	16.59	12.19
RMSE				
average	0.29	0.64	0.43	0.35
stdev	0.04	0.11	0.04	0.05
t-stat	7.30	5.55	9.73	7.02
MME-U				
average	0.34	0.68	0.54	0.42
stdev	0.02	0.03	0.02	0.02
t-stat	16.02	21.91	22.63	17.06
MME-O				
average	0.31	0.56	0.40	0.34
stdev	0.02	0.03	0.02	0.02
t-stat	14.49	20.21	18.82	14.84

TABLE 4.8(a)   GARCH forecast error results: $\beta = 0.80$

	Normal	$t(5)$	$t(10)$	$t(50)$
Mean				
average	−0.07	−0.29	−0.12	−0.05
stdev	0.03	0.04	0.02	0.02
t-stat	−2.56	−7.37	−5.03	−2.12
MAE				
average	0.21	0.39	0.22	0.20
stdev	0.02	0.03	0.02	0.01
t-stat	13.45	13.27	13.77	13.28
RMSE				
average	0.27	0.48	0.27	0.24
stdev	0.03	0.12	0.03	0.03
t-stat	7.62	3.96	7.70	7.48
MME-U				
average	0.36	0.57	0.38	0.34
stdev	0.02	0.03	0.02	0.02
t-stat	18.34	19.35	18.66	18.11
MME-O				
average	0.28	0.41	0.27	0.27
stdev	0.02	0.02	0.02	0.02
t-stat	14.89	18.76	15.43	14.51

TABLE 4.8(b)   SV forecast error results: $\beta = 0.80$

	Normal	$t(5)$	$t(10)$	$t(50)$
Mean				
average	−0.01	−0.34	−0.23	−0.03
stdev	0.02	0.04	0.02	0.02
t-stat	−0.40	−8.73	−9.72	−1.07
MAE				
average	0.19	0.43	0.29	0.19
stdev	0.02	0.03	0.02	0.02
t-stat	12.51	14.67	17.13	12.53
RMSE				
average	0.25	0.51	0.33	0.24
stdev	0.03	0.12	0.03	0.03
t-stat	7.24	4.18	9.57	7.29
MME-U				
average	0.32	0.61	0.48	0.32
stdev	0.02	0.03	0.02	0.02
t-stat	17.29	20.93	23.62	17.27
MME-O				
average	0.28	0.45	0.32	0.27
stdev	0.02	0.02	0.02	0.02
t-stat	13.78	20.41	18.85	13.79

TABLE 4.9(a)   GARCH forecast error results: $\beta = 0.75$

	Normal	$t(5)$	$t(10)$	$t(50)$
Mean				
average	−0.06	−0.29	−0.09	−0.06
stdev	0.02	0.03	0.02	0.02
t-stat	−2.97	−9.55	−4.16	−2.53
MAE				
average	0.18	0.36	0.20	0.18
stdev	0.01	0.02	0.01	0.01
t-stat	13.46	16.90	14.13	14.01
RMSE				
average	0.22	0.42	0.24	0.23
stdev	0.03	0.06	0.03	0.03
t-stat	7.80	7.05	7.70	8.09
MME-U				
average	0.33	0.56	0.36	0.33
stdev	0.02	0.02	0.02	0.02
t-stat	18.19	25.26	18.97	18.13
MME-O				
average	0.24	0.38	0.25	0.25
stdev	0.02	0.02	0.02	0.02
t-stat	14.16	19.76	15.16	14.75

TABLE 4.9(b)   SV forecast error results: $\beta = 0.75$

	Normal	$t(5)$	$t(10)$	$t(50)$
Mean				
average	−0.01	−0.36	−0.22	−0.04
stdev	0.02	0.03	0.02	0.02
t-stat	−0.54	−11.72	−9.47	−1.85
MAE				
average	0.17	0.42	0.28	0.19
stdev	0.01	0.02	0.02	0.01
t-stat	11.90	19.21	17.11	13.52
RMSE				
average	0.22	0.47	0.32	0.23
stdev	0.03	0.06	0.03	0.03
t-stat	7.12	8.00	9.63	7.99
MME-U				
average	0.29	0.61	0.47	0.32
stdev	0.02	0.02	0.02	0.02
t-stat	16.14	28.05	23.14	17.42
MME-O				
average	0.25	0.43	0.31	0.26
stdev	0.02	0.02	0.02	0.02
t-stat	13.28	22.37	19.10	14.61

The forecast assessment for each model is done on the minimum mean square error (MMSE) forecast, which is the forecast $\overline{y_{t+1}}$ that minimizes the expected square loss. The forecasts are generated by using the forecast function in Matlab, which estimates MMSE forecasts recursively following Baillie and Bollerslev (1992) and Box *et al.* (1994). These forecasts are then used to generate conditional mean and variance forecasts for the SV and GARCH models, respectively, in our simulation code.

In terms of the true model parameters used to simulate the EGARCH model, the Pagan and Schwert (1990) study reported a β estimate of 0.74 using US equity returns data (1834–1925 sample period) compared with the 0.98 we have estimated (see Tables 4.2 and 4.3) using the 1793–2014 period. For our simulation exercise, we have used the 1791–2014 period true model parameters (i.e., the true model), estimated using S&P 500 data (see Section 4.4).

The simulation results indicate that, not surprisingly, the SV model outperforms the GARCH model under the normal distribution assumption on all metrics considered. This result holds irrespective of the value of β studied. In addition, the results also show that the significance of forecast error metrics tends to be higher for the GARCH model compared with the case of SV.

However, under the t-distribution assumption, the relative assessment results start to become more mixed, with the GARCH model starting to outperform the SV model on almost all assessment metrics considered as lower values of β are used. For instance, using the $\beta = 0.75$ assumption coupled with a $t(5)$ and $t(10)$ distribution shock assumption, the GARCH model's superiority stretches across all metrics, including those designed to capture the forecast error's accuracy using asymmetric weighting schemes (i.e., MME-U and MME-O).

However, as the β value is increased, the simulation results start once again to converge towards the normal distribution results. Specifically, for the $\beta = 0.98$ assumption, we find that the SV model generates relatively lower relative forecast error statistics (irrespective of the specific t-distribution assumption used), together with generally lower significance levels as well compared with the GARCH model.

We think that the quality of stationarity under GARCH and SV model structures, when β is close to 1, can help shed light on the drivers behind the findings discussed above. Specifically, for the GARCH model, a β value of 0.98 is close to the stationarity bound depending on the ARCH parameter. However, for the SV model, stationarity is only dependent on the β parameter, as we know that for AR(1), we often need to be closer to 1 than 0.98 for the bound to be hit. However, a deeper understanding may involve the behaviour of near-random-walk processes for which, as far as we are aware, a theory for volatility models has not yet been developed. Our intuition is that as we get close to an I(1) process only the first two moments matter, and the non-existence of higher moments is not relevant. Some results that support this intuition are due to Boswijk (2001) and Ling and Li (1998). They show that with near-integrated volatility, maximum likelihood estimators converge to distributions all of whose moments exist. Whilst no results have been proven for forecasts, it is likely that these results will imply less dependence on fat tails.

4.7 CONCLUSION

This chapter addresses the question of what simple volatility model an econometrician should use when confronted with empirical data when forecasting. We argue that the best true model might be the one for which past empirical work has been the most convincing, which we believe to be the EGARCH(1,2) model in the context of US equity and bond markets. The econometrician considers only GARCH(1,1) and SV(1,1) as the two competitors. We then compare the relative performances of GARCH(1,1) vs. SV(1,1) when the true model is EGARCH(1,2). We also derive the moments of EGARCH(1,2), which can be used to compare with the moments of the other two models.

To generate artificial data from the true model, it needs to be estimated. We estimated the true model parameters (i.e., EGARCH(1,2)) using long-term returns data for both S&P 500 and US 10yr bonds. We also connected the observed shifts in model parameters during the various subsamples studied with the broader macroeconomic situation prevalent in the US economy.

Our analysis confirms the superiority of the SV model under the normal distribution assumption. However, using t-distributed shocks, the results vary and appear to depend on the value of β, which we believe is related to the behaviour of the given volatility models when β is close to 1.

Finally, we find that, based on conventional measures of forecast accuracy such as MSE, SV forecasts are very exposed to outliers relative to GARCH. This is partially a consequence of the need to exponentiate the SV forecasts (since SV is a model of log-volatility). Furthermore, we show how the presence of non-normality maps onto the time-series structure and we show that exponentiation under some circumstances leads to non-existence of population moments.

In terms of AD in volatility, it seems that simple estimators which ignore it will forecast satisfactorily, depending upon particular circumstances relating to actual distributions of errors. Whilst we have concerned ourselves with misspecification, we acknowledge that the best procedure here is to forecast with the actual asymmetrically dependent process; this, however, has numerous challenges, which we shall discuss in future work.

REFERENCES

Aiyar, S. (2012). From financial crisis to great recession: the role of globalized banks. *The American Economic Review*, 102, 225–230.

Amin, K. and Ng, V. (1993). ARCH processes and option valuation. Working Paper, University of Michigan.

Baillie, R. and Bollerslev, T. (1992). Prediction in dynamic models with time-dependent conditional variances. *Journal of Econometrics*, 52, 91–113.

Basak, S. and Shapiro, A. (2001). Value-at-risk-based risk management: optimal policies and asset prices. *Review of Financial Studies*, 14(2), 371–405.

BIS Semi-Annual Report (2014). Statistical release – OTC derivatives statistics at end-December 2013. Bank of International Settlements, Monetary and Economics Department.

Bernanke, B.S. (2005). The global saving glut and the US current account deficit. Sandridge Lecture, Virginia Association of Economists, Richmond, VA, March 10.

Bernanke, B.S. and Reinhart, V. (2004). Conducting monetary policy at very low short-term interest rates. *The American Economic Review*, 94, 85–90.

Black, F. (1976). Studies of stock price volatility changes. Proceedings of the 1976 Business Meeting of the Business and Economics Statistics Section, American Statistical Association, pp. 177–181.

Bollerslev, T. (1986). Generalized autoregressive conditional heteroscedasticity. *Journal of Econometrics*, 31, 307–327.

Borio, C.E.V., Kennedy, N. and Prowse, S.D. (1994). Exploring aggregate asset price fluctuations across countries: measurement, determinants, and monetary policy implications. BIS Economics Papers No. 40, April.

Boswijk, P.H. (2001). Testing for a unit root with near-integrated volatility. Tinbergen Institute Discussion Papers No. 01-077/4.

Box, G.E.P., Jenkins, G.M. and Reinsel, G.C. (1994). *Time Series Analysis: Forecasting and Control* (3rd edn). Prentice Hall, Englewood Cliffs, NJ.

Cox, D.R. (1981). Statistical analysis of time series: recent developments. *Scandinavian Journal of Statistics*, pp. 93–115.

Dassios, A. (1992). Asymptotic approximations to stochastic variance models. Mimeo, London School of Economics.

Duan, J.C. (1995). The GARCH option pricing model. *Mathematical Finance*, 5, 13–32.

Engle, R.F. (1982). Autoregressive conditional heteroskedasticity with estimates of the variance of UK inflation. *Econometrica*, 50, 987–1008.

Gande, A. and Parsley, D. (2004). Sovereign credit ratings, transparency and international portfolio flows. AFA 2006 Boston Meetings Paper.

Geske, R. and Johnson, H.E. (1984). The valuation of corporate liabilities as compound options: a correction. *Journal of Financial and Quantitative Analysis*, 19, 231–232.

Harvey, A.C. (1989). *Forecasting Structural Time Series and the Kalman Filter*. Cambridge University Press, Cambridge.

Harvey, A.C., Ruiz, E. and Shephard, N. (1994). Multivariate stochastic variance models. *Review of Economic Studies*, 61, 247–264.

Harvey, A.C. and Shephard, N. (1996). Estimation of an asymmetric model of asset prices. *Journal of Business and Economic Statistics*, 14, 429–434.

Heston, S.L. (1993). A closed-form solution for options with stochastic volatility with applications to bond and currency options. *The Review of Financial Studies*, 6, 327–343.

Kallsen, J.C. and Taqqu, M.S. (1995). Option pricing in ARCH-type models: with detailed proofs. Mimeo, Boston University.

Ling, S. and Li, W.K. (1998). Limiting distributions of maximum likelihood estimators for unstable autoregressive moving-average time series with general autoregressive heteroskedastic errors. *Annals of Statistics*, 26, 84–125.

Mandelbrot, B.B. (1963). The variation of certain speculative prices. *Journal of Business*, 36, 394–419.

Minsky, H.P. (1975). *John Maynard Keynes*. Columbia University Press, Columbia, OH.

Minsky, H.P. (1982). *Can 'It' Happen Again?* M.E. Sharpe, Armonk, NY.

Minsky, H.P. (1986). *Stabilizing An Unstable Economy*. Yale University Press, London.

Nelson, D.B. (1990). Stationarity and persistence in the GARCH(1,1) model. *Econometric Theory*, 6, 318–334.

Nelson, D.B. (1991). Conditional heteroskedasticity in asset returns: a new approach. *Econometrica*, 59, 347–370.

Neri, S. and Ropele, T. (2013). The macroeconomic effects of the sovereign debt crisis in the euro area. Bank of Italy Workshop, February 15.

Obstfeld, M. and Rogoff, K. (2009). Global imbalances and the financial crisis: products of common causes. Paper prepared for the Federal Reserve Bank of San Francisco Asia Economic Policy Conference, Santa Barbara, CA.

Pagan, A.R. and Schwert, G.W. (1990). Alternative models for conditional stock volatility. *Journal of Econometrics*, 45, 267–290.

Poon, S.-H. and Granger, C.W.J. (2003). Forecasting volatility in financial markets. *Journal of Economic Literature*, 41, 478–539.

Satchell, S.E. and Timmermann, A. (1993). Option pricing with GARCH and systematic consumption risk. Financial Economic Discussion Paper (FE/10), Birkbeck College, University of London.

Schmidt, C. (1996). Option pricing using EGARCH models. ZEW Discussion Papers, No. 96-20.

Schwert, G.W. (1989a). Business cycles, financial crises and stock volatility. Carnegie-Rochester Conference Series on Public Policy, 31, pp. 133–138.

Schwert, G.W. (1989b). Why does stock market volatility change over time? *Journal of Finance*, 44, 1115–1153.

Sentana, E. (1991). Quadratic ARCH models: a potential re-interpretation of ARCH models. LSE Financial Market Group Discussion Paper No. 122, pp. 1–45.

Shephard, N. (1996). *Time Series Models – In Econometrics, Finance and Other Fields*. Chapman & Hall, London.

Taylor, S. (1986). *Modelling Financial Time Series*. John Wiley, New York.

Additional Details Regarding Underlying Data Sources Used by Global Financial Data and Bloomberg

US 10yr government bond yields. The historical data has been sourced by Global Financial Data from Richard E. Sylla, Jack Wilson and Robert E. Wright, *Price Quotations in Early U.S. Securities Markets, 1790–1860; Hunt's Merchants Magazine* (1843–1853); *The Economist* (1854–1861); *The Financial Review* (1862–1918); Federal Reserve Bank, *National Monetary Statistics*, 1941, 1970 (annually thereafter); and Salomon Brothers, *Analytical Record of Yields and Yield Spreads*, 1995. The 'constant maturity' yield was sourced from Federal Reserve Bank, H-15 tables, which are available from 1953.

US equity returns. The original S&P indices were introduced by the Standard Statistics Corporation in 1923, covering 233 stocks in 26 sectors. Data were calculated on a weekly basis back to 1918. The daily indices were introduced in 1928 and consisted of a 90-stock average including 50 industrials, 20 rails and 20 utilities. The Standard and Poor's Composite combines a number of different indices. From 1791 to 1801, Global Financial Data has calculated an equal-weighted index using data from seven banks (Union National Bank of Boston, Massachusetts National Bank of Boston, First Bank of the United States, Bank of the State of New York, Bank of Pennsylvania, Bank of South Carolina and Bank of America), three insurance companies (New York Insurance Company, Insurance Co. of Pennsylvania and Insurance Co. of North America) and two transport companies (Philadelphia and Lancaster Turnpike Company and Schuylkill Permanent Bridge Company). Using Walter B. Smith and Arthur H. Cole, *Fluctuations in American Business, 1790–1860*, Harvard University Press, Cambridge, MA, 1935, the index combines the monthly price indices of Bank stocks (1802–1815), Bank and Insurance stocks (February 1815–December 1845), and Rails (1834–1862) from Smith and Cole and Railroads (1863–1870) from Frederick R. Macaulay, *The Movements of Interest Rates, Bond Yields and Stock Prices in the United States Since 1856*, National Bureau of Economic Research, New York, 1938. Where these indices overlap, the indices have been weighted according to the number of stocks included in the indices. Beginning in 1871, the Cowles/Standard and Poor's Composite index of stocks is used. The Standard and Poor's indices were first calculated in 1918, and the Cowles Commission back-calculated the series to 1871 using the *Commercial and Financial Chronicle*. For more information, see Standard and Poor's, *Security Price Index Record* and Cowles Commission for Research in Economics, *Common-Stock Indexes* (2nd edn), Principia Press, Bloomington, IN, 1939.

Proof of Theorem 4.1

By assumption $v_t : (0, \sigma_v^2)$ but we now need the moments of $\ln(\varepsilon_t^2)$. Using the mgf, we have immediately that

$$E[\exp(s \ln(\varepsilon_t^2))] = E[(\varepsilon_t^2)^s] = M(s).$$

Now the mean and variance of $\ln(\varepsilon_t^2)$ will be given as functions of the derivatives of $M(s)$, evaluated at $s = 0$.

Letting

$$K(s) = \ln M(s)$$

we have

$$K'(s) = \frac{M'(s)}{M(s)},$$

$$K''(s) = \frac{M(s)M''(s) - (M'(s))^2}{(M(s))^2}.$$

Consequently,

$$\ln(\varepsilon_t^2) : (K'(0), K''(0)).$$

Thus

$$\mu = K'(0) \text{ and } \delta^2 = K''(0).$$

Examining the composite error in our ARMA(1,1) representation, we have

$$v_t - \beta \ln(\varepsilon_t^2) : (-\beta\mu, \sigma_v^2 + \beta^2 \delta^2).$$

Also,

$$\ln(\varepsilon_{t+1}^2) : (\mu, \delta^2).$$

So, letting w_t and w_{t+1} be white noise processes such that

$$w_t : (0, d^2)$$

we have immediately that

$$g_{t+1} = \ln(\varepsilon_{t+1}^2) + v_t - \beta \ln(\varepsilon_t^2) = w_{t+1} - q w_t$$

is MA(1) and we need to solve for q and d.

In particular,

$$\mathrm{Var}(g_{t+1}) = d^2(1 + q^2) = \sigma_v^2 + (1 + \beta^2)K''(0)$$

and

$$\mathrm{Cov}(g_{t+1}, g_t) = -qd^2 = -\beta K''(0).$$

Therefore, solving the two equations $q = \beta K''(0)/d^2$ and $d^2(1 + (\beta K''(0)/d^2)^2) = \sigma_v^2 + (1 + \beta^2)$ $K''(0)$:

$$d^4 - d^2(\sigma_v^2 + (1 + \beta^2)K''(0)) + (\beta K''(0))^2 = 0.$$

Substituting, we see that the resulting quadratic has reciprocal roots. Taking a positive solution we arrive, after some calculation, at

$$d^2 = \frac{\sigma_v^2 + (1 + \beta^2)K''(0) + (\sigma_v^4 + (1 - \beta^2)^2(K''(0))^2 + 2\sigma_v^2(1 + \beta^2)K''(0))^{0.5}}{2}$$

and

$$q = \frac{2\,\beta K''(0)}{\sigma_v^2 + (1 + \beta^2)K''(0) + (\sigma_v^4 + (1 - \beta^2)^2(K''(0))^2 + 2\sigma_v^2(1 + \beta^2)K''(0))^{0.5}}.$$

Different distributional assumptions on v_t and ε_t will generate different μ and δ^2 but with $v_t : (0, \sigma_v^2)$.

Proof of Corollaries 4.1 and 4.2

PROOF OF COROLLARY 4.1

Under normality,

$$M(s) = E\left[\left(\chi^2_{(1)}\right)^s\right] = \frac{2^s \Gamma\left(\frac{1}{2} + s\right)}{\Gamma\left(\frac{1}{2}\right)}$$

with $K(s) = s \ln 2 + \ln \Gamma\left(\frac{1}{2} + s\right) - \ln \Gamma\left(\frac{1}{2}\right)$

giving

$$\mu = K'(0) = \ln 2 + \psi\left(\frac{1}{2}\right) \approx -1.27$$

$$\delta^2 = K''(0) = \psi'\left(\frac{1}{2}\right) \approx 4.93$$

where $\psi(\cdot)$ and $\psi'(\cdot)$ are the digamma and trigamma functions, respectively.

PROOF OF COROLLARY 4.2

Since v_t and ε_t have zero mean, we need to scale them to have the correct variance of σ^2_v for v_t and 1 for ε_t. Consequently, we let

$$v_t^2 = \frac{\sigma_v^2(n-2)\chi^2_{(1)}}{\chi^2_n} \quad \text{and} \quad \varepsilon_t^2 = \frac{(m-2)\chi^2_{(1)}}{\chi^2_n}.$$

Therefore,

$$\ln(\varepsilon_t^2) = \ln(m-2) + \ln \chi^2_{(1)} - \ln \chi^2_{(m)}$$

and thus

$$M(s) = (m-2)^s E\left[(\chi^2_{(1)})^s\right] E\left[(\chi^2_{(m)})^{-s}\right]$$

$$= (m-2)^s 2^s \frac{\Gamma\left(\frac{1}{2}+s\right) 2^{-s}\Gamma\left(\frac{m}{2}-s\right)}{\Gamma\left(\frac{1}{2}\right)\Gamma\left(\frac{m}{2}\right)}$$

and

$$K(s) = s\ln(m-2) + \ln\Gamma\left(\frac{1}{2}+s\right) + \ln\Gamma\left(\frac{m}{2}+s\right) - \ln\Gamma\left(\frac{1}{2}\right) - \ln\Gamma\left(\frac{m}{2}\right).$$

Consequently,

$$K'(s) = \ln(m-2) + \psi\left(\frac{1}{2}+s\right) - \psi\left(\frac{m}{2}-s\right),$$

$$K''(s) = \psi'\left(\frac{1}{2}+s\right) + \psi'\left(\frac{m}{2}-s\right).$$

Therefore,

$$\mu = K'(0) = \ln(m-2) + \psi\left(\frac{1}{2}\right) - \psi\left(\frac{m}{2}\right),$$

$$\delta^2 = \psi'\left(\frac{1}{2}\right) + \psi'\left(\frac{m}{2}\right).$$

Proof of EGARCH(1,2) mgf:

$$\ln\sigma_t^2 = \frac{\alpha}{1-\beta} + \sum_{j=0}^{\infty}\beta^j V_{t-j}$$

$$\sigma_t^2 = e^{\alpha/(1-\beta)} \prod_{j=0}^{\infty}\exp(\beta^j V_{t-j})$$

$$E[\sigma_t^{2s}] = \exp\left(\frac{s\alpha}{1-\beta}\right)\prod_{j=0}^{\infty} E\left[\exp(s\beta^j V_{t-j})\right]$$

$$V_{t-j} = \sum_{k=1}^{2}\alpha_k(\lambda\varepsilon_{t-j-k} + \delta(|\varepsilon_{t-j-k}| - E(|\varepsilon_{t-j-k}|)))$$

$$\beta^j V_{t-j} = \beta^j \sum_{k=1}^{2}\alpha_k(\lambda\varepsilon_{t-j-k} + \delta(|\varepsilon_{t-j-k}| - E(|\varepsilon_{t-j-k}|)))$$

$$= \beta^j[\alpha_1(\lambda\varepsilon_{t-1-j} + \delta(|\varepsilon_{t-1-j}| - E(|\varepsilon_{t-1-j}|)))]$$

$$+ \beta^j[\alpha_2(\lambda\varepsilon_{t-2-j} + \delta(|\varepsilon_{t-2-j}| - E(|\varepsilon_{t-2-j}|)))].$$

Consider

$$\sum_{j=0}^{\infty} \beta^j (\alpha_1(\lambda \varepsilon_{t-1-j}) + \alpha_2 \lambda \varepsilon_{t-2-j})$$

$$= \lambda \left[\alpha_1 \sum_{j=0}^{\infty} \beta^j \varepsilon_{t-j-1} + \alpha_2 \sum \beta^j \varepsilon_{t-2-j} \right]$$

$$= \lambda \left[\alpha_1 \varepsilon_{t-1} + \alpha_1 \sum_{j=1}^{\infty} \beta^j \varepsilon_{t-1-j} + \alpha_2 \sum_{j=0}^{\infty} \beta^j \varepsilon_{t-2-j} \right]$$

$$= \lambda \left[\alpha_1 \varepsilon_{t-1} + \alpha_1 \sum_{j=0}^{\infty} \beta^{j+1} \varepsilon_{t-1-(j+1)} + \alpha_2 \sum_{j=0}^{\infty} \beta^j \varepsilon_{t-2-j} \right]$$

$$= \lambda \left[\alpha_1 \varepsilon_{t-1} + (\alpha_1 \beta + \alpha_2) \sum_{j=0}^{\infty} \beta^j \varepsilon_{t-2-j} \right].$$

Also,

$$\sum_{j=0}^{\infty} \beta^j (\alpha_1 \delta(|\varepsilon_{t-1-j}| - E[|\varepsilon_{t-1-j}|]) + \alpha_2 \delta(|\varepsilon_{t-2-j}| - E[|\varepsilon_{t-2-j}|]))$$

$$= \delta[\alpha_1(|\varepsilon_{t-1}| - E[|\varepsilon_{t-1}|]) + (\alpha_1 \beta + \alpha_2) \sum_{j=0}^{\infty} \beta^j (|\varepsilon_{t-2-j}| - E(|\varepsilon_{t-2-j}|))].$$

Putting together:

$$\sum_{j=0}^{\infty} \beta^j V_{t-j} = \alpha_1(\lambda \varepsilon_{t-1} + \delta(|\varepsilon_{t-1}| - E(|\varepsilon_{t-1}|)))$$

$$+ (\alpha_1 \beta + \alpha_2) \sum_{j=0}^{\infty} \beta^j [\lambda \varepsilon_{t-2-j} + \delta(|\varepsilon_{t-2-j}| - E(|\varepsilon_{t-2-j}|))].$$

So

$$\exp\left(s \sum_{j=0}^{\infty} \beta^j V_{t-j} \right)$$

$$= \exp[s\alpha_1(\lambda \varepsilon_{t-1} + \delta(|\varepsilon_{t-1}| - E(|\varepsilon_{t-1}|)))]$$

$$\cdot \exp\left[s(\alpha_1 \beta + \alpha_2) \sum_{j=0}^{\infty} \beta^j [\lambda \varepsilon_{t-2-j} + \delta(|\varepsilon_{t-2-j}| - E(|\varepsilon_{t-2-j}|))] \right]$$

$$= \exp[s\alpha_1(\lambda \varepsilon_{t-1} + \delta(|\varepsilon_{t-1}| - E(|\varepsilon_{t-1}|)))]$$

$$\cdot \prod_{j=0}^{\infty} \exp(s(\alpha_1 \beta + \alpha_2)\beta^j [\lambda \varepsilon_{t-2-j} + \delta(|\varepsilon_{t-2-j}| - E(|\varepsilon_{t-2-j}|))]).$$

Thus:

$$E\left[\exp\left(s\sum_{j=0}^{\infty}\beta^j V_{t-j}\right)\right]$$

$$= E[\exp(s\alpha_1 W_{t-1})] \cdot \prod_{j=0}^{\infty} E[\exp(s(\alpha_1\beta + \alpha_2)\beta^j W_{t-2-j})]$$

where

$$W_{t-j} = \lambda\varepsilon_{t-j} + \delta(|\varepsilon_{t-j}| - E(|\varepsilon_{t-j}|)).$$

We now consider:

$$E[\exp(s\gamma_j W_{t-j})], \qquad j = 0, 1, 2, \ldots$$

$$\gamma_1 = \alpha_1, \ \gamma_2 = (\alpha_1\beta + \alpha_2)$$

$$\gamma_j = (\alpha_1\beta + \alpha_2)\beta^{j-2}, \ j \geq 3$$

$$E[\exp(s\gamma_j W_{t-j})]$$
$$= E[\exp(s\gamma_j[\lambda\varepsilon_{t-j} + \delta(|\varepsilon_{t-j}| - E(|\varepsilon_{t-j}|))])]$$
$$= E[\exp(\theta_1\varepsilon_{t-j} + \theta_2(|\varepsilon_{t-j}| - E(|\varepsilon_{t-j}|)))]$$
$$= \exp(-\theta_2 E[|\varepsilon_{t-j}|]) \cdot E[\exp(\theta_1\varepsilon_{t-j} + \theta_2|\varepsilon_{t-j}|)].$$

Now, let $\varepsilon_{t-j} \sim$ i.i.d. $N(0, 1)$ and thus we can easily show that

$$E(|\varepsilon_{t-j}|) = \sqrt{2/\pi}$$

and

$$E[\exp(\theta_1\varepsilon_{t-j} + \theta_2|\varepsilon_{t-j}|)]$$

$$= \int_{-\infty}^{\infty} \exp(\theta_1\varepsilon_{t-j} + \theta_2|\varepsilon_{t-j}|)\frac{1}{2\pi} e^{-\varepsilon_{t-j}^2/2} d\varepsilon_{t-j}$$

$$= \int_{-\infty}^{0} \exp(\theta_1\varepsilon_{t-j} - \theta_2\varepsilon_{t-j})\frac{1}{2\pi} e^{-\varepsilon_{t-j}^2/2} d\varepsilon_{t-j}$$

$$= \int_{0}^{\infty} \exp(\theta_1\varepsilon_{t-j} + \theta_2\varepsilon_{t-j})\frac{1}{2\pi} e^{-\varepsilon_{t-j}^2/2} d\varepsilon_{t-j}$$

$$= \int_{-\infty}^{0} \exp(-(\theta_2 - \theta_1)\varepsilon_{t-j})\frac{1}{2\pi} e^{-\varepsilon_{t-j}^2/2} d\varepsilon_{t-j} \qquad (4.C.1)$$

$$+ \int_{0}^{\infty} \exp((\theta_2 + \theta_1)\varepsilon_{t-j})\frac{1}{2\pi} e^{-\varepsilon_{t-j}^2/2} d\varepsilon_{t-j}. \qquad (4.C.2)$$

Integral A Consider the exponent

$$-\frac{\varepsilon_{t-j}^2}{2} - (\theta_2 - \theta_1)\varepsilon_{t-j}$$

$$= -\frac{1}{2}(\varepsilon_{t-j}^2 + 2(\theta_2 - \theta_1)\varepsilon_{t-j} + (\theta_2 - \theta_1)^2 - (\theta_2 - \theta_1)^2)$$

$$= \frac{1}{2}(\theta_2 - \theta_1)^2 - \frac{1}{2}(\varepsilon_{t-j} + (\theta_2 - \theta_1))^2.$$

Thus,

$$(4.C.1) \rightarrow e^{(\theta_2-\theta_1)^2/2} \int_{-\infty}^{0} \frac{1}{\sqrt{2\pi}} \exp\left(-\frac{1}{2}(\varepsilon_{t-j} + (\theta_2 - \theta_1))^2\right) d\varepsilon_{t-j}$$

$$\varepsilon_{t-j} \rightarrow u = \varepsilon_{t-j} + (\theta_2 - \theta_1)$$

i.e., $$\varepsilon_{t-j} = u - (\theta_2 - \theta_1)$$

$$d\varepsilon_{t-j} = du$$

$$(4.C.2) \rightarrow e^{(\theta_2-\theta_1)^2/2} \int_{-\infty}^{(\theta_2-\theta_1)} \frac{1}{\sqrt{2\pi}} e^{-u^2/2} du$$

$$= e^{(\theta_2-\theta_1)^2/2} \Phi(\theta_2 - \theta_1).$$

Similarly, we have

$$(4.C.2) \rightarrow \quad = e^{(\theta_2-\theta_1)^2/2} \Phi(\theta_2 + \theta_1).$$

Therefore,

$$E[\exp(\theta_1\varepsilon_{t-j} + \theta_2|\varepsilon_{t-j}|)]$$

$$= e^{(\theta_2-\theta_1)^2/2} \Phi(\theta_2 - \theta_1) + e^{(\theta_2+\theta_1)^2/2} \Phi(\theta_2 + \theta_1)$$

and finally

$$E[\exp(s\gamma_j W_{t-j})]$$

$$= e^{-\theta_2\sqrt{2/\pi}} [e^{(\theta_2-\theta_1)^2/2} \Phi(\theta_2 - \theta_1) + e^{(\theta_2+\theta_1)^2/2} \Phi(\theta_2 + \theta_1)].$$

Since

$$\theta_1 = s\gamma_j\lambda \quad \text{and} \quad \theta_2 = s\gamma_j\delta$$

we have

$$(\theta_2 - \theta_1) = s\gamma_j(\delta - \lambda)$$

$$(\theta_2 + \theta_1) = s\gamma_j(\delta + \lambda).$$

Thus

$$E[\exp(s\gamma_j W_{t-j})]$$

$$= \exp\left(-s\delta\sqrt{\frac{2}{\pi}}\gamma_j\right)\left[\exp\left(\frac{1}{2}(s^2\gamma_j^2(\delta-\lambda)^2)\right)\cdot\Phi(s\gamma_j(\delta-\lambda))\right.$$

$$+ \exp\left(\frac{1}{2}(s^2\gamma_j^2(\delta+\lambda)^2)\right)\cdot\Phi(s\gamma_j(\delta+\lambda))\bigg]$$

$$\exp(s\alpha_1 W_{t-1})\cdot\exp(s(\alpha_1\beta+\alpha_2)W_{t-2})$$

$$\cdot\exp(s(\alpha_1\beta+\alpha_2)\beta W_{t-3})\cdot\exp(s(\alpha_1\beta+\alpha_2)\beta^2 W_{t-4})$$

$$\gamma_1 = \alpha_1$$

$$\gamma_2 = (\alpha_1\beta+\alpha_2)$$

$$\gamma_j = (\alpha_1\beta+\alpha_2)\beta^{j-2}, \ j \geq 3$$

$$E[\exp(s\ln\sigma_t^2)] = E[\sigma_t^{2s}]$$

$$= \exp\left(\frac{s\alpha}{1-\beta}\right)E\left[\exp\left(s\sum_{j=0}^{\infty}\beta^j V_{t-j}\right)\right]$$

$$= \exp\left(\frac{s\alpha}{1-\beta}\right)\cdot E\left[\exp\left(s\sum_{j=0}^{\infty}\gamma_j W_{t-j}\right)\right]$$

$$= \exp\left(\frac{s\alpha}{1-\beta}\right)\cdot\prod_{j=0}^{\infty}E\left[\exp(s\gamma_j W_{t-j})\right]$$

where

$$E[\exp(s\gamma_j W_{t-j})] = \exp\left(-s\delta\sqrt{\frac{2}{\pi}}\cdot\gamma_j\right)$$

$$\cdot\left[\exp\left(\frac{1}{2}(s^2\gamma_j^2(\delta-\lambda)^2)\right)\Phi(s\gamma_j(\delta-\lambda))+\exp\left(\frac{1}{2}(s^2\gamma_j^2(\delta+\lambda)^2)\right)\Phi(s\gamma_j(\delta+\lambda))\right]$$

with $\gamma_1 = \alpha_1$, $\gamma_2 = (\alpha_1\beta+\alpha_2)$, $\gamma_j = (\alpha_1\beta+\alpha_2)\beta^{j-2}, \ j \geq 3$

$$\prod_{j=0}^{\infty}\left[\exp(-a_1\gamma_j)\left[\exp\left(\frac{b_2^2}{2}\gamma_j^2\right)\Phi(b_1\lambda_j)+\exp\left(\frac{b_2^2}{2}\gamma_j^2\right)\Phi(b_2\gamma_j)\right]\right]$$

$$e^{a_1\gamma_1}\left[\exp\left(\frac{b_1^2}{2}\gamma_1^2\right)\Phi(b_1\gamma_1)+\exp\left(\frac{b_2^2}{2}\gamma_1^2\right)\Phi(b_2\gamma_1)\right]$$

$$\cdot e^{a_1 \gamma_2} \left[\exp\left(\frac{b_1^2}{2} \gamma_2^2 \right) \Phi(b_1 \gamma_2) + \exp\left(\frac{b_2^2}{2} \gamma_2^2 \right) \Phi(b_2 \gamma_2) \right]$$

$$= e^{-a_1} \sum \gamma_j \prod_{j=0}^{\infty} \left(e^{\frac{b_1^2 \gamma_j^2}{2}} \Phi(b_1 \gamma_j) + e^{\frac{b_2^2 \gamma_j^2}{2}} \Phi(b_2 \gamma_j) \right)$$

$$a_1 = -s\delta \sqrt{\frac{2}{\pi}}$$

$$b_1 = s(\delta + \lambda)$$

$$b_2 = s(\delta + \lambda)$$

$$\sum_{j=0}^{\infty} \gamma_j = \alpha_1 + \sum_{j=2}^{\infty} (\alpha_1 \beta + \alpha_2) \beta^{j-2}$$

$$= \alpha_1 + (\alpha_1 \beta + \alpha_2) \sum_{j=2}^{\infty} \beta^{j-2} 1 + \beta + \beta^2 + \beta^3 + \dots$$

$$l = j - 2$$

$$j = l + 2$$

$$= \alpha_1 + (\alpha_1 \beta + \alpha_2) \sum_{l=0}^{\infty} \beta^l = \alpha_1 + \frac{(\alpha_1 \beta + \alpha_2)}{(1 - \beta)}$$

$$\sum_{j=0}^{\infty} \gamma_j = \alpha_1 + \frac{(\alpha_1 \beta + \alpha_2)}{1 - \beta}$$

$$= \frac{\alpha_1 (1 - \beta) + \alpha_1 \beta + \alpha_2}{1 - \beta}$$

$$= \frac{\alpha_1 + \alpha_2}{1 - \beta}$$

$$E[\sigma_t^{2s}] = \exp\left(\frac{s\alpha}{1 - \beta} \right) \cdot \exp\left(\frac{-s\delta \sqrt{2/\pi}(\alpha_1 + \alpha_2)}{1 - \beta} \right)$$

$$\cdot \prod_{j=0}^{\infty} \left(e^{\frac{b_1^2 \gamma_j^2}{2}} \Phi(b_1 \gamma_j) + e^{\frac{b_2^2 \gamma_j^2}{2}} \Phi(b_2 \gamma_j) \right).$$

CHAPTER 5

Hedging Asymmetric Dependence

Anthony Hatherley

Abstract

In this chapter we explore the various derivative contracts that could be traded to hedge portfolio-level asymmetric dependence (AD). Hedging AD directly involves trading multi-underlying derivative products with exposure to implied correlation skew. We review the various strategies that practitioners use in order to trade implied correlation. We subsequently propose a long–short equity derivative strategy involving corridor variance swaps that provides exposure to aggregate implied AD consistent with the adjusted J statistic. This strategy provides a more direct hedge against the drivers of AD, in contrast to the current practice of simply hedging the effects of AD with volatility derivatives.

5.1 INTRODUCTION

Although tail risk has been a topic of research for the better part of the past 20 years, it took a global financial crisis for tail risk to become common parlance in the investment industry. In recent years, methods to hedge the tail risk associated with asymmetric dependence (AD) have become increasingly important to investors. The management of tail risk can be approached in two ways: either dynamically, through the asset allocation process (see Hatherley and Alcock (2007), Alcock and Hatherley (2009) and Low et al. (2013), for example) or by buying insurance in the form of tailored derivative products.

In deciding on the appropriate hedge amongst the myriad of derivative products now available to investors, it is important to understand the sensitivities and limitations of many of the products as effective AD management tools. For example, Alcock and Hatherley (2017) demonstrate the existence of a significant AD risk premium, over and above the risk premium associated with β. The implication for risk management is that hedging linear correlation risk is unlikely to completely insulate a portfolio from market shocks that alter the non-linear (higher-order) component of dependence. A strategy that hedges the risk associated with linear dependence may be significantly different from the strategy an investor might otherwise put in place to manage changes in AD.

Implicit in many of the so-called tail-risk trades proposed by sell-side banks is that the outcome of a low probability, but potentially devastating market event that causes assets to devalue in a correlated fashion can be represented by an increase in volatility. As a result, it is common to see volatility-based derivative trades put forward as tail-risk hedge candidates. A classic example is a crash-put option written over an index where the payoff requires the spot of the underlying to fall dramatically. Of course, volatility can increase for various reasons aside from a tail event, and as a result, volatility-based AD hedges can often only proxy the risk associated with an actual change in AD.

Cross-asset hybrid derivatives have also been proposed as tail-risk hedge candidates. For example, a put option on an equity index can be modified to only become active when the level of gold is above a given threshold. In the case of a major downside event, the equity index falls and the market flies to the safety of gold, which, if structured correctly, will force the put option to knock in. Such a trade is short equity/gold correlation, and therefore will be cheaper than a vanilla put option if the equity/gold correlation initially is highly positive (Whittall, 2010). The trade will be an effective tail hedge if the equity/gold correlation is highly negative upon the occurrence of a significant negative market event. The risk to this specific example is that the initially high positive equity/gold correlation remains high during the life of the trade. This was observed during 2010, when global markets observed a period of high cross-asset correlation combined with historical low volatility. Williams (2014) attributes this unusual market state to the programme of 'quantitative easing' used by the US Federal Reserve, where money flooded the market and was put to work across the major asset classes.[1] The market intervention effectively distorted the historical relationship between asset classes, which in turn impacted the effectiveness of many hybrid tail-risk hedges.

More effective AD hedges require products that target exposure of the dependence characteristics between underlyings.

5.2 ASYMMETRIC DEPENDENCE IN IMPLIED EQUITY CORRELATION: THE IMPLIED CORRELATION SKEW

A number of multi-asset derivative products provide investors with exposure to correlation including dispersion trades, correlation swaps, basket options and best-of/worst-of products where the payoff is a function of the best-performing or worst-performing asset in a basket. These products can be used to trade realized correlation, but are often also implicitly impacted by higher-order dependence characteristics.

Multi-asset derivatives provide an exposure to implied correlation that is computed depending on the prevailing spot price of the basket's underlyings. The implied correlation for a given equity basket can be computed as the ratio of the basket implied volatility to a function of the basket's constituent single stock implied volatility. Starting with the standard definition for portfolio variance, let $\sigma_i \equiv \sigma_i(K, T)$ refer to the implied volatility of asset i at strike factor K and time to maturity, T:

$$\sigma_I^2 = \sum_i (w_i \sigma_i)^2 + \sum_{i \neq j} \sum w_i w_j \sigma_i \sigma_j \rho_{ij}(K, T).$$

If we set $\hat{\rho}(K, T) = \rho_{ij}(K, T)$:

$$\sigma_I^2 = \sum_i (w_i \sigma_i)^2 + \hat{\rho}(K, T) \sum_{i \neq j} \sum w_i w_j \sigma_i \sigma_j,$$

we obtain an estimate for implied correlation by solving for $\hat{\rho}(K, T)$:

$$\hat{\rho}(K, T) = \frac{\sigma_I^2 - \sum_i (w_i \sigma_i)^2}{\sum \sum_{i \neq j} w_i w_j \sigma_i \sigma_j} = \frac{\sigma_I^2 - \sum_i (w_i \sigma_i)^2}{\left(\sum_{ij} w_i w_j \sigma_i \sigma_j\right)^2 - \sum_i (w_i \sigma_i)^2}. \tag{5.1}$$

---

[1]This was referred to as the 'Bernanke put', reflecting the name sake of the US Federal Reserve governor at the time, Ben Bernanke, and the effect of the monetary policy on global markets, in effect placing an artificial floor on asset prices.

Thus, if the basket implied volatility is taken to refer to the implied volatility of an equity index, the implied correlation for a given strike, K and maturity T that is incorporated into the basket implied volatility can be computed using the implied volatilities of the index's constituent stocks.

Figure 5.1 depicts the implied correlation during calm market conditions (March 2015) and during stressed market conditions (January 2016) for the DAX 30 and the Eurostoxx 50 using implied volatilities for all constituents making up each respective index.[2] The stressed market period follows a sharp move downward in global markets associated with uncertainty around oil prices and pressure on major market economies like China and Europe.

By computing Equation (5.1) for different strike levels and maturities, we effectively build up an implied correlation surface. The following observations can be made:

1. For a given strike, longer-dated maturities tend to display higher implied correlation than shorter-dated maturities. This is consistent with assets that are more correlated over longer periods than over shorter periods.
2. Implied correlation tends to be higher for low strikes compared with high strikes. To understand this result, suppose we buy a basket put option with a strike of 70%. The derivative will finish in-the-money if the spot falls below the strike price by the maturity date. For a one-month option, a fall of 30% is likely to be regarded as a more dramatic event than a fall of 30% over 3 years. Such a dramatic event over a short period of time is likely to occur as a result of severe market stress, for example, the type that causes dependence to increase in a manner consistent with AD. For a basket put option with an even lower strike of 50%, the event required to cause this fall over one month must be even greater. In order to sell this type of option, market-makers would require a higher risk premium to account for the additional risk of AD. The difference in implied correlation between a low strike and a high strike is referred to as the implied correlation skew.
3. Reflecting the previous point, the implied correlation skew tends to be highest for shorter-dated maturities.
4. Implied correlation tends to increase during stressed market conditions compared with calm market conditions. However, the implied correlation skew relative to the at-the-money (ATM) implied correlation tends to be higher during calm market conditions. For example, in the case of the one-month DAX slice, the implied correlation skew measured between the 70% strike and the 100% strike is approximately 64% of the ATM implied correlation in March 2015, but decreases to approximately 39% of the ATM implied correlation in January 2016. This implies that if an unexpected fall in prices were to occur when the prevailing market condition is calm, then the market treats the impact on dependence asymmetrically between down moves and up moves. In contrast, if a fall in prices were to occur when the prevailing market condition is stressed, then the market is more likely to treat the impact on dependence symmetrically (or less asymmetrically) between down moves and up moves. This is consistent with Alcock and Hatherley (2017), who argue that in situations where a market drawdown occurs and an asset is revealed to possess AD with the market, market participants may be less disappointed were another drawdown to occur a short time later. This is because the downside-dependent behaviour of the asset, contingent upon a market drawdown, is now a known characteristic of the joint return distribution. As a consequence, we may observe a premium for LTAD during normal market conditions but this premium may change subsequent to the occurrence of a major market crash.

The results of Figure 5.1 indicate that the exposure to implied correlation will change as the spot moves. Higher implied correlation for low relative strikes would occur if a fall in the market were to cause the average correlation between the underlyings to increase, consistent with the concept of AD.

---

[2]In practice, it is possible to compute the implied correlation using a subset of the single stock volatilities making up the index. This is particularly true in smaller developed markets such as Australia, where index options are widely traded, but only the top 10% to 25% of stocks by market cap have listed options. In this instance, the implied correlation does not necessarily lie between the traditional correlation bounds of ± 1.

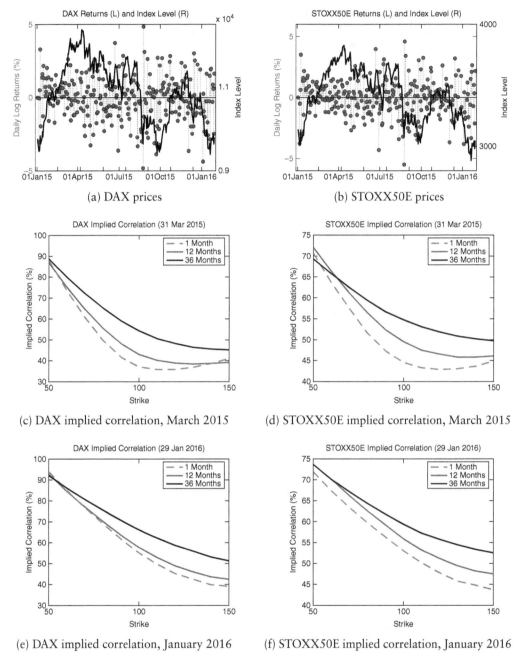

(a) DAX prices

(b) STOXX50E prices

(c) DAX implied correlation, March 2015

(d) STOXX50E implied correlation, March 2015

(e) DAX implied correlation, January 2016

(f) STOXX50E implied correlation, January 2016

FIGURE 5.1 Subplots (a) and (b) depict the DAX 30 and Eurostoxx prices and daily log returns between 3 January 2015 and 30 January 2016. Subplots (c) to (f) depict the implied correlation during calm market conditions (March 2015) and during stressed market conditions (January 2016) for the DAX 30 and the Eurostoxx 50 computed using Equation (5.1) for a range of strikes and maturities.

Therefore, a derivative product may be regarded as a possible candidate for an effective tail-risk hedge if that product displays sensitivity to implied correlation skew. Because no existing product trades directly in implied AD, isolating and trading correlation skew requires trades in combinations of multi-asset derivative products.

5.3 THE EFFECT OF CORRELATION SKEW ON PORTFOLIO CHOICE

To provide an indication of the effect that AD can have on a portfolio, and subsequently the need to hedge it, we consider the work of Buraschi *et al.* (2010), who demonstrate the significance of the hedge required to adequately account for correlation skew using a stochastic model for correlation risk. This is achieved by modelling the variance–covariance matrix as a Wishart process, originally introduced by Bru (1991), in conjunction with a standard bivariate stock process. By correlating the innovations driving the stock process and the variance–covariance process, the model allows for both the negative dependence between asset returns and volatility, known as Black's volatility leverage effect, as well as the negative dependence between returns and correlation. The latter characteristic, referred to as the correlation leverage effect (Roll, 1988), is synonymous with AD.

5.3.1 The Optimal Portfolio Incorporating Stochastic Correlation

Consider an (incomplete) economy consisting of two risky assets, $S = (S_1, S_2) \in \mathbb{R}^2$, and a riskless asset with instantaneous rate, $r \in \mathbb{R}_+$. Assume that the bivariate stock process is given by

$$dS(t) = I_S \left[(r\overline{1}_2 + \Lambda(\Sigma, t))dt + \Sigma^{1/2}(t)dW(t) \right],$$ (5.2)

where $I_S = Diag[S_1, S_2]$, $\overline{1}_2 = (1, 1)'$, $\Lambda(\Sigma, t)$ is a (possibly) state-dependent vector of risk premia and W represents a two-dimensional Brownian motion. The variance–covariance matrix, Σ, evolves according to a Wishart process:

$$d\Sigma(t) = [\Omega\Omega' + M\Sigma(t) + \Sigma(t)M']dt + \Sigma^{1/2}(t)dB(t)Q + Q'dB(t)'\Sigma^{1/2}(t),$$ (5.3)

where the negative semi-definite 2×2 square matrix, M, drives the mean reversion of the process towards the expected long-term variance–covariance matrix, represented by $\Omega\Omega'$, and the 2×2 square matrix, Q, determines the co-volatility features of the stochastic variance–covariance matrix of returns. Equation (5.3) therefore represents the matrix analogue of the square-root mean-reverting process.

The Brownian motion vectors, $W(t)$ and $B(t)$, are related in the following manner:

$$W(t) = Z(t)\sqrt{1 - \overline{\rho}'\overline{\rho}} + B(t)\overline{\rho},$$

where Z and B are independent two-dimensional Brownian motions and $\overline{\rho} = (\overline{\rho}_1, \overline{\rho}_2)'$ is a vector of correlation parameters $\overline{\rho}_i \in [-1, 1]$ such that $\overline{\rho}'\overline{\rho} \leq 1$. An investor with constant relative risk aversion utility over terminal wealth and relative risk aversion coefficient, γ, selects a portfolio, π, by solving

$$J(X_0, \Sigma_0) = \sup_{\pi} \mathbb{E}\left[\frac{X(T)^{1-\gamma}}{1-\gamma} \right],$$ (5.4)

subject to dynamic budget constraints on $X(T)$, the vector of wealth invested in each asset at a given time t. This wealth vector is assumed to evolve according to

$$dX(t) = X(t)[r + \pi(t)'\Lambda(\Sigma, t)]dt + X(t)\pi(t)'\Sigma^{1/2}(t)dW(t).$$ (5.5)

Assuming a constant market price of variance–covariance risk such that $\Lambda(\Sigma, t) = \Sigma(t)\lambda$ for $\lambda = (\lambda_1, \lambda_2)' \in \mathbb{R}^2$, the optimal portfolio, π, is given by

$$\pi = \frac{\lambda}{\gamma} + 2 \begin{pmatrix} A_{11} & A_{12} \\ A_{12} & A_{22} \end{pmatrix} \begin{pmatrix} q_{11}\bar{\rho}_1 + q_{12}\bar{\rho}_2 \\ q_{21}\bar{\rho}_1 + q_{22}\bar{\rho}_2 \end{pmatrix}, \tag{5.6}$$

where the symmetric matrix $A = A(t, T)$ relates to the solution of the system of matrix Riccati equations that characterize (5.4), while coefficients q_{ij} are the entries of the matrix Q appearing in the Wishart dynamics. See Buraschi *et al.* (2010) for a detailed proof of these results.

5.3.2 Characteristics and Model Intuition

Analogous to the results presented by Merton (1969), the optimal portfolio, π in Equation (5.6), is made up of myopic demand (λ/γ) and an intertemporal hedging adjustment that reflects the stochastic nature of the opportunity set. The coefficients, A_{ij}, represent the sensitivity of the marginal utility of wealth to the state variables, Σ_{ij}. Hence, A_{11} and A_{22} may be associated with the marginal utility of wealth to stochastic volatility (SV), while A_{12} may be associated with the marginal utility of wealth to stochastic correlation. The sign of these coefficients is negative for investors with risk-aversion parameters $\gamma > 1$ and λ such that $\lambda_1 \lambda_2 \geq 0$, indicating that investors experience a decrease in the marginal utility of wealth and an increase in either SV or stochastic correlation.

In addition to the marginal utility of wealth, the hedging portfolio is also driven by the extent to which the state variables, Σ_{ij}, are correlated with returns. To see this, we can compute the correlation between SV and stock return directly from the Wishart process (5.3) as:

$$corr_t \left(\frac{dS_1}{S_1}, d\Sigma_{11} \right) = \frac{q_{11}\bar{\rho}_1 + q_{21}\bar{\rho}_2}{\sqrt{q_{11}^2 + q_{21}^2}}, \tag{5.7}$$

where for any $i, j = 1, 2$, parameters q_{ij} denote the ijth element of matrix Q. Equation (5.7) can be used to model the empirical observation that volatility and returns are negatively correlated, for example. Analogously, correlation between stochastic correlation and returns is then given by

$$corr_t \left(\frac{dS_1}{S_1}, d\rho \right) = \frac{(q_{11}\bar{\rho}_1 + q_{21}\bar{\rho}_2)(1 - \rho^2(t))}{\sqrt{(\mathbb{E}_t[d\rho^2]/dt)\Sigma_{22}(t)}}, \tag{5.8}$$

where

$$d\rho = \frac{d\Sigma_{12}}{\sqrt{d\Sigma_{11}d\Sigma_{22}}}$$

and $\mathbb{E}_t[d\rho^2]$ is given by

$$\mathbb{E}_t[d\rho^2] = \left[(1 - \rho^2(t)) \left(\frac{q_{11}^2 + q_{21}^2}{\Sigma_{11}(t)} + \frac{q_{12}^2 + q_{22}^2}{\Sigma_{22}(t)} - 2\frac{q_{11}q_{12} + q_{21}q_{22}}{\sqrt{\Sigma_{11}(t)\Sigma_{22}(t)}}\rho(t) \right) \right] dt.$$

A negative value associated with Equation (5.8) is consistent with AD or correlation skew, where dependence increases with the occurrence of negative returns. A negative value in both Equations (5.7) and (5.8) will occur when $q_{11}\bar{\rho}_1 + q_{12}\bar{\rho}_2 < 0$.

5.3.3 Empirical Observations

Buraschi *et al.* (2010) quantify the demand for volatility and covariance hedging with the weekly and monthly allocation of wealth between the S&P500 Index Futures and the 30-year Treasury Bond Futures contract between January 1990 and October 2003. Their key results may be summarized as follows:

1. Estimation of Equation (5.3) indicates that the volatility and correlation leverage effects are driven by the negative coefficient associated with $\bar{\rho}$.
2. The coefficient q_{11}, associated with the equity index, tends to be significantly larger than q_{22}, associated with the bond index. The q_{11} coefficient is also significantly larger than q_{12} and q_{21}. Therefore, the correlation between stochastic correlation and equity returns in Equation (5.8) is going to be larger than the correlation between stochastic correlation and bond returns. As a result, Buraschi *et al.* (2010) conclude that 30-year Treasury bond returns are better instruments for hedging covariance risk.
3. Covariance hedging represents a substantial part of the total hedging demand and becomes increasingly important as the strength of leverage effect and the dimension of the investment opportunity set increases.
4. When allocating wealth between S&P500 Index Futures, Nikkei 225 Index Futures and the 30-year Treasury Bond Futures using a univariate SV model, the total hedging demand over a 10-year period for S&P500 futures for investors with a relative risk aversion of eight is approximately 4.8% of the myopic portfolio. Using the (multivariate) Wishart model, the total hedging demand for S&P500 futures is 28% and the covariance hedging demand is 16.9% of the myopic portfolio. As a result of the covariance hedging, the total hedging demand is around four to five times larger than in the univariate SV model case.

To summarize, Buraschi *et al.* (2010) show that if we assume the process followed by our assets adheres to a model that captures the risk associated with AD, then the calibration of this model implies an allocation amongst the assets that is significantly impacted by the market's AD characteristics. The demand for covariance hedging increases as the level of AD increases and as the number of assets in the portfolio increases. Furthermore, the magnitude of the required hedge is non-negligible. This reflects the work of Alcock and Hatherley (2017), who conclude that AD is as important as systematic risk in explaining the return variation in returns. It is also apparent from Buraschi *et al.* (2010) that assets that provide exposure to correlation that changes with spot are required to hedge AD risk, particularly in the case where we do not hold or are unable to hold fixed-income assets against our equity underlyings. This further necessitates the need for equity derivative products that are sensitive to correlation skew.

5.4 EQUITY CORRELATION PRODUCTS

A number of multi-asset derivative products provide investors with exposure to correlation including dispersion trades, correlation swaps, basket options and best-of/worst-of products. We briefly describe these products and the manner in which they provide exposure to implied correlation. For a more thorough treatment of these products, refer to Bouzoubaa and Osseiran (2008).

5.4.1 Dispersion

Dispersion trading involves taking a long (short) position in the volatility of a basket or index and pairing this with a short (long) position in the volatility of the basket's constituents. Taking DAX index dispersion trading as an example, a long exposure to correlation occurs if we buy DAX index volatility and sell a weighted basket of the DAX constituent volatilities. The short exposure to the single stock volatilities has the effect of mitigating the long exposure to the single stock volatility via the long index derivative exposure. What is left, therefore, is the (long) exposure to correlation.

Dispersion trades can also be executed with bespoke basket options against their constituents. This tends to be a popular inter-bank trade where the volatility exposure is traded as a basket call versus an equal weighted basket of constituent call options, typically referred to as a call-vs-call trade (Zetocha, 2015).

The correlation exposure of the dispersion trade can be represented by Equation (5.1). Here we see that a correlation exposure is obtained by computing a ratio of index and single stock volatilities, particularly if we compute

$$\rho_I \approx \frac{\sigma_I^2}{\left(\sum_{ij} w_i w_j \sigma_i \sigma_j\right)^2}. \tag{5.9}$$

Following Jacquier and Slaoui (2010), the profit and loss (P&L) for a delta-hedge dispersion strategy is given by

$$P\&L_{Disp} = P\&L_{Disp}^{\Gamma} + P\&L_{Disp}^{Vol}, \tag{5.10}$$

where the gamma P&L is given by

$$P\&L_{Disp}^{\Gamma} = \frac{1}{T} \sum_{i=1}^{n} \left[\left(\left(\frac{dS_i}{S_i}\right)^2 - \sigma_i^2 dt\right) \right](\alpha_i - w_i^2) + \frac{1}{T} \sum_{i \neq j} w_i w_j \sigma_i \sigma_j (\rho - \hat{\rho}) dt \tag{5.11}$$

and the volatility P&L is given by

$$P\&L_{Disp}^{Vol} = \sum_{i=1}^{n} \alpha_i \left(\text{Vega}_i d\sigma_i + \frac{1}{2} \text{Volga}_i \xi_i^2 \sigma_i^2 dt + \text{Vanna}_i \sigma_i S_i \rho_i \xi_i dt \right) \tag{5.12}$$

$$- \left(\text{Vega}_I d\sigma_I + \frac{1}{2} \text{Volga}_I \xi_I^2 \sigma_I^2 dt + \text{Vanna}_I \sigma_I S_I \rho_I \xi_I dt \right).$$

Here, Vega is the sensitivity of the derivative to changes in volatility, Volga is the sensitivity of Vega to changes in volatility, Vanna is the sensitivity of Vega to changes in spot, ρ and $\hat{\rho}$ are the average basket implied and realized correlation, respectively, ξ is the volatility convexity, w_i is the weight assigned to a stock making up the variance of the index, σ_I^2, and α_i is the weight associated with the exposure to the constituent underlyings when forming the dispersion trade. It is not necessary for the weight of each single stock exposure in the basket to equal the weight of the single stocks in making up the index, however, in the case where the weights are equal, Equation (5.11) simplifies to

$$P\&L_{Disp}^{\Gamma} = \frac{1}{T} \sum_{i \neq j} w_i w_j \sigma_i \sigma_j (\rho - \hat{\rho}) dt. \tag{5.13}$$

5.4.1.1 Trading Volatility The product chosen to trade volatility will ultimately have an impact on the price (in correlation points) at which correlation is traded when executing the dispersion strategy.

Straddle Dispersion A long straddle is formed by buying a put and a call option with the same strike and maturity on a given underlying. For an ATM straddle, the delta (the sensitivity of the derivative to changes in spot) of the structure will be close to zero at the beginning of the trade, implying that the combination of the ATM put and call can be used to take a directionless view of realized volatility.

One well-known downside to straddles is that they lose their delta neutrality as spot moves away from the strike level. For example, if spot shifts upwards by 20%, the call delta might shift from +0.5 to, say, +0.7. In contrast, the put option delta might move from −0.5 with spot at the strike to, say, −0.3 with spot up 20%. The new net delta of the structure with spot up 20% is therefore +0.4. Unless this delta is hedged regularly, the strategy is sensitive to changes in spot. Regular delta hedging increases the cost of trading dispersion due to the additional maintenance required and the transaction costs associated with trades in the underlying stocks.

Variance Swaps Dispersion Swap dispersion involves trading correlation via variance swaps, volatility swaps or gamma swaps. These swaps can provide a cleaner and simpler exposure to volatility than straddle dispersion, which in turn implies a cleaner exposure to correlation.

The payoff of a variance swap is given by

$$VarSwap = \mathcal{N} \left(\frac{1}{T} \int_0^T \sigma_t^2 dt - K^2 \right),$$

where $\mathcal{N}$ is the variance notional, often expressed in terms of the dollar notional per vega or volatility point, K^2 is the variance swap strike and

$$\int_0^T \sigma_t^2 dt \propto \sum_{i=1}^{N_A} \left[\ln \left(\frac{S(t_i)}{S(t_{i-1})} \right)^2 \right]$$

is the realized volatility between time 0 and T, where N_A is the number of trading days between 0 and T and $S(t_i)$ is the stock price at time i. The constant of proportionality is typically given by an annualization factor.

As shown by Demeterfi et al. (1999), the variance swap is replicated by a static position in a portfolio of European call and put options and a dynamic position in the underlying asset. The fair strike that ensures the variance swap has zero initial value is given by a weighted strip of European options:

$$K^2 = \frac{2e^{rT}}{T} \left(\int_0^{F_T} \frac{dK}{K^2} P(S_0, K, T) + \int_{F_T}^{\infty} \frac{dK}{K^2} C(S_0, K, T) \right),$$

where F_T is the forward value of the stock and P and C are put and call prices, respectively. A variance swap that is replicated with a portfolio of delta-hedged options that are weighted by the inverse of their squared strike produces a derivative that has constant cash gamma and vega that is constant in strike space (that is, zero vanna), but varies linearly with the time to maturity.

One well-known downside to the variance swap is that variance swaps are sensitive to jumps (Broadie and Jain, 2008). This can be problematic in the case where, for example, a company defaults and their stock price drops to zero. Such an event can cause realized volatility to explode, and as a result, it is market convention to cap variance swaps on single names at 250% of the uncapped variance swap fair strike. The payoff of the variance swap is then given by

$$VarSwap_{capped} = \mathcal{N} \left(\min \left[\frac{1}{T} \int_0^T \sigma_t^2 dt, 2.5 K_{uncapped}^2 \right] - K^2 \right).$$

Capping the realized variance is therefore akin to selling a call on realized variance and hence the variance swap is now priced as an option on variance. The capped variance swap is now exposed to vol-of-vol, otherwise known as volatility convexity. Unless the single names in the basket are weighted proportionally to each single stock's volatility convexity, the dispersion trade will have a net exposure to vol-of-vol when traded using capped variance swap contracts.

It is also worth noting that variance swaps will display a positive skew delta reflecting the negative skew typically found in equity implied volatility surfaces. The negative skew implies that out-of-the-money (OTM) puts tend to display larger vol that ATM options or even OTM calls. Therefore, the variance swap fair value will tend to display sensitivity to downward spot moves via the OTM puts. Like the exposure to vol-of-vol for capped variance swaps, dispersion trades with stock legs that are not weighted to account for this skew delta will invariably display a net skew delta exposure. Furthermore, if we assume that skew delta on an index can be decomposed in terms of the skew delta of the index's constituent underlyings, plus a term representing the skew correlation between the individual underlyings, then shorting a basket of variance swaps written on single name underlyings will ultimately imply that the skew delta exposure of the variance swap dispersion trade can be attributed to the skew correlation between the underlyings. The residual risk is the tendency for volatility to jointly explode when the spot price of the underlying crashes.

Volatility Swaps   The volatility swap can be loosely interpreted as a forward contract on future realized volatility of the underlying and is closely related to the variance swap where the volatility swap payoff is a function of the square root of the realized variance:

$$VolSwap = \mathcal{N}\left(\sqrt{\frac{1}{T}\int_0^T \sigma_t^2 dt} - K\right).$$

The volatility swap can be thought of as a variance swap with a convexity adjustment. To see this, consider the Taylor expansion for $\sqrt{x}$:

$$\sqrt{x} \approx \sqrt{x_0} + \frac{1}{2\sqrt{x_0}}(x - x_0) + \frac{1}{8\sqrt{x_0^3}}(x - x_0)^2.$$

Substituting the realized variance σ_R^2 for x and taking expectations, we are left with

$$\mathbb{E}[\sigma_R] \approx \sqrt{\mathbb{E}[\sigma_R^2]} + \frac{Var[\sigma_R^2]}{8\mathbb{E}[\sigma_R^2]^{3/2}}.$$

Therefore, the expected volatility is approximated by the square root of the expected variance plus an adjustment. Like the capped variance swap, the volatility swap is sensitive to volatility convexity where the change in volatility is a function of the volatility level. Unlike the variance swap, the volatility swap cannot be repriced with a replicating portfolio, implying that the volatility swap is harder to hedge, making these swaps less attractive (and therefore less liquid) than variance swaps.

Gamma Swaps   A gamma swap represents a slight modification of the variance swap and can be hedged with a strip of OTM options. The gamma swap payoff is given by

$$GammaSwap = \mathcal{N}\left(\frac{1}{T}\int_0^T \sigma_t^2 \frac{S_t}{S_0} dt - K^2\right),$$

where the gamma swap fair strike is given by

$$K = \frac{2}{T}\frac{e^{2rT}}{S_0}\left[\int_0^{F_T} \frac{dK}{K} P(S_0, K, T) + \int_{F_T}^{\infty} \frac{dK}{K} C(S_0, K, T)\right].$$

The gamma swap displays constant gamma, contrasting with variance swaps that display constant cash gamma. Because the realized variance is multiplied by the relative price, the gamma swap is less susceptible to jumps and therefore does not require a capped payoff. In essence, the weight associated with downside OTM puts is lowered and replaced with an exposure to the market level. Hence, the gamma swap is useful if the investor has a view on the direction of both spot and volatility.

Corridor Variance Swaps A corridor variance swap is a variance swap that accrues realized variance when the underlying is within a range, $[L, U]$. The realized variance is given by

$$RV_{corr} = \frac{252}{N} \sum_{i=1}^{N} \mathbb{I}_{\{L<S(t_{i-1})\leq U\}} \left[\ln \left(\frac{S(t_i)}{S(t_{i-1})} \right)^2 \right]$$

and the payoff is given by

$$CorrVar = \mathcal{N} \left(RV_{corr} - K^2_{corr} \right),$$

where K^2_{corr} is the corridor variance swap strike and T is the maturity of the trade in days. Therefore, if the stock lies outside the range $[L, U]$, the contribution to the value of realized variance is zero. As a result, the corridor variance swap should be worth less than or equal to the value of an ordinary variance swap. This contract can be used to take a view on both the direction and the volatility of the underlying. Carr and Lewis (2004) demonstrate that the corridor variance swap can be replicated with a static position on options and bonds, analogous to an ordinary variance swap.

Conditional Variance Swaps Related to the corridor variance swap, the conditional variance swap also accrues variance when the underlying is within a range, $[L, U]$, however this time, the contribution of observations lying outside the range is completely ignored in the realized variance calculation

$$RV_{cond} = \frac{252}{D} \sum_{i=1}^{N} \mathbb{I}_{\{L<S(t_{i-1})\leq U\}} \left[\ln \left(\frac{S(t_i)}{S(t_{i-1})} \right)^2 \right],$$

where D equals the number of days inside the range, $\sum \mathbb{I}_{\{L<S(t_{i-1})\leq U\}}$. The conditional variance swap payoff is therefore given by

$$CondVar = \mathcal{N} \frac{D}{T} \left(RV_{cond} - K^2_{cond} \right),$$

where K^2_{cond} is the conditional variance swap strike. Allen *et al.* (2006) show that the conditional variance swap can be written in terms of a corridor variance swap plus a range accrual product, that is:

$$CondVar = \mathcal{N} \frac{D}{T} \left(RV_{cond} - \frac{T}{D} K^2_{corr} + \frac{T}{D} K^2_{corr} - K^2_{cond} \right)$$

$$= \mathcal{N} \left(\frac{D}{T} RV_{cond} - K^2_{corr} \right) + \mathcal{N} \left(K^2_{corr} - \frac{D}{T} K^2_{cond} \right),$$

where the first part of the expression is equal to a corridor variance swap and the latter part is the range accrual. The range accrual can be hedged with a static strip of digital options, where the digital options are, in turn, approximated by put and call spreads.

For both the corridor and the conditional variance swap, it is possible to define an up-style contract where the range is defined by $[U, \infty]$, and a down-style contract where the range is defined by $[0, L]$. As a result, it is possible to take a view on the volatility skew by trading the up-style contract against the down-style contract. For example, a long skew exposure may be obtained by being long the down-style contract and short the up-style contract.

5.4.1.2 Dispersion Leg Weightings In forming a dispersion trade, the exposure to each constituent in the trade, α_i, need not equal the weight of the constituent making up the index leg, w_i. The choice of weights, α_i, will ultimately dictate the risk characteristics of the dispersion trade. For example, when $\alpha_i = w_i$, the vega on the index leg is unlikely to equal the weighted vega of the basket leg exposure. Hence, the P&L of the dispersion trade will have net non-zero vega.

A number of modifications to the single leg exposures, α, can be made to target particular risk characteristics.

Theta-Neutral Dispersion A theta-neutral dispersion trade occurs when the theta of the index leg equals the weighted theta of the single stock leg. In this case, implied volatility on the index leg is assumed to move by the same percentage as the single stock leg. Following Equation (5.9), theta-neutral dispersion can be interpreted as correlation-weighted dispersion, where the profit and loss of the trade depends on the difference between implied and realized correlation. This weighting strategy tends to produce a relatively clean correlation exposure compared with other leg weighting schemes, however the strategy does tend to be short vega and short cash gamma.

Vega-Neutral Dispersion A vega-neutral dispersion trade occurs when the vega of the index leg equals the weighted vega of the single stock leg. Vega neutrality assumes that the implied volatility of the index leg moves by the same absolute amount as the single stock leg, causing the contribution of vega to be zero in Equation (5.10). The dispersion strategy is net short theta and net long cash gamma.

Gamma-Neutral Dispersion Finally, gamma-neutral dispersion trades occur when the gamma of the index leg equals the gamma of the single stock leg. These trades tend to be short theta and short vega.

5.4.2 Correlation Swaps

Correlation swaps can be used to provide exposure to the average correlation among a basket of underlyings. The correlation swap payoff is given by

$$CorrSwap = \mathcal{N}(\rho_R - K_\rho),$$

where K_ρ is the correlation swap strike and ρ_R is the annualized average realized correlation amongst the basket underlyings, typically given by

$$\rho_R = \frac{\sum_{i \neq j} w_i w_j \hat{\rho}_{i,j}}{\sum_{i \neq j} w_i w_j}.$$

Like the variance swap, the correlation swap is therefore a forward contract written over realized correlation. Although the correlation swap can be used to provide a pure exposure to implied correlation, the lack of a replicating portfolio to replicate the payoff means that the correlation swap market tends to be highly illiquid. Bossu (2006) provides an approximation to the correlation swap payoff and illustrates how this pseudo-payoff can be quasi-replicated by variance dispersion trades. Demeterfi *et al.* (1999) demonstrate that the difference between the implied correlation of a dispersion trade and the strike of a correlation swap is given by Equation (5.12), namely the volatility P&L component of the dispersion trade. Hence, the correlation swap is similar to a theta-neutral dispersion strategy.

5.4.3 Worst-Of Options

A worst-of option is a derivative whose payoff is a function of the worst-performing underlying in a basket. For an n-asset basket, the payoff of a worst-of call is given by

$$WOCall = \max\{0, \min\{S_1(T), S_2(T), \dots, S_n(T)\} - K\}.$$

The more negatively correlated the assets, the lower the worst-of call payoff, implying that the worst-of call is long correlation (short dispersion). If we define correlation skew as the difference between the implied correlation for relative strikes less than 100% and the implied correlation for relative strikes greater than 100%, then the derivative is short correlation skew as the call increases in value if upside correlation (for strikes greater than 100%) increases.

Although a call option is typically also long volatility, the impact of higher volatility may also cause dispersion to increase, thereby reducing the price of the call. Therefore an event that increases both AD and implied correlation may have mixed effects on the price of the worst-of call.

Conversely, a worst-of put is given by

$$WOPut = \max\{0, K - \min\{S_1(T), S_2(T), \dots, S_n(T)\}\}.$$

Negative correlation amongst the assets increases the payoff of the worst-of put option, implying that a worst-of put option is short correlation (long dispersion) and short correlation skew. Like call options, put options are also long volatility, and in this case, long volatility skew. However, downside moves in spot that increase volatility are also likely to increase downside dependence, which decreases the value of the worst-of put option.

5.4.4   Basket Options

The payoff of the basket call option is given by

$$BasketCall = \max\left[0, \sum_{i=1}^{n} w_i S_i(T) - K\right], \tag{5.14}$$

where w_i is the weight of each constituent in the basket and $S_i(T)$ is the price of asset i at maturity T. The product is long vega, like an ordinary call, and long correlation, meaning that the value of the basket call increases if each of the assets appreciates over the life of the trade. Like worst-of options, if we assume that correlation skew is measured as the difference between the implied correlation for relative strikes less than 100% and the implied correlation for relative strikes greater than 100%, then the basket call option is short correlation skew since a decrease in correlation skew will occur if implied correlation for call strikes increases relative to the implied correlation for put strikes. The basket put option is defined similarly:

$$BasketPut = \max\left[0, K - \sum_{i=1}^{n} w_i S_i(T)\right], \tag{5.15}$$

which is also long vega and long correlation. Using the above definition of implied correlation skew, the basket put option is long correlation skew.

5.4.5   Derivative Strategies to Hedge AD

The multi-underlying derivatives described up to this point can be used to provide an exposure to correlation. At best they provide an implicit exposure to correlation skew and hence to AD risk. Given the existing universe of products, we propose two strategies that could be used to better target AD risk.

5.4.5.1   Basket Call Spread/Basket Risk Reversal   The implied correlation exposure of the basket option is a function of the strike of the option. A long basket call spread involves trading a long basket call with strike K_1 and a short basket call with strike K_2 where $K_1 < K_2$. The strategy payoff is therefore zero for basket prices less than K_1 at expiry, and capped at K_2 for basket prices greater than K_2 at expiry. The basket call spread is long correlation at strike level K_1 and short correlation at strike level K_2, implying that the call spread is long correlation skew. Note, however, that the strategy is also long delta, implying that we are implicitly bullish on the spot price of the basket. Since AD tends to be large during ordinary market conditions, such a strategy might be expected to be an effective hedge for increasing AD risk as the market settles into a period of quiet, consistent with the observations of Alcock and Hatherley (2017). As an alternative basket option strategy, selling a risk reversal involves buying a basket put with strike K_1 and selling a basket call with strike K_2, where $K_1 < K_2$. The basket risk reversal is long correlation skew since it is long downside correlation via the basket put and short upside correlation via the basket call. In addition, the product is short delta, implying that the risk reversal can be traded in the situation where we need to hedge a down move in the basket in conjunction with an increase in AD.

Although these trades will produce an exposure to correlation skew, the exposure is unlikely to be a clean one and will be subject to the risks inherent in outright basket option trades.

5.4.5.2 Conditional Variance Dispersion Spread

Alcock and Hatherley (2017) measure AD by computing correlations conditional on joint stock returns below a threshold and comparing them with correlations conditional on joint stock returns above a threshold. The spirit of this calculation can be replicated by manufacturing a long downside correlation exposure via a down-style conditional variance swap dispersion trade over the range $[0, K]$ and a short upside correlation exposure via an up-style conditional variance swap dispersion trade over the range $[K, \infty]$. We are therefore long downside correlation and short upside correlation and the strategy is therefore long correlation skew.

To be consistent with Alcock and Hatherley (2017), the basic dispersion spread trade should be modified such that we trade a weighted strip of down-style conditional variance swap dispersion trades against a weighted strip of up-style conditional variance swap dispersion trades where the weight decreases as we move away from the ATM level. For example, if we let $k = \{0, K/N, 2K/N, \dots, N\}$ refer to the range, $[0, K]$, that has been divided into N regions of size K/N, then a strip of down-style conditional variance swap dispersion trades amounts to trading

$$Disp^{Down} = \sum_{i=0}^{N-1} w_i Disp_{k_i, k_{i+1}}^{CondVar}, \quad k_i \in k$$

where i is the index of set k and $Disp_{L,U}^{CondVar}$ refers to a conditional variance swap dispersion defined between some lower bound, L and an upper bound, U. A similar expression can be formulated for trading up-style dispersion. By trading in a weighted fashion over the strike range, we are able to place more weight on the dependence characteristics close to the ATM strike and control the contribution to the overall dependence exposure from the wings. Typically, option liquidity in the wings can be thin, particularly for short-dated maturities. One would expect the accuracy of the implied correlation measured in the wings to be lower than when implied correlation is measured in more liquid strike ranges.

Given that variance swaps are sensitive to jumps, one would expect the downside conditional variance swap to be affected more by jumps than the upside conditional variance swap, since equities are more likely to jump downwards than upwards. A conditional variance dispersion spread may therefore produce an over-exposure to downside vol-of-vol. To mitigate this, it might be preferable, in principle, to trade upside and downside dispersion using conditional upside and conditional downside gamma swaps.

5.5 MODELS FOR CORRELATION SKEW

When trading derivatives that target implied correlation skew, it becomes increasingly important to keep track of the net exposure to correlation skew across all the exposures in a given portfolio. This necessitates a model for asset prices that is aware of implied correlation skew. A number of choices are available that achieve this. For example, Buraschi *et al.* (2010) demonstrate the ability of the multivariate Wishart process to capture the correlation that is a function of the change in spot price. This stochastic correlation model was developed independently in the context of derivative pricing by da Fonseca *et al.* (2007) and has been expanded upon by numerous authors, including, for example, Romo (2012a) in the case of pricing digital out-performance options, Romo (2012b) in the case of pricing worst-of options, and Branger and Muck (2012) in the case of pricing quanto options. One downside to the Wishart model for correlation skew is that the model struggles to replicate short-dated volatility skew (Zetocha, 2015). Alternative models that account for correlation skew include instantaneous correlation models, local correlation models and copula-based models. These models can be used to assess the impact of correlation skew on traditional multi-underlying derivatives and therefore the effectiveness of their ability to hedge AD. We consider these models briefly in this section.

5.5.1 Instantaneous Correlation Models

The instantaneous correlation model is part of the stochastic correlation model family where the correlation coefficient diffusion is based on a Jacobi process.

Consider a generic SV model (Gatheral, 2006):

$$dS_t = \mu_t S_t dt + \sqrt{v_t} S_t dW_t$$

$$dv_t = \alpha(S_t, v_t, t)dt + \eta\beta(S_t, v_t, t)dZ_t$$

where

$$dW_t dZ_t = \rho dt.$$

Traditional stochastic correlation models assume that the correlation between standard Brownian motions, dW_t and dZ_t, is constant. Following van Emmerich (2006), Delbaen and Shirakawa (2002) and Zetocha (2015), a simple extension is to assume that ρ is fully stochastic:

$$d\rho_t = a(t, \rho_t)dt + b(t, \rho_t)dK_t,$$

where $\rho_0 \in [-1, 1]$ and K is a standard Brownian motion. In order to ensure that ρ_t is bounded to $[-1, 1]$, the functional for $d\rho_t$ is given by

$$d\rho_t = \alpha(\bar{\rho} - \rho_t)dt + \beta\sqrt{(1 - \rho_t)(\rho_t - \rho_{min})}d\hat{W}_t, \tag{5.16}$$

where $\alpha, \beta > 0$ is the speed of mean reversion and volatility of instantaneous correlation, respectively, and $\hat{W}_t$ is a standard Brownian motion. In order to incorporate correlation skew, we assume that

$$dW_t d\hat{W}_t = \rho_{CS} dt,$$

where the constant, ρ_{CS}, is the correlation between correlation and the stock process. In principle, one may also account for correlation between correlation and volatility by writing

$$dZ_t d\hat{W}_t = \rho_{CV} dt,$$

where the constant, ρ_{CV}, is the correlation between correlation and the variance process. As an example of the implementation of this model, Zetocha (2015) considers N stocks where each stock follows a local volatility diffusion:

$$dS_t^i = \mu_t^i S_t^i dt + \sigma^i(S_t^i, t) S_t^i dW_t^i, \tag{5.17}$$

where each asset displays correlation:

$$dW_t^i dW_t^j = \rho_t dt,$$

$$dW_t^i d\hat{W}_t = \rho_{CS} dt,$$

where ρ_t evolves according to Equation (5.16). The value of ρ_{min} needed to ensure the semi-definiteness is given by

$$\rho_{min} = \frac{-1 + N\rho_{CS}^2}{N - 1}.$$

The advantage of this specific model implementation is that it's moments are analytically tractable, as shown by Zetocha (2015), and the correlation skew can be incorporated into the model transparently. On the downside, calibration of the model is troublesome by virtue of the fact that it is not common to observe liquidly traded instruments that display exposure to the risk factors that the model attempts to capture. Furthermore, the model can struggle to replicate index volatility levels in front months. In the latter case, Zetocha (2015) illustrates that the addition of a jump term to Equation (5.16) may be required to account for the magnitude of front-month correlation skew. However, while this improves the empirical model fit, it further increases the calibration burden in that a set of jump parameters must now be calibrated and maintained.

5.5.2 Local Correlation Modelling

Local correlation models extend local volatility modelling to multiple dimensions. Unlike stochastic models, the local correlation model assumes that correlation is a function of spot and is therefore driven by spot noise. A good summary of current local correlation methodologies is provided by Guyon (2013), who suggests that existing implementations fall into one of two categories. The first class infers local correlation from the local volatility properties of the index and its constituents, while the second focuses explicitly on correlation and assumes that correlation is a function of the index level.

Langnau (2010) provides an example of the first class of models, extending Dupire's local volatility model to the multi-asset case. Consider n assets that evolve according to the local volatility diffusion described in Equation (5.17), where

$$dW_t^i dW_t^j = \rho_{ij}(t) dt$$

describes the pairwise correlation between the ith and jth diffusion. For each asset, i, assume there exists a set of vanilla European options such that $\partial V_t^i(T, K)/\partial T$ and $\partial V_t^i(T, K)^2/\partial K^2$ exist and are continuous for all T and K, where V is the derivative value. Suppose further that the basket

$$dS_t^0 = \sum_{i=1}^{n} \alpha_i dS_t^i$$

can be weakly described by a univariate diffusion

$$dS_t^0 = \mu_t^0 S_t^0 dt + \sigma^0(S_t^0, t) S_t^0 dW_t^0,$$

where basket weights are given by $0 \leq \alpha_i \leq \infty$. The absence of dispersion arbitrage requires the drift term of the basket to match the weighted drift term of the constituents

$$S_t^0 \mu_t^0 = \sum_{i=1}^n \alpha_i \mu_t^i S_t^i,$$

and further, the local volatility of the index matches the weighted local volatility of the basket constituents

$$\left(\sum_{i=1}^n \alpha_i S_t^i \right)^2 \sigma^0(S_t^0, t)^2 = \sum_{i,j=1}^n \alpha_i \alpha_j S_t^i S_t^j \sigma^i(S_t^i, t) \sigma^j(S_t^j, t) \rho_{ij}(t).$$

If, in addition, there exists a ρ_{ij}^{down} such that $\rho_{ij}(t) \geq \rho_{ij}^{down}$ for all i, j and t, then a necessary condition for the absence of dispersion arbitrage is that

$$cov_{LB} = \sum_{i,j=1}^n \alpha_i \alpha_j S_t^i S_t^j \sigma^i(S_t^i, t) \sigma^j(S_t^j, t) \rho_{ij}^{down} \leq \left(\sum_{i=1}^n \alpha_i S_t^i \right)^2 \sigma^0(S_t^0, t)^2$$

$$\leq \sum_{i,j=1}^n \alpha_i \alpha_j S_t^i S_t^j \sigma^i(S_t^i, t) \sigma^j(S_t^j, t)$$

$$= cov_{UB}.$$

The local correlation model is then given by

$$\rho(t) = \hat{\rho}_{ij}((u^\star)^2),$$

where $u^\star$ is a function of the spot and is given by

$$u^\star = \begin{cases} \sqrt{-\dfrac{cov_{LB} - \sigma^0(S_t^0, t)^2 (S_t^0)^2}{cov_0 - \sigma^0(S_t^0, t)^2 (S_t^0)^2}} & \text{if } cov_0 - \sigma^0(S_t^0, t)^2 (S_t^0)^2 > 0, \\[4mm] \sqrt{-\dfrac{cov_0 - \sigma^0(S_t^0, t)^2 (S_t^0)^2}{cov_{UB} - \sigma^0(S_t^0, t)^2 (S_t^0)^2}} & \text{else.} \end{cases}$$

Here:

$$cov_0 \equiv \sum_{i,j=1}^n \alpha_i \alpha_j S_t^i S_t^j \sigma^i(S_t^i, t) \sigma^j(S_t^j, t) \rho_{ij}^{centre},$$

where ρ_{ij}^{centre} and ρ_{ij}^{down} define a family of correlation matrices such that

$$\hat{\rho}_{ij}(u) \equiv \begin{cases} \dfrac{\rho_{ij}^{down} + u^2 \rho_{ij}^{centre}}{1 + u^2} & u \leq u_0 \\[4mm] \dfrac{\rho_{ij}^{centre} + u^2 \rho_{ij}^{up}}{1 + u^2} & u > u_0 \end{cases}$$

for some threshold, u_0, where it is assumed that $\rho_{ij}^{up} = 1$.

Reghai (2010) provides an example of the second class of local correlation model. Assuming simplified spot dynamics:

$$dS_t^i = \sigma^i(S_t^i, t)S_t^i dW_t^i,$$

where the correlation between the Brownian motions is given by

$$\rho(\lambda)_t = (1 - \lambda(S_t^1, \dots, S_t^n, t)) \, \rho + \lambda(S_t^1, \dots, S_t^n, t)\Theta,$$

where ρ is a symmetric positive semi-definite matrix with diagonal of 1, Θ is an $n \times n$ matrix of ones and $\lambda(S_t^1, \dots, S_t^n, t)$ depends on state variables $(S^1, \dots, S^n)$. The implied local correlation, $\rho_{ij}(t)$, is effectively recast in terms of some baseline correlation matrix, ρ, and a state-dependent adjustment factor, λ. Reghai (2010) suggests parametrizing λ such that

$$\lambda(S_t^1, \dots, S_t^n, t) = \lambda_0 f(L_t, t),$$

where $L_t = h(S_t^1, \dots, S_t^n)$. Here, λ_0 is interpreted as a bump that perturbs f in a manner consistent with the current market conditions encapsulated by the state variable L_t. By writing f as a function of time, t, it becomes possible to impose different short-term and long-term dynamics that respond differently to market moves.

According to Guyon (2013), the downside to both the Langnau (2010) approach and the Reghai (2010) approach is that both methods can fail to produce a correlation matrix that is positive semi-definite. In response to this, Guyon (2013) parametrizes a local correlation model such that $a + b\lambda$ is local in the index level, where a and b can be chosen to ensure positive semi-definiteness at all times. The Reghai (2010) model is represented within this framework by setting $a = 0$ and $b = 1$, while the Langnau (2010) model is recovered with $a = \sum_i \sigma_i^2$ and $b = -\sum_{ij} \sigma_i \sigma_j$.

5.5.3 Copula Models

As indicated by Langnau (2010), a Gaussian copula is insufficient to explain the implied correlation skew that is built into index-implied volatility smiles. This indicates that the dependence structure in equity derivative markets is richer than the assumed Gaussian dependence structure upon which much of modern finance was built.

Lucic (2013) proposes the use of a product copula to account for correlation skew, where the dependence structure is modelled as the product of two Gaussian copulas (where Gaussian correlations are chosen in an attempt to match the empirical dependence characteristics). The downside to non-Gaussian copulas, like the product copula, as models for correlation skew is that the copula can only handle one maturity at a time and therefore cannot be used to price path-dependent options (Zetocha, 2015).

5.5.3.1 Developing the Multivariate Skew-T Copula

Notwithstanding this limitation, we consider the use of the multivariate skew-T (MST) copula as an alternative non-Gaussian copula that might be used to model higher-order dependence structures. The advantage of the skew-T over the product copula is that linear dependence and higher-order dependence can be represented separately within the same function. This makes it possible to attribute characteristics to linear dependence and higher-order dependence on the basis of their calibrated values.

Following the exposition described by Smith *et al.* (2012), an elliptical distribution can be transformed into a skew-elliptical distribution by conditioning on a hidden truncated random variable. Specifically, let

$$\begin{pmatrix} Z \\ \epsilon \end{pmatrix} \sim t_{2r}\left(\begin{pmatrix} 0 \\ 0 \end{pmatrix}, \Omega = \begin{pmatrix} \Gamma & 0 \\ 0 & I \end{pmatrix}, \nu \right),$$

where Z, ϵ are both $(r \times 1)$ vectors with a joint multivariate t-distribution with zero mode, v degrees of freedom and an $(r \times r)$ shape matrix, Ω. Following Sahu et al. (2003), consider the following transformation:

$$X = DZ + \epsilon,$$

$$Q = Z,$$

where $D = diag(\delta_1, \ldots, \delta_r)$ is a diagonal matrix where $\delta_i \in \mathbb{R}$ are skew parameters. It follows that

$$\begin{pmatrix} X \\ Q \end{pmatrix} = \begin{pmatrix} I & D \\ 0 & I \end{pmatrix} \begin{pmatrix} \epsilon \\ Z \end{pmatrix} \sim t_{2r} \left(\begin{pmatrix} 0 \\ 0 \end{pmatrix}, \Omega = \begin{pmatrix} \Gamma + D^2 & D \\ D & I \end{pmatrix}, v \right).$$

We say that $(X|Q > 0)$ is skew-T distributed, provided $Q_i > 0 \; \forall \; i$, and the resulting density is given by

$$f_{St}(x; \Gamma, D, v) = \frac{2^r}{det(\Gamma + D^2)^{1/2}} f_t \left((\Gamma + D^2)^{-\frac{1}{2}} x; v \right) \mathbb{P}(V > 0; x),$$

where $V \sim t_r(D(\Gamma + D^2)^{-1}x, \frac{S(x) + v}{r + v}(I - D(\Gamma + D^2)^{-1}D), r + v)$, $f_t(x; v)$ is a $t_r(0, I, v)$ density and $S(x) = x'(\Gamma + D^2)x$.

The first moment of the MST distribution is given by Smith et al. (2012) and Sahu et al. (2003) as

$$\mathbb{E}(X) = \mu^\star = \kappa(v)\delta, \quad \text{where } \kappa(v) = \left(\frac{v}{\pi} \right)^{1/2} \frac{\Gamma_f((v-1)/2)}{\Gamma_f(v/2)}, \tag{5.18}$$

where Γ_f is the gamma function. The second moment is given by

$$var(X) = \Sigma^\star = (\Gamma + D^2)\frac{v}{v-2} - \left[\kappa(v)^2 \iota\iota' - (\iota\iota' - I)\frac{2v}{\pi(v-2)} \right] \odot \delta\delta', \tag{5.19}$$

where $\delta = (\delta_1, \ldots, \delta_r)'$, $\iota = (1, \ldots, 1)'$ and $\odot$ is the Hadamard (i.e., dot) matrix multiplication operator. Equation (5.19) can be rewritten as

$$\Sigma^\star_{ii} = \Gamma_{ii} \left(\frac{v}{v-2} \right) + \delta_i^2 \left[\frac{v}{v-2} - \kappa(v)^2 \right], \tag{5.20}$$

$$\Sigma^\star_{ij} = \Gamma_{ij} \left(\frac{v}{v-2} \right) + \delta_i\delta_j \left[\frac{2}{\pi}\frac{v}{v-2} - \kappa(v)^2 \right], \tag{5.21}$$

where Γ_{ij} is the (i, j)th element of Γ. Equation (5.21) indicates that covariance is given by a traditional covariance matrix (Γ_{ij}) plus some adjustment coefficients associated with individual asset skew ($\delta_i\delta_j$) and a global parameter loosely reflecting global kurtosis (v).

To demonstrate how this may be used, we provide an alternative analysis of the effect of AD on the optimal portfolio in a one-period setting. We derive new mean-variance efficient frontier boundaries by extending the conclusions drawn by Cochrane (2005) using $\Sigma^\star$ in Equation (5.21) in place of Σ, the traditional covariance matrix.

Following the stochastic discount factor approach to asset pricing:

$$p = \mathbb{E}(mx)$$

$$= \mathbb{E}(m)\mathbb{E}(x) + cov(m, x),$$

suppose that the covariance between m and payoff x is actually governed by Equation (5.21):

$$p = \mathbb{E}(m)\mathbb{E}(x) + cov^{\star}(m, x)$$

$$= \mathbb{E}(m)\mathbb{E}(x) + cov(m, x)\left(\frac{v}{v-2}\right) + \delta_m \delta_x \left[\frac{2}{\pi}\frac{v}{v-2} - \kappa(v)^2\right]. \tag{5.22}$$

In the above, we measure the AD between an asset and the universal marginal rate of substitution, m, that is, the rate at which an investor is willing to substitute consumption at time t for consumption at time $t+1$:

$$m_{t+1} = \beta \frac{u'(c_{t+1})}{u'(c_t)}.$$

Because marginal utility decreases as consumption increases, if asset payoffs positively covary with consumption, asset prices will be lower, that is $cov(c, x) > 0$, but $cov(m, x) < 0$. By extension, in order to induce lower prices in assets with lower-tail AD, we require $(\delta_c, \delta_x) < 0$, implying $\delta_m > 0$, $\delta_x < 0$ and therefore their product $\delta_m \delta_x < 0$. Conversely, for upper-tail AD, to induce higher prices, we require $\delta_c < 0$, $\delta_x > 0$, implying $(\delta_m, \delta_x) > 0$ and therefore their product $\delta_m \delta_x > 0$. Dividing Equation (5.22) by p to convert to the return space, and letting

$$K = \left[\frac{2}{\pi}\frac{v}{v-2} - \kappa(v)^2\right],$$

Equation (5.22) becomes

$$1 = \mathbb{E}(m)\mathbb{E}(R^i) + \rho_{m,R^i}\sigma(R^i)\sigma(m)\left(\frac{v}{v-2}\right) + \delta_m \delta_{R^i} K$$

$$\Leftrightarrow \mathbb{E}(R^i) = R^f - \rho_{m,R^i}\frac{\sigma(m)}{\mathbb{E}(m)}\sigma(R^i)\left(\frac{v}{v-2}\right) - \frac{\delta_m}{\mathbb{E}(m)}\delta_{R^i} K$$

$$\Leftrightarrow |\mathbb{E}(R^i) - R^f| \le \frac{\sigma(m)}{\mathbb{E}(m)}\sigma(R^i)\left(\frac{v}{v-2}\right) - \frac{\delta_m}{\mathbb{E}(m)}\delta_{R^i} K, \tag{5.23}$$

where the last inequality follows since $|\rho| \le 1$. We can therefore plot the efficient frontier in $\mathbb{E}(R^i) - \sigma(R^i)$ space for a number of scenarios.

Case 1: $v \to \infty$, $\delta_i \to 0$, $\forall\, i$. This implies

$$|\mathbb{E}(R^i) - R^f| \le \frac{\sigma(m)}{\mathbb{E}(m)}\sigma(R^i).$$

The ratio $\sigma(m)/\mathbb{E}(m)$ represents the slope of the efficient frontier. See Figure 5.2. In this case, the excess return, $\mathbb{E}(R^i) - R^f$, is a function of return volatility, $\sigma(R^i)$, multiplied by a scaling factor.

Case 2: $v \downarrow 2$, $\delta_i \to 0$, $\forall\, i$. This implies

$$|\mathbb{E}(R^i) - R^f| \le \frac{\sigma(m)}{\mathbb{E}(m)}\sigma(R^i)\left(\frac{v}{v-2}\right).$$

Since $(v/(v-2)) > 1$, this has the effect of increasing the slope (Figure 5.3). In this case, the excess return, $\mathbb{E}(R^i) - R^f$, is a function of return volatility, $\sigma(R^i)$, multiplied by a much bigger scaling factor than in Case 1. Therefore, the return on the efficient frontier is made up of a traditional (systematic) risk component, plus global 'kurtosis' risk.

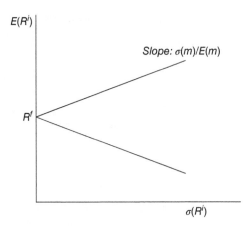

FIGURE 5.2   Traditional mean-variance frontier.

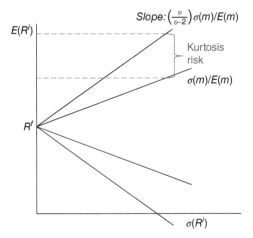

FIGURE 5.3   Mean-variance frontier with global kurtosis.

Case 3: $v \downarrow 2$, $\delta_i \neq 0$, $\forall\, i$. This implies

$$\left| \mathbb{E}(R^i) - R^f + \frac{\delta_m}{\mathbb{E}(m)} \delta_{R^i} K \right| \leq \frac{\sigma(m)}{\mathbb{E}(m)} \sigma(R^i) \left(\frac{v}{v-2} \right). \tag{5.24}$$

Therefore, the efficient frontier has the same slope as in Case 2, but the entire frontier is shifted by $-R^f \delta_m \delta_{R^i} K$ (Figure 5.4). The direction of the shift depends on the combined values of δ_m and δ_{R^i}. Specifically, if $(\delta_m, \delta_{R^i}) < 0$ as in the case of upper-tail AD, or $(\delta_m, \delta_{R^i}) > 0$ in the case where downside skewness in consumption is offset by upside skewness in asset returns, the efficient frontier shifts downwards, indicating that the presence of upper-tail AD should be associated with lower returns for a given level of risk (i.e., a discount). Conversely, if $\delta_m > 0$ and $\delta_{R^i} < 0$, as in the case of lower-tail AD, then

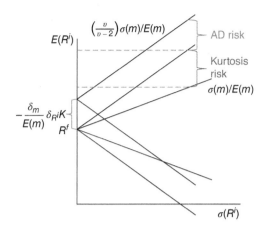

FIGURE 5.4 Mean-variance frontier with global kurtosis and AD.

the efficient frontier shifts upwards. Large absolute values of both δ_m and δ_{R^i} imply bigger movements in the efficient frontier than lower absolute values. Therefore, we conclude that returns compensate for traditional risk, kurtosis risk and tail risk. The direction of the shift in the efficient frontier depends on whether the asset displays upper-tail AD or lower-tail AD with consumption.

REFERENCES

Alcock, A. and Hatherley, A. (2009). Asymmetric dependence between domestic equity indices and its effect on portfolio construction. *Australian Actuarial Journal*, 15(1), 143–180.

Alcock, A. and Hatherley, A. (2017). Characterizing the asymmetric dependence premium. *Review of Finance*, 21(4), 1701–1737.

Allen, P., Einchcomb, S. and Granger, N. (2006). Conditional variance swaps. Product Note, JP Morgan.

Bossu, S. (2006). A new approach for modelling and pricing correlation swaps in equity derivatives. *Global Derivatives Trading & Risk Management*, May.

Bouzoubaa, M. and Osseiran, A. (2008). *Exotic Options and Hybrids: A Guide to Structuring, Pricing and Trading*. John Wiley & Sons, Hoboken, NJ.

Branger, N. and Muck, M. (2012). Keep on smiling? Volatility surfaces and the pricing of quanto options when all covariances are stochastic. *Journal of Banking and Finance*, 36(6), 1577–1591.

Broadie, M. and Jain, A. (2008). The effect of jumps and discrete sampling on volatility and variance swaps. *International Journal of Theoretical and Applied Finance*, 11(8), 761–797.

Bru, M.F. (1991). Wishart processes. *Journal of Theoretical Probability*, 4(4), 725–743.

Buraschi, A., Porchia, P. and Trojani, F. (2010). Correlation risk and optimal portfolio choice. *Journal of Finance*, 65(1), 393–420.

Carr, P. and Lewis, K. (2004). Corridor variance swaps. *Risk*, 17(2), 67–72.

Cochrane, J.H. (2005). *Asset Pricing*. Princeton University Press, Princeton, NJ.

Da Fonseca, J., Grasselli, M. and Tebaldi, C. (2007). Option pricing when correlations are stochastic: an analytic framework. *Review of Derivatives Research*, 10(2), 151–180.

Delbaen, F. and Shirakawa, H. (2002). An interest rate model with upper and lower bounds. *Asia-Pacific Financial Markets*, 9(3), 191–209.

Demeterfi, K., Derman, E., Kamal, M. and Zou, J. (1999). More than you ever wanted to know about volatility swaps. Goldman Sachs, Quantitative Strategies Research Notes.

Gatheral, J. (2006). *The Volatility Surface*. John Wiley & Sons, Hoboken, NJ.

Guyon, J. (2013). A new class of local correlation models. Working Paper, Bloomberg.

Hatherley, A. and Alcock, J. (2007). Portfolio construction incorporating asymmetric dependence structures: a user's guide. *Accounting & Finance*, 47(3), 447–472.

Jacquier, A. and Slaoui, S. (2010). Variance dispersion and correlation swaps. Working Paper.

Langnau, A. (2010). A dynamic model for correlation. *Risk*, April, 74–78.

Low, R.K.Y., Alcock, J., Faff, R. and Brailsford, T. (2013). Canonical vine copulas in the context of modern portfolio management: are they worth it? *Journal of Banking and Finance*, 37(8), 3085–3099.

Lucic, V. (2013). Correlation skew via product copula. Global Derivatives Conference, Amsterdam.

Merton, R. (1969). Lifetime portfolio selection: the continuous-time case. *Review of Economics and Statistics*, 51(3), 247–257.

Reghai, A. (2010). Breaking correlation breaks. *Risk*, October, 92–97.

Roll, R. (1988). The international crash of October 1987. *Financial Analysts Journal*, 44(5), 19–35.

Romo, J.M. (2012a). Pricing digital outperformance options with uncertain correlation. *International Journal of Theoretical and Applied Finance*, 14(5), 709–722.

Romo, J.M. (2012b). Worst-of options and correlation skew under a stochastic correlation framework. *International Journal of Theoretical and Applied Finance*, 15(7), 1–32.

Sahu, K.S., Dey, D.K. and Branco, M.D. (2003). A new class of multivariate skew distributions with applications to Bayesian regression models. *Canadian Journal of Statistics*, 31(2), 129–150.

Smith, M.S., Gan, Q. and Kohn, R.J. (2012). Modelling dependence using skew T copulas: Bayesian inference and applications. *Journal of Applied Econometrics*, 27, 500–522.

Van Emmerich, C. (2006). Modelling correlation as a stochastic process. Working Paper, Bergische Universitat Wuppertal.

Whittall, C. (2010). Correlation: opportunities and threats. *Risk*, October, 23–25.

Williams, M. (2014). The impact of quantitative easing on asset price comovement, in H. Fung and Y. Tse (eds), *International Financial Markets (Frontiers of Economics and Globalization)*, Vol. 13, pp. 139–163.

Zetocha, V. (2015). Jumping off the bandwagon: introducing jumps to equity correlation. Working Paper.

CHAPTER 6

Orthant Probability-Based Correlation

Mark Lundin[a] and Stephen Satchell[b]

[a]Director, Risk Management – Charles Schwab Investment Management (CSIM)
[b]Discipline of Finance, Sydney University and Trinity College, Cambridge

Abstract

We derive, from the basic characteristics of Pearson's product-moment correlation, an asymmetric method of dependence estimation which makes a distinction between desirable risk and undesirable risk. The method captures non-linear as well as linear dependence, but what distinguishes it most from other methods is its quantification of four bivariate correlations conditional on the signs of return pairs; distinct and different correlations when both assets perform positively, both perform negatively, or results are mixed (positive–negative or negative–positive). A potentially profitable by-product of this method is that it involves the estimation of correlation in different regimes simultaneously, and we offer the conjecture that this allows a more microscopic view of what is typically gauged in practice by other methods as a correlation amalgam. A t-value for orthant correlations is derived, so that a t-test can be conducted and p-values inferred from Student's t-distribution. Orthant-conditional correlations in the presence of imposed skewness and kurtosis and fixed liner correlations are shown. We conclude with a demonstration that this dependence measure also carries potentially profitable return information.

6.1 INTRODUCTION

In this chapter, a method for portfolio allocation which enhances performance by seeking asset combinations with higher dependence conditional on rising asset returns and lower dependence otherwise is investigated and developed. In doing so, the challenges of estimating dependence in the presence of skewness and excess kurtosis are confronted.

The dependence between the returns of financial market securities varies with time. This follows from the observation – readily available to anyone in possession of financial time series – that quantification of dependence by any means will differ for nearly any two particular assets one selects, over nearly any two different time periods. These differences are often subtle, sometimes appearing small or slow enough in trend to neglect without noticeable implications in either asset allocation or portfolio return. But they invariably become larger and more important in times of both crisis and opportunity. More surprising than this are the observations that asset return dependence varies conditionally on return magnitude and sign; that dependence is often asymmetric. This may at first strike one as a bit of esoteric trivia, but closer examination reveals material implications which affect investment performance in important ways. Erb *et al.* (1994) studied equity cross-correlations in relation to the coherence between business cycles in different countries for the period from 1970 to 1993 and found that correlations were higher during recessions than during growth periods, and that correlations were lower when two countries' business cycles were out of phase. Longin and Solnik (2001) modelled the multivariate distribution of large returns and estimated correlation for different threshold levels over the period from 1959 to 1996, revealing results which are compatible with the commonly held belief that correlation increases in bear markets, but not in bull markets. Ang and Chen (2002) found that correlations between domestic equity portfolios and the aggregate market, for the period between 1963 and 1998, were greater in downside markets than in upside markets, that asymmetries between upside and downside correlations existed between stocks in a single market as well as across markets internationally, and that there existed greater asymmetries among smaller stocks, value stocks and recent negatively performing stocks. There are clearly profits to be made and losses to be avoided by considering AD information, and by taking the trouble to estimate it more appropriately and precisely.

Dependence in the context of Markowitz's (1952) modern portfolio theory is, in practice, often taken to mean application of the ever-ubiquitous Pearson's (1896) product-moment correlation coefficient; ρ as applies to a population, or r as applies to a sample. Mean and variance self-adjusting, invariant to multivariate scales, it serves as a powerful single-pass algorithm. ρ^2 (as estimated by r^2) efficiently measures that part of the variance of one variable that is explained linearly by another variable, however any non-linear dependence between variables goes unmeasured. Misinterpretation of what Pearson's product-moment correlation actually estimates (as opposed to mis-estimation by the method itself) may lead to false conclusions in any implementation reliant on correlation. This is particularly relevant for the analysis of financial securities, whose return distributions are rarely close to normal; their non-linearities routinely manifest themselves through distributional asymmetries (skewness) and narrow 'peakedness' (kurtosis).

As with the variances and covariance from which Pearson's product-moment correlation coefficient is derived, the correlation between financial securities changes with time and presumably also with financial market conditions. Estimations of Pearson's r for different data samples produce differing results in ways which cannot be fully explained by statistical sampling fluctuations. It is possible that relevant information goes unmeasured, or that relevant information becomes smeared in a long-term average.

We discuss a correlation estimation method which gauges both linear and non-linear dependencies by ignoring distributional characteristics, relying instead on occupancy of the four quadrants of the Cartesian plane formed by the returns of two investments. A potentially profitable by-product of this method is that it involves the estimation of correlation in different regimes simultaneously, and we offer the conjecture that this allows a more microscopic view of what is typically gauged in practice by other methods as a correlation amalgam. Applied to financial securities, evidence is presented that this essentially risk-based estimation method includes return information which may allow portfolio performance improvement based on exploitable co-variability characteristics. From the perspective that a financial security may refer to an irreducible asset or itself be a portfolio of underlying assets, this discussion has important implications for security selection, portfolio construction, investment manager selection and asset allocation.

6.2   ORTHANT PROBABILITIES AND ORTHANT CORRELATION

Given a simple portfolio of two assets whose marginal returns form a joint distribution, (X, Y), four performance outcomes are possible for price changes over a finite time period: both assets' returns may be positive; the returns may contradict each other, with the first being positive and the second negative; the returns may contradict each other, with the first being negative and the second positive; or both assets' returns may be negative. For the bivariate normal distribution (two assets delivering random standard normal marginal distributions with zero means), the probability for each of these possibilities can be described separately through Sheppard's (1898, 1899) theorem of median dichotomy:

$$P_{11} = \text{Prob}[X > 0, Y > 0] = \frac{1}{4} + \frac{1}{2\pi} \sin^{-1}(\rho_{X,Y}), \tag{6.1}$$

$$P_{01} = \text{Prob}[X \leq 0, Y > 0] = \frac{1}{4} - \frac{1}{2\pi} \sin^{-1}(\rho_{X,Y}), \tag{6.2}$$

$$P_{00} = \text{Prob}[X \leq 0, Y \leq 0] = \frac{1}{4} + \frac{1}{2\pi} \sin^{-1}(\rho_{X,Y}), \tag{6.3}$$

$$P_{10} = \text{Prob}[X > 0, Y \leq 0] = \frac{1}{4} - \frac{1}{2\pi} \sin^{-1}(\rho_{X,Y}), \tag{6.4}$$

where $\rho_{X,Y}$ is the linear correlation between X and Y.

Equations (6.1)–(6.4) are often referred to as orthant normal probabilities. The term 'orthant' is used in reference to a framework which can be expanded to n dimensions, but for the two-dimensional case involving the returns of two financial securities there are four orthants or quadrants. The orthant probabilities arise from the conversion of the joint probability density function to polar coordinates and form one of the stronger links between probability theory and the vector and linear algebra descriptions of correlation.

Equations (6.1)–(6.4) apply to a mean = 0 bivariate normal distribution. It can be shown (see the proof in Appendix 6.A) that this also holds for the class of elliptical distributions which are mean zero and which can be described as conditionally scale bivariate normal, where the scale is a positive random variable with finite mean. This includes some members of the zero-mean elliptical family with excess kurtosis, including the bivariate t-distribution and mixtures of normal distributions with the same covariance matrix. These are closer to the distributions observed for the returns of financial assets, though Appendix 6.A is not strictly necessary for the results which follow. In these circumstances, rearranging Equations (6.1)–(6.4) and solving for correlation terms results in four different but equivalent definitions of a single correlation. If the joint distribution is bivariate normal, these equivalent orthant correlations are also equal to Pearson's product-moment correlation coefficient.

For cases involving other distributions, solving Equations (6.1)–(6.4) for the correlation variable will result in implied orthant correlations which would be equal under normality/ellipticity. Rearranging for correlation terms then, expressions of implied quadrant correlations can be expressed conditionally on the quadrants of the Cartesian plane of the bivariate X, Y distribution:

$$\rho_{11} = \rho_{X,Y}|[X > 0, Y > 0] = \sin\left(2\pi\left(P_{11} - \frac{1}{4}\right)\right), \tag{6.5}$$

$$\rho_{01} = \rho_{X,Y}|[X \leq 0, Y > 0] = \sin\left(2\pi\left(-P_{01} + \frac{1}{4}\right)\right), \tag{6.6}$$

$$\rho_{00} = \rho_{X,Y}|[X \leq 0, Y \leq 0] = \sin\left(2\pi\left(P_{00} - \frac{1}{4}\right)\right), \tag{6.7}$$

$$\rho_{10} = \rho_{X,Y}|[X > 0, Y \leq 0] = \sin\left(2\pi\left(-P_{10} + \frac{1}{4}\right)\right). \tag{6.8}$$

6.3   ORTHANT PROBABILITY TESTING

Before moving to a discussion on the interpretation and use of orthant or quadrant correlations, we address the issue of statistical significance. A t-value for quadrant correlations is derived so that a t-test can be conducted and p-values inferred from Student's t-distribution. In addition, we provide exact tests for forecasting hypotheses concerning orthant probabilities. Denoting

$$P_{00} = \text{Prob}(X \leq 0, Y \leq 0),$$

$$P_{11} = \text{Prob}(X > 0, Y > 0),$$

$$P_{01} = \text{Prob}(X \leq 0, Y > 0),$$

$$P_{10} = \text{Prob}(X > 0, Y \leq 0),$$

it follows that

$$P_{00} + P_{01} + P_{10} + P_{11} = 1.$$

If the probability density function, pdf(x, y), is symmetric around $(0, 0)$, then $P_{00} = P_{11}$, $P_{10} = P_{01}$ and $P_{00} + P_{10} = \frac{1}{2}$.

If we further assume that X, Y are bivariate elliptical with finite second moments, then it is well known that a transformation of the sample correlation coefficient, R, based on a sample of N observations, is distributed as Student's t. In particular, $t = \frac{R\sqrt{N-2}}{\sqrt{1-R^2}}$ has a t-distribution with $N - 2$ degrees of freedom. We present the following result.

Theorem 6.3.1 *To test if* $P_{11} = \text{Prob}(X > 0, Y > 0) = \frac{1}{4}$, $P_{00} = \text{Prob}(X \leq 0, Y \leq 0) = \frac{1}{4}$ *under the assumption of bivariate ellipticity with finite second moments. If* $\widehat{P}_{11}$ *is the sample estimator of* P_{11} *and* $\widehat{P}_{01}$ *is the sample estimator of* P_{01}, *then* $\tan\left(2\pi\left(\widehat{P}_{11} - \frac{1}{4}\right)\right)\sqrt{N-2}$ *has a t-distribution with $N - 2$ degrees of freedom and* $\tan\left(2\pi\left(\frac{1}{4} - \widehat{P}_{01}\right)\right)\sqrt{N-2}$ *has a t-distribution with $N - 2$ degrees of freedom.*

Proof: To test if $P_{11} = \text{Prob}(X > 0, Y > 0) = \frac{1}{4}$: using Equation (6.1), $\frac{1}{4} + \frac{1}{2\pi}\sin^{-1}(\rho_{X,Y}) = P_{11}$. In terms of sample data, $R = \sin\left(2\pi\left(\widehat{P}_{11} - \frac{1}{4}\right)\right)$.

Using the fact that $t = \frac{R\sqrt{N-2}}{\sqrt{1-R^2}}$ has a t-distribution with $N - 2$ degrees of freedom, we see that $t = \tan\left(2\pi\left(\widehat{P}_{11} - \frac{1}{4}\right)\right)\sqrt{N-2}$ has a t-distribution with $N - 2$ degrees of freedom.

To test if $P_{00} = \text{Prob}(X < 0, Y < 0) = \frac{1}{4}$: using Equation (6.1), $\frac{1}{4} - \frac{1}{2\pi}\sin^{-1}(\rho_{X,Y}) = P_{01}$. In terms of sample data, $R = \sin\left(2\pi\left(\frac{1}{4} - \widehat{P}_{01}\right)\right)$. Using the fact that $t = \frac{R\sqrt{N-2}}{\sqrt{1-R^2}}$ has a t-distribution with $N - 2$ degrees of freedom, we see that $t = \tan\left(2\pi\left(\frac{1}{4} - \widehat{P}_{01}\right)\right)\sqrt{N-2}$ has a t-distribution with $N - 2$ degrees of freedom. ∎

We can apply the above results to test the hit rate, defined as the proportion of times that the forecasts and the actuals have the same sign. From the above result, to test if the hit rate (HR) is 50%, we can define $\text{HR} = P_{00} + P_{11} = -\frac{1}{2} + \frac{1}{\pi}\sin^{-1}(\rho_{X,Y})$ and so $t = \tan\left(\pi\left(\widehat{\text{HR}} - \frac{1}{2}\right)\right)\sqrt{N-2}$ has a t-distribution with $N - 2$ degrees of freedom, where $\widehat{\text{HR}}$ is the sample hit rate.

6.4 CHARACTERISTICS OF ORTHANT CORRELATIONS

The four probability-dependent quadrant correlations of Equations (6.5)–(6.8) are shown graphically in the two-dimensional rectangular Cartesian coordinate system of Figure 6.1, where the horizontal axis corresponds to the return of a first asset and the vertical axis corresponds to the return of a second asset.

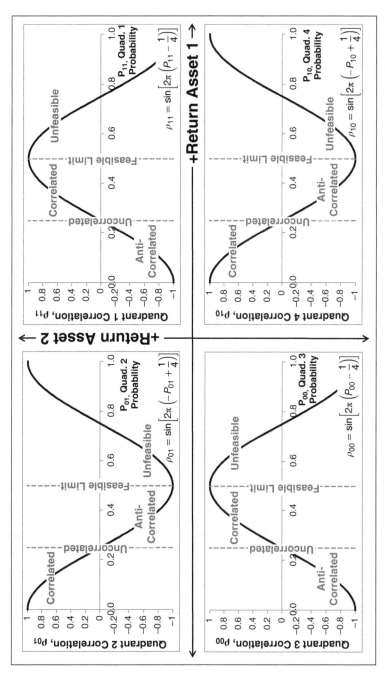

FIGURE 6.1 The relation between orthant correlations and orthant probabilities illustrated for the bivariate case of the return distributions of two financial assets, shown as a function of quadrant. A base-case neutral condition might be considered that of a bivariate standard normal (mean zero, variance one) distribution for which occupancy in each quadrant would be 25%, translating to a probability of 0.25 and leading to an orthant correlation of zero for all quadrants. Occupancies which differ from this 25% occupancy base-case of occupancy or probability will result in either increases or decreases in correlation, depending on the quadrant involved.

In the figure and subsequent text, we follow the Cartesian convention of numbering quadrants 1 to 4 by starting with the upper-right quadrant and moving counter-clockwise. If the joint probability distribution of asset returns is zero-mean and random bivariate normal (therefore, median equal to mean) and uncorrelated, then returns from both assets occupy each of the four quadrants with equal probability of 0.25. An increase or decrease in occupancy will directly change (decreasing or increasing) that of some other quadrant, as the sum of probabilities is one. In addition, any change in occupation or probability will necessarily affect quadrant correlations in the sinusoidal manner dictated by Equations (6.5)–(6.8), resulting either in an increase or a decrease in correlation in a manner which may be proportional or inversely proportional to probabilities. Increases in probability will increase or decrease correlation only up to a limit (probability of 0.5), beyond which the derivative of the function and changes in correlation will change sign. We interpret a quadrant occupancy of greater than 50% of the joint distribution, or a quadrant probability of greater than 0.5, as a region of asset combination infeasibility for which one of the assets is either so superior or so inferior that it should be taken alone as a portfolio itself or should be excluded from consideration as a portfolio choice. This commonly occurs when the median of one asset's marginal return distribution is extreme; either very positive or very negative.

Table 6.1 presents the results of application of both Pearson's product-moment correlation and the orthant correlations to joint distributions X, Y where X is the standard normal and Y is defined variously either as independent from X or defined jointly with X. In the first two lines of the table ($Y = \pm 1$), X is a mean-zero random normal distribution with unit variance, Y is a constant and X and Y are clearly independent. For rows three and four of Table 6.1 ($Y = \pm X$), X is a standard normal, $N(0, 1)$, and X and Y are linearly dependent. For rows five and six of Table 6.1 ($Y = \pm X^2$), X is a standard normal and X and Y are not linearly dependent, but are non-linearly dependent as defined in the first column. In rows seven and eight, X and Y are both standard normal, $N(0, 1)$, with linear correlation between them (gauged by Pearson's product-moment correlation) enforced to be 0 (in row seven) and 0.5 (in row eight).

For the case of $Y = 1$, from Table 6.1, Y is fully independent of X and Pearson's product-moment correlation coefficient reflects this with an estimation of zero. However, the orthant correlations consider

TABLE 6.1   Results of various benchmark cases of dependency between two distributions, X and Y, comparing the Pearson's product-moment correlation coefficient to the four quadrant orthant correlations for the bivariate joint distribution. The ability of orthant correlations to fully capture non-linearities, in comparison with Pearson's product-moment linear correlation, is especially apparent in the classic textbook case of $Y = X^2$ where there is full dependence between X and Y but no linear correlation exists

	Pearson's ρ	ρ_{11} (quad. 1)	ρ_{01} (quad. 2)	ρ_{00} (quad. 3)	ρ_{10} (quad. 4)
$Y = 1$	0	1	−1	−1	1
$Y = -1$	0	−1	1	1	−1
$Y = X$	1	1	1	1	1
$Y = -X$	−1	−1	−1	−1	−1
$Y = X^2$	0	1	−1	−1	1
$Y = -X^2$	0	−1	1	1	−1
$Y = N(0, 1)$	0	0	0	0	0
$Y = N(0, 1)$	0.5	0.5	0.5	0.5	0.5

the relation X, Y in the separate and isolated perspective of each of four quadrants, providing a more microscopic view which can be less readily open to interpretation. In this case, the occupancies or measured probabilities in quadrants one to four $(P_{11}, P_{01}, P_{00}, P_{10})$ are 0.5, 0.5, 0 and 0, respectively. As a result, correlation in the first quadrant, ρ_{11}, is equal to one due to occupancy in that quadrant of 50% of the distribution. Examination of Figure 6.1 reveals this to be 25% more than would be the case if X, Y were independent (in which case occupancy and probability would be just 25%). The second quadrant has an equally high occupancy (50%), but these samples fall into a category of opposite-signed samples $(-X, +Y)$ leading, unlike quadrant one, to full anti-correlation for ρ_{01} as occupation occurs in numbers greater than would be the case for random and independent median-zero joint distributions (or 25%). The absence of any observations in quadrant three (corresponding to negative returns for both assets) is interpreted by the orthant relations as full anti-correlation for ρ_{00}. If quadrant three was highly occupied then the conclusion would be the opposite. Likewise, in quadrant four, the absence of any observations is interpreted not in terms of what is present, but in terms of what is missing compared with a joint distribution for which the marginal medians are equal to zero (occupancy of 25% or probability of 0.25), and the result is full correlation for ρ_{10}.

The $Y = X$ case of Table 6.1 results in full correlation in all quadrants, which is both logical and in agreement with Pearson's product-moment correlation coefficient.

The continuous function $Y = X^2$ from Table 6.1 is a textbook example illustrating that linear correlation does not equate with dependence. In this case, full dependence between X and Y is obvious and yet Pearson's product-moment correlation coefficient (capturing only linear dependence) is equal to zero. Quadrant correlations for this case are non-zero, but are also equivalent to quadrant correlation results for the fully independent case of $Y = 1$. Quadrant correlations gauge the linear component of dependence as well as the non-linear, and when gauging correlation they make no distinction between functional or distributional forms, even distributions that do not exist or are more exotic in character.

Table 6.1 also includes two cases for which both X and Y are standard normal distributions (mean zero, variance one) and with Pearson's product-moment correlation enforced for the separate cases of 0 and 0.5. The results illustrate that orthant correlations revert to Pearson's product moment correlation coefficient, which fully captures linear dependence, for standard normal joint distributions. All four quadrant correlations are equal to each other for distributions whose medians are equal to their means, but for bivariate standard normal distributions they are also equal to Pearson's product-moment correlation coefficient. In any other circumstances quadrant correlations may produce results which are close to Pearson's correlation, but will almost never be exactly equal, typically as the result of non-linear dependencies between joint distributions which Pearson's linear correlation does not detect.

6.5 IN THE PRESENCE OF SKEWNESS AND KURTOSIS

Orthant or quadrant-conditional correlations in the presence of imposed skewness and kurtosis and fixed linear correlations are shown in Figure 6.2. The Vale–Maurelli (1983) implementation of Fleishman's (1978) method was used to generate bivariate joint distributions with pre-specified first to fourth marginal distribution moments, as well as Pearson product-moment linear correlations between the two. A multivariate SAS/IML 6.0 implementation of the Vale–Maurelli (1983) method, designed and incorporated in SAS by Wicklin (2013), was used for this purpose. The first marginal distribution was specified to be standard normal, $N(0,1)$, with zero skewness and zero excess kurtosis. In Figure 6.2(a) the second marginal distribution was specified as zero mean, unit variance, excess kurtosis of 10 and varying degrees of skewness. A fixed value of 10 for kurtosis, γ_4, was selected in order to allow a wide breadth of skewness, γ_3, since $\gamma_4 \geq \gamma_3^2 + 1$ (see Stuart and Ord (1994) and Vargo *et al.* (2010)). In Figure 6.2(b) the second marginal distribution was specified as zero mean, unit variance, zero skewness and varying degrees of kurtosis. In both cases, joint distributions were pre-specified to have fixed linear Pearson's product-moment correlation coefficients of 0.5 and all pre-specified values were enforced to five significant figures.

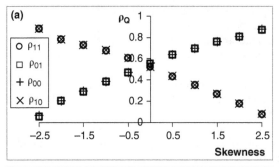

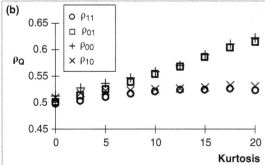

FIGURE 6.2 Orthant correlations of the four quadrants of joint bivariate distributions for various levels of non-linearity. (a) Orthant correlations are shown as a function of skewness between a standard normal $N(0,1)$ distribution (with zero skewness and zero excess kurtosis) and a distribution with mean zero, variance of one, excess kurtosis of 10 and skewness varying from -2.5 to 2.5. In all cases, linear correlation as measured by Pearson's product-moment correlation coefficient is pre-specified and fixed for each case of skewness at 0.5. Quadrant two and three correlations, ρ_{01} and ρ_{00}, appear linearly related to skewness and quadrant one and four correlations, ρ_{11} and ρ_{10}, inversely linearly related. (b) Orthant correlations are shown between a standard normal $N(0,1)$ distribution (with zero skewness and zero excess kurtosis) and a distribution with mean zero, variance of one, skewness of zero and various levels of excess kurtosis between 0 and 20. In all cases, linear correlation as measured by Pearson's product-moment correlation coefficient is fixed to 0.5.

The orthant correlation's quadrant sensitivity to skewness in Figure 6.2(a) is significant, with first and fourth quadrant correlations being inversely related and second and third quadrants directly related. Direct sensitivity to kurtosis is present in Figure 6.2(b) for all four quadrants, but appears to be of a lower magnitude compared with skewness for the regions of skewness and kurtosis which were tested.

We note that the sensitivities of orthant correlations to both skewness and kurtosis are also likely to be dependent on a number of other factors such as the distribution first and second moments and the linear dependence (in these tests imposed at 0.5) of joint distributions.

6.6 QUANTIFYING THE COMPLEMENTARITY OF ASSET CHARACTERISTICS

The absolute and relative benefit of holding assets is primarily apparent through their risk and return characteristics. A secondary and joint characteristic is the correlation between assets held, or the extent to which their variability is related. A commonly employed method for estimation of correlation is through Pearson's product-moment correlation coefficient, ρ, which can be estimated for a bivariate sample by Pearson's r. Pearson's product-moment correlation coefficient gauges only the part of variability in one asset which is linearly dependent on the variability of another. In the absence of non-linearities, or even in the presence of low levels of non-linearity, typically made apparent through distributional skewness and kurtosis, Pearson's product-moment correlation is a practical and powerful metric for optimizing portfolio 'fit' between assets. Unfortunately, linearity is rarely the case with financial return distributions, which more often than not exhibit skewness and excess kurtosis. In such cases any non-linear co-variability will go unquantified by Pearson's product-moment correlation, leading to underestimation of dependence. Orthant correlations present at least two advantages: they are agnostic to distributional form and, in addition, may present an opportunity for gauging co-variability on a more microscopic scale. The exploitation of both these advantages may find applications in portfolio construction and higher frequencies of arbitrage securities trading.

Figure 6.1 provides one possible starting point for the practical application of orthant correlations and its examination in the context of what is beneficial or detrimental to the goals of a practical application can act as a guide. From the perspective of a simple two-asset portfolio, occupancy of greater than 25% (the base case of a random-normal bivariate with zero median) of joint distributions is typically judged as desirable for the first quadrant of their joint distribution. Occupancy in the first quadrant, P_{11}, reflects positive returns in both assets and Figure 6.1 indicates that an occupancy of greater than 25% necessarily involves an increase of the correlation ρ_{11} between the two assets. For the purposes of this exercise, further making an assumption that the first asset is a fixed decision (for example, a previously existing, long-term portfolio investment whose sale is undesirable), higher occupancy in quadrant two, P_{01}, is also a desirable outcome; the second asset return, to some extent, compensating for the negative return of the first fixed asset. For quadrant two, such an increase in occupancy is linked to a decrease in the quadrant correlation ρ_{01} (see quadrant two of Figure 6.1). Occupancy of quadrant three, P_{00}, is the least desirable result (both assets delivering negative returns); a decrease below a probability of 25% is desirable and quadrant three of Figure 6.1 indicates that such a shift in occupancy and probability decrease would be linked to a decrease in the correlation, ρ_{00}, for that particular quadrant. Again assuming that holding asset one is a given constraint, occupancy in quadrant four of Figure 6.1 would by preference be lower than 25% and a decrease in occupancy and probability in quadrant four, P_{10}, is linked to an increase in the correlation, ρ_{10}, for that quadrant. Differing arguments and conclusions might be made for differing applications and perspectives, but the conclusions of these particular arguments are summarized in Table 6.2.

The conclusions from Table 6.2 might be quantified in a simple linear combination of orthant correlations:

$$\Delta\rho_Q = \rho_{11} - \rho_{01} - \rho_{00} + \rho_{10}. \tag{6.9}$$

As the quadrant correlations are bounded by +/−1, $\Delta\rho_Q$ will be bounded by +/−4, or $\Delta\rho_Q$ might be divided by four, making it bounded by +/−1 for greater ease of interpretation. Figure 6.3 provides insight into the sensitivity of $\Delta\rho_Q$, defined by Equation (6.9), to skewness and kurtosis. The returns of the first asset are distributed as a standard normal with Pearson's product-moment correlation enforced to be 0.5 with the second asset. In Figure 6.3(a) the second asset has a fixed excess kurtosis of 10,

TABLE 6.2 Summary of assessment of quadrant orthant correlation desirable changes for the particular case of a two-asset portfolio for which holding the first asset is a fixed assumption and the second asset is a candidate for portfolio addition. The rationale for 'desirability' of change is likely dependent on the particular application in mind and the rationale for this particular case is described in the text

Quadrant	Desirable probability change from $P_Q = 0.25$	Resulting correlation change from $\rho_Q = 0$
Q_1 ($R_{Asset\ 1} > 0$, $R_{Asset\ 2} > 0$)	Increase	Increase
Q_2 ($R_{Asset\ 1} \leq 0$, $R_{Asset\ 2} > 0$)	Increase	Decrease
Q_3 ($R_{Asset\ 1} \leq 0$, $R_{Asset\ 2} \leq 0$)	Decrease	Decrease
Q_4 ($R_{Asset\ 1} > 0$, $R_{Asset\ 2} \leq 0$)	Decrease	Increase

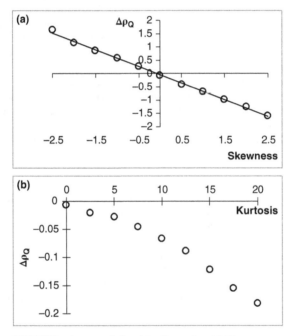

FIGURE 6.3 $\Delta\rho_Q$ as defined by Equation (6.9), as a function of excess kurtosis and skewness for the case of a bivariate joint distribution of asset returns in which the first asset is a standard normal distribution with mean zero, unit variance, zero skewness and zero kurtosis. In all cases, linear correlation as measured by the Pearson's product-moment correlation coefficient was fixed to 0.5. (a) The second distribution has zero mean, unit variance and excess kurtosis fixed at 10, while the skewness is varied. (b) The second distribution has zero mean, unit variance and skewness fixed at zero, while the excess kurtosis is varied.

mean of zero, variance of one and varying degrees of skewness. The inverse linear relation between $\Delta\rho_Q$ and skewness indicates that a negatively skewed second asset would be a more optimal portfolio combination, at least with an asset whose returns are distributed as a standard normal. In Figure 6.3(b) the returns of the second asset also have mean zero, variance one and an enforced linear correlation of 0.5 with the first asset, but zero skewness and varying degrees of kurtosis, revealing a non-linear and strictly negative relation between $\Delta\rho_Q$ and positive kurtosis.

Figure 6.4 shows $\Delta\rho_Q$ as a function of mean return for a portfolio of two assets, along with a best-fit line which gauges the linear dependence between the two. As part of a Monte Carlo study, 100,000 random joint bivariate events were generated for two standard normal $N(0,1)$ distributions and linear correlation (Pearson's r) was enforced to be 0.5. The joint return history was then subdivided into 1,000 non-overlapping subsets of 100 samples each. Means (=0), variances (=1), skewness (=0), excess kurtosis (=0) for both distributions, and Pearson's product-moment correlation (=0.5) were forced to a precision of five significant figures for each subset of data addressed separately. The mean of the sample distribution of 1,000 equally weighted portfolio combination asset returns was 1×10^{-17} and its standard deviation was 0.08548. The mean value of $\Delta\rho_Q$s was −0.0066 with a standard deviation of 0.5170. However, division of the total population into 1,000 smaller groups of 100 observations each allows for sampling fluctuations to occur and these lead to local variations in linear correlation from 0.5, non-zero portfolio returns and non-zero $\Delta\rho_Q$ values for the subsamples, even while the full sample of data has distribution mean value and $\Delta\rho_Q$ equivalent to zero and linear correlation of 0.5 to within five significant figures.

Figure 6.4 shows the relation between $\Delta\rho_Q$ and finite-period portfolio returns. A linear fit to the data indicates a strong linear dependence between the two ($R^2 = 0.4247$, or Pearson's linear correlation of 0.65). The average of portfolio returns jointly occurring with $\Delta\rho_Q > 0$ was 0.0509, whereas the average of portfolio returns jointly occurring with $\Delta\rho_Q < 0$ was −0.0485. Assuming that $\Delta\rho_Q$ for a

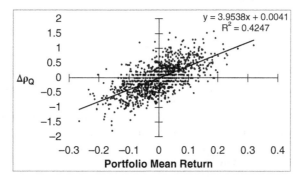

FIGURE 6.4 $\Delta\rho_Q$ as defined by Equation (6.9), as a function of the mean value of portfolio returns for an equally weighted combination of assets. Each of the 1,000 individual data points consists of a non-overlapping subset of 100 joint samples from a bivariate normal $N(0,1)$ distribution (with zero skewness and zero excess kurtosis) and linear correlation (as measured by Pearson's product-moment correlation coefficient) was fixed to 0.5 for the entire sample of 100,000 random joint samples. According to a least-squares best fit to a line (shown in the figure) and also as a result of t-tests, there are reliable indications of a significant relation between $\Delta\rho_Q$ and portfolio returns.

future investment period is known, it is theoretically possible to use the orthant correlation information of $\Delta\rho_Q$ as a return-enhancing information source. For example, a simple investment strategy of holding cash conditional on $\Delta\rho_Q < 0$, and holding an equal combination of the two assets conditional on $\Delta\rho_Q > 0$, would produce positive portfolio returns over the long term, even though asset returns over the long term would be zero. Going further, a simple investment strategy of short selling both assets for $\Delta\rho_Q < 0$, and holding an equal combination of the two assets when $\Delta\rho_Q > 0$, would produce an even more positive return result. For a limited time interval, it is not unusual for an asset combination to produce a weighted average portfolio combination return which is greater than either of the two assets. If the returns of two equally weighted assets are distributed as uncorrelated random standard normals, this would occur in 25% of joint samples. It is this level of probability, 25%, which has been referred to previously in this discussion as a 'base case' or neutral condition. Unfortunately, a separate 25% of samples would also result in the opposite condition of a portfolio return more negative than either asset and at issue is whether or not the long-term average of weighted returns can be systematically improved in comparison with the long-term average of weighted asset distribution expectation values, conditional on information related to asset co-variability. This might be considered unusual, and we note that systematically positive deviation of portfolio returns from the weighted average of asset returns only occurs in the presence of future return information which can be employed to guide either relative asset selection in a context of strategic asset allocation or tactical asset weighting in a context of active management.

t-Tests were performed in an attempt to gauge the confidence with which it can be concluded that the mean or expected values of distributions' portfolio mean returns, as shown in Figure 6.4, but conditional on $\Delta\rho_Q < 0$ and $\Delta\rho_Q > 0$, actually differ. Both pooled and unpooled t-tests were performed on the negative, $Z_{1,i} = 0.5 \times (\overline{X_i} + \overline{Y_i})|(\Delta\rho_Q < 0)$, and positive, $Z_{2,i} = 0.5 \times (\overline{X_i} + \overline{Y_i})|(\Delta\rho_Q > 0)$, conditional distributions of mean return values of the $i = 1, \ldots, 1{,}000$ subsets of portfolio combinations of asset one and asset two return distributions, X and Y. Subset portfolio mean returns were composed of equally weighted asset returns, equivalent to an equally weighted average of their means, $\overline{X_i}$ and $\overline{Y_i}$. Due to the fact that a limited sample of 100 values was used for each of the 1,000 data points in Figure 6.4, some granularity is apparent in the figure at values of $\Delta\rho_Q$ closer to zero. For the same reason, 71 out of 1,000 data points actually resulted in $\Delta\rho_Q = 0$. Of the remaining 929 non-zero values, 477 out of 1,000 samples in Figure 6.4 had $\Delta\rho_Q < 0$ and 452 samples had $\Delta\rho_Q > 0$. The underlying assumption of t-tests on the conditional distributions, Z_1 and Z_2, was that the means of the two distributions are the same, or compatible. A pooled Sasabuchi (1988a) t-test (which assumed equal variances of the two distributions) resulted in a t-value of 21.23 (with 927 degrees of freedom) and a corresponding p-value of 0.0001. The t-value is related to the size of the difference between the means for the two samples under comparison and the p-value is the probability of obtaining a t-value at this extreme or greater under the assumption of equivalent means. An unpooled Satterthwaite (1946)-style t-test (which assumes unequal variances) was performed and resulted in a t-value of 21.22 (with 922.04 degrees of freedom) and a corresponding p-value of 0.0001. Finally, a Cochran and Cox (1950)-style unpooled t-test (assuming unequal variances) was performed and resulted in a t-value of 21.22 and a corresponding p-value of 0.0001. The number of degrees of freedom for the Cochran and Cox t-test is undefined when the number of samples from each pair is unequal, which was the case here. Separately, a Steel and Torrie (1980) equality of variances test was performed and revealed a two-tailed F-value of 1.04 with a probability of being greater than F of 0.6748, which we interpret as an indication that there is insufficient evidence of unequal variances between Z_1 and Z_2. Examination of skewness and kurtosis in Z_1 and Z_2 revealed only slight non-normality and this was confirmed by visual examination of Q–Q plots of data quantiles versus normal distribution theoretical quantiles. All three t-tests resulted in highly significant p-values, supporting the conclusion of a significant difference between the means for the return distributions conditional about zero on $\Delta\rho_Q$.

There is a strong assumption behind the conclusion that quadrant correlations can be employed to produce a long-term average investment return which is greater than any of the individual asset long-term averages of returns. The assumption is that there exists perfect, or more realistically significant, knowledge of the quadrant correlations of investment sub-periods before those periods begin. The ability to forecast quadrant correlations, for example by taking recent historical values as forecasts of near-term future values, remains an open question. However, we do surmise that quadrant correlation values, as we presume is the case for asset variance and covariance, to which correlation is closely related, are more persistent and predictable than future security performance or mean return expectation values if only based on the observation that the former tends to vary much less (and more slowly) than the latter.

For comparison, Pearson's product-moment correlation coefficient, r, was estimated for the same subsets of simulation data from Figure 6.4 and the results are shown as a function of portfolio subset average return in Figure 6.5. The average of portfolio returns under the condition $r > 0.5$ was 0.0005 and for $r < 0.5$ was -0.0006, providing some indication that little or no portfolio return information is reflected by linear correlation. Figure 6.5 also shows the results of an unsuccessful attempt to perform a least-squares regression fit to a straight line and confirms that no significant, direct relation presents itself. The source of the relatively strong relation between portfolio returns and orthant correlations, as quantified by $\Delta\rho_Q$ and as shown in Figure 6.4, likely stems from the sensitivity of orthant correlations to non-linearities, or from the more granular information afforded by quadrant-dependent correlations, or both sources combined.

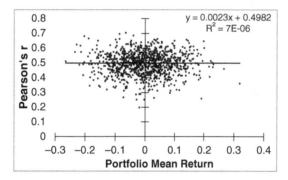

FIGURE 6.5 Linear correlation as measured by Pearson's product-moment correlation coefficient, as a function of the mean value of portfolio returns for an equally weighted combination of assets. Each of the 1,000 individual data points consists of a non-overlapping subset of 100 joint samples from a bivariate normal $N(0,1)$ distribution (with zero skewness and zero excess kurtosis) and linear correlation (as measured by Pearson's product-moment correlation coefficient) was fixed to 0.5 for the entire sample of 100,000 random joint samples. Both by eye and according to a least-squares best fit to a line (shown in the figure), there is no indication of a relation between Pearson's r and portfolio returns.

6.7   CONCLUSIONS

Orthant probabilities have been applied in order to gauge correlation of financial asset returns in a manner which is robust to the non-linearities which often manifest themselves through skewness and kurtosis, while also opening a more microscopic view on co-variability under differing (for example rising versus falling) market conditions. The case of a simple, two-asset investment portfolio has been used to demonstrate the potential for application of orthant correlations in investment management. A strategy involving investment in the two assets simulated for the results shown in Figure 6.4 when $\Delta \rho_Q > 0$, but remaining in cash otherwise, produced a long-run portfolio return greater than zero, with a convincing level of confidence, while both the long-run averages of asset returns and their weighted average were zero. This result could only be achieved through application of new information which directly explains asset return information which is not apparent with the application of Pearson's product-moment correlation. We preliminarily conclude that the upper limit for the potential of this method, paradoxically based in risk management, is to systematically deliver higher long-term portfolio returns than the long-term returns of individual assets themselves taken separately. We note that a practical overlay implementation of $\Delta \rho_Q$ – involving a large portfolio of assets – was described by Anderson *et al.* (2016), where back-testing revealed that roughly 2% per year would have been added to the returns of a risk-parity strategy, while portfolio market risk would have been reduced.

   In demonstrating this upper-limit potential, a strong assumption involving knowledge of future orthant correlations was made, but it can be argued that the forecast ability of correlation is at least as tenable as, or even more easily attainable than, the forecasting of asset returns which in practice is typically implicit (either quantitatively or qualitatively) in asset selection. This discussion was limited to the two-dimensional framework of quadrants and we see no closed-form solution involving more than four orthants. Therefore, we note that more work is likely required in order to achieve a multivariate extrapolation to larger portfolios. We view orthant correlation as a unique quantifier with a potential for portfolio construction which is complementary to return expectation value analysis.

   Some effort has been made to illustrate the character of correlations, particularly in the presence of skewness and excess kurtosis, and we note that $\Delta \rho_Q$ produces results which are different from those applying Pearson's correlation coefficient conditionally on the sign of returns. We attribute this difference to the fact that Pearson's product-moment correlation is known to less than fully capture dependence where excess kurtosis and skewness are present. Orthant probability-based correlations which rely on probabilities (or occupancies where empirical observations are concerned) make the method blind to distributional characteristics in their estimation of dependence.

   We view these efforts as a starting point in research and development and future study is called for. It is noted that much of our current Monte Carlo simulation has been performed under a forced linear correlation value of 0.5 (as gauged by Pearson's product-moment correlation); orthant correlation in the full correlation space merits further investigation. This is particularly relevant for the case of negative correlation which presumably exists with high prevalence in long–short security combinations. Likewise, the simple orthant correlations combination, $\Delta \rho_Q$, as defined in Equation (6.9), is viewed as one of many possible. We currently perceive that the manner in which orthant correlations are most optimally applied will be dependent on the application in mind.

   In this discussion, we have addressed the case of a fixed investment portfolio in the context of a search for a new portfolio candidate asset. In one straightforward scenario, quantifiers such as the $\Delta \rho_Q$ defined here, when estimated separately for various candidates, have a potential for adding value in a comparison-based asset selection process. In addition to asset selection and portfolio construction, we also note the potential for application of orthant correlations in the realm of high-frequency arbitrage trading, where bivariate or multivariate combinations of highly liquid assets might be selected or weighted according to quantifiers related to $\Delta \rho_Q$ in order to produce a systematic positive return largely or fully unrelated to security return analysis.

REFERENCES

Anderson, M., Chen, S., Croce, J., Eichholz, R., Lieberman, M., Lundin, M. *et al.* (2016). Risk management for return enhancement. *Risk*, technical paper, February.

Ang, A. and Chen, J. (2002). Asymmetric correlations of equity portfolios. *Journal of Financial Economics*, 63, 443–494.

Cochran, W.G. and Cox, G.M. (1950). *Experimental Designs*. John Wiley, New York.

Erb, C.B., Harvey, C.R. and Viskanta, T.E. (1994). Forecasting international equity correlations. *Financial Analysts Journal*, 50, 32–45.

Fleishman, A.I. (1978). A method for simulating non-normal distributions. *Psychometrika*, 43, 521–532.

Kendall, M.G. (1975). *Rank Correlation Methods* (4th edn). Charles Griffin and Co., London.

Longin, F. and Solnik, B. (2001). Extreme correlation of international equity markets. *Journal of Finance*, 56, 649–676.

Markowitz, H. (1952). Portfolio selection. *Journal of Finance*, 7(1), 77–91.

Pearson, K. (1896). Mathematical contributions to the theory of evolution. III. Regression, heredity and panmixia. *Philosophical Transactions of the Royal Society London, Series A*, 187, 253–318.

Sasabuchi, S. (1988a). A multivariate test with composite hypotheses determined by linear inequalities when the covariance matrix has an unknown scale factor. *Memoirs of the Faculty of Science, Kyushu University, Series A*, 42, 9–19.

Sasabuchi, S. (1988b). A multivariate test with composite hypotheses when the covariance matrix is completely unknown. *Memoirs of the Faculty of Science, Kyushu University, Series A*, 42, 37–46.

Satterthwaite, F.W. (1946). An approximate distribution of estimates of variance components. *Biometric Bulletin*, 2, 110–114.

Sheppard, W. (1898). On the geometrical treatment of the 'normal curve' of statistics, with especial reference to correlation and to the theory of error. *Proceedings of the Royal Society London*, lxii, 171–173.

Sheppard, W. (1899). On the application of the theory of error to cases of normal distributions and normal correlations. *Philosophical Transactions of the Royal Society London, Series A*, xcxii, 101–167.

Steel, R.G.D. and Torrie, J.H. (1980). *Principles and Procedures of Statistics* (2nd edn). McGraw-Hill, New York.

Stuart, A. and Ord, K. (1994). *Kendall's Advanced Theory of Statistics*, Vol. 1. Hodder Arnold, New York.

Vale, C.D. and Maurelli, V.A. (1983). Simulating multivariate non-normal distributions. *Psychometrika*, 48, 465–471.

Vargo, E., Pasupathy, R. and Leemis, L. (2010). Moment-ratio diagrams for univariate distributions. *Journal of Quality Technology*, 42(3), 276–286.

Wicklin, R. (2013). *Simulating Data with SAS*. SAS Institute, Cary, NC.

Proof of Application of Sheppard's Theorem to the Bivariate Elliptical

There exist elegant and simple specific proofs of Sheppard's theorem based on the geometry of the circle; we shall present a more complex argument which has the definite benefit of allowing us to consider more general distributions. As in the main text, we shall use the notation

$$P_{00} = \text{Prob}(X \leq 0, Y \leq 0),$$

$$P_{11} = \text{Prob}(X > 0, Y > 0),$$

$$P_{01} = \text{Prob}(X \leq 0, Y > 0),$$

$$P_{10} = \text{Prob}(X > 0, Y \leq 0).$$

It follows that

$$P_{00} + P_{01} + P_{10} + P_{11} = 1.$$

If the probability density function, pdf(x, y), is symmetric around $(0, 0)$, then $P_{00} = P_{11}$, $P_{10} = P_{01}$ and $P_{00} + P_{10} = \frac{1}{2}$.

Define

$$sgn(x) = \frac{1}{\pi} \int\limits_{-\infty}^{+\infty} \frac{e^{itx} dt}{it}$$

$$= 1, \text{ if } x > 0$$

$$= 0, \text{ if } x = 0$$

$$= -1, \text{ if } x < 0.$$

For proof, see Kendall (1975).
Also, let $S = E(sgn(x) \cdot sgn(y)) = P_{00} + P_{11} - P_{10} - P_{01}$.
Under symmetry about $(0, 0)$:

$$S = 2P_{00} - 2P_{10},$$

so

$$P_{00} = \frac{1}{4}(1 + S) \quad \text{and}$$

$$P_{10} = \frac{1}{4}(1 - S). \tag{6.A.1}$$

In order to compute

$$S = \frac{1}{\pi^2} \int_{-\infty}^{+\infty} \frac{dt_1}{it_1} \int_{-\infty}^{+\infty} \frac{dt_2}{it_2} \varphi(t_1, t_2),$$

where $\varphi(t_1, t_2) = E(e^{it_1 x + it_2 y})$, let

$$\begin{pmatrix} x \\ y \end{pmatrix} \sim N\left(\begin{pmatrix} 0 \\ 0 \end{pmatrix} \begin{pmatrix} 1 & \rho \\ \rho & 1 \end{pmatrix} \right),$$

then

$$\varphi(t_1, t_2) = E(e^{-1/2(t_1^2 + 2\rho t_1 t_2 + t_2^2)}).$$

(We note that, in the main body of the text we use the notation $\rho_{X,Y}$ in order to call attention to a correlation which may be conditional on X and Y. For ease of reading, this notation has been dropped in the context of this proof as it serves no functional purpose.)

Hence

$$S = \frac{1}{\pi^2} \int_{-\infty}^{+\infty} \frac{dt_1}{it_1} \int_{-\infty}^{+\infty} \frac{dt_2}{it_2} e^{-1/2(t_1^2 + 2\rho t_1 t_2 + t_2^2)}. \tag{6.A.2}$$

Now

$$\frac{\partial S(\rho)}{\partial \rho} = \frac{1}{\pi^2} \iint_{-\infty}^{+\infty} e^{-1/2(t_1^2 + 2\rho t_1 t_2 + t_2^2)} \partial t_1 \partial t_2,$$

and $S(0) = 0$, since $P_{00} = P_{11} = P_{01} = P_{10} = \frac{1}{4}$.

Also, from the properties of the normal distribution:

$$S'(\rho) = \frac{2}{\pi\sqrt{1 - \rho^2}},$$

so integrating w.r.t. ρ gives

$$S(\rho) = \frac{2\sin^{-1}(\rho)}{\pi}, \tag{6.A.3}$$

since

$$\frac{\partial \sin^{-1}\rho}{\partial \rho} = \frac{1}{\sqrt{1 - \rho^2}}.$$

Thus

$$P_{00} = \frac{1}{4}\left(1 + \frac{2}{\pi}\sin^{-1}(\rho)\right)$$

$$= \frac{1}{4} + \frac{1}{2\pi}\sin^{-1}(\rho)$$

and $P_{01} = \frac{1}{4} - \frac{1}{2\pi}\sin^{-1}(\rho)$ from Equations (6.A.1) and (6.A.3).

Let τ be our positive stochastic scale factor which we condition on. It is intuitively clear that if the conditional pdf is denoted

$$\begin{pmatrix} x \\ y \end{pmatrix} \bigg| \tau \sim N\left(0, \tau \begin{pmatrix} 1 & \rho \\ \rho & 1 \end{pmatrix}\right), \tag{6.A.4}$$

then

$$\text{Prob}(X > 0, y > 0|\tau) = \frac{1}{4} + \frac{1}{2\pi}\sin^{-1}(\rho)$$

$$\therefore \text{Prob}(X > 0, y > 0) = \frac{1}{4} + \frac{1}{2\pi}\sin^{-1}(\rho).$$

This can be further demonstrated by going through the steps from Equation (6.A.2) onwards, where (6.A.2) becomes

$$S = \frac{1}{\pi^2} \int_{-\infty}^{+\infty} \frac{dt_1}{it_1} \int_{-\infty}^{+\infty} \frac{dt_2}{it_2} e^{-\tau/2(t_1^2 + 2\rho t_1 t_2 + t_2^2)}.$$

6.A.1 EXTENSIONS

We have shown that Sheppard's theorem holds for a subset of the zero-mean elliptical family described by Equation (6.A.4). We now consider potential extensions.

Consider a mixture model for which, after standardizing the data, we can write the probability density function as

$$\text{pdf}(x, y) = \sum_{j=1}^{m} a_j N\left(\begin{pmatrix} 0 \\ 0 \end{pmatrix}, \Omega_j\right),$$

where $a_j \geq 0$, $\sum_{j=1}^{m} a_j = 1$, $\Omega_j = \begin{pmatrix} 1 & \rho_j \\ \rho_j & 1 \end{pmatrix}$ and $N\left(\begin{pmatrix} 0 \\ 0 \end{pmatrix}, \Omega_j\right)$, means distributed as bivariate normal with

mean $\begin{pmatrix} 0 \\ 0 \end{pmatrix}$ and covariance matrix Ω_j. This assumes that all of the m subpopulations have the same mean vector and same variance, but that they differ in correlation, thus they lie outside the elliptical family. Now their characteristic function is

$$\varphi(t_1, t_2) = \sum_{j=1}^{m} a_j e^{-1/2(t_1^2 + 2\rho_j t_1 t_2 + t_2^2)} \tag{6.A.5}$$

and computing S as before and differentiating w.r.t. $\rho_1 \ldots \rho_m$ we find

$$\frac{\partial^m S(\rho_1 \ldots \rho_m)}{\partial \rho_1 \ldots \partial \rho_m} = \sum_{j=1}^{m} \left(\frac{2a_j}{\pi\sqrt{1 - \rho_j^2}}\right).$$

Noting that $S(0,0 \ldots 0) = 0$ and integrating over $\rho_1 \ldots \rho_m$, we see that

$$S(\rho_1 \ldots \rho_m) = 2\sum_{j=1}^{m} \frac{a_j \sin^{-1}(\rho_j)}{\pi}$$

and

$$P_{00} = \frac{1}{4} + \frac{1}{2\pi} \sum_{j=1}^{m} a_j \sin^{-1}(\rho_j),$$

$$P_{01} = \frac{1}{4} - \frac{1}{2\pi} \sum_{j=1}^{m} a_j \sin^{-1}(\rho_j).$$

As before, if $\rho_j \to 1$ for $j = 1, \ldots, m$, then $\sin^{-1}(\rho_j) \to \frac{\pi}{4}$. Thus, since $\sum_{j=1}^{m} a_j = 1$, $P_{00} = \frac{1}{2}$ and $P_{01} = 0$.

It is also clear that this can be extended to consider cases where each subpopulation satisfies assumption (6.A.4); this now covers a fairly large family of distributions whose orthant probabilities can be computed explicitly. Also, since the characteristic function (6.A.5) is real, it means that the probability density function is symmetric about $(0, 0)$ and hence its medians and means are both zero.

CHAPTER 7

Risk Measures Based on Multivariate Skew Normal and Skew *t*-Mixture Models

Sharon X. Lee[a] and Geoffrey J. McLachlan[a]

[a]Department of Mathematics, University of Queensland

Abstract

It is widely recognized that financial stock returns do not always follow the normal distribution. Typically, they exhibit non-normal features such as skewness, heavy tails and kurtosis. In this chapter, we consider the application of multivariate non-normal mixture models for modelling the joint distribution of the log returns in a portfolio. Formulas are then derived for some commonly used risk measures including probability of shortfall (PS), Value-at-Risk (VaR), expected shortfall (ES) and tail-conditional expectation (TCE), based on these models.

Our focus is on skew normal and skew *t*-component distributions. These families of distributions are generalizations of the normal distribution and *t*-distribution, respectively, with additional parameters to accommodate skewness and/or heavy tails, rendering them suitable for handling the asymmetric distributional shape of financial data. As linear transformations of the quantities under consideration also have mixtures of skew-normal or skew *t*-distributions, the PS, VaR and TCE, and other risk measures of an asset portfolio, can be expressed explicitly in terms of the parameters of the fitted mixture models. This approach is demonstrated on a real example of a portfolio of Australian stock returns and the performances of these models are compared with the traditional normal mixture model.

7.1 INTRODUCTION

Risk measurement and forecast are important in investment management. Measures such as Value-at-Risk (VaR) and expected shortfall (ES) are widely used in the finance industry to evaluate market risk exposure. Typically, estimation of these measures relies on the assumption that the returns follow some parametric distribution. Traditional approaches have used the normal distribution for this purpose. However, it is well recognized in the literature that financial returns often have non-normal distributions. They generally exhibit features such as heavy tails, skewness and kurtosis. Studies have shown that approaches that model the returns using a normal distribution (whether explicitly or implicitly) may not perform satisfactorily when applied to real data.

To allow for greater flexibility in the shape of the underlying distribution, some authors have considered finite mixtures of normal distributions, and some slight improvements in the accuracy of risk measures have been observed (Venkataraman, 1997). Recently, Soltyk and Gupta (2011) have reported that further improvements can be made by adopting component densities that incorporate a skewness parameter, that is, by fitting a multivariate skew normal mixture model. However, in addition to asymmetry, empirical evidence has indicated that the distributions of financial returns also exhibit other features such as heavy tails and kurtosis. More recently, Lee and McLachlan (2013b) have considered the use of flexible asymmetric distributions as component distributions for modelling portfolio returns and observed that they provided a closer fit to the real data set in their example.

In this chapter, we examine the application of finite mixtures of skew-elliptical distributions for modelling stock returns and derive estimates for commonly used risk measures based on these models. Our focus will be on two of the most commonly used skew distributions, namely the skew normal and skew *t*-distributions. In particular, we adopt a quite general characterization of the skew normal and skew *t*-distributions, known as the canonical fundamental skew normal (CFUSN) and canonical fundamental skew *t* (CFUST) distributions, respectively. We point out that linear combinations of the variables in a random vector with a multivariate CFUSN (or CFUST) mixture distribution also have a mixture of CFUSN (or CFUST) distributions. These results provide a generalization to those of Bernardi (2013). More specifically, the restricted skew normal distribution considered in Bernardi (2013) is a special case of the CFUSN distribution. As the distribution of a portfolio of returns can now be expressed as a mixture model, simulation (as employed by Soltyk and Gupta (2011) and Lee and McLachlan (2013b)) is no longer required when estimating various risk measures. The cumulative distribution function (cdf) and quantile function (qf) can be calculated numerically from the density of the fitted model, and estimates of PS, VaR and TCE can be obtained from them.

We illustrate the usefulness of this approach in modelling a portfolio of three Australian shares. The model parameters can be estimated from the data using the expectation-maximization (EM) algorithm, and VaR and TCE estimates are then calculated based on the fitted model. Comparison of the performance of these models against traditional approaches is evaluated using backtesting.

The rest of this chapter is organized as follows. Section 7.2 provides an overview of multivariate skew normal and skew *t*-mixture models. In Section 7.3, we outline the result that linear combinations of random variables that have jointly finite mixtures of CFUSN and CFUST distributions also follow finite mixtures of CFUSN and CFUST distributions, respectively. Section 7.4 provides a summary of the definition of commonly used risk measures. The specific expressions for estimates of these measures based on the CFUSN and CFUST mixture models are derived in Section 7.4.1. An application to a portfolio of Australian stocks is illustrated in Section 7.5. Finally, a summary and some remarks are discussed in Section 7.6.

7.2 FINITE MIXTURE OF SKEW DISTRIBUTIONS

Skew distributions, in particular the skew normal and skew *t*-distributions, have received increasing attention in recent years. These families of distributions are extensions of the (univariate) skew normal distribution (Azzalini, 1985) with additional parameters to regulate skewness and other features. For a comprehensive survey of skew distributions, the reader is referred to the recent book by Azzalini and Capitanio (2014), the edited volume of Genton (2004) and the papers by Azzalini (2005), Arellano-Valle and Azzalini (2006) and Genton (2006). For finite mixtures of skew distributions, see Lee and McLachlan (2013a,c, 2014, 2015c).

To establish notation, let Y be a p-dimensional random vector. Then Y is said to follow a CFUSN distribution (Arellano-Valle and Genton, 2005) with location vector μ, scale matrix Σ and skewness matrix Δ if its density is given by

$$f_{\text{CFUSN}_{p,q}}(y; \mu, \Sigma, \delta) = 2^q \phi_p(y; \mu, \Sigma) \, \Phi_q(\Delta^T \Sigma^{-1}(y - \mu); 0, I_q - \Delta^T \Sigma^{-1}\Delta), \tag{7.1}$$

where $\phi_p(.;\mu,\Sigma)$ is the density of the p-variate normal distribution with mean vector μ and covariance matrix Σ, and $\Phi_p(.;\mu,\Sigma)$ is the corresponding distribution function. If Y follows the CFUSN distribution (7.1), we write $Y \sim CFUSN_{p,q}(\mu,\Sigma,\Delta)$. Note that Δ is an arbitrary $p \times q$ matrix. When $\Delta = 0$, (7.1) reduces to the multivariate normal distribution.

The density of a CFUST distribution can be defined in a similar manner by replacing the normal density and cdf in (7.1) with that of a t-distribution, given by

$$f_{CFUST_{p,q}}(y;\mu,\Sigma,\Delta,v) = 2^q t_p(y;\mu,\Sigma,v)\, T_q\left(\Delta^T\Sigma^{-1}(y-\mu)\sqrt{\frac{v+p}{v+d(y)}};0,\Lambda,v+p\right), \quad (7.2)$$

where $\Lambda = I_q - \Delta^T\Sigma^{-1}\Delta$ and $d(y) = (y-\mu)^T\Sigma^{-1}(y-\mu)$ is the squared Mahalanobis distance between y and μ with respect to Σ. Here we let $t_p(.;\mu,\Sigma,v)$ denote the p-dimensional t-density with location vector μ, scale matrix Σ and degrees of freedom v, and $T_p(.;\mu,\Sigma,v)$ is the corresponding distribution function. If Y follows the CFUST distribution (7.2), we can write $Y \sim CFUST_{p,q}(\mu,\Sigma,\Delta,v)$. Note that when $\Delta = 0$, the CFUST density reduces to the multivariate t-distribution. Also, by letting $v \rightarrow \infty$ in (7.2), we obtain the CFUSN density given in (7.1) above.

The above characterization in Equations (7.1) and (7.2) of the skew normal and skew t-distribution is quite flexible in shape. Figure 7.1 shows the contours of some bivariate forms of the CFUST distribution with $\mu = 0$ and $v = 3$. The CFUSN and CFUST distributions encompass some of the commonly used versions of skew normal and skew t-distributions, such as the formulations by Azzalini and Dalla Valle (1996), Branco and Dey (2001), Azzalini and Capitanio (2003), Lachos *et al.* (2010) and Sahu *et al.* (2003). In particular, the so-called restricted skew normal and skew t-distribution can be obtained by letting $\Delta = \delta$ in (7.1) and (7.2) respectively, where δ is a p-dimensional column vector. The restricted characterization is equivalent (after reparametrization) to the well-known classical version of the skew normal and skew t-distribution proposed by Azzalini and Dalla Valle (1996) and Azzalini and Capitanio (2003), as well as other versions (Branco and Dey, 2001; Lachos *et al.*, 2010); see Lee and McLachlan (2013c) for further details. The unrestricted characterization of skew normal and skew t-distribution as proposed by Sahu *et al.* (2003) is also a special case of the CFUSN and CFUST distribution, respectively. They are obtained by letting $\Delta = \text{diag}(\delta)$ in (7.1) and (7.2), that is, a diagonal matrix with diagonal elements specified by δ. Theoretical properties and discussions of the canonical fundamental characterization can be found in Arellano-Valle and Genton (2005) and Lee and McLachlan (2015c).

In this chapter, we consider the modelling of stock returns using finite mixtures of CFUSN and CFUST distributions. The density of a g-component finite mixture model is defined as a convex linear combination of g densities, given by

$$f(y;\Psi) = \sum_{h=1}^{g} \pi_h f(y;\theta_h), \quad (7.3)$$

where θ_h contains the unknown parameters of the hth component density which includes the distinct elements of μ_h, Σ_h and Δ_h (and v_h for the CFUST case), $\Psi = (\pi_1, \ldots, \pi_{g-1}, \theta_1^T, \ldots, \theta_g^T)^T$ is the vector of all unknown parameters of the mixture model, and the mixing proportions π_i are non-negative and sum to one. When component densities $f(y;\theta_i)$ in Equation (7.3) take the form of (7.1) and (7.2), we obtain a finite mixture of CFUSN (FM-CFUSN) distributions and of CFUST (FM-CFUST) distributions, respectively. Their density is given by

$$f(y;\Psi) = \sum_{h=1}^{g} \pi_h f_{CFUSN_{p,q}}(y;\mu_h,\Sigma_h,\Delta_h) \quad (7.4)$$

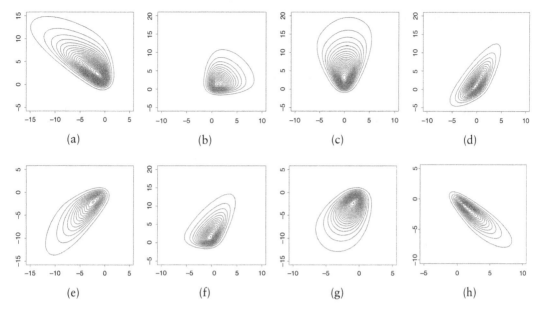

FIGURE 7.1 Contours of the density of some bivariate CFUST distribution with $\mu = 0$, $\nu = 3$ and other parameters as follows. For cases (a) to (f), $\boldsymbol{\Sigma}$ is the identity matrix. For cases (g) and (h), $\boldsymbol{\Sigma}$ has diagonal elements being 1 and off-diagonal elements being -0.75. The elements of $\boldsymbol{\Delta}$ from left to right, top to bottom are given by $(-5,0,3.5,3)$, $(3,0,0,4)$, $(2,-2,5,4)$, $(2,-2,5,-2)$, $(-3,-3,-5,-1)$, $(2,-2,5,0)$, $(0,-2,-3.5,-2)$ and $(2.5,1,-1.5,-2)$, respectively, for cases (a) to (h).

and

$$f(y; \boldsymbol{\Psi}) = \sum_{h=1}^{g} \pi_h f_{\text{CFUST}_{p,q}}(y; \boldsymbol{\mu}_h, \boldsymbol{\Sigma}_h, \boldsymbol{\Delta}_h, \nu_h), \qquad (7.5)$$

respectively. We write $Y \sim$ FM-CFUSN$_{p,q}(\boldsymbol{\Psi})$ and $Y \sim$ FM-CFUST$_{p,q}(\boldsymbol{\Psi})$ to denote that Y has a FM-CFUSN and FM-CFUST distribution, respectively.

Parameter estimation of the FM-CFUSN and FM-CFUST models can be carried out via the EM algorithm. The EM algorithm has become the standard tool for the calculation of maximum likelihood (ML) estimates of the parameters of a mixture model. It is an iterative procedure that alternates the E- and M-steps until some convergence criterion is satisfied. For brevity, the technical details of the approach are omitted here. A detailed description can be found in Leemaqz (2014) for the FM-CFUSN model and Lee and McLachlan (2015c) for the FM-CFUST model. An implementation for the FM-CFUST model in the R software is available freely from Lee and McLachlan (2015a, b).

7.3 LINEAR TRANSFORMATION OF SKEW NORMAL AND SKEW *t*-MIXTURES

We now outline some properties of the FM-CFUSN and FM-CFUST models that are useful for the application of modelling financial returns. To be more specific, we are interested in the distribution of a linear combination of the elements of a random variable that follows a FM-CFUSN or FM-CFUST distribution. Suppose that the p-dimensional random vector Y has either (7.4) or (7.5) as its distribution.

Then we are interested in the variable defined by the linear combination $Y^* = a^T Y$, where $a^T \in \mathbb{R}^p$. Focusing first on the case of FM-CFUSN, let $Y \sim CFUSN_{p,q}(\mu, \Sigma, \Delta)$ and let $\Phi_q(\cdot)$ denote the cdf of a q-dimensional standard normal distribution. Then the moment generating function (mgf) of Y is given by

$$M_Y(t) = 2^q \, e^{t^T \mu + \frac{1}{2} t^T \Sigma t} \, \Phi_q(\Delta^T t). \tag{7.6}$$

The proof can be found in Arellano-Valle and Genton (2005). It can be shown that the linear transformation of Y given by $Y^* = a^T Y$ is also a CFUSN distribution. This can easily be observed from its mgf, which is given by

$$M_{Y^*}(t) = 2^q \, e^{ta^T \mu + \frac{1}{2} t^2 a^T \Sigma a} \, \Phi_q(t\Delta^T a). \tag{7.7}$$

The proof follows immediately from (7.6) by noting that $M_{a^T Y}(t) = M_Y(ta)$. It follows from (7.7) that Y^* has a $CFUSN_{1,q}$ distribution with location parameter $a^T \mu$, scale parameter $a^T \Sigma a$ and skewness vector $a^T \Delta$. It is of interest to note that the density corresponding to (7.7) is a univariate density, but its skewness parameter is a q-dimension row vector. This implies this it is not the same as the classical univariate skew normal distribution, as the latter is a special case of this density with $q = 1$.

In the case of finite mixtures of CFUSN distribution, it can easily be shown that if $Y \sim FM\text{-}CFUSN_{p,q}(\Psi)$, then its mgf is in the form of a linear combination of (7.6), given by

$$M_Y(t) = \sum_{h=1}^{g} \pi_h \left[2^q e^{t^T \mu_h + \frac{1}{2} t^T \Sigma_h t} \Phi_q(\Delta_h^T t) \right]. \tag{7.8}$$

Applying a linear transformation to Y above leads to an mgf that can be expressed as a linear combination of (7.7) given by

$$M_{Y^*}(t) = \sum_{h=1}^{g} \pi_h \left[2^q \, e^{ta^T \mu_h + \frac{1}{2} t^2 a^T \Sigma_h a} \Phi_q(t\Delta_h^T a) \right]. \tag{7.9}$$

The above results can be summarized by the following theorem.

Theorem 7.3.1 (Linear Transformation of FM-CFUSN)   *Let Y be a p-dimensional random vector that follows a FM-CFUSN distribution, that is, $Y \sim FM\text{-}CFUSN_{p,q}(\Psi)$. Let a be a row vector with real elements. Then the linear transformation $Y^* = a^T Y$ has density given by*

$$f(y^*) = \sum_{h=1}^{g} \pi_h \, f_{CFUSN_{1,q}}(y^*; \mu_h^*, \sigma_h^{*2}, \delta_h^{*T}),$$

where $\mu^* = a^T \mu_h$, $\sigma^{*2} = a^T \Sigma_h a$ and $\delta^{*T} = a^T \Delta_h$, for $h = 1, \dots, g$.

In a similar manner, it can be shown that the linear transformation of a FM-CFUST distribution also has a FM-CFUST distribution. The proof follows directly from its mgf. However, the mgf of a CFUST distribution cannot be expressed in closed form. It is given as an integral involving the mgf of the CFUSN distribution. Let $Y \sim CFUST_{p,q}(\mu, \Sigma, \Delta, v)$, then its mgf is given by

$$M_Y(t) = 2^q \int_0^{\infty} e^{\frac{1}{2w} t^T \Sigma t} \Phi_q\left(\frac{1}{\sqrt{w}} \Delta^T t\right) d\, G(w), \tag{7.10}$$

where $G(w)$ denotes the cdf of a gamma$\left(\frac{v}{2}, \frac{v}{2}\right)$ random variable. As in the case of the CFUSN distribution, the CFUST distribution is closed under linear transformation, meaning that a linear transformation of the variables in a CFUST random variable also has a CFUST distribution. It follows that the mgf of $Y^* = a^T Y$ is given by

$$M_{Y^*}(t) = 2^q \int_0^\infty e^{\frac{1}{2w} t^T A \Sigma A^T t} \Phi_q\left(\frac{1}{\sqrt{w}} \Delta^T A^T t\right) d\, G(w). \tag{7.11}$$

Note that the location, scale and skewness parameters are transformed in the same way as for a CFUSN distribution, but the degrees of freedom remain unchanged. This implies that Y^* follows a $\text{CFUST}_{1,q}$ distribution with location parameter $a^T \mu$, scale parameter $a^T \Sigma a^T$, skewness vector $a^T \Delta$ and v degrees of freedom. Generalizing Equations (7.10) and (7.11) to the case of finite mixture models is straightforward and analogous to the generalization of (7.6) and (7.7) to (7.8) and (7.9), respectively. The mgf for $Y \sim \text{FM-CFUST}_{p,q}(\Psi)$ and $Y^* = a^T Y$ is given by

$$M_Y(t) = \sum_{h=1}^g \pi_h \left[2^q \int_0^\infty e^{\frac{1}{2w} t^T \Sigma_h t} \Phi_q(\frac{1}{\sqrt{w}} \Delta_h^T t) d\, G(w) \right] \tag{7.12}$$

and

$$M_{Y^*}(t) = \sum_{h=1}^g \pi_h \left[2^q \int_0^\infty e^{\frac{1}{2w} t^T A \Sigma_h A^T t} \Phi_q(\frac{1}{\sqrt{w}} \Delta_h^T A^T t) d\, G(w) \right], \tag{7.13}$$

respectively. A summary is given in the following theorem.

Theorem 7.3.2 (Linear Transformation of FM-CFUST)   *Let Y be a p-dimensional random vector that follows a FM-CFUST distribution, that is, $Y \sim \text{FM-CFUST}_{p,q}(\Psi)$. Let a be a row vector with real elements. Then the linear transformation $Y^* = a^T Y$ has density given by*

$$f(y^*) = \sum_{h=1}^g \pi_h f_{\text{CFUST}_{1,q}}(y^*; \mu_h^*, \sigma_h^{*2}, \delta_h^{*T}, v_h), \tag{7.14}$$

where $\mu^* = a^T \mu_h$, $\sigma^{*2} = a^T \Sigma_h a$ and $\delta^{*T} = a^T \Delta_h$, for $h = 1, \dots, g$.

It should be noted that the component densities in (7.14) above are not identical to a classical univariate skew t-distribution. The latter is a special case of (7.14) and can be obtained by letting $q = 1$.

7.4   RISK MEASURES

We consider here some commonly used risk measures, namely the probability of shortfall (PS), Value-at-Risk (VaR), expected tail loss (ETL) and tail-conditional expectation (TCE). The PS is the probability that the return of a portfolio falls below a target value. Let Y_R denote the return of a portfolio. Note that Y_R is a scalar random variable. Then the PS for a target y^* is defined as

$$PS_{Y_R}(y^*) = P(Y_R \le y^*). \tag{7.15}$$

The VaR is one of the most popular measures of risk. It can be interpreted as the estimated worse loss over a specified time period and a given significance (or confidence) level. A more mathematical interpretation is that the probability of incurring a loss greater than the VaR for the specified time period is bounded by the significance level α. For example, if $\alpha = 0.05$ and the time period is one day, then a VaR of one million dollars can be interpreted as implying that the probability of incurring a loss in excess of one million dollars for this portfolio over this day is bounded by 0.01. A formal definition of VaR is given by

$$VaR_{Y_R}(\alpha) = -\sup\{y^* : P(Y_R < y^*) \leq \alpha\}, \tag{7.16}$$

that is, it is the negative of the largest value of y^* such that the probability of Y_R is below y^* is bounded by α. In practice, the significance level is typically 0.01 or 0.05. Note that VaR is a positive value, representing a positive amount of 'losses'.

As the VaR has several shortcomings, such as not satisfying the property of subadditivity, Artzner *et al.* (1997) proposed the use of an alternative risk measure known as the ES. This measure is also known by various other names, such as the Conditional Value-at-Risk (CVaR), Average Value-at-Risk (AVaR) and ETL. We will adopt the latter name throughout this chapter. Unlike VaR, the ETL is a coherent risk measure and takes into account loss beyond the VaR level. By definition, the ETL is the expected loss given that the loss is beyond a specified VaR. More formally, it can defined as

$$ETL_{Y_R}(\alpha) = \frac{1}{\alpha} \int_0^\alpha VaR_{Y_R}(\gamma)d\gamma, \tag{7.17}$$

where $VaR_{Y_R}(\alpha)$ is the VaR of Y_R as defined in Equation (7.16) above. Hence, the ETL can be interpreted as a measure of the average of the loss that exceeds the specified VaR.

A similar measure to the ETL is the TCE. This measure is also known as the Tail Value-at-Risk (TVaR) and conditional tail expectation (CTE). The TCE is defined as the expected loss below a specified significance level, given by

$$TCE_{Y_R}(\alpha) = -E\{Y_R \mid Y_R \leq -VaR_{Y_R}(\alpha) \}, \tag{7.18}$$

where $E(A \mid B)$ denotes the conditional expectation of A given B. It can be observed from the definitions above that the ETL and TCE are very similar and, indeed, they are equivalent if the distribution of Y_R is continuous. It should also be noted that the value of the TCE is always greater than the value of the VaR for a given Y_R.

7.4.1 Risk Measures Based on Skew Mixture Models

Explicit expressions for (7.15) to (7.17) based on the FM-CFUSN and FM-CFUST distributions can be derived using the results in Section 7.3. Let Y be a p-dimensional random vector containing the p assets in the portfolio. Then the aggregate return is given by the sum of the individual returns, that is

$$Y_R = \sum_{i=1}^p Y_i = 1_p^T Y, \tag{7.19}$$

where Y_i is the return of the ith asset. Hence Y_R is a linear transformation of Y.

7.4.2 Skew Normal Mixture Models

Focusing first on the case of skew normal mixture models, we let the joint distribution of the portfolio be a FM-CFUSN distribution, that is, $Y \sim \text{FM-CFUSN}_{p,q}(\Psi)$. Then the distribution of the aggregate return Y_R is given by

$$f(Y_R) = \sum_{h=1}^g \pi_h \, f_{\text{CFUSN}_{1,q}} \left(y^*; \mu_h^*, \sigma_h^{*2}, \delta_h^{*T} \right), \tag{7.20}$$

where

$$\mu_h^* = \sum_{i=1}^{p} (\mu_h)_i, \tag{7.21}$$

$$\sigma_h^{*2} = \sum_{i=1}^{p} \sum_{j=1}^{p} (\Sigma_h)_{ij}, \tag{7.22}$$

$$\delta_h^* = \left[\sum_{j=1}^{p} (\Delta_h)_{1j}, \sum_{j=1}^{p} (\Delta_h)_{2j}, \dots, \sum_{j=1}^{p} (\Delta_h)_{qj} \right]. \tag{7.23}$$

That is, μ_h^* and σ_h^{*2} are the sum of the elements of μ_h and Σ_h, respectively, and δ_h^* is the row vector given by summing up the elements in each column of Δ_h. Let the cdf of the above FM-CFUSN distribution be denoted by $F_{\text{FM-CFUSN}_{p,q}}(\cdot)$, and the corresponding qf be denoted by $F_{\text{FM-CFUSN}_{p,q}}^{-1}(\alpha)$. It follows that the PS for the FM-CFUSN is given by

$$PS_y(y^*) = F_{\text{FM-CFUSN}_{p,q}}(y^*). \tag{7.24}$$

For the VaR, it follows from Equation (7.16) that the VaR for a specified significance level α is equivalent to the negative of the quantile of order α of the cdf of Y_R. That is, it can be expressed as

$$VaR_y(\alpha) = -F_{\text{FM-CFUSN}_{p,q}}^{-1}(\alpha) \tag{7.25}$$

for the FM-CFUSN case.

As mentioned previously, the ETL and TCE are identical when Y follows the FM-CFUSN distribution, as the latter is a continuous distribution. By definition (7.18), the conditional expectation on the right-hand side can be interpreted as the first moment of Y_R truncated above by the negative of $VaR_{Y_R}(\alpha)$. It follows that the TCE of Y_R is given by the first moment of a truncated CFUSN mixture model; that is,

$$TCE_{Y_R}(\alpha) = -E[X] = -\frac{\int_{-\infty}^{-VaR_{Y_R}(\alpha)} Y_R \, f_{\text{CFUSN}}(Y_R; \Psi) \, dY_R}{f_{\text{CFUSN}}(VaR_{Y_R}(\alpha); \Psi)}, \tag{7.26}$$

where X is a random variable that has a truncated FM-CFUSN distribution with parameter Ψ, being truncated above by the negative of $VaR_{Y_R}(\alpha)$.

7.4.3 Skew *t*-Mixture Models

Analogous to Section 7.4.2, the PS, VaR and TCE measures in the case where Y follows a FM-CFUST distribution can be expressed in terms of the cdf, qf and first truncated moment, respectively, of a FM-CFUST random variable. Let the joint distribution of the p stocks in the portfolio be a FM-CFUST distribution, that is, $Y \sim \text{FM-CFUST}_{p,q}(\Psi)$. Then the distribution of aggregate return Y_R is given by

$$f(Y_R) = \sum_{h=1}^{g} \pi_h \, f_{\text{CFUST}_{1,q}}(y^*; \mu_h^*, \sigma_h^{*2}, \delta_h^{*T}, v_h), \tag{7.27}$$

where μ_h^*, σ_h^{*2} and δ_h^{*T} are as defined in Equations (7.21), (7.22) and (7.23) above. Similarly, we denote by $F_{\text{FM-CFUST}_{p,q}}(\cdot)$ the cdf of a FM-CFUST distribution, and $F_{\text{FM-CFUST}_{p,q}}^{-1}(\alpha)$ is the corresponding qf.

The PS measure in this case is given by the cdf corresponding to (7.27) evaluated at $Y_R = y^*$, where y^* is the target; that is,

$$PS_{Y_R}(y^*) = F_{\text{FM-CFUST}_{p,q}}(y^*). \tag{7.28}$$

For a specified significance level of α, the VaR for Y_R is given by the negative of the qf of (7.27) evaluated at α; that is,

$$VaR_{Y_R}(\alpha) = -F^{-1}_{\text{FM-CFUST}_{p,q}}(\alpha). \tag{7.29}$$

The TCE for Y_R is given by the first truncated moment of (7.27). It can be expressed as

$$TCE_{Y_R}(\alpha) = -E[X] = -\frac{\int_{-\infty}^{-VaR_{Y_R}(\alpha)} Y_R\, f_{\text{CFUST}}(Y_R; \boldsymbol{\Psi})\, dY_R}{f_{\text{CFUST}}(VaR_{Y_R}(\alpha); \boldsymbol{\Psi})}, \tag{7.30}$$

where X here is a random variable that has a truncated FM-CFUST distribution with parameters $\boldsymbol{\Psi}$ and truncated above by the negative of $VaR_{Y_R}(\alpha)$.

7.5 APPLICATION TO AN AUSTRALIAN PORTFOLIO

7.5.1 The Data Set

We consider a portfolio of three shares listed on the Australian Stock Exchange (ASX) as analysed in Lee and McLachlan (2013b). Briefly, the data consist of the monthly returns for three shares: Flight Centre Limited (FLT), Westpac Banking Corporation (WBC) and Australia and New Zealand Banking Group Limited (ANZ). The time period is from 1 January 2000 to 28 June 2013. The monthly returns of each share were calculated on the adjusted closing prices, and the results are recorded as a percentage. A plot of the data is given in Figure 7.2(a). The summary statistics of the stock returns (Table 7.1) suggest that the data do not satisfy the normality assumption, with mild skewness and excess kurtosis present in all three returns.

7.5.2 Evaluation of Risk Measures

To evaluate the performance of VaR estimators, we shall consider three of the most commonly used statistical tests available, namely the unconditional coverage test (or backtesting), the (Markov) independence test and the exceeding ratio (ER). The backtest (Kupiec, 1995) is a strategy for testing the unconditional coverage property of a VaR estimate model; that is, it is concerned with whether or not the observed and expected violation rates are statistically different. Specifically, the test examines the proportion of violations, given by $r = v/n$, where v denotes the number of violations in the data and n is the number of observations, and determines whether it is statistically different from the expected rate of $\alpha \times 100\%$ of the sample. A violation occurs if the actual loss exceeds the VaR, as implied by the model for the given level of significance. Under the null hypothesis that the model is adequate, v follows a binomial distribution, leading to a likelihood ratio (LR) test statistic of the form

$$\text{LR}_{bt} = 2 \log \left[\left(\frac{1-r}{1-\alpha} \right)^{n-v} \left(\frac{r}{\alpha} \right)^{v} \right], \tag{7.31}$$

which has a asymptotic chi-squared distribution with one degree of freedom. Hence the test would reject a VaR model if it generates too many or too few violations. The backtest, however, cannot detect whether a VaR model satisfies the independence property.

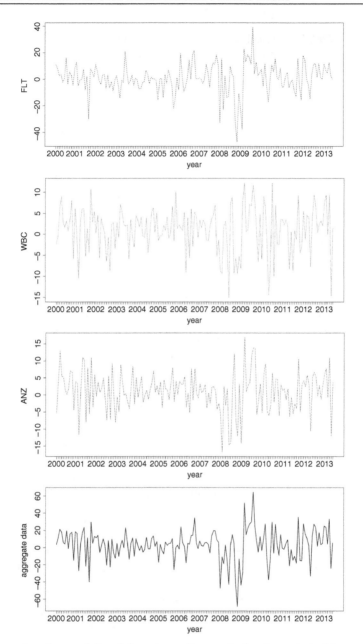

FIGURE 7.2 Time series of a portfolio of three Australian stocks for the period of January 2000 to June 2013. The top three panels correspond to the return of each of three individual stocks: Flight Centre Limited (FLT; dashed line), Westpac Banking Corporation (WBC; dotted line), Australia and New Zealand Banking Group Limited (ANZ; dash-dot line). The bottom panel shows the aggregate return (solid line) overlaid by the three stocks.

TABLE 7.1 Summary statistics of the monthly returns of three Australian stocks for period of early 2000 to mid-2013

	FLT	WBC	ANZ
Min.	−47.13	−15.06	−16.73
Max.	39.08	12.24	16.87
Mean	0.8562	16.87	1.102
Std. Dev.	11.48	5.496	5.858
Skewness	−0.7944	−0.5709	−0.3418
Kurtosis	5.8182	3.173	3.613

Christoffersen (1998) proposed a more elaborate test that examines whether or not a VaR violation process is serially dependent. The underlying assumption is that, for a good and accurate VaR model, the probability of observing a VaR violation should not depend on whether or not a violation has occurred for the previous observation, that is, the sequence of violations should be independently distributed. The LR test statistic for the independence test can be expressed as

$$
\text{LR}_{idp} = -2 \log \left[\frac{(1-q)^{N_1+N_2} q^{N_3+N_4}}{(1-q_1)^{N_1} q_1^{N_3} (1-q_2^{N_2}) q_2^{N_4}} \right], \tag{7.32}
$$

where N_1 denotes the number of observations with no violation followed by no violation, N_2 denotes the number of observations with violation followed by no violation, N_3 denotes the number of observations with no violation followed by a violation, and N_4 denotes the number of observations in which a violation has occurred followed by another violation. The proportions q, q_1 and q_2 are defined, respectively, as the proportion of observations in which a violation has occurred, the proportion for which a violation is observed given no violation has occurred in the previous observation, and the proportion for which a violation is observed given a violation had occurred in the previous observation. More formally, they are given by $q = \frac{N_3+N_4}{N_1+N_2+N_3+N_4}$, $q_1 = \frac{N_3}{N_1+N_3}$ and $q_2 = \frac{N_4}{N_2+N_4}$. The null hypothesis of $q_1 = q_2$ can be tested against the alternative of first-order Markov independence, and the LR statistic (7.32) again has a χ_1^2 distribution.

There are existing strategies for handling financial return series that are serially dependent. One popular approach is to apply a GARCH filter to the returns before fitting a skew model, then perform defiltering on the fitted density to obtain a conditional risk forecast for the return; see, for example, Hu and Kercheval (2007).

Finally, we consider also the ER (Choi and Min, 2011), defined as the ratio of the estimated number of violations over the expected number of violations; that is,

$$
ER = \frac{v}{\alpha n}. \tag{7.33}
$$

An ER value greater than one indicates the model is under-forecasting the VaR, and an ER value less than one indicates an over-forecast VaR estimate.

7.5.3 Performance of the Fitted Models

For this illustration, we compare the performance of finite mixtures of multivariate normal (FM-MN) distributions, the FM-CFUSN model and the FM-CFUST model, in fitting this trivariate data set. To determine the optimal number of components g, each mixture model is fitted with g ranging from 1 to 4, and the best model is selected on the basis of BIC. The value of q is taken to be 3, corresponding to the number of stocks in the portfolio. Estimation of VaR and TCE can be obtained via numerical methods, as described in Section 7.3 based on the fitted parameters of the mixture model. Except for the FM-MN models for which BIC selected $g = 2$ number of components, the other two mixture models require only a single component. Figure 7.3 shows the contours of the density of the fitted models for

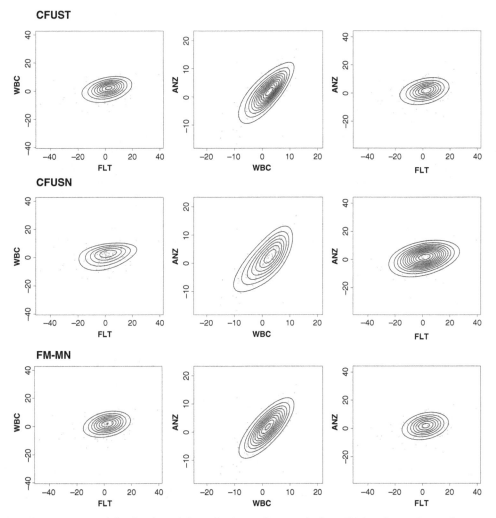

FIGURE 7.3 Contours of the fitted models to the Australian stock data. Each column shows the bivariate plot of a pair of stocks in the portfolio. The top panel shows the contours given by the fitted CFUST model. The middle panel shows the contours given by the fitted CFUSN model. The bottom panel shows the contours given by the fitted FM-MN model.

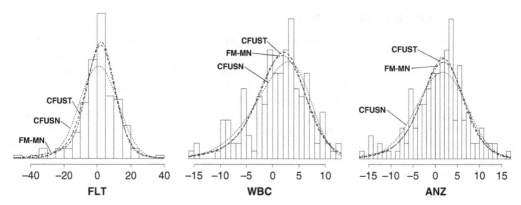

FIGURE 7.4 Histogram of the three stocks in the portfolio overlaid with the marginal density of the fitted models. The dashed, dotted, and dash-dot curves are given by the fitted CFUST, CFUSN and FM-MN models, respectively.

each bivariate combination of the variables of the data. It can be observed that the CFUST and CFUSN distributions can capture the asymmetric shape of the distribution of Y, in particular in the bivariate plots of the pair (ANZ, WBC). The estimated marginal density for each individual return is shown in Figure 7.4. In the figure for FLT, it can be observed that the fit given by the CFUSN model did not handle the left tail as well as the CFUST and FM-MN models. The latter, however, requires two components to accommodate for the heavy tail on the left, whereas a single CFUST component would suffice in this case. Similar behaviour can be observed by the fitted distributions to the WBC and ANZ returns plotted in Figure 7.4, although the differences between the three models is not as evident. The estimated density for the aggregate return Y_R, calculated based on the fitted multivariate models, is shown in Figure 7.5.

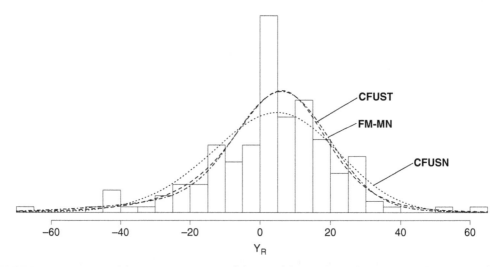

FIGURE 7.5 Histogram of the aggregate return of the portfolio. The overlaid lines are the density of Y_R calculated based on the fitted models, where the dashed, dotted, and dash-dot curve corresponds to the CFUST, CFUSN and FM-MN model, respectively.

TABLE 7.2 Performance of various mixture models on estimating the 5% VaR of three Australian stocks. The backtesting and independence values refer to the *P*-value of the respective tests. The empirical VaR is $29.64

	FM-MN	CFUSN	CFUST
VaR	27.14	27.26	28.68
ER	1.12	1.12	1.12
Backtesting	0.74	0.74	0.74
Independence	1.00	1.00	1.00

Inspection of the left tail in this figure shows that the CFUSN model finds it challenging to model the heavy tail accurately for this data set.

The estimated 5% VaR value given by the FM-MN model and two skew mixture models is reported in the first row of Table 7.2. Given that the empirical VaR calculated from the data is $29.64, it can be observed that the CFUST model gives the closest estimate. All the models considered did not fail the backtesting and independence test (rows 3 and 4 in Table 7.2). The ER indicates that all models over-estimated the VaR, but it is evident from Figure 7.6 that the estimates given by the CFUST model are closer to the empirical curve for a range of α values of interest. The results for the case of 1% significance level are reported in Table 7.3. Again, the estimates given by the CFUSN and CFUST models are closer to the empirical value than the FM-MN model. The ER and the results of the backtesting and independence test are identical for all three models in this case, as the number of violations in the data that exceed the estimated VaR is the same for all models. A plot comparing the estimates of TCE given by the three models for different α values is shown in Figure 7.7. As expected, it can be observed from this figure that the estimates given by the fitted skew distributions follow more closely the curve of the empirical VaR (solid line) than that given by the normal mixture model.

TABLE 7.3 Performance of various mixture models on estimating the 1% VaR of three Australian stocks. The backtesting and independence values refer to the *P*-value of the respective tests. The empirical VaR is $45.45

	FM-MN	CFUSN	CFUST
VaR	55.89	54.15	51.71
ER	0.62	0.62	0.62
Backtesting	0.60	0.60	0.60
Independence	0.96	0.96	0.96

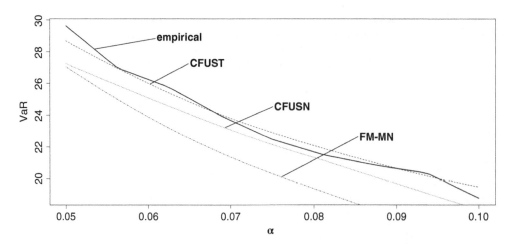

FIGURE 7.6 Estimates of VaR provided by various fitted models. The solid line corresponds to the empirical value, whereas the dashed, dotted, and dash-dot line represent the estimate given by the fitted CFUST, CFUSN and FM-MN model, respectively.

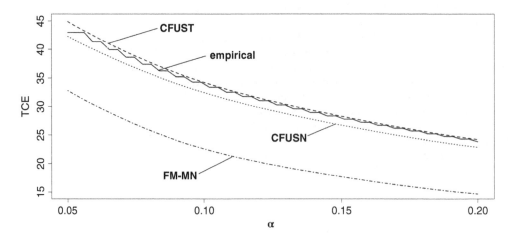

FIGURE 7.7 Estimates of TCE given by various skew mixture models. The solid line corresponds to the empirical value, whereas the dashed, dotted, and dash-dot line represent the estimate given by the CFUST, CFUSN and FM-MN models, respectively.

7.6 SUMMARY AND CONCLUSIONS

In this chapter, we have presented the application of finite mixtures of skew normal and skew t-distributions for modelling asset returns. The families of these distributions are natural extensions of the normal distribution, with additional parameters to accommodate a range of non-normal features.

Results of the illustrative example suggest that the accuracy of risk measures such as VaR can be improved by adopting these flexible parametric families of distributions. In particular, the fitting of mixtures of CFUST distributions is shown to outperform the FM-CFUSN and FM-MN models in this example. It is also observed that the FM-MN model needed two-component normal distributions in order to accommodate the skewness and heavy tails in the data, whereas only a single component is required for the more flexible skew distributions.

REFERENCES

Arellano-Valle, R.B. and Genton, M.G. (2005). On fundamental skew distributions. *Journal of Multivariate Analysis*, 96, 93–116.

Arellano-Valle, R.B. and Azzalini, A. (2006). On the unification of families of skew-normal distributions. *Scandinavian Journal of Statistics*, 33, 561–574.

Artzner, P., Delbaen, F., Eber, J. *et al.* (1997). Thinking coherently. *Risk*, 10, 68–71.

Azzalini, A. (1985). A class of distributions which includes the normal ones. *Scandinavian Journal of Statistics*, 12, 171–178.

Azzalini, A. (2005). The skew-normal distribution and related multivariate families. *Scandinavian Journal of Statistics*, 32, 159–188.

Azzalini, A. and Dalla Valle, A. (1996). The multivariate skew-normal distribution. *Biometrika*, 83, 715–726.

Azzalini, A. and Capitanio, A. (2003). Distributions generated by perturbation of symmetry with emphasis on a multivariate skew t distribution. *Journal of the Royal Statistical Society, Series B*, 65, 367–389.

Azzalini, A. and Capitanio, A. (2014). *The Skew-Normal and Related Families*. Institute of Mathematical Statistics Monographs. Cambridge University Press, Cambridge.

Bernardi, M. (2013). Risk measures for skew normal mixtures. *Statistics & Probability Letters*, 83, 1819–1824.

Branco, M.D. and Dey, D.K. (2001). A general class of multivariate skew-elliptical distributions. *Journal of Multivariate Analysis*, 79, 99–113.

Choi, P. and Min, I. (2011). A comparison of conditional and unconditional approaches in Value-at-Risk estimation. *Journal of the Japanese Economic Association*, 62, 99–115.

Christoffersen, P.F. (1998). Evaluating interval forecasts. *International Economic Review*, 39, 841–862.

Genton, M.G. (ed.) (2004). *Skew-Elliptical Distributions and Their Applications: A Journey Beyond Normality*. Chapman & Hall/CRC, Boca Raton, FL.

Genton, M.G. (2006). Discussion of: The skew-normal distribution and related multivariate families, by. A. Azzalini. *Scandinavian Journal of Statistics*, 9, 1–37.

Hu, W. and Kercheval, A. (2007). Risk management with generalized hyperbolic distributions. Proceedings of the 4th IASTED International Conference on Financial Engineering and Applications, pp. 19–24.

Kupiec, P. (1995). Techniques for verifying the accuracy of risk management models. *Journal of Derivatives*, 3, 73–84.

Lachos, V.H., Ghosh, P. and Arellano-Valle, R.B. (2010). Likelihood based inference for skew normal independent linear mixed models. *Statistica Sinica*, 20, 303–322.

Lee, S. and McLachlan, G.J. (2014). Finite mixtures of multivariate skew t-distributions: some recent and new results. *Statistics and Computing*, 24, 181–202.

Lee, S.X. and McLachlan, G.J. (2013a). Model-based clustering and classification with non-normal mixture distributions. *Statistical Methods and Applications*, 22, 427–454.

Lee, S.X. and McLachlan, G.J. (2013b). Modelling asset return using multivariate asymmetric mixture models with applications to estimation of value-at-risk, in J. Piantadosi, R.S. Anderssen and J. Boland (eds), *MODSIM 2013* (20th International Congress on Modelling and Simulation, Adelaide, Australia), pp. 1228–1234.

Lee, S.X. and McLachlan, G.J. (2013c). On mixtures of skew-normal and skew t-distributions. *Advances in Data Analysis and Classification*, 7, 241–266.

Lee, S.X. and McLachlan, G.J. (2015a). EMMIXcskew: an R package for the fitting of a mixture of canonical fundamental skew t-distributions. arXiv: 1509.02069 [stat.CO].

Lee, S.X. and McLachlan, G.J. (2015b). EMMIXcskew: fitting mixtures of CFUST distributions. R package version 0.9–2.

Lee, S.X. and McLachlan, G.J. (2015c). Finite mixtures of canonical fundamental skew t-distributions: the unification of the restricted and unrestricted skew t-mixture models. *Statistics and Computing*. doi: 10.1007/s11222-015-9545-x.

Leemaqz, S.X. (2014). Finite mixture modelling using multivariate skew distributions. Ph.D. thesis, School of Mathematics and Physics, University of Queensland, Australia.

Sahu, S.K., Dey, D.K. and Branco, M.D. (2003). A new class of multivariate skew distributions with applications to Bayesian regression models. *Canadian Journal of Statistics*, 31, 129–150.

Soltyk, S. and Gupta, R. (2011). Application of the multivariate skew normal mixture model with the EM algorithm to Value-at-Risk, in F. Chan, D. Marinova and R.S. Anderssen (eds), *MODSIM 2011* (19th International Congress on Modelling and Simulation, Perth, Australia), pp. 1638–1644.

Venkataraman, S. (1997). Value at risk for a mixture of normal distributions: the use of quasi-Bayesian estimation techniques. *Economic Perspectives*, 21, 2–13.

CHAPTER 8

Estimating Asymmetric Dynamic Distributions in High Dimensions*,#

Stanislav Anatolyev[a], Renat Khabibullin[b] and Artem Prokhorov[c]

[a]New Economic School and CERGE-EI
[b]Barclays Capital
[c]University of Sydney Business School, St. Petersburg State University and Innopolis University

Abstract

We consider estimation of dynamic joint distributions of large groups of assets. Conventional likelihood functions based on 'off-the-shelf' distributions quickly become inaccurate as the number of parameters grows. Alternatives based on a fixed number of parameters do not permit sufficient flexibility in modelling asymmetry and dependence. This chapter considers a sequential procedure, where the joint patterns of asymmetry and dependence are unrestricted, yet the method does not suffer from the curse of dimensionality encountered in non-parametric estimation. We construct a flexible multivariate distribution using tightly parameterized lower-dimensional distributions coupled by a bivariate copula. This effectively replaces a high-dimensional parameter space with many simple estimations with few parameters. We provide theoretical motivation for this estimator as a pseudo-MLE with known asymptotic properties. In an asymmetric GARCH-type application with regional stock indexes, the procedure provides excellent fit when dimensionality is moderate, and remains operational when the conventional method fails.

8.1 INTRODUCTION

The problem of estimating conditional, or dynamic, distributions for a group of assets is very important to a wide range of practitioners, in particular in the areas of risk management and portfolio optimization. The key problem is how to allow for arbitrary asymmetry and dependence in high dimensions while preserving a feasible parameterization. Traditional multivariate likelihood-based estimators are often impractical in these settings due to high dimensionality or small samples, or both. The existing multivariate densities that allow for asymmetric shapes tend to be tightly parameterized. For example, the multivariate skewed Student-t distribution of Bauwens and Laurent (2005) allows for

---

*Helpful discussions with Eric Renault, Tommaso Proietti, Dmytro Matsypura and Oleg Prokopyev are gratefully acknowledged.
#Research for this paper was supported by a grant from the Russian Science Foundation (Project No. 16-18-10432).

different degrees of asymmetry along each dimension, but the degrees of freedom are constrained to be the same along all dimensions. Thus, a more natural benchmark is provided by the copula approach, which allows for greater flexibility as far as the density shape is concerned.

Now consider the problem of constructing a high-dimensional distribution using the copula approach. Suppose we wish to estimate a d-dimensional Student-t distribution. This is equivalent to estimating d univariate Student-t marginals and a Student-t d-copula. The problem has at least $d(d-1)/2$ parameters. The conventional approach is to construct a joint log-density from this d-dimensional distribution and use it in a maximum likelihood (ML) routine. However, for large d and moderate sample sizes, the likelihood is highly unstable, Hessians are near singular, estimates are inaccurate and global convergence is hard to achieve.

One solution is to use copulas which have tighter parameterizations. However, the functional form of such copulas limits the nature of dependence they can accommodate (Nelsen, 2006, Section 4.6). Another solution is to use 'vine copulas' (Aas et al., 2009) when the d-variate density is decomposed into a product of up to $d(d-1)/2$ bivariate densities. However, there are still $O(d^2)$ parameters in the joint likelihood; in addition, the required ordering of components is rarely available, especially in the time-series context. Yet another alternative is to use the factor copula approach (Oh and Patton, 2013). However, the joint density obtained lacks a close form; in addition, it is unclear whether the convolution of distributions imposed by the factor copula covers all classes of joint distributions one may wish to model.

The method we describe in this chapter replaces the initial estimation problem with a sequence of bivariate problems. This procedure was first outlined by Anatolyev et al. (2014) and can be thought of as recovering the joint distribution from the distributions of all lower-dimensional sub-vectors comprising the original random vector. We start with univariate distributions and estimate all copula-based bivariate distributions that can be constructed from them. Then we couple each univariate marginal with one of the bivariate distributions to get all possible trivariate distributions involving three given marginals. Then we model the average. At every subsequent step we couple each univariate marginal with a lower-dimensional distribution from the previous step and average over these combinations. This provides sufficient flexibility as we can model asymmetry and dependence differently in each step.

Theoretical justification for this procedure comes from the theory of composite and quasi-likelihoods (see, e.g., Varin et al., 2011 for a review) and the theory of compatible copulas (see, e.g., Nelsen, 2006). The averaging over combinations comes from the theory of model average estimators (see, e.g., Clemen, 1989 for an early review). The procedure is related to the work by Sharakhmetov and Ibragimov (2002) and de la Pena et al. (2006), who provide a representation of multivariate distributions in terms of sums of U-statistics of independent random variables, where the U-statistics are based on functions defined over all subvectors of the original random vector. The procedure is also somewhat similar in spirit to Engle's (2009) approach of estimating a vast-dimensional DCC model by merging estimates of many pairwise models, either all of them or a number of selected ones. In contrast to Engle (2009), we reconstruct the dynamics of the entire multivariate distribution, rather than focusing on the dynamics of the conditional second moment.

Our method uses many individual optimization problems at each step. However, each such problem involves substantially fewer parameters than the conventional estimation problem where the entire dependence structure is parameterized. For the Student-t example above, we will show in the application section that the conventional MLE will have difficulty even when dimensions are moderate (i.e., when d is between 5 and 10). In contrast, our procedure requires running MLEs for only bivariate Student-t's.

In parametric estimation, fewer parameters means functional form biases. If we take an 'off-the-shelf' distribution with a high d and a tight parameterization, it will typically be tied to a convenient functional form indexed by a handful of parameters and the patterns of asymmetry and dependence it can accommodate will be limited. As an example, consider a one-parameter Gumbel–Hougaard d-copula. This is a multivariate Archimedean copula with Kendall's τ in the range $[0,1)$, incapable of capturing discordance or lower-tail dependence (see, e.g., Nelsen, 2006, Section 4.6). An important advantage of our approach is greater flexibility in modelling asymmetry and dependence – because of the many steps, we have more degrees of freedom in choosing parameterizations.

In this chapter we look in more detail at the asymptotic properties of our estimator. We show that this estimator can be viewed as a traditional pseudo-maximum likelihood estimator (PMLE). We also look at the estimator in the framework of the generalized method of moments (GMM) estimation in order to study the consequences of multiple-stage estimation on asymptotic efficiency and standard error construction.

The chapter proceeds by describing the algorithm in Section 8.2. Section 8.3 considers theoretical properties of our estimator. Section 8.4 describes a typical parameterization that arises in a multivariate setting with dynamic and skewed distributions. It also gives details on the compounding functions and goodness-of-fit tests that seem appropriate in this setting. Section 8.5 presents an empirical application of the sequential method. Section 8.6 concludes.

8.2 SEQUENTIAL PROCEDURE

Suppose the group contains d assets. The new methodology can be described in the following sequence of steps.

> **Step 1.** Estimate the univariate marginals by fitting suitable parametric distributions
>
> $$\hat{F}_1, \hat{F}_2, \ldots, \hat{F}_d,$$
>
> where $\hat{F}_j = F(\hat{\theta}_j)$ for each $j = 1, \ldots, d$. This step involves d MLE problems and is standard for parametric modelling of dynamic multivariate distributions using copulas. The conventional next step would be to apply a d-copula to the marginals but, as discussed in the Introduction, this often results in an intractable likelihood.
>
> **Step 2.** Using $\hat{F}_j$'s, estimate bivariate distributions for all distinct pairs (i, j)
>
> $$\hat{F}_{12}, \hat{F}_{13}, \ldots, \hat{F}_{1K}, \hat{F}_{23}, \ldots, \hat{F}_{d-1,d}$$
>
> using a suitable parametric copula family as follows:
>
> $$\hat{F}_{ij} = C^{(2)}\left(\hat{F}_i, \hat{F}_j; \hat{\theta}_{ij}\right),$$
>
> where $C^{(2)}(\cdot, \cdot; \cdot)$ is a bivariate symmetric copula.[1]
>
> In bivariate settings, this step is also standard, and final. For $d > 2$, we repeat it for all asset pairs, effectively obtaining all possible contributions of the pairwise composite likelihood. There are $d(d-1)/2$ distinct pairs, as a symmetric copula for (i, j) is identical to the copula of (j, i). Hence, this step involves at least that many ML estimations.
>
> An alternative that provides even more flexibility is to use an asymmetric copula, in which case $C^{(2)}\left(\hat{F}_i, \hat{F}_j; \hat{\theta}_{ij}\right) \neq C^{(2)}\left(\hat{F}_j, \hat{F}_i; \hat{\theta}_{ji}\right)$. Then, the number of estimations increases

---

[1]Here and further a *symmetric* copula $C(.,.)$ means that $C(u, v) = C(v, u)$. This is the terminology used, for example, in Nelsen (2006). With reference to copulas it is sometimes equivalent to *exchangeable* copulas and not to be confused with *radially symmetric* copulas, which means that $C(u, v) = u + v - 1 + C(1 - u, 1 - v)$. All of the copulas we used, including symmetric in the sense above, are not radially symmetric so they allow for asymmetry in the joint distribution.

to $d(d-1)$ and in order to obtain a single distribution involving, say, index i and index j, we use the average of the two copulas as follows:

$$\widehat{F}_{ij} = \frac{C^{(2)}\left(\widehat{F}_i, \widehat{F}_j; \widehat{\theta}_{ij}\right) + C^{(2)}\left(\widehat{F}_j, \widehat{F}_i; \widehat{\theta}_{ji}\right)}{2}.$$

Aside from simple averaging, data-driven weighting schemes (e.g., based on information criteria) exist (see, e.g., Burnham and Anderson, 2002, Chapter 4), but we leave this aside for the moment.

It is easy to see that steps 1 and 2 produce pseudo-ML estimators of $\widehat{\theta}_j$'s and $\widehat{\theta}_{ij}$'s. So, for each pair (i, j) we have a pseudo-ML estimator of their distribution. It could be tempting to stop here and to construct the joint distribution over all marginals by aggregating $\widehat{F}_{ij}$ over $i, j = 1, \ldots, d$ (e.g., by averaging). This would be similar to other types of composite likelihood-based estimators (see, e.g., Cox and Reid, 2004; Varin and Vidoni, 2005, 2006, 2008). However, it will impose a restrictive dependence structure on the joint distribution and result in a poorer fit. We return to this point in Section 8.3.1.

Step 3. Using $\widehat{F}_j$ and $\widehat{F}_{ij}$, estimate trivariate distributions for each combination of i and (j, k)

$$C^{(3)}\left(\widehat{F}_i, \widehat{F}_{jk}; \widehat{\theta}_{ijk}\right),$$

where $C^{(3)}\left(\widehat{F}_i, \widehat{F}_{jk}; \widehat{\theta}_{ijk}\right)$ is a suitable copula-type *compounding function* (not necessarily symmetric) that captures dependence between the ith asset and the (j, k)th pair of assets. There are $d(d-1)(d-2)/2$ possible combinations of $\widehat{F}_i$'s with disjoint pairs $\widehat{F}_{jk}$, so this is the number of estimations involved in this step.

Similar to step 2, we construct a single distribution for triplet (i, j, k) by averaging over the three available estimates as follows:

$$\widehat{F}_{ijk} = \frac{C^{(3)}\left(\widehat{F}_i, \widehat{F}_{jk}; \widehat{\theta}_{ijk}\right) + C^{(3)}\left(\widehat{F}_j, \widehat{F}_{ik}; \widehat{\theta}_{jik}\right) + C^{(3)}\left(\widehat{F}_k, \widehat{F}_{ij}; \widehat{\theta}_{kij}\right)}{3}.$$

This formula is an extension of that for $\widehat{F}_{ij}$. It uses triplets of observations to construct the composite likelihood contributions and it applies equal weights when averaging since we have no information-theoretic argument to prefer one estimated distribution over another.

Step m, $m < d$. Using the $\widehat{F}_i$'s and $\widehat{F}_{i_1, \ldots, j-1, j+1, \ldots, i_m}$, estimate an m-dimensional distribution for each m-tuple. There are $d!/(d-m)!(m-1)!$ possible combinations of $\widehat{F}_i$'s with disjoint $(m-1)$-variate marginals. Let $i_1 < i_2 < \ldots < i_m$. Obtain a model average estimate of the distribution for the $(i_1, i_2, \ldots, i_m)$th m-tuple:

$$\widehat{F}_{i_1 i_2 \ldots i_m} = \frac{1}{m} \sum_{l=1}^{m} C^{(m)}\left(\widehat{F}_l, \widehat{F}_{i_1, \ldots, l-1, l+1, \ldots, i_m}; \widehat{\theta}_{l, i_1, \ldots, l-1, l+1, \ldots, i_m}\right),$$

where $C^{(m)}$ is an mth-order compounding function which is set to be a suitable asymmetric bivariate copula.

Step d. Estimate the d-variate distribution:

$$\widehat{F}_{12\ldots d} = \frac{1}{d} \sum_{l=1}^{d} C^{(d)}\left(\widehat{F}_l, \widehat{F}_{1, \ldots, l-1, l+1, \ldots, d}; \widehat{\theta}_{l, 1, \ldots, l-1, l+1, \ldots, d}\right),$$

where $C^{(d)}$ is a dth-order compounding function. There are d such functions to be estimated.

As the compounding functions are regular bivariate copulas, it follows that, by construction, $\hat{F}_{1,2,\ldots,d}$ is non-decreasing on its support, bounded and ranges between 0 and 1. Hence, $\hat{F}_{1,2,\ldots,d}$ can be viewed as an estimate of the joint cumulative distribution function obtained using sequential composite likelihoods. In essence this cdf is a result of sequential applications of bivariate copulas to univariate cdf's and bivariate copulas.

Nothing guarantees that such a sequential use of copulas preserves the copula properties, that is, nothing guarantees that the mth-order compounding functions are also m-copulas, $m = 3, \ldots, d$. In fact, there are several well-known impossibility results concerning construction of high-dimensional copulas by using lower-dimensional copulas as arguments of bivariate copulas (see, e.g., Quesada-Molina and Rodriguez-Lallena, 1994; Genest *et al.*, 1995b). Basically, the results suggest that copulas are rarely compatible, that is, if one uses a k-copula and an l-copula as arguments of a bivariate copula, the resulting $(k + l)$-variate object does not generally meet all the requirements for being a copula (see, e.g., Nelsen, 2006, Section 3.5).

Strictly speaking, the compounding functions constructed in steps 3 to d may fail to be m-copulas unless we use a compatible copula family. However, the resulting estimator $\hat{F}_{12\ldots d}$ is a distribution and thus implies a d-copula. Therefore we do not require the compounding functions to qualify for being m-copulas as long as they can provide a valid pseudo-likelihood. In the theory section, we discuss the assumptions underlying this estimator. In practice, in order to ensure that we use a valid pseudo-likelihood we choose in steps 3 to d a flexible asymmetric bivariate copula family that passes goodness-of-fit diagnostics.

As an alternative we could use copula functions which *are* compatible. Consider, for example, the Archimedean copulas. These copulas have the form $C(u_1, \ldots, u_d) = \psi^{[-1]}(\psi(u_1) + \ldots + \psi(u_d))$, where $\psi(\cdot)$ is a function with certain properties and $\psi^{[-1]}(\cdot)$ is its inverse. Under a certain monotonicity condition on ψ sometimes referred to as a nesting condition (see, e.g., Theorem 4.6.2 of Nelsen, 2006) this functional form allows us to go from $C(u_1, u_2)$ to the d-copula by repeatedly replacing one of the two arguments with $u_m = C(u_{m+1}, u_{m+2})$, $m = 2, \ldots, d - 1$. However, as discussed in the Introduction, the range of dependence such d-copulas can capture is limited and hence we do not use it in the empirical section.[2]

In each step of the procedure we operate only with two types of objects: a multivariate distribution of a smaller (by one) dimension and a univariate distribution. This allows for the number of parameters used in each compounding function to be really small, while the total number of parameters in the joint distribution remains rather large and ensures the flexibility needed to model general asymmetry and dependence. This clarifies the claims made in the Introduction about the advantages of this procedure over the standard single-copula or full-likelihood-based estimation. The conventional methods often produce intractable likelihoods due to dimensionality, or they may be overly restrictive due to a tight parameterization. Our procedure allows us to maintain a high degree of flexibility while trading the dimensionality of the parameter space for numerous simpler estimations.

Finally, if we are faced with an extremely large number of assets our method permits a reduction of the number of estimations by following the approach of Engle *et al.* (2008) and considering *random* pairs, triples, etc., instead of *all* possible pairs, triples, etc., as proposed here.

8.3 THEORETICAL MOTIVATION

8.3.1 Composite Pseudo-likelihood and Model Averaging

Fundamentally, our method of obtaining $\hat{F}_{12\ldots d}$ falls within a subcategory of sequential pseudo-MLE known as composite likelihood methods (see, e.g., Cox and Reid, 2004; Varin and Vidoni, 2005). Composite likelihood estimators construct joint pseudo-likelihoods using components of the true data

---

[2]In the application, we have considered using the Clayton copula as an Archimedean alternative to Student's t copula. However, in spite of being a comprehensive copula, it did not pass our goodness-of-fit diagnostics and so we do not report these results here.

generating process such as all pairs (see, e.g., Caragea and Smith, 2007; Varin, 2008) or pairwise differences (see, e.g., Lele and Taper, 2002), and sometimes employing weights on the likelihood components to improve efficiency (see, e.g., Heagerty and Lele, 1998).

Unlike existing composite likelihood approaches, we estimate components of the composite likelihood sequentially, for all possible multivariate marginals of the joint distribution, and employ weighting to combine alternative composite densities. So our estimator is related to the literature on sequential copula-based pseudo-MLE (see, e.g., Joe, 2005; Prokhorov and Schmidt, 2009b) and to the literature on Bayesian model averaging and optimal forecast combination (see, e.g., Clemen, 1989; Geweke and Amisano, 2011).

Consider the sequential procedure for $d = 3$ and ignore for the moment the combinatorics and the weighting. Let $H(x_1, x_2, x_3)$ and $h(x_1, x_2, x_3)$ denote the joint distribution and density, respectively. We wish to estimate these objects. Let $F_j = F(x_j)$ and $f_m = f(x_j), j = 1, 2, 3$, denote the univariate marginal cdf's and pdf's. Note that the conventional 3-copula factorization would lead to the following expression for the log joint density:

$$\ln h(x_1, x_2, x_3) = \sum_{j=1}^{3} \ln f_j + \ln c(F_1, F_2, F_3), \qquad (8.1)$$

where $c(u_1, u_2, u_3)$ is a 3-copula density.

Now let $C^{(3)}(u_1, u_2)$ denote the copula function used in step 3 of our procedure, where u_2 is set equal to the copula obtained in step 2, and let $c^{(3)}(u_1, u_2)$ denote the copula density corresponding to $C^{(3)}(u_1, u_2)$. The following result shows that the log joint density (without the weighting) has a useful factorization, analogous to Equation (8.1).

Proposition 8.3.1 *Suppose* $H(x_1, x_2, x_3) = C^{(3)}(F_3(x_3), C^{(2)}(F_2(x_2), F_1(x_1)))$. *Assume* $\ln c^{(2)}(u_1, u_2)$ *is Lipschitz continuous. Then,*

$$\ln h(x_1, x_2, x_d) = \sum_{j=1}^{3} \ln f_j + \ln c^{(2)}(F_2, F_1) + \ln c^{(3)}\left(F_3, C^{(2)}(F_2, F_1)\right)$$

$$+ O\left(c^{(2)}(F_2, F_1)^{-1}\right) \qquad (8.2)$$

Proof: see Appendix 8.A for proofs.   ∎

In essence, Proposition 8.3.1 shows that under a standard continuity condition, one can reconstruct a trivariate log density, up to an approximation error, by combining likelihood contributions obtained from individual marginals using bivariate copulas as in our algorithm. The approximation error is inversely related to $c^{(2)}(F_2, F_1)$, so it is small in areas of the support where $c^{(2)}$ concentrates a lot of mass and is big in flat areas of the copula density.

Now suppose we stop at step 2, as discussed in Section 8.2. Effectively, this means we omit the third term on the right-hand side of Equation (8.2). The approximation error is now larger and its magnitude is no longer inversely related to values of copula densities. We also omit a valid contribution to the likelihood in the form of the log-copula density from step 3. This may have efficiency implications even if we use model averaging.

Clearly there are many possible combinations of marginals that can be used to form a joint distribution $H(x_1, x_2, x_3)$. For example, $C^{(3)}$ can also be formed as $C^{(3)}\left(F_1, C^{(2)}(F_2, F_3)\right)$, or as $C^{(3)}\left(F_2, C^{(2)}(F_1, F_3)\right)$. Each such combination of marginals will produce a different log-density so it is important to pool them optimally. This question of density pooling is central in the literature on combining multiple prediction densities (see, e.g., Hall and Mitchell, 2007; Geweke and Amisano, 2011), where optimal weights, also known as scoring rules, are worked out in the context of information theory. As an example, define $c_j^{(3)}$ as follows:

$$c_j^{(3)} \equiv c^{(3)}\left(F_j, C_k^{(2)}\right),$$

where $j, k = 1, 2, 3, j \neq k$ and $C_k^{(2)} \equiv C^{(2)}(F_k, F_l), l \neq k, l \neq j$. Then, it is possible in principle to obtain the optimal weights ω_j as solutions to the following problem:

$$\max_{\omega_j : \sum \omega_j = 1} \sum_{\text{sample}} \ln \sum_j \omega_j c_j^{(3)}. \tag{8.3}$$

Such scoring rules make the ω_j's a function of the $c_j^{(3)}$'s and may be worth pursuing in large samples. However, it has been noted in this literature that often a simple averaging performs better due to the estimation error in ω's (see, e.g., Stock and Watson, 2004; Elliot, 2011). Moreover, in our setting, problem (8.3) would need to be solved at each step, imposing a heavy computational burden. Therefore, in our procedure we use a simple average of $C^{(m)}$'s, or equivalently, a simple average of $c^{(m)}$'s.

8.3.2 Asymptotics

We now turn to the asymptotic properties of our estimator. Let $\hat{\theta}$ contain all $\hat{\theta}$'s from the steps described in Section 8.2. Assume that $\hat{F}_{12\ldots d}(x_1, \ldots, x_d)$ is a proper distribution. Then, by the celebrated Sklar (1959) theorem, the distribution $\hat{F}_{12\ldots d}(x_1, \ldots, x_d)$ implies a d-copula $K(u_1, \ldots, u_d; \hat{\theta})$ and the corresponding estimator of density $\hat{f}_{12\ldots d}(x_1, \ldots, x_d)$ implies a d-copula density $k(u_1, \ldots, u_d; \hat{\theta})$. (We denote the implied copula distribution and density functions by K and k, respectively, to distinguish them from the true copula distribution $C(u_1, \ldots, u_d)$ and true copula density $c(u_1, \ldots, u_d)$.) The following result gives explicit formulas for the implied copula (density).

Proposition 8.3.2 *Let $\hat{F}_m^{-1}(u_m), m = 1, \ldots, d$, denote the inverse of the marginal cdf $\hat{F}_m$ from step 1 and let $\hat{f}_m$ denote the pdf corresponding to $\hat{F}_m$. Then, the copula implied by $\hat{F}_{12\ldots d}$ can be written as follows:*

$$K(u_1, \ldots, u_d; \hat{\theta}) = \hat{F}_{12\ldots d}(\hat{F}_1^{-1}(u_1), \ldots, \hat{F}_d^{-1}(u_d))$$

$$k(u_1, \ldots, u_d; \hat{\theta}) = \frac{\hat{f}_{12\ldots d}(\hat{F}_1^{-1}(u_1), \ldots, \hat{F}_d^{-1}(u_d))}{\prod_{m=1}^d \hat{f}_m(\hat{F}_m^{-1}(u_m))}.$$

Proposition 8.3.2 gives the form of the flexible parametric d-variate *pseudo*-copula implied by $\hat{F}_{12\ldots d}(x_1, \ldots, x_d)$.[3] So if we estimated θ using the conventional one-step MLE rather than the sequential MLE algorithm of Section 8.2, the asymptotic properties of our estimator would be the well-studied properties of copula-based *pseudo*- or *quasi*-MLE (see, e.g., Genest *et al.*, 1995a; Joe, 2005; Zhao and Joe, 2005; Prokhorov and Schmidt, 2009b). Sequential estimation only affects the asymptotic variance of θ. The following proposition summarizes these results.

---

[3]Here, by *pseudo*-copula we mean a possibly misspecified copula function. The same term is sometimes used in reference to an empirical copula obtained using univariate empirical cdf's and to a copula-type function that satisfies most but not all copula properties (see, e.g., Fermanian and Wegkamp, 2012; Fang and Madsen, 2013).

Proposition 8.3.3 *The MLE estimator $\hat{\theta}$ minimizes the Kullback–Leibler divergence criterion,*

$$\hat{\theta} = \arg\min_{\theta} \mathbb{E} \ln \frac{c(u_1, \ldots, u_d)}{k(u_1, \ldots, u_d; \theta)},$$

where c is the true copula density and expectation is with respect to the true distribution. Furthermore, under standard regularity conditions, $\hat{\theta}$ is consistent and asymptotically normal. If the true copula belongs to the family $k(u_1, \ldots, u_d; \theta)$, it is consistent for the true value of θ. If the copula family is misspecified, the convergence occurs to a pseudo-true value of θ, which minimizes the Kullback–Leibler distance.

It is worth noting that it is still possible in principle to follow the conventional MLE approach here. That is, we can still attempt to find $\hat{\theta}$ by maximizing the log-likelihood based on the following joint log-density:

$$\ln h(x_1, \ldots, x_d) = \sum_{j=1}^{d} \ln f_j(\theta_j) + \ln k(F_1(\theta_1), \ldots, F_d(\theta_d); \theta), \tag{8.4}$$

where θ_j's denote parameters of the univariate marginals. However, the dimension of θ in this problem is greater than for the initial problem in Equation (8.1) and so if the initial problem is intractable, this method will be as well.

Proposition 8.3.3 outlines the asymptotic properties of $\hat{\theta}$ and thus of $\hat{F}_{12\ldots d}$. However, it does not provide the asymptotic variance of $\hat{\theta}$. In order to address the issue of the relative efficiency of our procedure, we rewrite our problem in the GMM framework.

It is well known that the MLE can quite generally be written as a method of moments problem based on the relevant score functions. As an example, we look at the ingredients of our procedure for $d = 3$. The first step is the MLE for $F_j \equiv F_j(\theta_j), j = 1, 2, 3$; the second step is the MLE for $c^{(2)}(\hat{F}_2, \hat{F}_3; \theta_{23})$, where $\hat{F}_j \equiv F_j(\hat{\theta}_j)$; the third step is the MLE for $c^{(3)}(\hat{F}_1, \hat{C}^{(2)}; \theta_{123})$, where $\hat{C}^{(2)} \equiv C^{(2)}(\hat{F}_2, \hat{F}_3; \hat{\theta}_{23})$. The corresponding GMM problems can be written as follows:

$$1. \ \mathbb{E} \begin{bmatrix} \nabla_{\theta_1} \ln f_1(\theta_1) \\ \nabla_{\theta_2} \ln f_2(\theta_2) \\ \nabla_{\theta_3} \ln f_3(\theta_3) \end{bmatrix} = 0,$$

$$2. \ \mathbb{E}[\nabla_{\theta_{23}} \ln c^{(2)}(\hat{F}_2, \hat{F}_3; \theta_{23})] = 0,$$

$$3. \ \mathbb{E}[\nabla_{\theta_{123}} \ln c^{(3)}(\hat{F}_1, \hat{C}^{(2)}(\hat{F}_2, \hat{F}_3); \theta_{123})] = 0,$$

where ∇ denotes the gradient of the score function.

The GMM representation provides several important insights. First, it shows that at steps 2 and 3 we treat the quantities estimated in the previous step as if we knew them. The fact that we estimate them affects the asymptotic variance of $\hat{\theta}_{23}$ and $\hat{\theta}_{123}$, and the correct form of the variance should account for that. The appropriate correction and simulation evidence of its effect are provided, for example, by Joe (2005) and Zhao and Joe (2005).

Second, it shows that each estimation in the sequence is an exactly identified GMM problem. That is, each step introduces as many new parameters as new moment conditions. One important implication of this is that the (appropriately corrected for the preceding steps) asymptotic variance of the sequential estimator is identical to the asymptotic variance of the one-step estimator, which is obtained by solving the optimal GMM problem based on all moment conditions at once (see, e.g., Prokhorov and Schmidt, 2009a). Such an optimal GMM estimator may be difficult to obtain in practice due to the large number of moment conditions, but this efficiency bound is the best we can do in terms of relative efficiency with the moment conditions implied by our sequential MLE problems.

Finally, it is worth noting that this efficiency bound does not coincide with the Fisher bound, implied by the MLE based on the full likelihood in Equation (8.4), even if the copula k is correctly specified. The corresponding GMM problem for that likelihood includes moment conditions of the form

$$\mathbb{E}\left[\nabla_{\theta_j} \ln k(F_1(\theta_1), \ldots, F_d(\theta_d); \theta)\right] = 0, \quad j = 1, \ldots, d,$$

which are not used in the sequential procedure. Therefore, the sequential procedure cannot be expected to be fully efficient.

8.4   PARAMETERIZATIONS

This section describes the models and distributions used in the empirical implementation of our sequential procedure. The particular choices of parameterizations are tied to our data set and should be perceived as suggestive. However, we believe that they are flexible enough to produce good fits when applied to log-returns data – these are models and distributions characterized by asymmetry, skewness, fat tails and dynamic dependence.

Assume that the following sample of log-returns is available: $\{y_t = \{y_{it}\}_{i=1}^d\}_{t=1}^T$, where y_{it} is the individual log-return of the ith asset at time t, d is the total number of assets and T is the length of the sample.

8.4.1   Univariate Distributions

We would like to use skewed and thick-tailed distributions to model univariate marginals. Azzalini and Capitanio (2003) propose one possible generalization of Student's t-distribution which is able to capture both these features. Moreover, their transformation does not restrict the smoothness properties of the density function, which is useful for quasi-maximum likelihood optimization. The pdf of their skew t-distribution is

$$f_Y(y) = 2\, t_\nu(y)\, T_{\nu+1}\left[\gamma \frac{y - \xi}{\omega} \left(\frac{\nu + 1}{\nu + Q_y}\right)^{1/2}\right],$$

where

$$Q_y = \left(\frac{y - \xi}{\omega}\right)^2,$$

$$t_\nu(y) = \frac{\Gamma((\nu + 1)/2)}{\omega\,(\pi\nu)^{1/2}\Gamma(\nu/2)}(1 + Q_y/\nu)^{-(\nu+1)/2}$$

and $T_{\nu+1}(x)$ denotes the cdf of the standard t-distribution with $\nu + 1$ degrees of freedom. The parameter γ reflects the skewness of the distribution. Equivalently, denote

$$Y \sim St_1(\xi, \omega, \gamma, \nu).$$

It is worth noting the first three moments of the distribution when $\xi = 0$,

$$E(Y) = \omega\bar{\mu},$$

$$E(Y^2) = \bar{\sigma^2} = \omega^2 \frac{v}{v-2},$$

$$E(Y^3) = \bar{\lambda} = \omega^3\bar{\mu}\, \frac{3+2\gamma^2}{1+\gamma^2}\, \frac{v}{v-3},$$

where

$$\bar{\mu} := \frac{\gamma}{\sqrt{1+\gamma^2}} \left(\frac{v}{\pi}\right)^{1/2} \frac{\Gamma((v-1)/2)}{\Gamma(v/2)}.$$

The last moment equation indicates that by varying γ one can change the skewness of the distribution. Also, it follows from the first two equations that the first moment of Y is different from 0 and its second central moment is not equal to 1. It is therefore useful to define the standardized skew t-distribution by adjusting $St_1(\xi, \omega, \gamma, v)$ for zero expectation and unit variance through setting ξ and ω in the following way:

$$\omega = \left(\frac{v}{v-2} - \bar{\mu}^2\right)^{-1/2},$$

$$\xi = -\omega\bar{\mu}.$$

Denote the standardized skew t-distribution by $St(\gamma, v)$, its cdf by $F^{St}_{\gamma,v}$ and pdf by $f^{St}_{\gamma,v}$. We augment this distribution with the NAGARCH structure for the conditional variance equation (see, e.g., Engle and Ng, 1993):

$$y_{it} = \mu_i + \sqrt{h_{it}}\varepsilon_{it}, \qquad \varepsilon_{it} \sim \text{ i.i.d. } St(\gamma_i, v_i),$$

$$h_{it} = \omega_i + \alpha_i\left(y_{i,t-1} - \mu_i + \kappa_i\sqrt{h_{i,t-1}}\right)^2 + \beta_i h_{i,t-1},$$

where the h_{it}'s are the conditional variances of the y_{it}'s and $(\mu_i, \gamma_i, v_i, \omega_i, \alpha_i, \beta_i, \kappa_i)$ is the set of parameters. It is worth noting that the parameter κ_i reflects the leverage effect and is expected to be negative.

Using this structure we can write the cdf of y_{it} as follows:

$$F_i(y_{it}) = F^{St}_{\gamma_i,v_i}\left(\frac{y_{it} - \mu_i}{h_{it}^{1/2}}\right).$$

Then, the log-likelihood function for each univariate marginal will have the following form:

$$\ln L_i = \sum_{t=2}^{T}\left\{\ln f^{St}_{\gamma_i,v_i}\left(\frac{y_{it} - \mu_i}{h_{it}^{1/2}}\right) - \frac{1}{2}\ln h_{it}\right\}.$$

There are seven parameters in this likelihood function for each i.

8.4.2 Bivariate Copulas

Here we chose the following p-copula adapted from Ausin and Lopes (2010):

$$C_{\eta,R}(u_1, \ldots, u_p) = \int_{-\infty}^{T_\eta^{-1}(u_1)} \cdots \int_{-\infty}^{T_\eta^{-1}(u_p)} \frac{\Gamma\left(\frac{\eta+p}{2}\right)\left(1 + \frac{v'R^{-1}v}{\eta-2}\right)^{-\frac{\eta+p}{2}}}{\Gamma\left(\frac{\eta}{2}\right)\sqrt{(\pi(\eta-2))^p|R|}}\, d\mathbf{v},$$

where $T_\eta^{-1}(\cdot)$ is the inverse of the standardized Student t cdf, p is number of assets in the group under consideration, η is the number of degrees of freedom and R is the correlation matrix. Denote the expression under the integral by $f_{\eta,R}(\mathbf{v})$ – it is the pdf of the standardized multivariate Student t-distribution. Except for comparison with the benchmark involving $p = d$, we will use only the bivariate version of this copula ($p = 2$).

Following Ausin and Lopes (2010), we assume that the dynamic nature of the correlation matrix R is captured by the following equation:

$$R_t = (1 - a - b)\overline{R} + a\Psi_{t-1} + bR_{t-1},$$

where $a \geq 0$, $b \geq 0$, $a + b \leq 1$, $\overline{R}$ is a positive definite constant matrix with ones on the main diagonal and Ψ_{t-1} is such a matrix whose elements have the following form:

$$\Psi_{ij,t-1} = \frac{\sum_{h=1}^m x_{it-h} x_{jt-h}}{\sqrt{\sum_{h=1}^m x_{it-h}^2 \sum_{h=1}^m x_{jt-h}^2}},$$

where

$$x_{it} = T_\eta^{-1}\left(F_{\gamma_i,\nu_i}^{St}\left(\frac{y_{it} - \mu_i}{h_{it}^{1/2}}\right)\right).$$

The advantage of defining R_t in this way is that it guarantees positive definiteness. This circumvents the need to use additional transformations (see, e.g., Patton, 2006, who uses the logistic transformation).

Substituting the marginal distributions into the assumed copula function, we obtain the following model for the joint cdf of a vector of financial log-returns $\mathbf{y}_t = (y_{1t}, \dots, y_{pt})$:

$$F(\mathbf{y}_t) = C_{\eta,R_t}(F_1(y_{1t}), \dots, F_p(y_{pt})). \tag{8.5}$$

We also derive the joint pdf by differentiating Equation (8.5):

$$f(\mathbf{y}_t) = f_{\eta,R_t}(T_\eta^{-1}(F_1(y_{1t})), \dots, T_\eta^{-1}(F_p(y_{pt})))$$
$$\times \prod_{i=1}^p \left\{ \frac{1}{t_\eta\left(T_\eta^{-1}(F_i(y_{it}))\right)} f_{\gamma_i,\nu_i}^{St}\left(\frac{y_{it} - \mu_i}{h_{it}^{1/2}}\right) \frac{1}{h_{it}^{1/2}} \right\}.$$

Then, the log-likelihood function for the conventional full ML estimation can be written as follows:

$$\ln L = \sum_{t=m+1}^T \ln f_{\eta,R_t}\left(T_\eta^{-1}(F_1(y_{1t})), \dots, T_\eta^{-1}(F_p(y_{pt}))\right)$$
$$+ \sum_{t=m+1}^T \sum_{i=1}^p \left\{ -\ln t_\eta\left(T_\eta^{-1}(F_i(y_{it}))\right) + \ln f_{\gamma_i,\nu_i}^{St}\left(\frac{y_{it} - \mu_i}{h_{it}^{1/2}}\right) - \frac{1}{2}\ln h_{it} \right\}.$$

In the conventional one-step full MLE, $p = d$ and the number of parameters in this likelihood is $d(d-1)/2 + 3$ from the copula part plus $7d$ from the marginal parts.

In our sequential alternative to the FMLE, we first estimate the skew t-marginal distributions using only the last two terms in the likelihood – they do not depend on the copula parameters. Then, the likelihoods we use in steps 2 to d are based on the bivariate version of this log-likelihood with given $\widehat{F}_i(y_{it})$'s. This version is simpler; it can be written as follows:

$$
\ln L_{ij} = \sum_{t=m+1}^{T} \ln f_{\eta,R_t}\left(T_\eta^{-1}\left(\widehat{F}_i(y_{it})\right), T_\eta^{-1}\left(\widehat{F}_j(y_{jt})\right)\right)
$$

$$
- \sum_{t=m+1}^{T} \left\{ \ln t_\eta\left(T_\eta^{-1}\left(\widehat{F}_i(y_{it})\right)\right) + \ln t_\eta\left(T_\eta^{-1}\left(\widehat{F}_j(y_{jt})\right)\right) \right\}.
$$

It has only four parameters.

8.4.3 Compounding Functions

The two arguments of the bivariate copula in step 2 are similar objects – they are the marginal distributions of two assets. This is the reason why we use a symmetric copula for the bivariate modeling in step 2. In contrast, the compounding functions in steps 3 to d operate with two objects of different nature: one is a marginal distribution of one asset and the other is a joint distribution of a group of assets. Thus, in general it makes sense to use asymmetric copulas as compounding functions in these steps.

Khoudraji (1995) proposes a method of constructing asymmetric bivariate copulas from symmetric bivariate copulas using the following transformation:

$$
C^{(asym)}(u,v) = u^\alpha v^\beta C^{(sym)}\left(u^{1-\alpha}, v^{1-\beta}\right), \quad 0 \le \alpha, \beta \le 1,
$$

where $C^{(sym)}(u,v)$ is a generic symmetric copula and $C^{(asym)}(u,v)$ is the corresponding asymmetric copula. We utilize this result to obtain what we call the asymmetrized bivariate standardized t-copula:

$$
C_{\eta,\rho}^{(t,asym)}(u,v) = u^\alpha v^\beta \int_{-\infty}^{T_\eta^{-1}(u^{1-\alpha})} \int_{-\infty}^{T_\eta^{-1}(v^{1-\beta})} \frac{\Gamma\left(\frac{\eta+2}{2}\right)\left(1 + \frac{x^2+y^2-2\,\rho\,x\,y}{(\eta-2)(1-\rho^2)}\right)^{-\frac{\eta+2}{2}}}{\Gamma\left(\frac{\eta}{2}\right)\pi(\eta-2)\sqrt{1-\rho^2}} dx\,dy,
$$

where u denotes the marginal distribution of an asset, v denotes the distribution of a group of assets and we assume a similar time-varying structure on the correlation coefficient as in Section 8.4.2. The form of the compounding function in the mth step will then be

$$
C^{(m)}\left(\widehat{F}_l, \widehat{F}_{i_1,\dots,l-1,l+1,\dots,i_m}; \theta_{l,i_1,\dots,l-1,l+1,\dots,i_m}\right) = C_{\eta,\rho}^{(t,asym)}\left(\widehat{F}_l, \widehat{F}_{i_1,\dots,l-1,l+1,\dots,i_m}\right),
$$

where $\theta_{l,i_1,\dots,l-1,l+1,\dots,i_m} = (\alpha,\beta,\eta,\rho,a,b)'$ is the parameter set (the last three parameters come from the time-varying structure of the correlation matrix R containing in the bivariate case only one correlation coefficient ρ). Correspondingly, there are only six parameters to estimate in each optimization problem of the sequential procedure, regardless of the dimensionality of the original problem.

8.4.4 Goodness-of-Fit Testing

In order to assess the adequacy of distributional specifications, we conduct goodness-of-fit (GoF) testing. For this purpose we use the conventional approach based on probability integral transforms (PIT) first proposed by Rosenblatt (1952). The approach is based on transforming the time series of log-returns into a series that should have a known pivotal distribution in the case of correct specification and then testing the hypothesis that the transformed series indeed has that known distribution.

To assess the quality of fit of marginals, we use the approach of Diebold *et al.* (1998), who exploit the following observation. Suppose there is a sequence $\{y_t\}_{t=1}^T$ which is generated from distributions $\{F_t(y_t|\Omega_t)\}_{t=1}^T$, where $\Omega_t = \{y_{t-1}, y_{t-2}, \ldots\}$. Then, under the usual condition of a non-zero Jacobian with continuous partial derivatives, the sequence of probability integral transforms $\{F_t(y_t|\Omega_t)\}_{t=1}^T$ is i.i.d. $U(0,1)$. Diebold *et al.* (1998) propose testing the uniformity property and the independence property separately by investigating the histogram and correlograms of the moments up to order 4. We follow this approach, with the exception that the statistical tests rather than the graphical analyses are conducted in order to separately test the uniformity and independence properties. In particular, we run Kolmogorov–Smirnov tests of uniformity and F-tests of serial uncorrelatedness.

The goodness-of-fit tests for bivariate copulas are based on a similar approach proposed by Breymann *et al.* (2003), which also relies on PIT. Let $\mathbf{X} = (X_1, \ldots, X_d)$ denote a random vector with marginal distributions $F_i(x_i)$ and conditional distributions $F_{i|i-1\ldots1}(x_i|x_{i-1}, \ldots, x_1)$ for $i = 1, \ldots, d$. The PIT of vector $\mathbf{x}$ is defined as $T(\mathbf{x}) = T(x_1, \ldots, x_d) = (T_1, \ldots, T_d)$ such that $T_1 = F_1(x_1)$, $T_p = F_{p|p-1\ldots1}(x_p|x_{p-1}, \ldots, x_1)$, $p = 2, \ldots, d$. One can show that $T(\mathbf{X})$ is uniformly distributed on the p-dimensional hypercube (Rosenblatt, 1952). This implies that $T_1, \ldots, T_p$ are uniformly and independently distributed on $[0, 1]$. This approach has been extended to the time-series setting (see, e.g., Patton, 2006). Again, we exploit the Kolmogorov–Smirnov tests for uniformity and F-tests for serial uncorrelatedness. Note, however, that there exist $p!$ ways of choosing conditional distributions of a p-variate vector. For pairwise copulas, this means two such ways: $X_2 \mid X_1$ and $X_1 \mid X_2$. We examine both of them for all pairs.

8.5 EMPIRICAL APPLICATION

This section demonstrates how to apply the new sequential technique to model a joint distribution of DJIA constituents. We have considered larger numbers of stocks but to illustrate the advantage of our method over conventional ones (and to save space) we start with $d = 5$. For univariate marginals, we exploit skewed t-distributions with a NAGARCH structure for conditional variance; for bivariate distributions, we exploit the asymmetrized time-varying t-copula, which is also the copula we use for benchmark comparisons when estimating p-variate distributions with $p > 2$. We have considered other copulas but found this copula to produce the best fit. The Kolmogorov–Smirnov goodness-of-fit tests conducted at each step of the procedure show that these parametric distributions provide a good fit for individual asset returns as well as jointly for their combinations. Eventually, we compare our new methodology with the conventional benchmark – a single five-dimensional time-varying t-copula-based estimation.

8.5.1 Data

We choose the following five stocks from among DJIA constituents (as of 8 June 2009): GE – General Electric Co.; MCD – McDonald's Corp.; MSFT – Microsoft Corp.; KO – Coca-Cola Co.; PG – Procter & Gamble Co. The selection is based on a high level of liquidity and availability of historical prices. Daily data from 3 January 2007 to 31 December 2007 are collected; we focus on this period to avoid dealing with the turbulence that followed. The stock prices are adjusted for splits and dividends, and then the log-returns are constructed and used in estimation. The plots of relative price dynamics, histograms of log-returns and sample statistics of log-returns for the five stocks are presented in Figures 8.1 and 8.2 and in Table 8.1. One can see that the unconditional sample distributions in some cases demonstrate skewness and heavy tails, which justifies the selection of the skew t-distribution for modelling marginals.

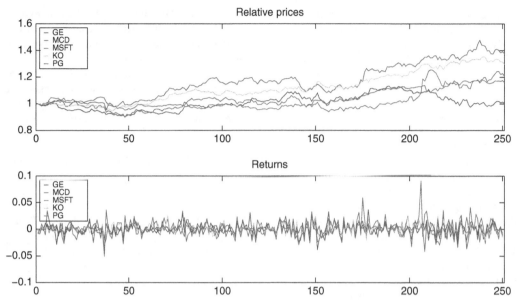

FIGURE 8.1 Relative prices and returns dynamics for GE, MCD, MSFT, KO and PG from 3 January to 31 December 2007.

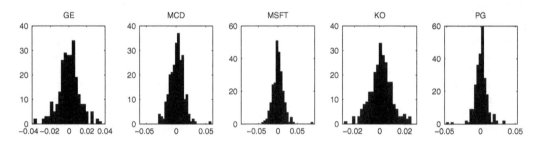

FIGURE 8.2 Histograms of the returns.

TABLE 8.1 Summary statistics of the returns

	GE	MCD	MSFT	KO	PG
Minimum	−0.0384	−0.0298	−0.0421	−0.0285	−0.0506
Maximum	0.0364	0.0589	0.0907	0.0254	0.0359
Mean × 10^{-3}	0.0248	1.2831	0.7575	1.0363	0.5987
Standard deviation	0.0115	0.0116	0.0143	0.0087	0.0091
Skewness (zero-skewness: p-value)	−0.0349 (0.8216)	0.2617 (0.0912)	0.9461 (0.0000)	0.0512 (0.7408)	−0.6106 (0.0001)
Kurtosis (zero-ex. kurtosis: p-value)	3.9742 (0.0017)	4.8977 (0.0000)	8.7270 (0.0000)	3.6313 (0.0416)	9.2954 (0.0000)

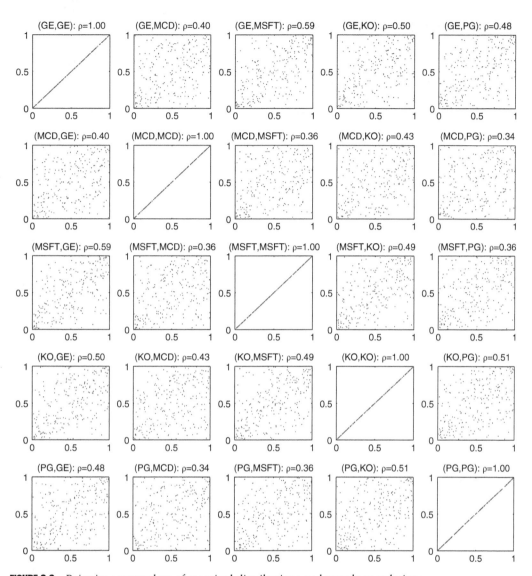

FIGURE 8.3 Pairwise scatter plots of marginal distributions and sample correlations.

The scatter plots and correlations on Figure 8.3 show that, as expected, all of the stocks are positively correlated. The correlation between MSFT and PG is smaller than for most of the other stocks – these two stocks belong to different sectors (Technology and Consumer Goods).[4] At the same time, the correlation between KO and PG is greater than between the other stocks, due to the fact that they both belong to the Consumer Goods sector.

---

[4] See http://finance.yahoo.com for a classification.

8.5.2 Estimates of Univariate Distributions

We use the skew-t-NAGARCH model for the marginals in order to accommodate the asymmetries, heavy tails, leverage effects and volatility clustering that are observed in stock log-returns. For marginal distributions, we choose the initial value of the conditional variance h_{i1} in the GARCH process to be equal to the sample unconditional variance of log-returns.

The estimates of the parameters of marginal distributions are summarized in Table 8.2. As before, μ denotes mean return, ω is unconditional variance, α reflects the ability to predict conditional variance using current innovations, β is a measure of persistence of conditional variance, κ is leverage effect, the reciprocal of v captures heavy tails and γ represents skewness. The mean return μ is fairly close to the sample mean. There is a substantial degree of persistence in the conditional variance process for four out of the five series. There is excess kurtosis in all series. The skewness parameter γ and the leverage effects are largely insignificant; however, we keep them in the model because of the non-zero skewness found (see Table 8.1) and because it is now standard in the literature to account for these stylized facts.

The Kolmogorov–Smirnov tests of uniformity applied to the transformed series show that at the 95% confidence level the hypothesis of uniformity is not rejected. The quantitative results along with the diagrams are presented in Figure 8.4. The model passes these tests.

Next, we conduct the tests for serial correlation of the transformed series. Diebold et al. (1998) recommend that it is sufficient in practice to investigate the moments up to order 4. We follow this suggestion and test the hypothesis about the joint insignificance of coefficients in the regression of each

TABLE 8.2 Maximum likelihood parameter estimates for marginal distributions (robust standard errors are in parentheses)

	GE	MCD	MSFT	KO	PG
$\mu \times 10^{-3}$	−0.032	1.340	0.660	0.750	0.574
	(0.615)	(0.709)	(0.886)	(0.673)	(0.645)
$\omega \times 10^{-5}$	0.569	5.845	0.852	0.667	0.608
	(0.581)	(1.893)	(0.809)	(0.740)	(0.523)
α	0.106	0.153	0.041	0.142	0.107
	(0.062)	(0.090)	(0.024)	(0.082)	(0.052)
β	0.861	0.379	0.915	0.787	0.837
	(0.084)	(0.130)	(0.055)	(0.139)	(0.063)
κ	−0.074	−0.530	−0.174	−0.032	−0.168
	(0.364)	(0.394)	(0.796)	(0.740)	(0.606)
v	6.482	9.672	5.898	8.098	3.305
	(2.325)	(4.976)	(2.360)	(4.046)	(0.734)
γ	−0.014	−0.431	0.176	−0.236	−0.106
	(0.077)	(0.706)	(0.533)	(0.950)	(0.482)

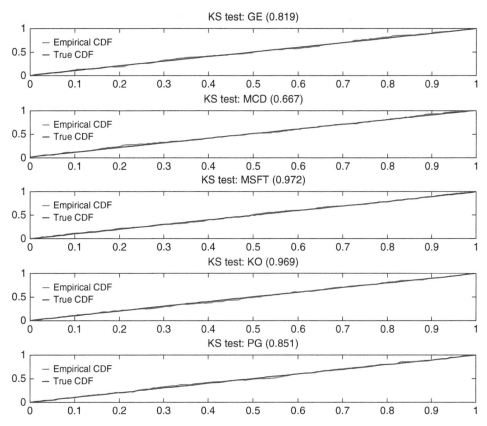

FIGURE 8.4 Kolmogorov–Smirnov tests of marginal distributions (*p*-values in parentheses).

moment on its 20 lags using the F-test. The results are presented in Table 8.3. The hypotheses of no serial correlation are not rejected at the 95% confidence level in nearly every case; the exception is the fourth central moment of the KO stock, for which the hypothesis is not rejected at the 99% confidence

TABLE 8.3 *p*-values of F-tests for serial correlation

Central moment	GE	MCD	MSFT	KO	PG
1	0.701	0.454	0.762	0.336	0.310
2	0.763	0.805	0.448	0.070	0.437
3	0.567	0.672	0.763	0.611	0.657
4	0.887	0.774	0.635	0.032	0.172

level. In addition, all the Ljung–Box tests carried out to test for autocorrelation in the residuals of the marginals' specification do not reject the hypothesis of no serial correlation either. This also indicates a good fit of the selected parametric forms of the marginal distributions.

8.5.3 Estimates of Pairwise Copulas

The pairwise copula parameter estimates are summarized in Table 8.4 and the results of pairwise Kolmogorov–Smirnov tests are presented in Figures 8.5 and 8.6. All Kolmogorov–Smirnov tests are passed at any reasonable confidence level. This indicates that the time-varying t-copula used for modelling bivariate distributions fits quite well and can be used in step 2 of the sequential approach.

As before, the hypothesis of no serial correlation can be tested by checking the joint insignificance of the coefficients in the regression of each of the first four moments on their 20 lags using the F-test.

TABLE 8.4 Maximum likelihood parameter estimates for pairwise copulas (robust standard errors are in parentheses)

	GE, MCD	GE, MSFT	GE, KO	GE, PG	MCD, MSFT
η	9.627	7.948	6.107	14.236	9.883
	(7.732)	(3.006)	(2.390)	(11.290)	(8.488)
a	0.074	0.089	0.002	0.038	0.159
	(0.075)	(0.113)	(0.002)	(0.023)	(0.096)
b	0.399	0.001	0.486	0.913	0.385
	(0.241)	(0.130)	(0.306)	(0.031)	(0.226)
$\bar{\rho}$	0.418	0.625	0.513	0.557	0.429
	(0.062)	(0.042)	(0.050)	(0.076)	(0.073)
	MCD, KO	**MCD, PG**	**MSFT, KO**	**MSFT, PG**	**KO, PG**
η	11.825	6.011	5.672	6.926	10.760
	(9.397)	(2.476)	(2.226)	(2.968)	(9.417)
a	0.072	0.170	0.031	0.197	0.053
	(0.087)	(0.091)	(0.225)	(0.152)	(0.076)
b	0.447	0.394	0.462	0.000	0.342
	(0.288)	(0.266)	(2.057)	(0.169)	(0.209)
$\bar{\rho}$	0.417	0.368	0.556	0.469	0.504
	(0.059)	(0.080)	(0.056)	(0.065)	(0.050)

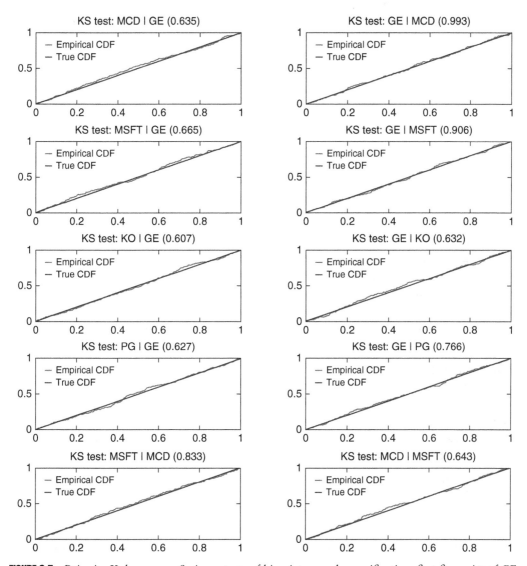

FIGURE 8.5 Pairwise Kolmogorov–Smirnov tests of bivariate copula specification: first five pairs of GE, MCD, MSFT, KO and PG (*p*-values in parentheses).

Additionally, in the bivariate setting we included the lagged moments of the other PIT series in the regression to test for independence. All the results (not shown here to save space) suggest that the hypotheses of no serial correlation cannot be rejected at any reasonable confidence level in every case and that the bivariate specification we chose fits well.

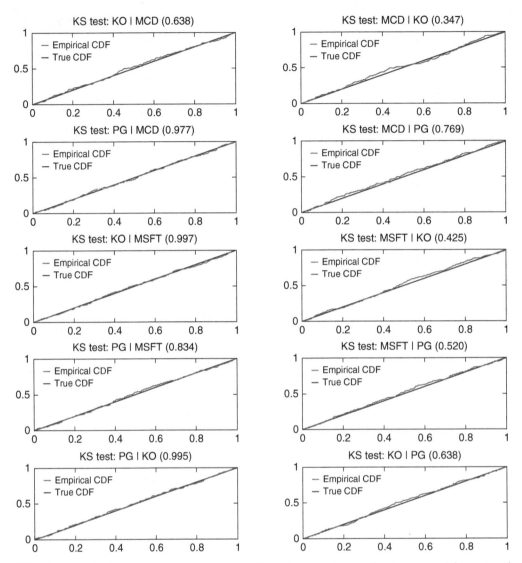

FIGURE 8.6 Pairwise Kolmogorov–Smirnov tests of bivariate copula specification: second five pairs of GE, MCD, MSFT, KO and PG (*p*-values in parentheses).

8.5.4   Estimates of Compounding Functions

Tables 8.5, 8.6 and 8.7 contain parameter estimates in the *t*-copula-based approach for groups of assets of different size. We do not present standard errors for the estimates to save space. Also, we omit the plots and *p*-values for the Kolmogorov–Smirnov tests. The tests support our choice of the asymmetrized bivariate *t*-copula as a compounding function and show an exceptional fit.

TABLE 8.5 Maximum likelihood parameter estimates of the compounding functions for groups of three assets (standard errors omitted)

$C(\cdot;\cdot)$	α	β	η	$\bar{\rho}$	a	b
(GE; MCD, MSFT)	0.044	0.322	8.612	0.884	0.004	0.992
(MCD; GE, MSFT)	0.007	0.011	8.557	0.408	0.124	0.351
(MSFT; GE, MCD)	0.008	0.001	8.828	0.503	0.143	0.092
(GE; MCD, KO)	0.002	0.251	8.544	0.499	0.001	0.249
(MCD; GE, KO)	0.000	0.112	9.928	0.403	0.059	0.399
(KO; GE, MCD)	0.017	0.008	61.964	0.446	0.048	0.334
(GE; MCD, PG)	0.023	0.114	14.379	0.468	0.109	0.059
(MCD; GE, PG)	0.009	0.028	5.197	0.338	0.114	0.423
(PG; GE, MCD)	0.001	0.194	5.306	0.472	0.106	0.275
(GE; MSFT, KO)	0.076	0.224	8.508	0.670	0.076	0.128
(MSFT; GE, KO)	0.007	0.007	6.867	0.536	0.036	0.232
(KO; GE, MSFT)	0.031	0.162	8.459	0.602	0.004	0.314
(GE; MSFT, PG)	0.002	0.161	10.151	0.638	0.015	0.946
(MSFT; GE, PG)	0.030	0.001	10.296	0.498	0.101	0.034
(PG; GE, MSFT)	0.057	0.251	8.786	0.612	0.060	0.242
(GE; KO, PG)	0.046	0.069	13.185	0.496	0.001	0.033
(KO; GE, PG)	0.009	0.001	23.245	0.497	0.066	0.484
(PG; GE, KO)	0.001	0.234	7.505	0.612	0.136	0.016
(MCD; MSFT, KO)	0.005	0.219	6.018	0.469	0.119	0.362
(MSFT; MCD, KO)	0.003	0.001	9.917	0.436	0.054	0.402
(KO; MCD, MSFT)	0.129	0.025	19.673	0.541	0.026	0.286
(MCD; MSFT, PG)	0.133	0.315	8.481	0.588	0.358	0.136
(MSFT; MCD, PG)	0.001	0.000	6.562	0.407	0.078	0.606
(PG; MCD, MSFT)	0.001	0.128	5.165	0.425	0.120	0.561
(MCD; KO, PG)	0.000	0.004	6.686	0.320	0.154	0.324
(KO; MCD, PG)	0.231	0.020	19.575	0.577	0.066	0.605
(PG; MCD, KO)	0.000	0.405	4.553	0.587	0.164	0.365
(MSFT; KO, PG)	0.002	0.001	6.930	0.473	0.125	0.015
(KO; MSFT, PG)	0.002	0.001	23.721	0.530	0.067	0.251
(PG; MSFT, KO)	0.022	0.143	8.385	0.544	0.159	0.221

TABLE 8.6 Maximum likelihood parameter estimates of the compounding functions for groups of four assets (standard errors omitted)

$C(\cdot;\cdot)$	α	β	η	$\overline{\rho}$	a	b
(GE; MCD, MSFT, KO)	0.057	0.326	8.580	0.630	0.007	0.646
(MCD; GE, MSFT, KO)	0.005	0.180	8.326	0.440	0.137	0.244
(MSFT; GE, MCD, KO)	0.022	0.110	8.443	0.508	0.058	0.238
(KO; GE, MCD, MSFT)	0.015	0.062	8.540	0.466	0.023	0.477
(GE; MCD, MSFT, PG)	0.026	0.137	8.868	0.523	0.096	0.103
(MCD; GE, MSFT, PG)	0.046	0.201	8.464	0.447	0.189	0.390
(MSFT; GE, MCD, PG)	0.007	0.008	8.666	0.423	0.185	0.047
(PG; GE, MCD, MSFT)	0.025	0.235	6.492	0.511	0.092	0.494
(GE; MCD, KO, PG)	0.026	0.269	10.768	0.447	0.092	0.188
(MCD; GE, KO, PG)	0.023	0.228	8.492	0.400	0.163	0.320
(KO; GE, MCD, PG)	0.140	0.073	8.825	0.440	0.101	0.304
(PG; GE, MCD, KO)	0.048	0.400	8.507	0.675	0.079	0.730
(GE; MSFT, KO, PG)	0.013	0.109	8.563	0.553	0.004	0.706
(MSFT; GE, KO, PG)	0.004	0.004	9.226	0.475	0.105	0.130
(KO; GE, MSFT, PG)	0.022	0.073	9.093	0.506	0.064	0.316
(PG; GE, MSFT, KO)	0.022	0.225	8.615	0.591	0.120	0.186
(MCD; MSFT, KO, PG)	0.022	0.356	8.839	0.481	0.229	0.112
(MSFT; MCD, KO, PG)	0.023	0.056	8.487	0.418	0.100	0.345
(KO; MCD, MSFT, PG)	0.041	0.022	8.652	0.450	0.066	0.757
(PG; MCD, MSFT, KO)	0.035	0.327	8.487	0.564	0.102	0.552

TABLE 8.7 Maximum likelihood parameter estimates of the compounding functions for groups of five assets (standard errors omitted)

$C(\cdot;\cdot)$	α	β	η	$\overline{\rho}$	a	b
(GE; MCD, MSFT, KO, PG)	0.175	0.265	10.818	0.546	0.157	0.227
(MCD; GE, MSFT, KO, PG)	0.189	0.410	9.088	0.578	0.247	0.199
(MSFT; GE, MCD, KO, PG)	0.394	0.301	8.580	0.463	0.309	0.285
(KO; GE, MCD, MSFT, PG)	0.285	0.585	8.680	0.433	0.312	0.321
(PG; GE, MCD, MSFT, KO)	0.045	0.252	8.499	0.520	0.051	0.782

8.5.5 Comparison with the Conventional Copula Approach

Now we compare the proposed approaches with the conventional single copula approach to dynamic modelling of joint distributions. The conventional alternative would be to estimate a time-varying five-dimensional t-copula using ML.

The parameter estimates for the conventional benchmark method are summarized in Table 8.8. As before, we have run serial correlation tests – they are not reported due to their large number – and almost all of them passed at the 95% confidence level. This means that, for our five time series, there is no obvious leader in the goodness-of-fit competition. Moreover, the number of estimations in our procedure is much larger than in the conventional method. In this example, a five-dimensional distribution requires solving 80 low-dimensional problems in the sequential procedure.[5] The conventional approach would require solving just one, but it would involve estimating 43 parameters in total.[6] Hence, for moderate dimensions such as $d = 5$, the conventional method may be preferred in terms of computer time, provided it is operational (it *was* quicker in this example). However, this changes as we increase the dimensionality of the problem, which is what we will do next.

When we repeat the above exercise for $d = 6, \ldots, 15$, the number of parameters in the conventional MLE based on the d-copula grows according to $O(d^2)$, while the number of additional parameters in each step of the new sequential procedure remains fixed at 6. The number of estimations in the sequential procedure also grows with d (potentially faster than d^2); however, this number can be made small in steps 3 and above, if we consider a random subset of all available combinations in each step. Table 8.9 contains the number of parameters to be estimated in a single optimization problem when we use the new and the conventional method.

TABLE 8.8 Maximum likelihood parameter estimates of time-varying five-dimensional t-copula for the returns (robust standard errors are in parentheses)

		$\{\bar{R}_{ij}\}$	1	2	3	4	5
		GE	1.000	0.425	0.621	0.502	0.510
			(0.000)	(0.055)	(0.042)	(0.055)	(0.049)
η	13.426	MCD	0.425	1.000	0.415	0.398	0.367
	(4.380)		(0.055)	(0.000)	(0.056)	(0.055)	(0.062)
a	0.030	MSFT	0.621	0.415	1.000	0.539	0.465
	(0.035)		(0.042)	(0.056)	(0.000)	(0.053)	(0.057)
b	0.157	KO	0.502	0.398	0.539	1.000	0.495
	(0.308)		(0.055)	(0.055)	(0.053)	(0.000)	(0.049)
		PG	0.510	0.367	0.465	0.495	1.000
			(0.049)	(0.062)	(0.057)	(0.049)	(0.000)

---

[5]There are 5 estimation problems at step 1, 20 distributions of all possible pairs in step 2, 30 combinations of $\hat{F}_i$ with $\hat{F}_{jk}$ in step 3, 20 combinations of $\hat{F}_i$ with $\hat{F}_{jkl}$ in step 4, and 5 combinations of $\hat{F}_i$ with $\hat{F}_{jklm}$.

[6]Each skew-t marginal has 6 parameters and the t-copula has 13 distinct parameters.

TABLE 8.9 Growth of the number of parameters in a
single optimization problem for the conventional and
for the sequential methods based on the t-copula

Dimension	Conventional	Sequential
3	6	6
4	9	6
5	13	6
6	18	6
7	24	6
8	31	6
9	39	6
10	48	6
11	58	6
12	69	6
13	81	6
14	94	6
15	108	6

In our application, we discovered that the conventional approach fails to produce reliable convergence when d reaches and exceeds 10. At the same time, the new approach remains functional. Although there are a lot of optimization problems to solve, each such problem is relatively simple and takes very little time. In this application, each of the sequential estimations took only a few seconds, while the high-dimensional standard estimation with d close to 10 takes minutes and fails if the dimension is greater than 10.[7]

8.6   CONCLUDING REMARKS

We have proposed a sequential MLE procedure which reconstructs a joint distribution by sequentially applying a copula-like compounding function to estimates of marginal distributions. We have discussed the theoretical justification of the use of compounding functions and averaging and outlined the asymptotic properties of our estimator. We have shown in an application that this is a reasonable alternative to the conventional single-copula approach, especially when the dimension is higher than moderate.

The issues with conventional ML are not only computational (Hessian non-invertibility, local maxima, etc.). It is often a problem to find a multivariate distribution that accommodates certain features

---

[7]A Matlab module handling arbitrary dimension and data sets under both conventional and sequential methodology is available at https://sites.google.com/site/artembprokhorov/papers/reconstruct.zip.

(e.g., asymmetry and extreme dependence in higher dimensions) while remaining tractable. Moreover, finite-sample-based ML estimation of highly parameterized multivariate distribution is inaccurate due to the curse of dimensionality.

The proposed method falls short of solving all the issues. For example, the full version of the algorithm requires more computing time than conventional ML (when it works) and the standard errors of the sequential procedure suffer from the 'generated regressor' problem. However, the new method allows us to estimate distributions with arbitrary patterns of dependence and to parameterize dependence between a scalar and a subvector.

The standard way to study the performance of our algorithm relative to the vine copula and factor copula approaches mentioned in the Introduction is by means of simulations. However, it is unclear what criterion to use for such comparisons. The difficulty is not only in coming up with a feasible version of a MISE-type distance for a d-variate function. The operational version of this measure would need to be applicable to sequential estimators. We leave the development and implementation of such criteria for future research.

Alternative methods of constructing a joint distribution from objects of lower dimensions may come from work by de la Pena *et al.* (2006) and Li *et al.* (1999). De la Pena *et al.* (2006) provide a characterization of arbitrary joint distributions using sums of U-statistics of independent random variables. Their terms in the U-statistic are functions $g(\cdot)$ defined over subvectors of the original multidimensional vector. Li *et al.* (1999) discuss the notion of the linkage function $L(\cdot)$, which is a multidimensional analogue of the copula function. Linkage functions link uniformly distributed random vectors rather than uniformly distributed scalar random variables.

Functions $g(\cdot)$ and $L(\cdot)$ are the lower-dimensional objects that may be used in a similar estimation procedure to ours. However, except for some special cases, the closed-form expressions of these objects are unknown and their properties are not so well studied as the properties of copula functions. For this reason, we leave the study of such alternative methods of modelling joint distributions for future research.

REFERENCES

Aas, K., Czado, C., Frigessi, A. and Bakken, H. (2009). Pair-copula constructions of multiple dependence. *Insurance: Mathematics and Economics*, 44, 182–198.

Anatolyev, S., Khabibullin, R. and Prokhorov, A. (2014). An algorithm for constructing high dimensional distributions from distributions of lower dimension. *Economics Letters*, 123, 257–261.

Ausin, M.C. and Lopes, H.F. (2010). Time-varying joint distribution through copulas. *Computational Statistics and Data Analysis*, 54, 2383–2399.

Azzalini, A. and Capitanio, A. (2003). Distributions generated by perturbation of symmetry with emphasis on a multivariate skew t-distribution. *Journal of the Royal Statistical Society, Series B*, 65, 367–389.

Bauwens, L. and Laurent, S. (2005). A new class of multivariate skew densities, with application to generalized autoregressive conditional heteroscedasticity models. *Journal of Business and Economic Statistics*, 23, 346–354.

Breymann, W., Dias, A. and Embrechts, P. (2003). Dependence structures for multivariate high-frequency data in finance. *Quantitative Finance*, 3, 1–14.

Burnham, K.P. and Anderson, D.R. (2002). *Model Selection and Multimodel Inference: A Practical Information-Theoretic Approach*. Springer, New York.

Caragea, P.C. and Smith, R.L. (2007). Asymptotic properties of computationally efficient alternative estimators for a class of multivariate normal models. *Journal of Multivariate Analysis*, 98, 1417–1440.

Clemen, R. (1989). Combining forecasts: a review and annotated bibliography. *International Journal of Forecasting*, 5, 559–583.

Cox, D. and Reid, N. (2004). A note on pseudolikelihood constructed from marginal densities. *Biometrika*, 91, 729–737.

de la Pena, V.H., Ibragimov, R. and Sharakhmetov, S. (2006). Characterizations of joint distributions, copulas, information, dependence and decoupling, with applications to time series. *IMS Lecture Notes – Monograph Series*, 49, 183–209.

Diebold, F.X., Gunther, T.A. and Tay, A.S. (1998). Evaluating density forecasts with applications to financial risk management. *International Economic Review*, 39, 863–883.

Elliot, G. (2011). Averaging and the optimal combination of forecasts. UCSD Working Paper.

Engle, R. (2009). High dimension dynamic correlations, in J.L. Castle and N. Shephard (eds), *The Methodology and Practice of Econometrics: A Festschrift in Honour of David F. Hendry*. Oxford University Press, Oxford.

Engle, R.F. and Ng, V.K. (1993). Measuring and testing the impact of news on volatility. *Journal of Finance*, 48, 1749–1778.

Engle, R.F., Shephard, N. and Sheppard, K.K. (2008). Fitting vast dimensional time-varying covariance models. NYU Working Paper FIN-08-009.

Fang, Y. and Madsen, L. (2013). Modified Gaussian pseudo-copula: applications in insurance and finance. *Insurance: Mathematics and Economics*, 53, 292–301.

Fermanian, J.-D. and Wegkamp, M.H. (2012). Time-dependent copulas. *Journal of Multivariate Analysis*, 110, 19–29.

Genest, C., Ghoudi, K. and Rivest, L.-P. (1995a). A semiparametric estimation procedure of dependence parameters in multivariate families of distributions. *Biometrika*, 82, 543–552.

Genest, C., Quesada-Molina, J. and Rodriguez-Lallena, J. (1995b). De l'impossibilite de construire des lois a marges multidimensionnelles donnees a partir de copules. Comptes rendus de l'Academie des sciences de Paris Series I, Vol. 320. Elsevier, Paris.

Geweke, J. and Amisano, G. (2011). Optimal prediction pools. *Journal of Econometrics*, 164, 130–141.

Hall, S.G. and Mitchell, J. (2007). Combining density forecasts. *International Journal of Forecasting*, 23, 1–13.

Heagerty, P.J. and Lele, S.R. (1998). A composite likelihood approach to binary spatial data. *Journal of the American Statistical Association*, 1099–1111.

Joe, H. (1997). *Multivariate Models and Multivariate Dependence Concepts*. Chapman and Hall/CRC, Boca Raton, FL.

Joe, H. (2005). Asymptotic efficiency of the two-stage estimation method for copula-based models. *Journal of Multivariate Analysis*, 94, 401–419.

Khoudraji, A. (1995). Contributions à l'étude des copules et à la modélisation des valeurs extrêmes bivariées. Ph.D. dissertation, Université Laval.

Lele, S. and Taper, M.L. (2002). A composite likelihood approach to (co)variance components estimation. *Journal of Statistical Planning and Inference*, 103, 117–135.

Li, H., Scarsini, M. and Shaked, M. (1999). Dynamic linkages for multivariate distributions with given nonoverlapping multivariate marginal. *Journal of Multivariate Analysis*, 68, 54–77.

Nelsen, R.B. (2006). *An Introduction to Copulas*, 2nd edn. Springer Series in Statistics, Vol. 139. Springer, Berlin.

Oh, D.H. and Patton, A.J. (2013). Simulated method of moments estimation for copula-based multivariate models. *Journal of American Statistical Association*, 108, 689–700.

Patton, A.J. (2006). Modelling asymmetric exchange rate dependence. *International Economic Review*, 47, 527–556.

Prokhorov, A. and Schmidt, P. (2009a). GMM redundancy results for general missing data problems. *Journal of Econometrics*, 151, 47–55.

Prokhorov, A. and Schmidt, P. (2009b). Likelihood-based estimation in a panel setting: robustness, redundancy and validity of copulas. *Journal of Econometrics*, 153, 93–104.

Quesada-Molina, J. and Rodriguez-Lallena, J. (1994). Some advances in the study of the compatibility of three bivariate copulas. *Statistical Methods and Applications*, 3, 397–417.

Rosenblatt, M. (1952). Remarks on a multivariate transformation. *Annals of Mathematical Statistics*, 23, 470–472.

Sharakhmetov, S. and Ibragimov, R. (2002). A characterization of joint distribution of two-valued random variables and its applications. *Journal of Multivariate Analysis*, 83, 389–408.

Sklar, A. (1959). Fonctions de répartition à *n* dimensions et leurs marges. *Publications de l'Institut de Statistique de l'Université de Paris*, 8, 229–231.

Stock, J.H. and Watson, M.W. (2004). Combination forecasts of output growth in a seven-country data set. *Journal of Forecasting*, 23, 405–430.

Varin, C. (2008). On composite marginal likelihoods. *Advances in Statistical Analysis*, 92, 1–28.

Varin, C. and Vidoni, P. (2005). A note on composite likelihood inference and model selection. *Biometrika*, 92, 519–528.

Varin, C. and Vidoni, P. (2006). Pairwise likelihood inference for ordinal categorical time series. *Computational Statistics and Data Analysis*, 51, 2365–2373.

Varin, C. and Vidoni, P. (2008). Pairwise likelihood inference for general state space models. *Econometric Reviews*, 28, 170–185.

Varin, C., Reid, N. and Firth, D. (2011). An overview of composite likelihood methods. *Statistica Sinica*, 21, 5–42.

Zhao, Y. and Joe, H. (2005). Composite likelihood estimation in multivariate data analysis. *Canadian Journal of Statistics*, 33, 335–356.

Proof of Proposition 8.1: We provide the proof for $d = 3$. Arguments for $d > 3$ are analogous. Lipschitz continuity of $\ln c^{(m)}$ implies

$$\frac{d\, c^{(m)}(u_1, u_2)}{d\, u_j} \leq B c^{(m)}(u_1, u_2), \quad m = 1, \dots, d, \quad j = 1, 2.$$

Since $H(x_1, x_2, x_3) = C^{(3)}\left(F_1, C^{(2)}(F_2, F_3)\right)$, we have

$$h(x_1, x_2, x_3) \equiv \frac{\partial^3 H(x_1, x_2, x_3)}{\partial x_1 \partial x_2 \partial x_3}$$
$$= h_c(x_1.x_2, x_3) + \epsilon(x_1, x_2, x_3),$$

where

$$h_c(x_1.x_2, x_3) \equiv f_1\, f_2\, f_3 \frac{\partial^2 C^{(3)}\left(F_1, C^{(2)}(F_2, F_3)\right)}{\partial F_1 \partial C^{(2)}} \frac{\partial^2 C^{(2)}(F_2, F_3)}{\partial F_2 \partial F_3}$$
$$= f_1\, f_2\, f_3\, c^{(2)}(F_2, F_3)\, c^{(3)}(F_1, C^{(2)}(F_1, F_2))$$

$$\epsilon(x_1, x_2, x_3) \equiv f_1\, f_2\, f_3 \frac{\partial^3 C^{(3)}\left(F_1, C^{(2)}(F_2, F_3)\right)}{\partial F_1 [\partial C^{(2)}]^2} \frac{\partial C^{(2)}(F_2, F_3)}{\partial F_2} \frac{\partial C^{(2)}(F_2, F_3)}{\partial F_3}.$$

Note that $0 \leq \partial C^{(2)}(F_2, F_3)/\partial F_i \leq 1, i = 2, 3$. Therefore,

$$\epsilon(x_1, x_2, x_3) \leq f_1\, f_2\, f_3 \frac{\partial^3 C^{(3)}\left(F_1, C^{(2)}(F_2, F_3)\right)}{\partial F_1 [\partial C^{(2)}]^2} = f_1\, f_2\, f_3 \frac{\partial c^{(3)}(F_3, C^{(2)})}{\partial C^{(2)}}$$
$$\leq B f_1\, f_2\, f_3\, c^{(3)}(F_3, C^{(2)})$$
$$= \frac{B}{c^{(2)}(F_2, F_1)}\, h_c(x_1, x_2, x_3),$$

where the second line follows from $\ln c^{(3)}(u_1, u_2)$ being Lipschitz with constant B.

It follows that

$$\ln h(x_1, x_2, x_3) - \ln h_c(x_1, x_2, x_3) \leq B \frac{1}{c^{(2)}(F_2, F_1)}. \qquad \blacksquare$$

Proof of Proposition 8.2: The result follows trivially from application of Sklar's (1959) theorem to $\hat{F}_{12\ldots d}$.

Proof of Proposition 8.3: These are standard results cited, for example, in Chapter 10 of Joe (1997) or by Joe (2005).

CHAPTER 9

Asymmetric Dependence, Persistence and Firm-Level Stock Return Predictability

Jamie Alcock[a] and Petra Andrlikova[a]

[a]The University of Sydney Business School

Abstract

We examine whether excess returns can be predicted using information about asymmetric dependence (AD) of firm returns. AD is a significant predictor in all the stock markets examined; it can predict future excess returns up to 15 months ahead in the USA, UK and Australia. Our results are not biased by potential persistence of AD, as we find no evidence of autocorrelation in the firm AD across all markets. We further test whether one time series of AD from any of the stock markets considered is useful in forecasting AD from other stock markets. We find significant spillover effects of AD between the US and Australian stock markets. The level of AD in the USA influences future levels of AD in Australia.

Consistent with the concept of efficient markets, few firm-specific characteristics have been shown to significantly predict excess firm-level returns in out-of-sample empirical tests. In this chapter, we provide striking out-of-sample evidence that asymmetric dependence (AD) has been able to predict firm-level excess returns through a significant historical sample period (1959–2015).

We provide evidence of return predictability using AD information from multiple financial markets and across different asset classes. We analyse the power of AD to predict stock returns of US equities, US real-estate investment trusts (REITs), Australian listed equities and equities listed in the UK. We find that AD measured by the Alcock and Hatherley (2017) adjusted J statistic (J^{Adj}) is a significant predictor of future excess returns in all the tested financial markets. We also explore whether AD can predict stock excess returns in longer horizons and use future excess returns from the next 3 to 15 months. We reveal that the firm-level AD predicts returns of up to 15 months ahead in the USA, UK and Australia.

J^{Adj} is strongly significant in our predictive regressions with a high t-statistic. However, the traditional tests of stock return predictability may falsely reject the null hypothesis too frequently in the presence of persistent regressors (Mankiw and Shapiro, 1986; Elliott and Stock, 1994; Stambaugh, 1999; Campbell and Yogo, 2006). In order to validate our results, we explore the persistence of our chosen AD metric by testing the autoregressive properties of the J^{Adj} time-series processes using standard econometric tests. We also focus on the higher-order autoregressive (AR) components to study the patterns and cyclical behaviour of the autocorrelations of AD. We do this for AD, as well as for upper-tail and lower-tail AD autoregressive processes. We find no evidence of a significant persistence of AD in any of the financial time series analysed. No persistence increases the validity of our predictability results.

We also explore migration probabilities of the two distinct types of AD: lower-tail asymmetric dependence (LTAD) and upper-tail asymmetric dependence (UTAD). The information about the type of AD is crucial for an investor, as it completely changes the outlook on return prediction. All our predictive regressions suggest that LTAD (UTAD) is associated with positive (negative) future excess returns. We find that if a listed firm exhibits LTAD today, it is more likely to be LTAD in 12 months ahead. This holds across all the financial markets examined. This higher migration probability of LTAD may be explained by a higher prevalence of LTAD.

Finally, we explore the autoregressive properties of AD in a multivariate setting using the vector autoregression (VAR) model. We once again do not find any sign of a significant serial autocorrelation of AD. We also focus our attention on spillover effects of AD and examine whether there are any connections between the aggregate levels of AD across the four financial markets. We test for Granger causality and explore the dynamics in the AD levels between the markets using the VAR model. We find that there are substantial spillover effects between US and Australian equities. Specifically, the aggregate level of AD in the USA can predict future levels of AD of Australian-listed firms.

The first section of this chapter presents the empirical results of return predictability, using AD as a predictor, controlling for common factors, such as Capital Asset Pricing Model (CAPM) β, size, value, idiosyncratic risk, momentum, coskewness and cokurtosis. In the second part of this chapter, we focus on exploring the persistence of AD measure. At the end of this chapter, we analyse spillover effects of the aggregate levels of AD from all the four financial markets.

9.1   PREDICTIVE POWER OF ASYMMETRIC DEPENDENCE

We explore the power of AD to predict excess returns in the USA, UK and Australia and provide a summary of our empirical results in Table 9.1. J^{Adj} is the only factor (except cokurtosis) that is significant across all the financial markets, suggesting that AD plays an important role in predicting firm-level excess returns in all the countries analysed. Moreover, in all the stock markets, the coefficients associated with J^{Adj} from Fama and MacBeth (1973) regressions have the highest value of t-statistic that exceeds the Harvey *et al.* (2014) critical value of 3.0.

We further observe that the standard CAPM β cannot predict future returns 1 month ahead in US equities and US REITs, but affects future 1-month returns of Australian and UK equities. Our results suggest that in Australia and the UK, higher values of the CAPM β are associated with lower future 1-month excess returns, which is consistent with the existing literature (Fletcher, 1997; Brammer *et al.*, 2006; Gregory *et al.*, 2013).

The magnitude of the predictive power of AD differs substantially across countries. Investors in Australian equities have the highest sensitivity of future (1-month) returns to AD. The average level of AD of stock returns of Australian equities is associated with a predicted risk premium of approximately 5.9%. In contrast, average AD is associated with a future excess return of 2.5% in the next 1 month. Future excess returns of US REITs are less sensitive to AD; the average level of AD can predict 1% of future 1-month excess returns.

Cokurtosis is another factor significant in all the stock markets. Cokurtosis is positively correlated with future 1-month excess returns. The evidence about the price of other factors analysed is mixed. In three out of four of the financial markets (US equities, US REITs and UK equities), the level of idiosyncratic risk negatively influences future excess returns. The CAPM β, past return and coskewness are relevant only in half of the analysed stock markets.

TABLE 9.1   We measure risk premia using Fama and MacBeth (1973) regressions estimated every month rolling forward. We use the next 1-month monthly excess return as dependent variable. All regressors are winsorized at the 1% and 99% level at each month. We restrict our attention to stocks listed on the NYSE between January 1959 and December 2015, US REITs listed on the NYSE between January 1972 and December 2013, stocks listed on the ASX between June 1992 and June 2014, and UK stocks listed between January 1987 and May 2015, respectively. Statistical significance is determined using Newey and West (1987) adjusted t-statistics, given in parentheses, to control for overlapping data using the Newey and West (1994) automatic lag selection method to determine the lag length. All coefficients are reported as effective annual rates

	US Equities	US REITs	AUS Equities	UK Equities
Int	0.276	0.173	0.005	0.150
	[3.584]	[1.887]	[0.115]	[1.222]
β	0.020	−0.127	−0.094	−0.095
	[0.805]	[2.035]	[1.999]	[2.443]
Log-size	−0.016	−0.011	−0.001	−0.005
	[3.153]	[1.583]	[0.096]	[0.945]
BM	−0.002	0.025	0.067	0.013
	[0.600]	[1.280]	[4.777]	[1.769]
Past Ret	−1.129	1.214	2.219	0.285
	[3.672]	[2.187]	[5.543]	[0.781]
Idio	−7.802	−0.493	−1.985	−3.384
	[6.165]	[0.380]	[1.738]	[4.600]
Cosk	0.155	0.167	0.178	0.288
	[3.023]	[1.689]	[1.650]	[3.233]
Cokurt	0.021	0.073	0.055	0.041
	[2.178]	[2.579]	[2.034]	[2.701]
J^{Adj}	−0.007	−0.005	−0.014	−0.010
	[6.170]	[3.287]	[6.576]	[6.429]

9.1.1   Data and Method

We collect daily return data from CRSP and DataStream. We restrict our attention to US stocks listed on the NYSE between January 1959 and December 2015, US REITs listed on the NYSE between January 1959 and December 2015, UK stocks listed between January 1987 and May 2015, and Australian equities listed on the ASX between June 1992 and June 2014. Accounting and firm-financial data is collected from Compustat and DataStream.

We use local proxies for the risk-free rates and market returns. For US equities and US REITs, we use the CRSP value-weighted return of all NYSE, AMEX and NASDAQ stocks as a market proxy and the

1-month T-bill rate as a proxy for the risk-free rate, collected from the WRDS Fama–French database. For UK equities, we use the daily UK 3-month Treasury bill rate as a proxy for the risk-free rate and the FTSE100 index return as a proxy for market return. The daily observations on UK 3-month Treasury bill rate and FTSE100 index are collected from DataStream. For Australian equities, we proxy market returns using the S&P ASX 200 index and the risk-free rate with the 90-day bank accepted bill rate.

In all the predictive regressions, we calculate the control variables for a given month, t, in the following manner. The firm coskewness, cokurtosis are estimated using past 12 months of excess daily returns. Firm size is the average of the log value of market value calculated over the past 12 months of daily observations. The book-to-market ratio is the average BM from the past 12 months of daily observations. The idiosyncratic risk is measured as the standard deviation of CAPM residuals estimated using daily excess returns from the past 12 months. Monthly excess returns are calculated from the continuously compounded excess daily returns. We use daily risk-free rates to obtain the excess returns.

We use predictive regressions where value-weighted cross-sectional regressions are computed every month rolling forward. At a given month, t, the average of the mean of the next 1, 3, 6, 9, 12 and 15 months of excess monthly returns is regressed against β, idiosyncratic risk ('Idio'), coskewness ('Cosk'), cokurtosis ('Cokurt'), $J^{Adj}-$ and $J^{Adj}+$ estimated using the past 12 months of daily excess return data. We also include the average past 12-monthly excess return. We use the Newey and West (1987) adjusted t-statistics to determine the statistical significance while controlling for overlapping data using the Newey and West (1994) automatic lag selection method to determine the lag length. We winsorize all regressors at the 1% and 99% level at each month.

On the following pages, we analyse each financial market individually and in a closer detail. We also look at the predictive power of the two types of AD: LTAD and UTAD. We also use longer horizons than in the traditional Fama and MacBeth (1973) procedure to explore the ability of AD to predict future excess returns of 1 to 15 months ahead.

9.1.2   US Equities

Previous academic research in finance has revealed many cross-sectional relationships of future stock returns of equities listed in the USA. McLean and Pontiff (2016) identify 97 predictors of cross-sectional stock returns and show that the predictability of stock returns decreases significantly in the post-publication period. Their finding is consistent with investors learning about mispricing from academic publications. Cochrane (1999) argues that if the predictability factor describes a risk to the investor, it is likely to persist.

We aim to analyse the power of yet another predictor, AD, measured using the Alcock and Hatherley (2017) adjusted J statistic (J^{Adj}). In order to verify whether the predictability of AD is persistent, we use future excess returns of US equities from up to 15 months ahead.

We evaluate whether past estimates of AD affect future returns of US equities and present our results in Table 9.2. We first employ the traditional Fama and MacBeth (1973) approach and analyse the relation between past AD, estimated using the past 12 months of daily excess returns data, and the next month excess return. Surprisingly, we do not find a significant coefficient for the CAPM β. However, we do observe a significant coefficient associated with J^{Adj}.

The typical future 1-month excess return associated with average levels of LTAD, adjusted for scale, is a substantial 289.43% of the (insignificant) excess return predicted by CAPM β, providing additional support in favour of a substantial importance of AD in predicting firm excess returns relative to the market risk. The scaled predicted excess return for an average level of UTAD is 179.53% of that for β. The average level of lower- (upper-)tail AD of US equities is associated with a positive (negative) future 1-month return of 5.185% (3.285%).

We further test whether past estimates of AD affect excess returns 3, 6, 9, 12 and 15 months into the future. We find strong evidence that our estimates of AD (J^{Adj}) are able to predict excess returns up to 6 months in advance. Further, our estimates of LTAD ($J^{Adj}-$) are able to predict excess returns up to

TABLE 9.2 We measure risk premia using the Fama and MacBeth (1973) asset-pricing procedure where value-weighted cross-sectional regressions are computed every month rolling forward. At a given month, t, the average of the mean of the next 1, 3, 6, 9, 12 and 15 months of excess monthly returns is regressed against β, idiosyncratic risk ('Idio'), coskewness ('Cosk'), cokurtosis ('Cokurt'), $J^{Adj}-$ and $J^{Adj}+$ estimated using the past 12 months of daily excess return data. We also include the average past 12-monthly excess return ('Past Ret'). The relevant book-to-market ratio ('BM') at time t for a given stock is computed using the last available (most recent) book value entry. Size ('Log-size') is computed at the same date that the book-to-market ratio is computed. We proxy the market portfolio with the CRSP value-weighted return of all NYSE, AMEX and NASDAQ stocks and the risk-free rate with the 1-month T-bill rate. We restrict our attention to stocks listed on the NYSE between January 1959 and December 2015. Statistical significance is determined using Newey and West (1987) adjusted t-statistics, given in parentheses, to control for overlapping data using the Newey and West (1994) automatic lag selection method to determine the lag length. All coefficients are reported as effective annual rates

	1 month		3 months		6 months		9 months		12 months		15 months	
	III'	IV'	III'	IV'	III'	IV'	III'	IV'	III'	IV'	III'	IV'
Int	0.276	0.269	0.172	0.170	0.098	0.095	0.078	0.076	0.065	0.062	0.065	0.063
	[3.584]	[3.449]	[2.646]	[2.596]	[1.670]	[1.619]	[1.382]	[1.336]	[1.214]	[1.162]	[1.268]	[1.236]
β	0.020	0.016	-0.006	-0.007	-0.022	-0.023	-0.025	-0.026	-0.027	-0.028	-0.027	-0.028
	[0.805]	[0.672]	[0.307]	[0.346]	[1.168]	[1.218]	[1.429]	[1.450]	[1.756]	[1.773]	[1.949]	[1.967]
Log-size	-0.016	-0.017	-0.013	-0.014	-0.010	-0.010	-0.009	-0.009	-0.008	-0.009	-0.008	-0.009
	[3.153]	[3.229]	[2.975]	[2.997]	[2.524]	[2.557]	[2.400]	[2.429]	[2.351]	[2.366]	[2.474]	[2.505]
BM	-0.002	-0.002	0.003	0.003	0.004	0.004	0.005	0.005	0.005	0.005	0.005	0.005
	[0.600]	[0.628]	[0.952]	[0.940]	[1.313]	[1.317]	[1.496]	[1.501]	[1.609]	[1.617]	[1.631]	[1.640]
Past Ret	-1.129	-1.123	-0.894	-0.894	-0.709	-0.710	-0.691	-0.694	-0.695	-0.696	-0.737	-0.737
	[3.672]	[3.650]	[3.560]	[3.554]	[3.302]	[3.309]	[3.434]	[3.450]	[3.628]	[3.631]	[4.188]	[4.183]
Idio	-7.802	-7.778	-4.002	-4.011	-1.652	-1.644	-0.990	-0.991	-0.678	-0.677	-0.676	-0.680
	[6.165]	[6.166]	[5.866]	[5.873]	[3.858]	[3.863]	[2.725]	[2.740]	[2.109]	[2.127]	[2.242]	[2.270]
Cosk	0.155	0.162	0.059	0.064	0.036	0.039	0.020	0.022	0.013	0.014	0.013	0.014
	[3.023]	[3.120]	[2.422]	[2.584]	[1.776]	[1.911]	[1.100]	[1.215]	[0.779]	[0.874]	[0.835]	[0.893]
Cokurt	0.021	0.025	0.012	0.013	0.009	0.011	0.008	0.009	0.009	0.009	0.009	0.009
	[2.178]	[2.446]	[1.476]	[1.603]	[1.401]	[1.566]	[1.374]	[1.468]	[1.586]	[1.631]	[1.897]	[1.925]
J^{Adj}	-0.007		-0.002		-0.001		-0.0005		-0.0004		-0.0004	
	[6.170]		[4.346]		[2.306]		[1.540]		[1.355]		[1.401]	
$J^{Adj}-$		-0.010		-0.003		-0.002		-0.001		-0.001		-0.001
		[6.188]		[4.684]		[3.028]		[2.435]		[1.989]		[1.984]
$J^{Adj}+$		-0.005		-0.0016		-0.0003		-0.0001		-0.0001		-0.0002
		[4.536]		[2.185]		[0.444]		[0.190]		[0.152]		[0.391]

15 months in advance. When an investor uses AD estimates generated using only data available to her at time t, she is able to predict returns up to $t + 15$ months ahead.

Other factors that display a power to predict US stock returns in the period between 1959 and 2015 are firm size, past returns (momentum), idiosyncratic risk, coskewness and cokurtosis. Most of these factors can predict future returns up to 15 months ahead, except cokurtosis, which only affects excess returns in the next 1 month.

Our results are largely consistent with Stambaugh (2003), Ang *et al.* (2006), Avramov and Chordia (2006), Liu and Zhang (2008) and Fu (2009). Stambaugh (2003), Liu and Zhang (2008) and Fu (2009) employ the Fama and MacBeth (1973) approach and find that the CAPM β is not significant in predicting 1-month future excess returns. Stambaugh (2003) and Liu and Zhang (2008) further identify a negative (although insignificant) coefficient associated with market risk (β), which is consistent with our results from the Fama and MacBeth (1973) regression.

In the same 1-month predictive regressions, we further explore that size is negatively related to the level of future excess returns, which is confirmed by Avramov and Chordia (2006) and Fu (2009). The book-to-market ratio does not influence future excess returns one month in advance, which is in contrast with, for example, Avramov and Chordia (2006), who find that the book-to-market ratio is an important factor with a strong and positive effect on the level of future excess returns.

9.1.3   US REITs

Studying the effects of AD on returns of US REITs is particularly interesting. REITs are typically considered to be defensive assets (Glascock *et al.*, 2004), highly leveraged and required to distribute at least 90% of the taxable income to their investors. The effects of market downturn may be more pronounced in the US REIT market.

We estimate the sensitivity of future 1-month excess returns to our AD measure (J^{Adj}) using the Fama and MacBeth (1973) intertemporal asset-pricing procedure, 3-month predictive regressions and 6-month predictive regressions and report our results in Table 9.3. We use a sample of REITs listed on the NYSE between 1992 and 2013. The significant factors from the Fama and MacBeth (1973) regression are J^{Adj}, β, past excess return and cokurtosis. After controlling for β, size, book-to-market ratio, past returns, idiosyncratic risk, coskewness and cokurtosis, J^{Adj} is negatively correlated with future 1-month excess returns, see Table 9.3. The coefficient of J^{Adj} from the Fama and MacBeth (1973) regression has the highest value of t-statistic that exceeds the Harvey *et al.* (2014) critical value of 3.0.

Our resulting Fama and MacBeth (1973) regression coefficients associated with control variables are consistent with the existing literature. Ooi *et al.* (2009) confirm that CAPM β is insignificant in predicting the mean excess return of US REITs over the next 12 months. Their conclusions about the effects of book-to-market ratio, size and momentum are also qualitatively similar to ours in terms of the coefficient sign and significance. Our results further relate to Liow and Addae-Dapaah (2010), who find a negative yet insignificant coefficient attached to the CAPM β and provide evidence that size and idiosyncratic risk are not relevant predictors of future excess returns, using a sample of US REITs between 1998 and 2008.

We also explore the power of J^{Adj} to predict future excess returns over longer investment horizons (Table 9.3, columns 3 and 4). We find that J^{Adj} can predict excess returns up to 3 months ahead. The findings that AD can predict future excess returns are in line with Huang and Wu (2015), who show that by accounting for AD in US REITs, an investor can outperform the market and generate higher excess returns than the market.

We quantify the price associated with LTAD and UTAD separately and re-run our regressions using the $J^{Adj}-$ and $J^{Adj}+$ measure of LTAD and UTAD. After controlling for other factors, our measures for LTAD ($J^{Adj}-$) and UTAD ($J^{Adj}+$) are correlated with future excess returns, see Table 9.4. $J^{Adj}-$ and $J^{Adj}+$ are negatively correlated with US REIT future excess returns. This implies that a higher degree of LTAD (UTAD) leads to higher (lower) future excess returns.

TABLE 9.3 We measure risk premia using the Fama and MacBeth (1973) asset-pricing procedure and 3-month and 6-month predictive regressions estimated every month rolling forward. At a given month, t, the average 1-month, 3-month and 6-month excess monthly return is regressed against β, β^-, β^+, idiosyncratic risk ('Idio'), coskewness ('Cosk'), cokurtosis ('Cokurt') and J^{Adj} estimated using the previous 12 months of daily excess return data, size ('Log-size'), book-to-market ratio ('BM') and the average past 12-monthly excess return ('Past Ret'), computed as at time t. We proxy the market portfolio with the CRSP value-weighted return of all NYSE, AMEX and NASDAQ stocks and the risk-free rate with the 1-month T-bill rate. All regressors are winsorized at the 1% and 99% level at each month. We restrict our attention to REIT stocks listed on the NYSE between January 1972 and December 2013. Statistical significance is determined using Newey and West (1987) adjusted t-statistics, given in parentheses, to control for overlapping data using the Newey and West (1994) automatic lag selection method to determine the lag length. All coefficients are reported as effective annual rates

	Fama and MacBeth (1973)	Predictive regressions 3m	6m
Int	0.173	0.208	0.199
	[1.887]	[2.971]	[2.663]
β	−0.127	−0.086	−0.062
	[2.035]	[1.960]	[1.253]
Size	−0.011	−0.013	−0.013
	[1.583]	[2.669]	[2.320]
BM	0.025	0.021	0.020
	[1.280]	[1.497]	[1.240]
Past Ret	1.214	1.836	1.932
	[2.187]	[4.247]	[3.268]
Idio	−0.493	−0.111	0.372
	[0.380]	[0.095]	[0.342]
Cosk	0.167	0.051	0.067
	[1.689]	[0.890]	[1.095]
Cokurt	0.073	0.053	0.047
	[2.579]	[2.929]	[1.867]
J^{Adj}	−0.005	−0.002	−0.001
	[3.287]	[2.455]	[1.023]

TABLE 8.4 We measure risk premia using the Fama and MacBeth (1973) asset-pricing procedure and 3-month and 6-month predictive regressions estimated every month rolling forward. At a given month, t, the average 1-month, 3-month and 6-month excess monthly return is regressed against β, β^-, β^+, idiosyncratic risk ('Idio'), coskewness ('Cosk'), cokurtosis ('Cokurt'), $J^{Adj}-$ and $J^{Adj}+$ estimated using the previous 12 months of daily excess return data, size ('Log-size'), book-to-market ratio ('BM') and the average past 12-monthly excess return ('Past Ret'), computed as at time t. We proxy the market portfolio with the CRSP value-weighted return of all NYSE, AMEX and NASDAQ stocks and the risk-free rate with the 1-month T-bill rate. All regressors are winsorized at the 1% and 99% level at each month. We restrict our attention to REIT stocks listed on the NYSE between January 1972 and December 2013. Statistical significance is determined using Newey and West (1987) adjusted t-statistics, given in parentheses, to control for overlapping data using the Newey and West (1994) automatic lag selection method to determine the lag length. All coefficients are reported as effective annual rates

	Fama and MacBeth (1973)	Predictive regressions	
		3m	6m
Int	0.196	0.228	0.211
	[2.010]	[2.809]	[2.633]
β	−0.120	−0.081	−0.060
	[1.940]	[1.630]	[1.206]
Size	−0.012	−0.014	−0.014
	[1.691]	[2.515]	[2.372]
BM	0.023	0.020	0.020
	[1.146]	[1.246]	[1.279]
Past Ret	1.188	1.820	1.904
	[2.120]	[3.674]	[3.210]
Idio	−0.559	−0.074	0.429
	[0.430]	[0.059]	[0.391]
Cosk	0.159	0.058	0.076
	[1.625]	[0.909]	[1.255]
Cokurt	0.072	0.051	0.046
	[2.555]	[2.491]	[1.841]
$J^{Adj}-$	−0.003	−0.0003	−0.00001
	[1.541]	[0.145]	[0.008]
$J^{Adj}+$	−0.017	−0.014	−0.007
	[2.429]	[2.228]	[1.214]

We test the predictive ability of $J^{Adj}-$ and $J^{Adj}+$ using 3-month and 6-month future returns. $J^{Adj}+$ can predict excess returns up to 3 months ahead whilst $J^{Adj}-$ is insignificant across all our predictive regressions from Table 9.4.

AD is a significant predictor explaining out-of-sample excess returns of listed US REITs up to 3 months ahead. The statistical significance of the coefficient attached to J^{Adj} is strong relative to the other factors considered and exceeds Harvey *et al.*'s (2014) critical value of 3.0.

9.1.4 AUS Equities

Most of the stock return predictability studies are based on US data. We aim to verify the robustness of our results using non-US data and test the ability of J^{Adj} to predict future returns of Australian equities. In Australia, investors' sensitivity to certain risk factors may be different to those in the US market. That is because Australia is a more concentrated market. Australian-listed equities typically have a lower leverage and liquidity. The sovereign risk is also higher when compared with the US market (Faff, 2004).

We use the standard Fama and MacBeth (1973) procedure and report our results in the first two columns of Table 9.5. As well as being a good robustness test, this also provides an insight into whether an investor can extract information about future returns from AD measures in Australia. The typical level of AD can explain 548 bp of future 1-month excess return. This compares with 636 bp explained by the typical level of the CAPM β. Using our definition of the typical premium, we find that J^{Adj} is more influential in predicting 1-month future returns than any other factor considered except for the CAPM β. All of our measures of different types of AD (J^{Adj}, $J^{Adj}-$ and $J^{Adj}+$) are strongly significant in the Fama and MacBeth (1973) intertemporal regressions with t-statistics exceeding the Harvey *et al.* (2014) level of 3.0.

Our results from the Fama and MacBeth (1973) regressions are consistent with the hypothesis that firms with high book-to-market ratio require additional returns to compensate investors for additional risk. Vo (2015) provides a survey of existing literature examining the Fama–French three-factor model applied on Australian-listed equities. Our regression coefficient on book-to-market ratio is qualitatively similar yet smaller in magnitude compared with results from existing literature (Fama and French, 1998; Halliwell *et al.*, 1999; Faff, 2001; Gaunt, 2004; Faff, 2004; Gharghori *et al.*, 2007; Kassimatis, 2008; O'Brien *et al.*, 2010; Brailsford *et al.*, 2012). We do not find any evidence that small Australian firms are associated with higher future returns based on the Fama and MacBeth (1973) procedure.

We further explore the predictive power of J^{Adj} using 3-month, 6-month, 9-month, 12-month and 15-month future excess returns as the dependent variable. Our results are qualitatively similar across different regression specifications, Table 9.5. J^{Adj} is significant in predicting future returns up to 15 months in advance. When we incorporate the measures of LTAD ($J^{Adj}-$) and UTAD ($J^{Adj}+$) into our predictive regressions, we observe a similar trend. The t-statistics of both $J^{Adj}-$ and $J^{Adj}+$ decrease with longer investment horizons.

$J^{Adj}-$ can predict excess returns up to 12 months ahead, whereas $J^{Adj}+$ predicts excess returns up to 3 months ahead. The CAPM β is also important for investors as the t-statistic of the coefficient associated with the CAPM β increases with longer investment horizons and exceeds the Harvey *et al.* (2014) level of 3.0 with mean excess returns with horizons of 9 to 15 months.

9.1.5 UK Equities

We conduct the same analysis as in the previous three cases and test the ability of J^{Adj} to predict future returns of excess returns of UK-listed equities. We use the standard Fama and MacBeth (1973) procedure and predictive regressions with longer investment horizons. In Table 9.6, we repeat the predictive regressions using 1-month (Fama and MacBeth, 1973), 3-month, 6-month, 9-month, 12-month and 15-month future excess returns as the dependent variable.

TABLE 9.5 We measure risk premia using the Fama and MacBeth (1973) asset-pricing procedure where value-weighted cross-sectional regressions are computed every month rolling forward. At a given month, t, the average of the mean of the next 1, 3, 6, 9, 12 and 15 months of excess monthly returns is regressed against β, idiosyncratic risk ('Idio'), coskewness ('Cosk'), cokurtosis ('Cokurt'), $J^{Adj}-$ and $J^{Adj}+$ estimated using the past 12 months of daily excess return data. We also include the average past 12-monthly excess return ('Past Ret'). The relevant book-to-market ratio ('BM') at time t for a given stock is computed using the last available (most recent) book value entry. Size ('Log-size') is computed at the same date that the book-to-market ratio is computed. We proxy the market portfolio with the S&P ASX 200 index and the risk-free rate with the 90-day bank accepted bill rate. We restrict our attention to stocks listed on the ASX between June 1992 and June 2014. Statistical significance is determined using Newey and West (1987) adjusted t-statistics, given in parentheses, to control for overlapping data using the Newey and West (1994) automatic lag selection method to determine the lag length. All coefficients are reported as effective annual rates

	1 month		3 months		6 months		9 months		12 months		15 months	
	III′	IV′	III′	IV′	III′	IV′	III′	IV′	III′	IV′	III′	IV′
Int	0.005	0.015	0.094	0.098	0.083	0.078	0.091	0.087	0.088	0.086	0.100	0.096
	[0.115]	[0.319]	[1.756]	[1.760]	[1.538]	[1.390]	[1.715]	[1.586]	[1.740]	[1.670]	[2.073]	[1.962]
β	−0.094	−0.096	−0.106	−0.107	−0.108	−0.107	−0.107	−0.109	−0.102	−0.103	−0.090	−0.091
	[1.999]	[2.067]	[2.691]	[2.690]	[2.913]	[2.870]	[3.039]	[3.071]	[3.091]	[3.122]	[3.012]	[3.048]
Log-size	−0.001	0.000	−0.014	−0.014	−0.011	−0.010	−0.012	−0.012	−0.011	−0.011	−0.011	−0.011
	[0.096]	[0.026]	[2.158]	[2.169]	[1.659]	[1.417]	[1.840]	[1.874]	[1.843]	[1.873]	[2.072]	[2.061]
BM	0.067	0.066	0.065	0.065	0.067	0.067	0.058	0.057	0.053	0.053	0.047	0.047
	[4.777]	[4.763]	[4.108]	[4.102]	[3.945]	[3.956]	[3.668]	[3.655]	[3.601]	[3.581]	[3.492]	[3.489]
Past Ret	2.219	2.182	2.241	2.233	1.775	1.762	1.376	1.384	1.049	1.064	0.790	0.793
	[5.543]	[5.535]	[4.892]	[4.904]	[4.398]	[4.413]	[4.304]	[4.313]	[4.067]	[4.067]	[3.593]	[3.629]
Idio	−1.985	−2.026	−1.711	−1.710	−1.332	−1.304	−0.838	−0.781	−0.573	−0.548	−0.553	−0.516
	[1.738]	[1.768]	[1.811]	[1.799]	[1.502]	[1.464]	[1.075]	[1.001]	[0.796]	[0.763]	[0.800]	[0.752]
Cosk	0.178	0.176	0.061	0.064	0.046	0.073	0.017	0.018	0.022	0.014	−0.003	0.001
	[1.650]	[1.629]	[0.995]	[1.034]	[1.159]	[1.434]	[0.511]	[0.551]	[0.546]	[0.404]	[0.077]	[0.016]
Cokurt	0.055	0.053	0.071	0.072	0.062	0.061	0.061	0.064	0.060	0.061	0.053	0.055
	[2.034]	[1.902]	[3.281]	[3.231]	[3.021]	[2.737]	[3.183]	[3.168]	[3.111]	[3.076]	[2.999]	[2.975]
J^{Adj}	−0.014		−0.005		−0.003		−0.002		−0.002		−0.001	
	[6.576]		[3.906]		[3.700]		[3.284]		[2.769]		[2.308]	
$J^{Adj}-$		−0.012		−0.004		−0.003		−0.003		−0.002		−0.002
		[5.906]		[3.107]		[2.499]		[2.483]		[2.043]		[1.940]
$J^{Adj}+$		−0.020		−0.008		−0.004		−0.001		−0.001		−0.0004
		[5.114]		[3.112]		[1.974]		[0.766]		[0.579]		[0.276]

TABLE 9.6 We measure risk premia using the Fama and MacBeth (1973) asset-pricing procedure where value-weighted cross-sectional regressions are computed every month rolling forward. At a given month, t, the average of the mean of the next 1, 3, 6, 9, 12 and 15 months of excess monthly returns is regressed against β, idiosyncratic risk ('Idio'), coskewness ('Cosk'), cokurtosis ('Cokurt'), $J^{Adj}-$ and $J^{Adj}+$ estimated using the past 12 months of daily excess return data. We also include the average past 12-monthly excess return ('Past Ret'). The relevant book-to-market ratio ('BM') is computed using the last available (most recent) book value entry. Size ('Log-size') is computed at the same date that the book-to-market ratio is computed. We proxy the market portfolio with the FTSE 100 index and the risk-free rate with the 3-month UK Treasury bill rate. We restrict our attention to UK stocks listed between January 1987 and May 2015. Statistical significance is determined using Newey and West (1987) adjusted t-statistics, given in parentheses. All coefficients are reported as effective annual rates Newey and West (1994) automatic lag selection method to determine the lag length.

	1 month		3 months		6 months		9 months		12 months		15 months	
	III'	IV'	III'	IV'	III'	IV'	III'	IV'	III'	IV'	III'	IV'
Int	0.150	0.102	0.160	0.123	0.192	0.163	0.201	0.180	0.209	0.191	0.218	0.202
	[1.222]	[0.817]	[1.202]	[0.920]	[1.489]	[1.270]	[1.625]	[1.459]	[1.817]	[1.664]	[2.044]	[1.912]
β	-0.095	-0.105	-0.087	-0.096	-0.089	-0.096	-0.086	-0.092	-0.079	-0.083	-0.070	-0.074
	[2.443]	[2.652]	[2.345]	[2.548]	[2.486]	[2.639]	[2.540]	[2.661]	[2.620]	[2.731]	[2.627]	[2.746]
Log-size	-0.005	-0.004	-0.008	-0.007	-0.010	-0.009	-0.011	-0.010	-0.011	-0.011	-0.012	-0.011
	[0.945]	[0.763]	[1.252]	[1.163]	[1.611]	[1.535]	[1.758]	[1.690]	[1.934]	[1.877]	[2.165]	[2.121]
BM	0.013	0.013	0.018	0.019	0.019	0.019	0.017	0.017	0.014	0.014	0.012	0.012
	[1.769]	[1.826]	[2.211]	[2.250]	[2.248]	[2.255]	[2.122]	[2.093]	[1.926]	[1.918]	[1.672]	[1.664]
Past Ret	0.285	0.292	0.479	0.488	0.257	0.274	0.027	0.035	-0.123	-0.119	-0.159	-0.157
	[0.781]	[0.797]	[1.405]	[1.417]	[0.854]	[0.902]	[0.100]	[0.129]	[0.510]	[0.491]	[0.739]	[0.724]
Idio	-3.384	-3.327	-2.127	-2.047	-1.227	-1.169	-0.800	-0.768	-0.582	-0.550	-0.450	-0.427
	[4.600]	[4.590]	[3.435]	[3.400]	[2.264]	[2.194]	[1.563]	[1.498]	[1.233]	[1.162]	[1.059]	[0.993]
Cosk	0.288	0.296	0.110	0.114	0.075	0.078	0.046	0.049	0.043	0.045	0.036	0.038
	[3.233]	[3.279]	[2.281]	[2.325]	[1.905]	[1.949]	[1.452]	[1.530]	[1.637]	[1.692]	[1.463]	[1.503]
Cokurt	0.041	0.047	0.029	0.034	0.025	0.029	0.021	0.024	0.019	0.022	0.018	0.020
	[2.701]	[2.931]	[2.546]	[2.820]	[2.208]	[2.427]	[1.955]	[2.105]	[1.911]	[2.031]	[2.066]	[2.185]
J^{Adj}	-0.010		-0.004		-0.003		-0.002		-0.001		-0.001	
	[6.429]		[4.856]		[3.480]		[2.982]		[2.625]		[2.164]	
$J^{Adj}-$		-0.014		-0.008		-0.005		-0.004		-0.003		-0.002
		[6.028]		[4.770]		[3.918]		[3.559]		[3.388]		[3.294]
$J^{Adj}+$		-0.0062		-0.0006		0.0005		0.0004		0.0006		0.0007
		[3.853]		[0.446]		[0.428]		[0.366]		[0.604]		[0.737]

We find that AD is significantly priced in excess returns of UK-listed equities. The *t*-statistic attached to J^{Adj} in the Fama and MacBeth (1973) pricing regression is 6.429, which not only exceeds the usual level of 1.96 but also exceeds the Harvey *et al.* (2014) level of 3.0. The negative coefficient of J^{Adj} (−0.010) implies that higher levels of AD lead to a decrease in future 1-month excess return.

One explanation for the negative coefficient of J^{Adj} is that LTAD is associated with a premium and UTAD attracts a discount. We quantify the price of LTAD and UTAD separately by regressing excess returns against $J^{Adj}-$ and $J^{Adj}+$. The premium (discount) associated with a one-unit increase in LTAD (UTAD) is 1.1% (1.2%).[1] Our results are consistent with Skiadas (1997) agents, who may feel disappointed (elated) by holding a LTAD (UTAD) asset.

The typical level of AD can explain 250 bp of future 1-month excess returns. This compares with 590 bp explained by the typical level of the CAPM β. J^{Adj} is significant in predicting future returns up to 15 months in advance. J^{Adj} can predict a bigger proportion of future returns than any other significant factor considered except β and idiosyncratic risk. The CAPM β predicts excess returns up to 15 months in advance, whereas the idiosyncratic risk and cokurtosis can predict returns up to 6 months ahead. Some other factors, such as firm size and book-to-market ratio, also affect future returns in UK equities.

The market price of risk is significant in all of our regressions from Table 9.6. The regression coefficient associated with the CAPM β is negative, which suggests that higher levels of today's β are related with lower future excess returns. Our evidence of the price of the other commonly considered risk factors is consistent with the existing literature (Fletcher, 1997; Brammer *et al.*, 2006; Gregory *et al.*, 2013). For example, Gregory *et al.* (2013) also find that the size effect on 1-month future excess returns, using the Fama and MacBeth (1973) asset-pricing procedure, is not present in UK equities. The evidence on the value effect is mixed. We find that the book-to-market ratio is not a significant predictor of future returns, which is in contrast with Gregory *et al.* (2013) and Brammer *et al.* (2006).

Furthermore, in regressions IV from Table 9.6, we examine the predictive power of LTAD ($J^{Adj}-$) and UTAD ($J^{Adj}+$). Interestingly, we find that only LTAD and not UTAD can predict excess returns of UK equities with horizons longer than 1 month. $J^{Adj}-$ explains returns of up to 15 months in advance. $J^{Adj}-$ is the only predictor with a coefficient having a *t*-statistic exceeding the Harvey *et al.* (2014) hurdle rate of 3.0 in all the predictive regression from Table 9.6.

9.2 PERSISTENCE OF ASYMMETRIC DEPENDENCE

The traditional tests of stock return predictability may reject null hypotheses too frequently if the predictor variable is persistent (Campbell and Yogo, 2006). This may influence all of our results about return predictability from Section 9.1. We have provided evidence that in our predictive regressions from all the financial markets, J^{Adj} is strongly significant with a high *t*-statistic value. In the ordinary least-squares regression, however, the conventional critical values for the *t*-test depend on the assumption that the *t*-statistic is standard normal in large samples. Existing literature shows that the *t*-statistics, based on either simulations or analytical solutions, are not standard normal if the predictor variable is persistent (Mankiw and Shapiro, 1986; Elliott and Stock, 1994; Stambaugh, 1999).

We explore any potential persistence that may influence our inference about return predictability by studying the autoregressive properties of AD across all the analysed financial markets. We start examining the persistence in AD by estimating the coefficients of the AR processes of the time series of the values of the J^{Adj} statistic for each listed firm in our sample. We use non-overlapping estimates of J^{Adj} calculated using daily data from 12-month rolling window periods. We display the resulting ACF calculated using mean AR coefficients based on all listed firms in each financial market in Figure 9.1.

---

[1]Estimated using the Fama and MacBeth (1973) approach.

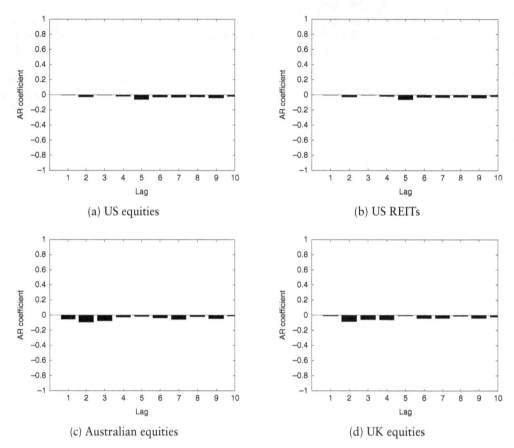

FIGURE 9.1   The autocorrelation function is computed using the J^{Adj} statistic computed on 12-month non-overlapping periods using daily excess returns. One lag represents a 12-month period. At a given month, t, J^{Adj} is estimated using the previous 12 months of daily excess return data. We restrict our attention to stocks listed on the NYSE between January 1959 and December 2015 in panel (a), US REITs listed on the NYSE between January 1972 and December 2013 in panel (b), stocks listed on the ASX between June 1992 and June 2014 in panel (c), and UK stocks listed between January 1987 and May 2015 in panel (d), respectively.

9.2.1   Data and Method

We collect daily US, UK and Australian return data from CRSP and DataStream. At each month t, we calculate the J^{Adj} as proposed by Alcock and Hatherley (2017) using daily excess returns from the past 12 months. We estimate the coefficients of the AR(10) process of the J^{Adj} time series of firms in all the financial markets separately. We calculate mean AR coefficients for each market and report our results graphically in the form of ACF using the mean AR coefficients. An AR coefficient that is close to zero may not necessarily mean a low level of serial autocorrelation. It may be the case that half of the sample exhibit a strong and positive autocorrelation and the other half of the firm J^{Adj} is significantly and negatively autocorrelated. We therefore calculate the proportion of significant AR coefficients that are positive (negative) and significant.

We also explore conditional migration probabilities of the two types of AD: lower-tail and upper-tail AD. A positive value of J^{Adj} indicates UTAD and a negative value of J^{Adj} indicates LTAD

(Alcock and Hatherley, 2017). We separate the UTAD and LTAD by creating $J^{Adj}+$ and $J^{Adj}-$ using the indicator function $\mathbb{I}_c$, which takes the value 1 when condition c is satisfied and zero otherwise:

$$J^{Adj}+ = J^{Adj}\mathbb{I}_{J^{Adj}>0}, \tag{9.1}$$

$$J^{Adj}- = J^{Adj}\mathbb{I}_{J^{Adj}<0}. \tag{9.2}$$

We use non-overlapping 12-month periods of daily data to estimate $J^{Adj}-$ and $J^{Adj}+$. We calculate migration probabilities for each firm from our sample individually. Next, we calculate the mean migration probabilities between LTAD ($J^{Adj}-$) and UTAD ($J^{Adj}+$) firm characteristics across all firms from the same financial market separately; that is, for US equities, US REITs, Australian equities as well as UK equities.

We extend our analysis of the J^{Adj} AR properties and employ the VAR(2) model, which allows us to assess the autoregressive characteristics in a multivariate setting. We regress a vector of the J^{Adj} measure using equity data from all four financial markets on lagged non-overlapping values of J^{Adj} from the same four financial markets. J^{Adj} is estimated using 12 months of daily data.

9.2.2 Serial Autocorrelation of the J^{Adj} Statistic

There is no evident sign of persistence in J^{Adj} in any of the financial markets. The mean value of AR coefficients of lags 1 to 10 is lower than 0.1 in absolute value.[2] US equities and US REITs exhibit a mean AR coefficient close to zero for all the lags. Australian and UK equities have a slightly higher level of negative autocorrelation at all lags. The mean values are however greater than -0.1, which implies that there is no evidence of a significant serial correlation of J^{Adj} in these equity markets.

The ACF from Figure 9.1 may not reflect all the important information about serial correlation of AD. For example, if one group of firms has a strong and negative autocorrelation in AD and another group of firms also exhibits strong but positive autocorrelation of AD, the mean autocorrelation AR coefficients across all firms will be close to zero even in the presence of strong serial correlation of most firms. We therefore also calculate the proportion of firms with significant AR coefficients, focusing mainly on the proportion of firms with significant and positive AR coefficients and the proportion of firms with significant and negative AR coefficients. We test for significance using the Ljung–Box test, where the null hypothesis is an independent distribution of time series with no serial correlation. The number of significant coefficients from Table 9.7 represents the number of firms, where we reject the null hypothesis of no autocorrelation at the standard confidence level ($\alpha = 0.05$).

Our findings from Table 9.7 confirm our observation from Figure 9.1 that listed firms in the USA, UK and Australia do not exhibit any strong autocorrelation since only a small proportion of firms have significant AR coefficients. The proportion of significant coefficients is around 5% in all the countries, which suggests that this significance is fairly random.

9.2.3 Migration Probabilities: Lower-Tail and Upper-Tail Asymmetric Dependence

As our next step in studying the persistence of AD, we explore the empirical probability that a firm with past LTAD continues to exhibit LTAD. This is not the same as persistence captured by AR processes discussed previously. Henceforth, we are only concerned with migrations between the lower-tail and upper-tail AD firm-return observations.

---

[2] Each lag represents one year because we use non-overlapping data and J^{Adj} is estimated using 12 months of daily data.

TABLE 8.7 The J^{Adj} statistic is estimated using a 12-month rolling window of daily returns. We estimate the AR(10) model for each firm in the sample and calculate the proportion of firms with significant AR coefficients. We restrict our attention to stocks listed on the NYSE between January 1959 and December 2015 (Panel A), US REITs listed on the NYSE between January 1972 and December 2013 (Panel B), stocks listed on the ASX between June 1992 and June 2014 (Panel C), and UK stocks listed between January 1987 and May 2015 (Panel D), respectively

Panel A	AR(1)	AR(2)	AR(3)	AR(4)	AR(5)	AR(6)	AR(7)	AR(8)	AR(9)	AR(10)
All	82	77	87	93	105	105	103	100	110	114
Proportion	4.88%	4.58%	5.18%	5.53%	6.25%	6.25%	6.13%	5.95%	6.54%	6.78%
Positive	51	62	45	63	39	58	42	41	43	55
Proportion	6.32%	8.24%	5.47%	8.13%	6.46%	8.01%	6.00%	5.77%	6.75%	7.58%
Negative	31	15	42	30	66	47	61	59	67	59
Proportion	3.55%	1.61%	4.89%	3.31%	6.13%	4.91%	6.22%	6.08%	6.42%	6.18%

Panel B	AR(1)	AR(2)	AR(3)	AR(4)	AR(5)	AR(6)	AR(7)	AR(8)	AR(9)	AR(10)
All	3	6	4	2	2	2	4	5	5	7
Proportion	3.57%	7.14%	4.76%	2.38%	2.38%	2.38%	4.76%	5.95%	5.95%	8.33%
Positive	1	5	1	2	0	2	1	2	2	2
Proportion	2.13%	9.62%	2.22%	4.26%	0.00%	8.00%	4.35%	7.14%	7.41%	8.00%
Negative	2	1	3	0	2	0	3	3	3	5
Proportion	5.41%	3.13%	7.69%	0.00%	4.44%	0.00%	4.92%	5.36%	5.26%	8.47%

Panel C	AR(1)	AR(2)	AR(3)	AR(4)	AR(5)	AR(6)	AR(7)	AR(8)	AR(9)	AR(10)
All	16	15	19	18	17	19	17	22	21	27
Proportion	3.21%	3.01%	3.82%	3.61%	3.41%	3.82%	3.41%	4.42%	4.22%	5.42%
Positive	4	8	5	12	7	13	4	8	5	16
Proportion	2.01%	5.06%	2.99%	5.15%	3.11%	6.28%	2.17%	3.70%	2.62%	6.87%
Negative	12	7	14	6	10	6	13	14	16	11
Proportion	4.01%	2.06%	4.23%	2.26%	3.66%	2.06%	4.14%	4.96%	5.21%	4.15%

Panel D	AR(1)	AR(2)	AR(3)	AR(4)	AR(5)	AR(6)	AR(7)	AR(8)	AR(9)	AR(10)
All	23	15	25	25	24	26	26	27	28	33
Proportion	4.50%	2.94%	4.89%	4.89%	4.70%	5.09%	5.09%	5.28%	5.48%	6.46%
Positive	11	12	6	9	11	14	6	18	14	11
Proportion	4.38%	7.19%	3.09%	4.71%	4.47%	6.73%	2.99%	7.63%	7.33%	5.00%
Negative	12	3	19	16	13	12	20	9	14	22
Proportion	4.62%	0.87%	5.99%	5.00%	4.91%	3.96%	6.45%	3.27%	4.38%	7.56%

Migration probabilities between the two types of AD are an important piece of information from the investor perspective, as LTAD is typically related to a return premium and UTAD attracts a return discount (Alcock and Hatherley, 2017). The information about whether a firm exhibits LTAD or UTAD in a given time period thus completely changes the outlook on return prediction (expected premium or discount). We estimate the migration probabilities between LTAD and UTAD as follows, and report our results in Table 9.8.

We find that if a listed firm exhibits LTAD, it has a higher probability of being LTAD 12 months in the future. Listed firms from our sample exhibiting UTAD are only slightly more likely to be UTAD in 12 months. This implies that the LTAD characteristic is more stable than the UTAD characteristic. This difference can also be explained by the fact that the LTAD return characteristic is more prevalent among listed firms, which holds for all the financial markets. The higher prevalence of LTAD implies that the probability of any firm being LTAD is naturally higher and not caused by persistence of the LTAD characteristic.

TABLE 9.8 J^{Adj} is estimated using a 12-month rolling window of daily returns. We calculate the probability of migrations between $J^{Adj}-$ and $J^{Adj}+$ using non-overlapping data. We restrict our attention to stocks listed on the NYSE between January 1959 and December 2015, US REITs listed on the NYSE between January 1972 and December 2013, stocks listed on the ASX between June 1992 and June 2014, and UK stocks listed between January 1987 and May 2015, respectively

US equities	$J^{Adj}-$	$J^{Adj}+$
$J^{Adj}-$	71.878%	28.122%
$J^{Adj}+$	62.024%	37.976%

US REITs	$J^{Adj}-$	$J^{Adj}+$
$J^{Adj}-$	70.953%	29.047%
$J^{Adj}+$	50.135%	49.865%

Australian equities	$J^{Adj}-$	$J^{Adj}+$
$J^{Adj}-$	83.143%	16.857%
$J^{Adj}+$	76.263%	23.737%

UK equities	$J^{Adj}-$	$J^{Adj}+$
$J^{Adj}-$	69.239%	30.761%
$J^{Adj}+$	65.460%	34.540%

9.3   SPILLOVER EFFECTS

The aggregate levels of AD in various financial markets exhibit diverse time-series patterns. Figure 9.2 displays the value of mean J^{Adj} measured using data on US-listed equities (US), US REITs, Australian-listed equities (AUS) and UK-listed equities (UK).

We can observe from Figure 9.2 that the aggregate level of AD of US REITs closely follows the trend of the level of AD of US equities until 2005. After 2005, the aggregate level of J^{Adj} is greater in US REITs than US equities, which suggests that US REITs exhibit higher (in value and not magnitude) exceedance correlations in the upper tail of the joint-return distribution than the US equities.[3]

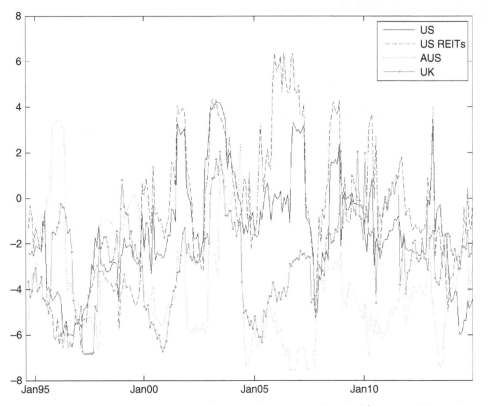

FIGURE 9.2   We calculate the aggregate level of AD as the average value of J^{Adj} across all firms from each financial market. At a given month, t, J^{Adj} is estimated using the past 12 months of daily excess return data. The aggregate levels of AD are winsorized at the 1% and 99% level. We restrict our attention to dates when data from NYSE, ASX and UK stocks is available, which starts from June 1992 and ends in December 2014. This figure presents a time series of the development of the aggregate level of J^{Adj} for the four different financial markets.

---

[3]This is because a positive value of J^{Adj} is associated with UTAD and the US REIT-aggregate level of J^{Adj} becomes more positive after 2005 than the aggregate level of J^{Adj} of US equities.

Another interesting finding from Figure 9.2 can be seen in the development of Australian and UK AD in the years preceding the 2007–2008 financial crisis. The aggregate level of AD in Australia and the UK seems to be negatively related to the AD level in the USA. In order to verify our observations from the time-series plot and examine these linkages in greater detail, we test whether past levels of AD influence current levels of AD for different combinations of markets from our sample.

The evidence of spillover effects in the level of AD is limited. Most of the existing literature is focused on spillover effects between returns. For example, Durand *et al.* (2001) find that changes in US returns explain more than 20% of daily variance of Australian market returns and Australian returns are Granger-caused by US returns. Durand *et al.* (2013) argue that this causality may be explained by Australian investors overreacting to US market-return changes. We aim to contribute to this literature by providing evidence of the interconnectedness of the financial markets in terms of AD.

First, we use the Granger-causality test (Granger, 1969) to examine whether one time series is useful in forecasting another. The results from the Granger-causality test are displayed in Table 9.9. The lag length is chosen using the Bayesian information criterion. The null hypothesis of this test is that there is no Granger causality. Our critical value (c_v) for the F-test is 3.88 for all the combinations of time series from Table 9.9. Our results suggest that we cannot reject the null hypothesis ($F < c_v$) of no Granger causality for any of the combination of time series.

TABLE 9.9 We calculate the aggregate level of AD as the average value of J^{Adj} across all firms from each financial market. At a given month, t, J^{Adj} is estimated using the past 12 months of daily excess return data. The aggregate levels of AD are winsorized at the 1% and 99% level. We restrict our attention to dates when data from NYSE, ASX and UK stocks is available, which starts from June 1992 and ends in December 2014. This table presents coefficients from the VAR(2) model of Equation (9.5) estimated using maximum likelihood

Causality	F
US → AUS	0.864
AUS → US	1.192
US → UK	2.625
UK → US	0.047
US → US REIT	2.536
US REIT → US	3.507
AUS → UK	0.868
UK → AUS	0.814

Based on our results from the Granger causality, we conclude that there is no Granger causality based on the bivariate combinations of time series of aggregate AD levels. To explore the multivariate dynamics of the time-series effects of the four analysed financial markets in greater detail, we also estimate the VAR model (Sims, 1980). The advantage of multivariate causality testing using the VAR model is that it can avoid spurious correlations, which may increase the validity of the Granger-causality test. This is because the VAR model includes more variables that may be responsible for the causality effects (Lütkepohl, 1982).

Let $\mathbf{x}_t$ define the vector of the time series of the aggregate levels of J^{Adj},

$$\mathbf{x}_t = \begin{pmatrix} x_{1,t} \\ x_{2,t} \\ x_{3,t} \\ x_{4,t} \end{pmatrix}, \tag{9.3}$$

where $x_{1,t}$ represents the aggregate level of J^{Adj} in US equities, $x_{2,t}$ is the aggregate level of J^{Adj} in US REITs, $x_{3,t}$ is the aggregate level of J^{Adj} in Australian equities, and $x_{4,t}$ is the aggregate level of J^{Adj} in UK equities, respectively. We can formally describe the VAR model with two lags as

$$\mathbf{x}_t = A + B\mathbf{x}_{t-1} + C\mathbf{x}_{t-2} + \mathbf{u}_t, \tag{9.4}$$

where A is a (4×1) vector of intercepts, B is the (4×4) matrix of regression coefficients associated with the AR(1) parameters, C is the (4×4) matrix of the AR(2) coefficients, and $\mathbf{u}_t$ is the (4×1) vector of regression errors for all four model equations. The VAR(2) model from Equation (9.4) can be expressed in longer form as

$$\begin{pmatrix} x_{1,t} \\ x_{2,t} \\ x_{3,t} \\ x_{4,t} \end{pmatrix} = \begin{pmatrix} A_1 \\ A_2 \\ A_3 \\ A_4 \end{pmatrix} + \begin{pmatrix} B_{1,1} & B_{1,2} & B_{1,3} & B_{1,4} \\ B_{2,1} & B_{2,2} & B_{2,3} & B_{2,3} \\ B_{3,1} & B_{3,2} & B_{3,3} & B_{3,3} \\ B_{4,1} & B_{4,2} & B_{4,3} & B_{4,3} \end{pmatrix} \begin{pmatrix} x_{1,t-1} \\ x_{2,t-1} \\ x_{3,t-1} \\ x_{4,t-1} \end{pmatrix}$$

$$+ \begin{pmatrix} C_{1,1} & C_{1,2} & C_{1,3} & C_{1,4} \\ C_{2,1} & C_{2,2} & C_{2,3} & C_{2,3} \\ C_{3,1} & C_{3,2} & C_{3,3} & C_{3,3} \\ C_{4,1} & C_{4,2} & C_{4,3} & C_{4,3} \end{pmatrix} \begin{pmatrix} x_{1,t-2} \\ x_{2,t-2} \\ x_{3,t-2} \\ x_{4,t-2} \end{pmatrix} + \begin{pmatrix} u_{1,t} \\ u_{2,t} \\ u_{3,t} \\ u_{4,t} \end{pmatrix}. \tag{9.5}$$

We estimate the parameters of the VAR(2) model from Equation (9.5) using maximum likelihood (ML) estimation and report our results in Table 9.10. Each lag represents one month. We choose to estimate a VAR model with parameters of up to two lags. In our system of equations, there are 36 coefficients to be estimated. Most of the AR coefficients are not significant, which suggests a low persistence of AD and a low level of spillover effects between the financial markets. We find that coefficients $B_{1,1}$, $B_{2,2}$, $B_{4,4}$ and $C_{3,3}$ are positive and significant, which is not surprising since the J^{Adj} estimation requires 12 months of daily data, and these coefficients represent the effect of lagged values from the same financial market.

Nevertheless, our results also indicate that there are some significant spillover effects between the US and the Australian stock market. We find that the level of AD of US equities influences the level of AD of Australian equities, since the coefficients $B_{3,1}$ and $C_{3,1}$ are significant. Our results are consistent with Durand *et al.* (2001), who provide evidence that US returns Granger-cause Australian returns.

Interestingly, the relationship between the level of US AD from the previous month and the current level of AD of Australian equities is positive, whereas the level of US AD from the previous two months

TABLE 9.10 We calculate the aggregate level of AD as the average value of J^{Adj} across all firms from each financial market. At a given month, t, J^{Adj} is estimated using the past 12 months of daily excess return data. The aggregate levels of AD are winsorized at the 1% and 99% level. We restrict our attention to dates when data from NYSE, ASX and UK stocks is available, which starts from June 1992 and ends in December 2014. This table presents coefficients from the VAR(2) model of Equation (9.5) estimated using ML. We report the estimated coefficients (Est), standard error of estimates (SE) and t-statistic (t-stat)

	Est	SE	t-stat
A_1	−0.270	0.138	−1.959
A_2	−0.494	0.151	−3.272
A_3	−0.243	0.127	−1.919
A_4	−0.202	0.170	−1.189
$B_{1,1}$	0.736	0.097	**7.592**
$B_{1,2}$	0.030	0.061	0.493
$B_{1,3}$	−0.010	0.071	−0.135
$B_{1,4}$	0.016	0.079	0.209
$B_{2,1}$	0.121	0.106	1.137
$B_{2,2}$	0.894	0.067	**13.352**
$B_{2,3}$	−0.008	0.078	−0.099
$B_{2,4}$	−0.167	0.086	−1.944
$B_{3,1}$	0.239	0.089	**2.682**
$B_{3,2}$	0.149	0.056	**2.647**
$B_{3,3}$	0.649	0.065	**9.958**
$B_{3,4}$	−0.123	0.072	−1.703
$B_{4,1}$	−0.164	0.120	−1.376
$B_{4,2}$	−0.044	0.075	−0.584
$B_{4,3}$	0.003	0.087	0.033
$B_{4,4}$	0.869	0.097	**8.986**
$C_{1,1}$	0.092	0.099	0.936
$C_{1,2}$	−0.050	0.060	−0.829
$C_{1,3}$	0.018	0.070	0.263
$C_{1,4}$	0.059	0.080	0.738
$C_{2,1}$	−0.036	0.108	−0.337
$C_{2,2}$	−0.042	0.066	−0.636
$C_{2,3}$	0.015	0.077	0.191
$C_{2,4}$	0.066	0.088	0.747
$C_{3,1}$	−0.213	0.091	**−2.350**
$C_{3,2}$	−0.134	0.055	**−2.414**
$C_{3,3}$	0.226	0.065	**3.499**
$C_{3,4}$	0.125	0.074	1.692
$C_{4,1}$	0.084	0.121	0.692
$C_{4,2}$	0.010	0.074	0.134
$C_{4,3}$	0.023	0.087	0.260
$C_{4,4}$	0.095	0.099	0.961

has a negative correlation with the current level of AD of Australian equities. We find similar effects of the level of AD in US REITs on the level of AD of Australian equities, which may be explained by the fact that US REITs are a subset of all US-listed equities. We do not find any evidence of other spillover effects between the stock markets considered.

9.4 CONCLUSION

In this chapter, we deal with three distinct properties of AD: predictive power of AD, persistence of AD and spillover effects of AD between financial markets. We first analyse whether AD has a statistical power to predict stock returns. We use the traditional Fama and MacBeth (1973) procedure and assess whether AD can predict future excess returns in the next one month. We find that AD measured by J^{Adj} is a significant predictor of future stock returns in all the stock markets considered, that is in the US-, Australian- and UK-listed equities. Our results are not only valid for the listed equities, but hold also for US REITs. Moreover, we find that the AD characteristic of US, Australian and UK equities predicts returns up to 15 months ahead.

Second, we verify our results by examining the persistence of AD. This is important for our inference about return predictability, since the standard predictability tests may reject the null hypothesis too frequently if the predictor is persistent (Campbell and Yogo, 2006). We study the serial dependence structure of individual firm time series of AD. We find that there is no evident positive or negative autocorrelation of AD in any of the analysed stock markets, which suggests that the AD predictor is not persistent. This finding increases the validity of our predictability results.

Third, we study the spillover effects between the four financial markets, namely between the US-, Australian- and UK-listed equity and US REITs. We find that there are spillover effects between the US and the Australian stock markets. The level of AD in the USA influences the level of AD in Australia. We do not find any other significant spillover effects in AD between the financial markets. Using the multivariate setting of the VAR model, we confirm that there is no significant serial autocorrelation of AD in any of the four financial markets examined.

REFERENCES

Alcock, J. and Hatherley, A. (2017). Characterizing the asymmetric dependence. *Review of Finance*, 21(4), 1701–1737.

Ang, A., Hodrick, R.J., Xing, Y. and Zhang, X. (2006). The cross-section of volatility and expected returns. *Journal of Finance*, 61(1), 259–299.

Avramov, D. and Chordia, T. (2006). Asset pricing models and financial market anomalies. *Review of Financial Studies*, 19(3), 1001–1040.

Brailsford, T., Gaunt, C. and O'Brien, M.A. (2012). Size and book-to-market factors in Australia. *Australian Journal of Management*, 37, 261–281.

Brammer, S., Brooks, C. and Pavelin, S. (2006). Corporate social performance and stock returns: UK evidence from disaggregate measures. *Financial Management*, 35(3), 97–116.

Campbell, J.Y. and Yogo, M. (2006). Efficient tests of stock return predictability. *Journal of Financial Economics*, 81(1), 27–60.

Cochrane, J.H. (1999). Portfolio advice for a multifactor world. *Economic Perspectives*, 23, 59–78.

Durand, R.B., Kee, K.S. and Watson, I. (2001). Who moved Asian-Pacific stock markets? A further consideration of the impact of the US and Japan. *Australian Journal of Management*, 26(2), 125–145.

Durand, R., Newby, R., Tant, K. and Trepongkaruna, S. (2013). Overconfidence, overreaction and personality. *Review of Behavioral Finance*, 5(2), 104–133.

Elliott, G. and Stock, J.H. (1994). Inference in time series regression when the order of integration of a regressor is unknown. *Econometric Theory*, 10(3&4), 672–700.

Faff, R. (2001). An examination of the Fama and French three-factor model using commercially available factors. *Australian Journal of Management*, 26(1), 1–17.

Faff, R. (2004). A simple test of the Fama and French model using daily data: Australian evidence. *Applied Financial Economics*, 14(2), 83–92.

Fama, E.F. and MacBeth, J.D. (1973). Risk, return, and equilibrium: empirical tests. *Journal of Political Economy*, 607–636.

Fama, E.F. and French, K.R. (1998). Value versus growth: The international evidence. *Journal of Finance*, 53(6), 1975–1999.

Fletcher, J. (1997). An examination of the cross-sectional relationship of beta and return: UK evidence. *Journal of Economics and Business*, 49(3), 211–221.

Fu, F. (2009). Idiosyncratic risk and the cross-section of expected stock returns. *Journal of Financial Economics*, 91(1), 24–37.

Gaunt, C. (2004). Size and book to market effects and the Fama French three factor asset pricing model: evidence from the Australian stockmarket. *Accounting & Finance*, 44(1), 27–44.

Gharghori, P., Chan, H. and Faff, R. (2007). Are the Fama–French factors proxying default risk? *Australian Journal of Management*, 32(2), 223–249.

Glascock, J.L., Michayluk, D. and Neuhauser, K. (2004). The riskiness of REITs surrounding the October 1997 stock market decline. *Journal of Real Estate, Finance and Economics*, 28(4), 339–354.

Granger, C.W. (1969). Investigating causal relations by econometric models and cross-spectral methods. *Econometrica: Journal of the Econometric Society*, 424–438.

Gregory, A., Tharyan, R. and Christidis, A. (2013). Constructing and testing alternative versions of the Fama–French and Carhart models in the UK. *Journal of Business, Finance & Accounting*, 40(1&2), 172–214.

Halliwell, J., Heaney, R. and Sawicki, J. (1999). Size and book to market effects in Australian share markets: a time series analysis. *Accounting Research Journal*, 12(2), 122–137.

Harvey, C.R., Liu, Y. and Zhu, H. (2014). … and the cross-section of expected returns. Technical Report, National Bureau of Economic Research.

Huang, M. and Wu, C.-C. (2015). Economic benefits and determinants of extreme dependences between REIT and stock returns. *Review of Quantitative Finance and Accounting*, 44(2), 299–327.

Kassimatis, K. (2008). Size, book to market and momentum effects in the Australian stock market. *Australian Journal of Management*, 33(1), 145–168.

Liow, K.H. and Addae-Dapaah, K. (2010). Idiosyncratic risk, market risk and correlation dynamics in the US real estate investment trusts. *Journal of Housing Economics*, 19(3), 205–218.

Liu, L.X. and Zhang, L. (2008). Momentum profits, factor pricing, and macroeconomic risk. *Review of Financial Studies*, 21(6), 2417–2448.

Lütkepohl, H. (1982). Non-causality due to omitted variables. *Journal of Econometrics*, 19(2), 367–378.

Mankiw, N.G. and Shapiro, M.D. (1986). Do we reject too often? Small sample properties of tests of rational expectations models. *Economics Letters*, 20(2), 139–145.

McLean, R.D. and Pontiff, J. (2016). Does academic research destroy stock return predictability? *Journal of Finance*, 71(1), 5–32.

Newey, W.K. and West, K.D. (1987). A simple, positive semi-definite, heteroskedasticity and autocorrelation consistent covariance matrix. *Econometrica*, 55(3), 703–708.

Newey, W.K. and West, K.D. (1994). Automatic lag selection in covariance matrix estimation. *Review of Economic Studies*, 61(4), 631–653.

O'Brien, M.A., Brailsford, T. and Gaunt, C. (2010). Interaction of size, book-to-market and momentum effects in Australia. *Accounting & Finance*, 50(1), 197–219.

Ooi, J.T., Wang, J. and Webb, J.R. (2009). Idiosyncratic risk and REIT returns. *Journal of Real Estate, Finance and Economics*, 38(4), 420–442.

Sims, C.A. (1980). Macroeconomics and reality. *Econometrica: Journal of the Econometric Society*, 1–48.

Skiadas, C. (1997). Conditioning and aggregation of preferences. *Econometrica*, 65(2), 347–367.

Stambaugh, R.F. (1999). Predictive regressions. *Journal of Financial Economics*, 54(3), 375–421.

Stambaugh, R.F. (2003). Liquidity risk and expected stock returns. *Journal of Political Economy*, 111(3), 642–685.

Vo, D.H. (2015). Which factors are priced? An application of the Fama French three-factor model in Australia. *Economic Papers: A Journal of Applied Economics and Policy*, 34(4), 290–301.

CHAPTER 10

The Most Entropic Canonical Copula with an Application to 'Style' Investment

Ba Chu[a] and Stephen Satchell[b]

[a]Department of Economics, Carleton University
[b]Discipline of Finance, Sydney University and Trinity College, Cambridge

Abstract

We propose a new approach to recover relative entropy measures of dependence from limited information by constructing the most entropic copulas (MECs) and their canonical form, namely, the most entropic canonical copula (MECC). In the empirical study, we focus on an application of the MECC theory to a 'style investing' problem for an investor with a constant relative risk aversion (CRRA) utility function allocating wealth between the Russell 1000 'growth' and 'value' indices. We found that, using the data in hand, the gains from using the MECC (vis-à-vis commonly used parametric copulas) to model the dependence between the indices' returns for our investment strategies are economically and statistically significant for the case with/without short-sales constraints.

10.1 INTRODUCTION

Modelling dependence between asset returns is crucial in a number of financial applications. For a number of standard distributions in the elliptical family, dependence is simply measured by Pearson's correlation coefficient. In practice, however, asset returns do not always belong to the elliptical family, and thus the dependence structure does not always show out of the joint distribution function under consideration. It would be useful to separate the statistical properties of each return from their dependence structure. Copulas provide us with a viable way to achieve this goal. As we shall see from our literature review here, dependence modelling via copulas has not been fully explored. The present chapter is a step in this direction.

There has been growing interest in constructing measures of dependence between non-elliptical random variables. Among other works, the work which essentially influences the present chapter is Joe (1989b), which proposes the relative entropy (RE) measures of dependence as a general method to capture dependence (as they can be used for a mixture of continuous, ordinal-categorical and nominal-categorical random variables). Many nonparametric estimators of the RE measures of dependence have been proposed and shown to be consistent under regularity conditions (see, *inter alia*, Joe, 1989a; Robinson, 1991; Skaug and Tjøstheim, 1996). The goal for the current chapter is, however, to develop a different method; that is, we employ the maximum entropy (ME) principle and copula theory to recover the RE measures of dependence from limited information. The motivation of our approach is that, despite having some prior knowledge about dependence between financial indices by examining data, financial analysts still do not have enough information to effectively infer complex aspects of tail dependence in a multivariate distribution; thus, it is useful to use the ME principle to construct the RE measures of dependence in an informationally minimum way.

To place the results obtained and the viewpoints taken in this chapter into proper perspective, we shall now give a brief indication of the works in entropy and copulas. Because the literature in this regard appears to be rather vast, we shall unfortunately be able to take into account only a very limited, certainly nonrepresentative, part of it. However, detailed indications of various economic and statistic aspects or applications of ME distributions and copulas can be found in several monographs, for instance, Zong (2006), Nelsen (1998), Cherubini *et al.* (2004) and Poon *et al.* (2007).

Using the entropy principle of Shannon (1948) to compute probability densities has been widely accepted in economics (see, e.g., Golan, 2002, 2007 and references therein for the background, discussions, and applications of the ME principle).[1] Rockinger and Jondeau (2002) use the ME principle to formulate risk-adjusted return distributions with autoregressive conditional volatility, skewness and kurtosis. Maasoumi and Racine (2002) employ metric entropy measures of nonlinear dependence to examine return predictability. Hang (1993) proposes a ME method to approximate flexible regression functions. Wu and Stengos (2005) develop a partially adaptive method based on the ME densities to estimate non-elliptical error distributions, and show, by Monte Carlo simulations, that the proposed estimators perform well. Closer in spirit to the present chapter is the paper by Miller and Liu (2002), who use the Kullback–Leibler cross entropy (KLCE) distance to recover joint distributions, while disposing only of information on certain joint moments. We shall discuss the main differences between the present chapter and the paper by Miller and Liu (2002) following a brief review of some works on copulas.

Copulas provide a promising way to model asymmetric dependence (AD) between random variables without being influenced by their marginal distributions (or *marginals* for brevity). Because the choice of copulas is not constrained by marginals, copulas are useful in many financial applications (e.g., AD modelling – Patton (2006); risk and portfolio management – Patton (2004) and Jondeau and Rockinger (2006), among others). By Sklar's (1959) theorem, any joint distribution can be decomposed into its *marginals* and a *copula* that completely summarizes the structure of dependence – thus, a copula is a more informative measure of dependence for non-elliptical random variables (e.g., financial asset returns). Although many parametric and nonparametric goodness-of-fit tests for copulas (see, e.g., Fermanian, 2005; Scaillet, 2007; Chen, 2007, among others) *or* copula approximations (see, e.g., Sancetta and Satchell, 2004) have been proposed, it is still quite a challenging task to determine which copula best fits a data set. Therefore, the purposes of the current chapter are clear. First, we propose an entropy method to recover a set of the most entropic copulas (MECs) from prior information, and show that the MECs are equivalent to the RE measures of dependence. Second, we can construct an equivalent class of minimum KLCE joint distributions from a MEC.

In this chapter, the MEC is defined as a copula, $\hat{c}(u, v)$, which, given an amount of prior information on dependence, maximizes the amount of information that we will be receiving (putting it simply, suppose that we do not assume any prior information at all, a natural candidate of the MEC is obviously uv – that is, the random variables are independent – thus, the RE measure of dependence is zero). Since a copula is a joint uniform distribution, we compute the MEC by maximizing the Shannon entropy of a joint distribution with its domain in a unit cube subject to the constraints that this joint distribution has Uniform[0,1] marginals, and that the measures of association are equal to their nonparametric estimates (or rank correlations) [e.g., Blest's rank correlations (see Genest and MacKay, 1986;

---

[1] Interested readers may be referred to two special issues (vol. 107 and 138) of the *Journal of Econometrics* for further contributions.

Blest, 2000)]. In addition, there exists, in the class of the MECs, a simple form called the most entropic canonical copula (MECC).

Now, we are in a position to discuss the *similarity* and *differences* between the present chapter and Miller and Liu (2002). The similarity is that the Shannon entropy of a copula (used in this paper) is, by the Sklar theorem, equivalent to the KLCE of a multivariate distribution (used in Miller and Liu, 2002). Some readers may at this point conclude that the former is just a special case of the latter, because the KLCE of a multivariate uniform distribution turns out to be the Shannon entropy. Notwithstanding this view, Shannon (1948) is usually credited with formulating the first mathematical measure of information. And following the Sklar theorem, the KLCE of any multivariate distribution can be, as shown in Section 10.2, translated into the Shannon entropy of a copula. Therefore, we can posit at this point that they are in fact *dual* problems.

However, the first difference is that, while Miller and Liu (2002) solve the problem of minimizing the KLCE of a multivariate distribution, we solve the problem of maximizing the Shannon entropy of a copula. The second difference is that, while Miller and Liu (2002) specify prior information on dependence by using sample joint moments, we do so by using rank correlations. An advantage of rank correlations over sample joint moments is that the former are 'robust' in the sense that they are less sensitive to outliers – thus, we may say that the MECs are 'robust' copulas. Moreover, since our approach and the approach of Miller and Liu (2002) are dual, a minimum KLCE joint distribution can be derived by substituting an arbitrary set of marginals into the MECC. As the RE measure of dependence specified by the MECC is invariant to specifications of marginals, the joint distributions derived from a MECC must have the same structure of dependence.

In empirical analysis, we applied the MECC theory to examine the problem of an investor with CRRA investing in two 'style' equity portfolios (i.e., Russell 1000 'growth' and 'value' indices, which are typical of high-risk/low-return and low-risk/high-return indices, respectively).[2] This problem is of practical interest because 'style investing', where portfolio managers rotate between 'value' and 'growth' stocks, has recently become popular in Wall Street. In the broad context of optimal asset allocation using copulas, our study is an extension of a recent empirical study of Patton (2004), who focuses on the 'large caps' and 'small caps' investment problem.

'Value' stocks often beat 'growth' ones – 'value' stocks have higher mean and lower variance than 'growth' ones (see, e.g., Basu, 1977; Fama and French, 1998, among others). However, this story is not quite true, as we can see from Table 10.1 where, in the in-sample period, the Russell 1000 'growth' index has higher mean and variance than the Russell 1000 'value' index; thus, it may well be that there are extended periods when 'growth' stocks seem to outperform 'value' stocks. Moreover, from the corporate finance perspective, 'value' stocks (or stocks issued by firms with low price–earnings ratios) are often associated with high costs of equity and high risk of the projects undertaken by the firms (see, e.g., Damodaran, 2004). Since high costs of equity implies that an investor who holds 'value' stocks does require higher returns as compensation for bearing high risk,[3] the low risk of 'value' stocks, which one often observes, may be a consequence of using sample variance as a measure of risk that inevitably underestimates the actual risk. Hence, we may not always achieve superior performance by simply tilting the equity allocation towards the 'value' portfolio (Ibbotson and Riepe, 1997). In this spirit, the first purpose of this empirical application is that, based on different dynamic investment models, we examine the variations in the shares of a portfolio optimally allocated to Russell 1000 'growth' and 'value' indices when risk is assumed to be time-varying and captured by the high-order moments of a conditional skewed distribution.

---

[2]The full-sample means and the full-sample standard deviations are 0.0051 and 0.0497 for the 'growth' index and 0.0072 and 0.0382 for the 'value' index, respectively.

[3]Moreover, according to the efficient market hypothesis, since fundamental variables are already factored into stock prices, the only factor yielding higher returns is higher risk.

TABLE 10.1 Descriptive sample statistics

	Full sample		In-sample		Out-of-sample	
	Russell 1000 Growth	Russell 1000 Value	Russell 1000 Growth	Russell 1000 Value	Russell 1000 Growth	Russell 1000 Value
Mean	0.0051	0.0072	0.0204	0.0162	−0.0041	0.0017
Std. Dev.	0.0497	0.0382	0.0435	0.0371	0.0511	0.0380
Skewness	−0.4504	−0.8437	0.1295	−0.6131	−0.5721	−1.0374
25% quantile	−0.0187	−0.0141	−0.0043	0.0023	−0.0267	−0.0191
75% quantile	0.0371	0.0302	0.0420	0.0409	0.0282	0.0244
Kurtosis	1.4665	2.1669	1.4216	1.1533	1.2462	2.8422
Min	−0.1514	−0.1529	−0.0828	−0.0802	−0.1514	−0.1529
Max	0.1580	0.1103	0.1580	0.1103	0.1211	0.0761
Kolmogorov–Smirnov p-value	0.0802	0.0972	0.1027	0.1480	0.0999	0.0776
Sample correlation	0.8091		0.8866		0.7621	

Notes: 'Kolmogorov–Smirnov' refers to the test for normality of the unconditional return distributions. The full-sample period runs from June 1995 to July 2006, the in-sample period from June 1995 to September 1999 and the out-of-sample period from October 1999 to July 2006.

The impact of dynamic dependence between asset returns in a portfolio on the optimal weights is evident.[4] Thus, effectively capturing this dependence pattern, which may be rather complex, is crucial for asset allocation. In the present 'style' investing problem, the 'growth' and 'value' returns, after being adjusted for fundamental risks, are less correlated than their underlying fundamentals; dependence between the risk-adjusted (or standardized) excess returns is more complex than that between the underlying fundamentals (Barberis and Shleifer, 2003; Barberis *et al.*, 2005). Hence, the second purpose of this empirical application is to show that this dependence can be well calibrated by the MECC, thus significantly improving investment gains.

Due to some considerable computational constraints, *first* we were compelled to ignore the ubiquitous issue of parameter and model uncertainty on investment decisions (see, e.g., Brandt, 2004). We are aware that this issue can be approached with the Bayesian estimation and model averaging method at a considerable computational cost, even so it is not certain that the Bayesian portfolios will outperform the $1/N$ portfolio (see DeMiguel *et al.*, 2009). *Second*, we considered only a one-period-ahead investment problem. This is a common problem in optimal asset allocation (see, e.g., Patton, 2004, among others). We used Hansen (1994)'s skewed t distribution to capture four time-varying central moments (means, variances, skewness and kurtosis) of the standardized residuals of the TGARCH-type models of the 'value' and 'growth' returns; and the copulas (normal, Clayton, Gumbel and MECC), which

---

[4]For instance, in the mean-variance framework, the optimal proportions of a portfolio allocated to individual assets are functions of the expected returns, the variances and the linear correlations.

have parameter(s) depending on the latent underlying fundamentals of the returns, to model AD between the standardized residuals. While the normal, Clayton or Gumbel copula has only one parameter, the MECC may have many parameters, depending on how much prior information we want to impose. Also note that this framework is a special case of the copula-based multivariate models (see, e.g., Patton, 2004, 2006; Jondeau and Rockinger, 2006).

We measure the gains from using the MECC by comparing the expected utility of a portfolio based on the MECC with that based on the normal, Clayton or Gumbel copula; we test for their statistical significance by using bootstrap methods. We find clear evidence that using the MECC leads to gains that are economically and statistically significant, and indeed these gains are sensitive to the amount of prior information specified in terms of rank correlations.

Although, in the present chapter, we mostly concentrate on the bivariate MECC, the multivariate MECC can feasibly be computed by maximizing the multivariate Shannon entropy subject to prior information expressed via multivariate rank correlations. Hence, the results presented here are in line with those for the multivariate case. The rest of this chapter is organized as follows. Section 10.2 includes brief descriptions of entropy and copulas. Section 10.3 defines the MEC and the MECC, and proposes their approximators with asymptotic properties. The main results are presented in Theorems 10.3.1–10.3.3. Some simulations and an empirical application are presented in Sections 10.4 and 10.5, confirming that our approach is feasible. Section 10.6 concludes this chapter. Last but not least, to make the current chapter as short and informative as possible, we shall delegate the results essential for the chapter and results of a technical flavour to the appendices. Also, to keep the empirical section parsimonious and solid, we shall unfortunately not allow ourselves to report some trivial statistical results. Nevertheless, they are all available from us upon request.

10.2 MAXIMUM ENTROPY AND COPULAS

This section provides a brief explanation of entropy and copulas. We refer to the appendices for further details.

The *Shannon entropy* has been used as an information criterion to construct the probability densities for economic or financial variables such as stock returns, income, GDP, etc. (see, *inter alia*, Zellner and Highfield, 1988; Wu, 2003; Wu and Perloff, 2007). A univariate ME density is generally obtained by maximizing the Shannon entropy, $-\int p(x) \log p(x) dx$, with respect to $p(x)$ under probability and moment constraints. A bivariate ME density can be obtained by minimizing the KLCE under joint moment constraints (see, e.g., Joe, 1989b; Miller and Liu, 2002):

$$\min_{f} KLCE(f : g) = \min_{f} \int_{\mathbb{R}^2} f(X, Y) \log \frac{f(X, Y)}{g_1(X)g_2(Y)} dX dY \qquad (10.1)$$

subject to

$$\int_{\mathbb{R}^2} h(X, Y)f(X, Y) dX dY = \mu_0,$$

where f is a bivariate density, g_1 and g_2 are marginal densities, and h is an arbitrary function such that $\mu_0 < \infty$.

The *copula* is proposed by Sklar (1959) as a method to construct joint distributions with given marginals. The advantage of copulas is that dependence between random variables can be parametrically specified entirely independently from their marginals. Throughout this chapter, we denote a bivariate copula of (u, v) by $C(u, v)$ and its density by $c(u, v)$. Since, by definition, $C(1, 1) = 1$, $C(u, 1) = u$ and $C(1, v) = v$, a copula, $C(u, v)$, must be a bivariate Uniform[0,1] distribution with Uniform[0,1] marginals. In the same way, a multivariate copula is a multivariate Uniform[0,1] distribution. By Sklar's theorem, the exact link between a copula, $C(u, v)$, and a joint distribution, $F(X, Y)$, is $F(X, Y) = C(G_1(X), G_2(Y))$, where G_1 and G_2 are the marginals.

As we have mentioned in the Introduction, we use measures of association and rank correlations in constructing the MEC, thus it is useful, at this stage, to discuss those quantities. Measures of association are, unlike joint moments, invariant under nonlinear transformations of the underlying random variables, and thus they are natural measures of dependence for non-elliptical random variables (see the appendices for formal definitions of measures of association). A measure of association is, in general, defined as $\tau = \int_0^1 h(u, v) dC(u, v)$, where h is a bivariate function such that $\tau < +\infty$. This measure, based on C, is also referred to as the *copula-based measure of dependence*. In practice, τ can be estimated by the rank statistic $\hat{\tau} = \frac{1}{T} \sum_{t=1}^{T} h\left(\frac{R_t}{T}, \frac{S_t}{T}\right)$, where (R_t, S_t) denotes the rank of (X_t, Y_t) in the sample of size T. A pro of using rank statistics as nonparametric measures of nonlinear dependence is that they are robust – where 'robust' means to be insensitive to contamination and to maintain a high efficiency for heavier-tailed elliptical distributions as well as for multivariate normal distributions. For helpful ideas on the topic of rank statistics, we refer to the monograph by Hajek and Sidak (1967).

In particular, if $h(u, v)$ is a self-decomposable function [i.e., $h(u, v) = J(u)J(v)$], we obtain:

$$\hat{\tau} = \frac{1}{T} \sum_{t=1}^{T} J\left(\frac{R_t}{T}\right) J\left(\frac{S_t}{T}\right),$$

where J is also called a standardized score function (see, e.g., Puri *et al.*, 1970). For instance, when the score function is $J(u) = \sqrt{12}(u - 1/2)$, then $\hat{\tau} = \frac{12}{T(T^2-1)} \sum_{t=1}^{T} \left(R_t - \frac{T+1}{2}\right)\left(S_t - \frac{T+1}{2}\right)$ is Spearman's rank correlation with asymptotic mean given by Spearman's rho. Other special cases of the above-mentioned rank statistic include Blest's rank correlations (see, e.g., Genest and Plante, 2003), which are summarized in the following table:

Measures of association	Rank correlation
Spearman's rho: $\rho_S = 12 \int_{[0,1]^2} uvc(u, v)dudv - 3$ and $\rho_S \in [-1, 1]$	$\hat{\rho}_S = \frac{12}{T^3-T} \sum_{t=1}^{T} R_t S_t - 3\frac{T+1}{T-1}$
Blest's measure I: $v_1 = 2 - 12 \int_{[0,1]^2} (1 - u)^2 vc(u, v)dudv$ and $v_1 \in [-1, 1]$	$\hat{v}_1 = \frac{2T+1}{T-1} - \frac{12}{T^2-T} \sum_{t=1}^{T} \left(1 - \frac{R_t}{T+1}\right)^2 S_t$
Blest's measure II: $v_2 = 2 - 12 \int_{[0,1]^2} u(1 - v)^2 c(u, v)dudv$ and $v_2 \in [-1, 1]$	$\hat{v}_2 = \frac{2T+1}{T-1} - \frac{12}{T^2-T} \sum_{t=1}^{T} R_t\left(1 - \frac{S_t}{T+1}\right)^2$
Blest's measure III: $\eta = 6 \int_{[0,1]^2} u^2 v^2 c(u, v)dudv - \frac{1}{5}$ and $\eta \in [0, 1]$	$\hat{\eta} = \frac{6}{T^2-T} \sum_{t=1}^{T} \left(\frac{R_t}{T+1}\right)^2 \left(\frac{S_t}{T+1}\right)^2 - \frac{(1/5)T+1}{T-1}$
Blest's measure IV: $\phi = \int_{[0,1]^2} [10(1 - u)^3 v - 3u^2 v^2]c(u, v)dudv - 9/10$ and $\phi \in [-1, 1]$	$\hat{\phi} = \frac{1}{T^2-T} \sum_{t=1}^{T} \left[\left(1 - \frac{R_t}{T+1}\right)^3 \frac{S_t}{T+1} - \left(\frac{R_t}{T+1}\right)^2 \left(\frac{S_t}{T+1}\right)^2\right] - \frac{0.9T+1}{T-1}$

Nonetheless, it is worth mentioning that not every rank correlation can be formulated in terms of the above general rank statistic $\hat{\tau}$. For instance, the statistic $\hat{R}_g$, which was proposed by Gideon and

Hollister (1987) as a coefficient of rank correlation resistant to outliers even in a small sample, has the form

$$\hat{R}_g = \frac{1}{[T/2]} \left(\max_t \sum_{s=1}^{t} \mathbf{1}(p_s < T + 1 - t) - \max_t \sum_{s=1}^{T} \mathbf{1}(R_s \le t < S_s) \right),$$

where p_s is the value of S_t, with the subscript t satisfying $R_t = s$, and $[\cdot]$ is the greatest integer notation. In addition, $\hat{R}_g$ estimates a copula-based measure of dependence, $R_g = 2\int_{[0,1]^2} [\sup_{w \in [0,1]} \mathbf{1}(u \le w, v < 1 - w) - \sup_{w \in [0,1]} (\mathbf{1}(u \le w) - \mathbf{1}(u \le w, v < w))]c(u, v)dudv$.

In the present chapter, we use the bivariate Shannon entropy of a copula, given by

$$\mathbf{W}(c) = -\int_{[0,1]^2} c(u, v) \log c(u, v)dudv, \quad \text{where } c(u, v) = \frac{\partial^2 C(u, v)}{\partial u \partial v}. \tag{10.2}$$

By Sklar's theorem, the Shannon entropy of a copula is equivalent to the KLCE, that is

$$\mathbf{W}(c) = -KLCE(f : g).$$

Hence, minimization of the KLCE and maximization of the bivariate Shannon entropy are dual problems. Let $\hat{c}(u, v)$ denote the MEC; we define the *RE measure of dependence* recovered from limited information as $-\mathbf{W}(\hat{c})$. Generally speaking, a multivariate Shannon entropy can be defined in an obvious way, and this dual relationship holds.

10.3   PROPOSED METHOD

10.3.1   The Most Entropic Copula as a Bivariate Distribution with Uniform[0,1] Marginals

The bivariate MEC (or the MEC) is obtained by maximizing the bivariate Shannon entropy (10.2) under the following two constraints: (1) the marginals of $c(u, v)$ are Uniform[0,1] and (2) the measures of association, defined in Section 10.2, are set equal to the corresponding rank correlations. We call this Problem A.

$$\text{Problem A:} \qquad \text{Maximizing} \quad \mathbf{W}(c) = -\int_{[0,1]^2} c(u, v) \log c(u, v)dudv \tag{10.3}$$

subject to

$$\int_{[0,1]^2} c(u, v)dudv = 1, \tag{10.4}$$

$$\int_{(0,u]}\int_{[0,1]} c(x, v)dxdv = u, \forall u \in [0, 1], \tag{10.5}$$

$$\int_{[0,1]}\int_{(0,v]} c(u, y)dudy = v, \forall v \in [0, 1], \tag{10.6}$$

$$\int_{[0,1]^2} h(u, v)c(u, v)dudv = \hat{\Theta}_T, \tag{10.7}$$

where Equation (10.4) implies that $c(u, v)$ is a joint density on the unit circle; Equations (10.5) and (10.6) imply that the marginals of $c(u, v)$ are Uniform[0,1] distributions; Equation (10.7) contains constraint(s) on the joint moment(s) of u and v – where $h(u, v)$ is a vector of functions so that the left-hand side of Equation (10.7) becomes some quadrants of measures of association, which are defined in Section 10.2, and $\hat{\Theta}_T$ (sometimes, we omit the 'T' for brevity) are some linear forms of rank correlations (for instance, given a restriction on Spearman's rho, we have $h(u, v) = uv$ and $\hat{\Theta} = \frac{\hat{\rho_S}+3}{12}$). We may have more than one constraint like Equation (10.7). Examples include Blest's coefficients or Gideon and Hollister's (1987) coefficient. Note that this approach is naturally *semiparametric* because the MEC maximizes the Shannon entropy, which is parametric, under the moment restriction (10.7), which requires nonparametric estimators (i.e., rank correlations).

In the sequel, let $\hat{c}(u, v) = c(u, v, \hat{\Lambda})$, where $\hat{\Lambda}$ is a vector of coefficients, represent the solution to Problem A. By Sklar's theorem, given a pair of marginals, $G_1(X)$ and $G_2(Y)$, we can construct a bivariate distribution $\hat{F}(X, Y) = \hat{C}(G_1(X), G_2(Y))$, where $\hat{C}(u, v) = \int_0^u \int_0^v \hat{c}(u, v) du dv$, thus the bivariate density is $\hat{f}(X, Y) = \hat{c}(G_1(X), G_2(Y)) g_1(X) g_2(Y)$, where $g_1(X) = \frac{\partial G_1(X)}{\partial X}$ and $g_2(Y) = \frac{G_2(Y)}{\partial Y}$.

Remark 10.3.1 $\hat{F}(X, Y)$ *is a coupling function of $G_1(X)$ and $G_2(Y)$. Dependence between X and Y is completely specified through the MEC, without being influenced by $G_1(X)$ and $G_2(Y)$. By the dual relationship between the Shannon entropy of copulas and the KLCE of joint distribution, $\hat{F}(X, Y)$ must be a minimum KLCE bivariate distribution.*

Assuming that the mappings $u = G_1(X) : \mathbb{R} \to [0, 1]$ and $v = G_2(Y) : \mathbb{R} \to [0, 1]$ are continuous and bijective, we can reformulate Problem A as follows:

Problem B: Minimizing $KLCE(f : g) = \int_{\mathbb{R}^2} f(X, Y) \log \frac{f(X, Y)}{g_1(X) g_2(Y)} dX dY$ (10.8)

subject to

$$\int_{\mathbb{R}^2} f(X, Y) dX dY = 1,$$ (10.9)

$$\int_{-\infty}^{x} \int_{\mathbb{R}} f(X, Y) dX dY = G_1(x), \forall\, x \in \mathbb{R},$$ (10.10)

$$\int_{\mathbb{R}} \int_{-\infty}^{y} f(X, Y) dX dY = G_2(y), \forall\, y \in \mathbb{R},$$ (10.11)

$$\int_{\mathbb{R}^2} h(G_1(X), G_2(Y)) f(X, Y) dX dY = \hat{\Theta},$$ (10.12)

where Equations (10.8)–(10.12), by Sklar's theorem, follow from Equations (10.2)–(10.7). Also note that Equations (10.10) and (10.11) ensure that G_1 and G_2 are the marginals of $\hat{F}(X, Y)$.

We can immediately see that Problem B is more difficult to solve than Problem A. There are two reasons: the first reason is that, while Equations (10.5) and (10.6) contain continuums of integrals with varying end-points on [0,1], Equations (10.10) and (10.11) contain those on $\mathbb{R}$; the second reason is that, in Problem B, we need to repeat the minimization algorithm when the marginals G_1 and G_2 change (even if the joint moments are fixed), whereas in Problem A, due to the separation property of copula theory, we can generate a new minimum KLCE distribution by simply plugging new marginals into the MEC.

The MECs (accordingly the MECC) can be approximated by replacing the continuums of varying end-points in Equations (10.5) and (10.6) by sets of definite integrals. We present an approximate solution to Problem A with one constraint on dependence (or $h(u, v)$ is a scalar function, $h(u, v)$) in Theorem 10.3.1. The case with many constraints is an obvious extension.

Theorem 10.3.1 *The MEC, $\hat{c}(u,v)$, can be approximated by an approximator, $\hat{c}_n(u,v)$, as follows:*

$$\hat{c}(u,v) = \lim_{n\to\infty} \hat{c}_n(u,v)$$

with

$$\hat{c}_n(u,v) = \frac{\mathcal{E}_n(u,v)}{\int_{[0,1]^2} \mathcal{E}_n(u,v)dudv}, \tag{10.13}$$

where

$$\mathcal{E}_n(u,v) = \exp\left\{ -\sum_{k=0}^{2^n-1} \left[\hat{\lambda}_k(\Phi(k-2^n u) + \Phi(2^n u - k - 1)) + \hat{\gamma}_k(\Phi(k-2^n v) + \Phi(2^n v - k - 1)) \right]\right.$$

$$\left. - \hat{\lambda}_{2^n} h(u,v) - b_0 \check{c}(u,v) \right\} \tag{10.14}$$

and $\hat{\Lambda} = \left[\{\hat{\lambda}_k\}_{k=0}^{2^n}, \{\hat{\gamma}_k\}_{k=0}^{2^n-1} \right]$ are the minimal values of the potential function

$$Q_n(\Lambda, \hat{\Theta}) = \int_{[0,1]^2} \exp\left\{ -\sum_{k=0}^{2^n-1} \left[\lambda_k(\Phi(k-2^n u) + \Phi(2^n u - k - 1) - 1 + 2^{-n}) \right.\right.$$

$$\left. + \gamma_k(\Phi(k-2^n v) + \Phi(2^n v - k - 1) - 1 + 2^{-n}) \right]$$

$$\left. - \lambda_{2^n}(h(u,v) - \hat{\Theta}) - b_0 \check{c}(u,v) \right\} dudv \text{ for a given } b_0 \text{ and } \check{c}(u,v). \tag{10.15}$$

Note that $\Phi(x) = \frac{1}{2\sqrt{\pi}} \int_{-\infty}^x \exp\{-\frac{1}{2}y^2\}dy$ is the cumulative standard normal distribution function and $\check{c}(u,v)$ is an arbitrary copula, which may involve a nuisance parameter that needs to be estimated.
In particular, the MEC $\hat{c}(u,v)$ can be symmetrized by letting λ_k be equal to γ_k ($\forall k = 1, \ldots, (2^n - 1)$) and $h(u,v)$ be a symmetric function.

Proof: The proof is presented in Appendix 10.C. ∎

As we can see, the MEC density nests an arbitrary copula, $\check{c}(u,v)$ (cf. Equation (10.14)). Indeed, the MEC depends on both b_0 and $\check{c}(u,v)$, thus no uniqueness is obtained. However, we can obtain a canonical form, which is called the *MECC*, by setting b_0 to zero. This idea of a *canonical* model can be traced back to Jeffreys,[5] who proposed using the *principle of simplicity* for deductive inference – that is, for any given set of data, there is usually an infinite number of possible laws that will 'explain' the data precisely, and the simplest model should be chosen.

It is worth noting that the potential function $Q_n(\Lambda, \hat{\Theta})$ in the above theorem is a multivariate convex function of Λ, thus in general has a unique minimum because it is the product of (positive) univariate convex functions.

---

[5] Jeffreys, H. (1961). *Theory of Probability.* Clarendon Press, Oxford, pp. 2–3.

We can claim that the MECC, $\hat{c}(u, v)$, is equivalent to a maximum likelihood estimator (MLE). Now, we need to verify this claim. Given a bivariate sample (X_t, Y_t) for $t = 1, \ldots, T$, the average maximum log-likelihood function is given by

$$\ell(\hat{\Lambda}) = \frac{1}{T} \sum_{t=1}^{T} \log \hat{c}_n(u_t, v_t, \hat{\Lambda})$$

$$= \frac{1}{T} \sum_{t=1}^{T} \log \mathcal{E}_n(u_t, v_t) - \log \int_{[0,1]^2} \mathcal{E}_n(u, v) du dv,$$

where $\hat{c}_n(u_t, v_t, \hat{\Lambda})$, or $\hat{c}_n(u_t, v_t)$, is defined in Equation (10.13),

$$u_t = \frac{1}{T} \sum_{s=1}^{T} 1(X_s \leq X_t) = \frac{R_t}{T+1},$$

and

$$v_t = \frac{1}{T} \sum_{s=1}^{T} 1(Y_s \leq Y_t) = \frac{S_t}{T+1},$$

in which R_t and S_t are the ranks of X_t and Y_t in the sample, respectively. Assuming that T is greater than n and that n is large enough, in view of Equation (10.14) with $b_0 = 0$, we obtain the following representation:

$$\ell(\hat{\Lambda}) = -\frac{1}{T} \sum_{t=1}^{T} \left(\hat{\lambda}_{-1} + \sum_{k=0}^{2^n-1} \left(\left[\hat{\lambda}_k (\Phi(k - 2^n u_t) + \Phi(2^n u_t - k - 1)) + \hat{\gamma}_k (\Phi(k - 2^n v_t) \right. \right. \right.$$

$$\left. \left. \left. + \Phi(2^n v_t - k - 1)) \right] + \hat{\lambda}_{2^n} h(u_t, v_t) \right) \right)$$

$$\approx - \left(\hat{\lambda}_{-1} + \frac{2}{2^n} \sum_{k=0}^{2^n-1} (\hat{\lambda}_k + \hat{\gamma}_k) + \hat{\lambda}_{2^n} \frac{1}{T} \sum_{t=1}^{T} h(u_t, v_t) \right)$$

$$= -W(\hat{c}(u, v)),$$

where $\hat{\lambda}_{-1} = \log \int_{[0,1]^2} \mathcal{E}_n(u, v) du dv$; '$\approx$' follows because $\frac{1}{T} \sum_{t=1}^{T} (\Phi(k - 2^n u_t) + \Phi(2^n u_t - k - 1)) \approx \frac{1}{2^n}$ $\forall k = 0, \ldots, (2^n - 1)$, and the last equality holds because $\int_{[0,1]^2} h(u, v) c(u, v) du dv$ is set equal to its consistent rank estimator, $\frac{1}{T} \sum_{t=1}^{T} h(R_t/(T+1), S_t/(T+1))$. Hence, the claim has been verified.

In order to implement Theorem 10.3.1, we need to define the function $h(u, v)$. For instance, we can do this via the association between the MECC and the Falier–Gumbel–Mogernstern (FGM) copula. In the sequel, let (X_1, Y_1) and (X_2, Y_2) denote two independent copies of a pair of random variables, (X, Y). The dependence of (X_1, Y_1) is specified via a copula, $C(u, v)$, while that of (X_2, Y_2) is specified via the FGM copula, $\tilde{C}(u, v)$. The measure of association between (X_1, Y_1) and (X_2, Y_2) is, thus, defined as follows:

$$\tau_{FGM} = 12 \int_{[0,1]^2} \tilde{C}(u, v) dC(u, v) - 3$$

$$= 12 \left\{ (1 + \theta) \int_{[0,1]^2} uv c(u, v) du dv + \theta \int_{[0,1]^2} u^2 v^2 c(u, v) du dv - \theta \left(\int_{[0,1]^2} u^2 v c(u, v) du dv \right. \right.$$

$$\left. \left. + \int_{[0,1]^2} uv^2 c(u, v) du dv \right) \right\} - 3. \tag{10.16}$$

Hence, prior information can be specified by imposing a constraint on τ_{FGM}. However, we can impose constraints on the quadrants of τ_{FGM} instead, and these constraints can be written in terms of Blest's measures. This way allows for more flexibility, and also avoids the need to estimate θ. We have:

$$\int_{[0,1]^2} uvc(u,v)dudv = \frac{\hat{\rho}_S + 3}{12},$$
$$(10.17)$$

$$\int_{[0,1]} u^2 vc(u,v)dudv = \frac{2\hat{\rho}_S - \hat{v}_1 + 2}{12},$$

$$\int_{[0,1]^2} uv^2 c(u,v)dudv = \frac{2\hat{\rho}_S - \hat{v}_2 + 2}{12},$$

$$\int_{[0,1]^2} u^2 v^2 c(u,v)dudv = \frac{\hat{\eta} + 1/5}{6}.$$
$$(10.18)$$

Now, we can define Problem A+.

Problem A+: Equations (10.3)–(10.6) and Equations (10.17), (10.18).

The solution to Problem A+ is presented in Corollary 10.1. The proof of Corollary 10.1 immediately follows from Theorem 10.3.1 by replacing $h(u,v)$ with appropriate quadrants of u and v.

Corollary 10.1 *Given linear forms of rank correlations,* $\hat{\Theta} = \left\{ \frac{\hat{\rho}_S + 3}{12}, \frac{2\hat{\rho}_S - \hat{v}_1 + 2}{12}, \frac{2\hat{\rho}_S - \hat{v}_2 + 2}{12}, \frac{\hat{\eta} + 1/5}{6} \right\}$, *the MEC is defined in Equation (10.13) with*

$$\mathcal{E}_n(u,v) = \exp \left\{ -\sum_{k=0}^{2^n-1} \left[\hat{\lambda}_k \left(\Phi(k - 2^n u) + \Phi(2^n u - k - 1) \right) \right. \right.$$

$$\left. + \hat{\gamma}_k \left(\Phi(k - 2^n v) + \Phi(2^n v - k - 1) \right) \right] - \hat{\lambda}_{2^n} uv - \hat{\lambda}_{2^n+1} u^2 v - \hat{\lambda}_{2^n+2} uv^2$$

$$\left. - \hat{\lambda}_{2^n+3} u^2 v^2 - b_0 \tilde{c}(u,v) \right\},$$
$$(10.19)$$

where $\hat{\Lambda} = \left[\{\hat{\lambda}_k\}_{k=0}^{2^n+3}, \{\hat{\gamma}_k\}_{k=0}^{2^n-1} \right]$ *are the minimal values of the potential function*

$$Q_n(\Lambda, \hat{\Theta}) = \int_{[0,1]^2} \exp \left\{ -\sum_{k=0}^{2^n-1} [\lambda_k \left(\Phi(k - 2^n u) + \Phi(2^n u - k - 1) - 1 + 2^{-n} \right) + \gamma_k \left(\Phi(k - 2^n v) \right. \right.$$

$$\left. + \Phi(2^n v - k - 1) - 1 + 2^{-n}) \right] - \lambda_{2^n}(uv - \frac{\hat{\rho}_S + 3}{12}) - \lambda_{2^n+1}(u^2 v - \frac{2\hat{\rho}_S - \hat{v}_1 + 2}{12})$$

$$\left. - \lambda_{2^n+2}(uv^2 - \frac{2\hat{\rho}_S - \hat{v}_2 + 2}{12}) - \lambda_{2^n+3}(u^2 v^2 - \frac{\hat{\eta} + 1/5}{6}) - b_0 \tilde{c}(u,v) \right\} dudv$$

for a given b_0 *and* $\tilde{c}(u,v)$.
$$(10.20)$$

The MECC is obtained by setting $b_0 = 0$. In particular, $\hat{c}(u,v)$ can be symmetrized by letting λ_k be equal to γ_k $(\forall k = 1, \dots, (2^n - 1))$ and λ_{2^n+1} be equal to λ_{2^n+2}.

Note that computation of the MECC requires approximating the potential function (10.20) by Gaussian quadratures. (Further details are presented in Appendix 10.C.) And we used a global optimization technique (namely the stochastic search algorithm proposed by Csendes, 1988)[6] to minimize this potential function.

10.3.2 Large Sample Properties of the Most Entropic Canonical Copula

As shown in Theorem 10.3.1, the approximated MECC densities are members of an exponential family parameterized by Lagrangian multipliers, Λ. Since the true measures of dependence, $\Theta^0 = \int_{[0,1]^2} b(u,v)c(u,v)dudv$, are unknown, a sample of size T is then used to form their consistent estimates, $\hat{\Theta}_T$, as seen in Equation (10.7). As a result, the sampling properties of $\hat{\Lambda}_T$ can be derived from those of $\hat{\Theta}_T$. Let $Q_n(\Lambda, \Theta)$ represent a potential function with the dependence parameters Θ. Let $\hat{\Lambda}_T$ and Λ^0 denote the minimum values of $Q_n(\Lambda, \Theta)$ for given $\Theta = \hat{\Theta}_T$ and $\Theta = \Theta^0$, respectively and let the Hessian matrices of $Q_n(\Lambda, \Theta)$ be $\mathcal{H}_{1,n}(\Lambda, \Theta) = \nabla_{\Lambda\Lambda'} Q_n(\Lambda, \Theta)$ and $\mathcal{H}_{2,n}(\Lambda, \Theta) = \nabla_{\Lambda\Theta'} Q_n(\Lambda, \Theta)$. The following assumptions are maintained:

AS1. $\hat{\Theta}_T \xrightarrow{p} \Theta^0 \in int(\mathcal{M})$, where $\mathcal{M}$ is some non-empty compact set and $dim(\mathcal{M})$ is the number of measures of association. Further,

$$\mathcal{N} = \{\Lambda \in \mathbb{R}^{dim(\Lambda)} : \nabla_\Lambda Q_n(\Lambda, \Theta) = 0, \forall \, \Theta \in \mathcal{M}\}$$

is also a non-empty, compact set, where $dim(\Lambda)$ is the number of the Lagrangian multipliers in $Q_n(\Lambda, \Theta)$, thus the number of marginal constraints is $dim(\Lambda) - dim(\mathcal{M})$.

AS2. The mapping from $\mathcal{M}$ to $\mathcal{N}$ is a diffeomorphism (i.e., one-to-one, continuous and onto in both directions).

AS3. $Q_n(\Lambda, \Theta)$ is a strictly convex function of Λ for all $\Theta \in \mathcal{M}$, and is uniformly continuous (in probability) with respect to Θ, i.e.,

$$\sup_{\Lambda \in \mathcal{N}} \left| Q_n(\Lambda, \hat{\Theta}_T) - Q_n(\Lambda, \Theta^0) \right| \xrightarrow{p} 0 \text{ as } |\hat{\Theta}_T - \Theta^0| \xrightarrow{p} 0.$$

AS4. The vector of rank correlations, $\hat{\Theta}_T$, is asymptotically normal, i.e.,

$$T^{1/2}(\hat{\Theta}_T - \Theta^0) \xrightarrow{d} N(0, \Psi), \tag{10.21}$$

where Ψ denotes an asymptotic variance–covariance matrix.

AS2 and AS3 ensure that the potential function $Q_n(\hat{\Lambda}, \hat{\Theta}_T)$ has a minimum value, $\hat{\Lambda}$, for a given estimator, $\hat{\Theta}_T$. AS1 and AS4 are satisfied by many important estimators, including Blest's measures of rank correlations, which we are using in this chapter.

Theorem 10.3.2 *Suppose that AS1–AS4 hold, we have:*

$$\hat{\Lambda}_T \xrightarrow{p} \Lambda^0, where \; \Lambda^0 \in int(\mathcal{N})$$

---

[6]The C++ implementation of the algorithm was downloaded from http://www.inf.u-szeged.hu/~csendes/Reg/regform.php.

and

$$T^{1/2}(\widehat{\boldsymbol{\Lambda}}_T - \boldsymbol{\Lambda}^0) \xrightarrow{d} N(\mathbf{0}, \mathcal{H}_{1,n}^{-1}(\boldsymbol{\Lambda}^0, \boldsymbol{\Theta}^0)\mathbf{I}\boldsymbol{\Psi}'\boldsymbol{\Gamma}'\mathcal{H}_{1,n}^{-1}(\boldsymbol{\Lambda}^0, \boldsymbol{\Theta}^0)'),$$

where $\mathbf{I}$ *is a* $dim(\boldsymbol{\Lambda}^0) \times dim(\boldsymbol{\Theta}^0)$ *diagonal matrix.*

Proof: The proof is presented in Appendix 10.C.   ∎

Theorem 10.3.2 suggests that the efficiency of the estimates $\widehat{\boldsymbol{\Lambda}}_T$ can be, in general, improved by increasing the number of constraints. Nevertheless, using too many constraints may cause the Hessian matrix $\mathcal{H}_{1,n}(\boldsymbol{\Lambda}^0, \boldsymbol{\Theta}^0)$ to quickly approach singularity (see Wu and Stengos, 2005), thus the asymptotic variance of $T^{1/2}(\widehat{\boldsymbol{\Lambda}}_T - \boldsymbol{\Lambda}^0)$ increases – the efficiency decreases.

10.4 SIMULATION

In this section, we provide some short simulations to examine the approximation error of the MECC density $\widehat{c}_n(u, v)$.

We note that, since computing the MECC only involves approximating Equations (10.5) and (10.6) with continuums of integrals with finite end-points, approximation errors are certainly invariant to rank correlations $\widehat{\rho}_S, \widehat{v}_1, \widehat{v}_2$ and $\widehat{\eta}$. Therefore, we first computed a MECC, $\widehat{C}_n(u, v)$, by using the rank correlations between Russell 1000 'growth' and 'value' indices. (Obviously, we may use any other values for the rank correlations, without essentially changing the approximation error.)

Next, we need to verify that $\widehat{C}_n(u, v)$ has Uniform[0,1] marginals (i.e., we need to check if $\widehat{C}_n(u, 1)$ and $\widehat{C}_n(1, v)$ become closer to the diagonal line as n gets large enough). We first generated two bivariate samples, $(u, \widehat{C}_n(u, 1))$ and $(v, \widehat{C}_n(1, v))$, from the approximated MECC, then formed linear regressions, $\widehat{C}_n(u, 1) = \widehat{a}_u + \widehat{\beta}_u u$ and $\widehat{C}_n(1, v) = \widehat{a}_v + \widehat{\beta}_v v$.

We observe that, as the number of marginal constraints increases from 2^5 to 2^{10}, the regression lines approach the diagonal lines (cf. Figure 10.1) – that is, $\widehat{a}_u$ and $\widehat{a}_v$ decrease from 0.2076 and 0.2962 to 0.0654 and 0.0887, respectively, while $\widehat{\beta}_u$ and $\widehat{\beta}_v$ increase from 0.623 and 0.701 to 1.097 and 1.1047, respectively. In addition, we found that the approximated MECC is sufficiently accurate with 2^6 marginal constraints (cf. Figure 10.1(b)). Hence, we used 2^6 marginal constraints to construct the MECC in Section 10.5.

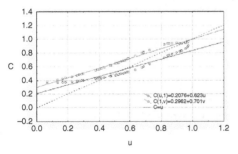

(a) Number of marginal constraints is 2^5 (b) Number of marginal constraints is 2^6

FIGURE 10.1   Approximate marginal densities ($C(u, 1)$ and $C(1, v)$ on the vertical axis) of the MECC, which are constructed from rank correlations, $\widehat{\rho}S = 0.4248$, $\widehat{v}_1 = 0.4967$, $\widehat{v}_2 = 0.5430$ and $\widehat{\eta} = -0.1520$, are plotted against u and v (on the horizontal axis).

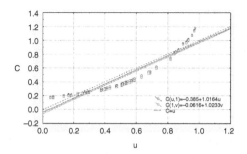

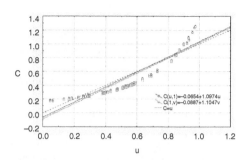

(c) Number of marginal constraints is 2^8 (d) Number of marginal constraints is 2^{10}

FIGURE 10.1   (*Continued*)

10.5   APPLICATION TO ASSET ALLOCATION

We analyse a CRRA investor's problem of allocating wealth between two 'style' portfolios – a portfolio of 'growth' stocks and a portfolio of 'value' stocks (see, e.g., Fama and French, 1998 for the definitions).

As shown in Basu (1977), 'value' portfolios outperform 'growth' ones by about 4% in terms of the Sharpe ratio, and this outperformance is *not* due to systematic risk. In fact, it is, on the one hand, due to time-varying risk (see, e.g., Petkova and Zhang, 2005). On the other hand, it may well be due to the fact that assets in different styles are less correlated than their underlying fundamentals [e.g., dividend yield, price–earning ratio and book–market ratio, etc. (cf. Campbell *et al.*, 2005, among others)], and that dependence among 'style' assets is complex (Barberis and Shleifer, 2003). Therefore, our investor's problem is a typical problem of optimal investment beyond linear risk and linear dependence. Consequently, we need to deviate from the mean-variance framework by accounting for possibly complex nonlinear risk and dependence. We then show, by empirical analysis, that the MECC can capture this complex nonlinear dependence, which may not be well captured by other copulas, consequently leading to an increase of economic gains.

We use monthly (from June 1995 to July 2006) data of the Russell 1000 index.[7] This index comprises 1,000 large US companies, which are determined by their market capitalizations and ranked by their adjusted book-to-price ratios. A probability methodology is then used to split the index into 'growth' and 'value' subindices – that is, each company is assigned a probability of being a 'growth' or a 'value' one. The 'growth' index thus contains the companies with greater-than-average growth orientations, higher-than-average P/B and P/E ratios, lower-than-average dividend yields and higher-than-average forecast earnings growth; the 'value' index contains the companies which are not 'growth' ones. We use the period of June 1995 to September 1999 (namely, the in-sample period) to develop our models, and the remaining period (namely, the out-of-sample period) for out-of-sample evaluation.

Table 10.1 shows that the continuously compounded 'growth' and 'value' returns in excess of the 3-month Treasury bill (T-bill) rate, a proxy of risk-free interest rate (hereafter, we shall write 'returns' for brevity, and specify otherwise) are not normally distributed in the entire sample period. (The Kolmogorov–Smirnov test rejects the normality for both series.) Moreover, the 'value' return has higher mean and lower variance than the 'growth' return in the entire sample and out-of-sample periods, but this pattern is *not* clear in the in-sample period; and these returns also display non-negligible linear correlation. In fact, this result is consistent with the claim by Ibbotson and Riepe (1997) that

---

[7]All the data used in the current chapter were downloaded from Bloomberg and Datastream.

'"value" trumps growth, with the caveat that "growth" stocks can outperform "value" stocks over an extended of time'.

First of all, to get a preliminary idea about the degree of AD between these returns, we used the measures of asymmetric linear correlation (i.e., the 'exceedance' correlations, see, e.g., Longin and Solnik, 2001; Ang and Chen, 2002) and a test for asymmetries proposed by Hong et al. (2007). Let $\rho^+(c)$ and $\rho^-(c)$ denote the 'exceedance' correlations between the 'growth' return, $r_{1,t}$, and the 'value' return, $r_{2,t}$, at a threshold level c, defined as follows:

$$\rho^+(c) = \mathrm{corr}(r_{1,t}, r_{2,t}|r_{1,t} > c, r_{2,t} > c), \tag{10.22}$$

$$\rho^-(c) = \mathrm{corr}(r_{1,t}, r_{2,t}|r_{1,t} < -c, r_{2,t} < -c). \tag{10.23}$$

Figure 10.2 shows that the differences between the sample 'exceedance' correlations (of these returns) are non-negligible under various cutoff quantiles. We also conducted the test for asymmetry with 24 'exceedance' levels (not reported), and found that the p-value is close to zero, confirming that there is strong evidence of asymmetric correlation. Furthermore, this asymmetric correlation varies significantly over time (cf. Figure 10.3).

Next, to parameterize our statistical models, following the conventional literature in return predictability, we used six well-known predictive variables that drive equity return fluctuations. The first variable is the 3-month T-bill rate (r_t^f), used by Fama (1981) as a proxy for shocks to expected economic growth. The second and third variables are dividend–price ratio (DY) and price–earnings ratio (PER), both used by Campbell and Shiller (1988) and Fama and French (1988), among others, as proxies for shocks to expected stock returns. The fourth and fifth variables are the term spread (TS) – the difference between the 10-year government bond yield and the 3-month T-bill rate – and the default spread (DS) – the difference between Moody's Baa and Aaa corporate bond yields. The sixth variable is the log consumption–aggregate wealth (or human capital plus asset holdings) ratio (Cay); according

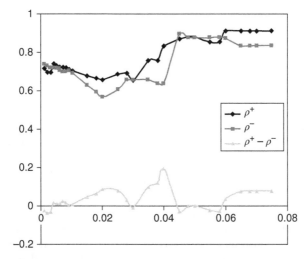

FIGURE 10.2 Asymmetric correlation between the excess returns on Russell 1000 Growth and Value. The horizontal axis shows cutoff quantiles, the vertical axis shows *exceedance* correlations between these returns, and ρ^+ and ρ^- denote the positive and negative *exceedance* correlations, respectively.

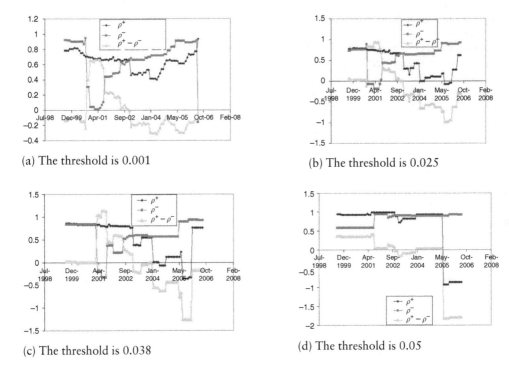

(a) The threshold is 0.001

(b) The threshold is 0.025

(c) The threshold is 0.038

(d) The threshold is 0.05

FIGURE 10.3 Moving-window asymmetric correlation between the excess returns on Russell 1000 Growth and Value. The horizontal axis shows time periods, the vertical axis shows *exceedance* correlations between these returns, and ρ^+ and ρ^- denote the positive and negative *exceedance* correlations, respectively.

to Lettau and Ludvigson (2001), *Cay* is a good predictor of future stock returns, especially in short and intermediate horizons. (See, *inter alia*, Ait-Sahalia and Brandt, 2001 for a comprehensive review of predictive variables used in the extant literature.)

Using real data with a window size of 50 observations, we recursively estimated the model (10.24)–(10.25), which we will explain in the next subsection, and then computed the rolling-sample 'exceedance' correlations between two standardized excess returns [(return-conditional mean)/volatility] for three threshold levels, $0.001, 0.005$ and 0.01. Figure 10.4 shows that the discrepancies between those (positive and negative) 'exceedance' correlations vary near zero; moreover, because model (10.25) can, by its nature, capture asymmetric volatility, these discrepancies are smaller and more stable than the discrepancies between rolling-sample 'exceedance' correlations between the returns (cf. Figure 10.3).

Since the sample linear correlations between the standardized excess returns (not reported) are less than those between the returns, the standardized excess returns could be less contemporaneously dependent than the returns, which should be correlated as much as their underlying fundamentals – this is true to the extent that the underlying fundamentals are *completely* factored into prices. This empirical finding is consistent with the postulation that 'assets in the same style will comove too much while assets in different styles comove too little' and that 'the market (standardized excess) returns on "value" and "growth" stocks are less correlated than the fundamentals of "value" and "growth" stocks, in turn adjusted for market fundamentals' (see Barberis and Shleifer, 2003). Moreover, this type of dependence is too complex to be measured. In this sense, the MECC is of practical interest because of its flexible specification.

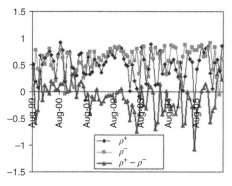

(a) The threshold is 0.001

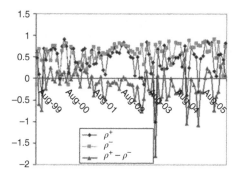

(b) The threshold is 0.005

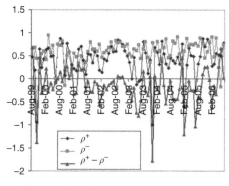

(c) The threshold is 0.01

FIGURE 10.4 Moving-window asymmetric correlation between the risk-adjusted (or standardized) excess returns on Russell 1000 Growth and Value. The horizontal axis shows time periods, the vertical axis shows *exceedance* correlations between these returns, and ρ^+ and ρ^- denote the positive and negative *exceedance* correlations, respectively.

Since, as we have just discussed, standardized excess 'style' returns comove a little, copulas with asymmetric structure (e.g., Clayton and Gumbel copulas) do not always provide better goodness-of-fit than the normal copula. We shall show in Section 10.5.2 that the dependence between these returns is best captured by the MECC, and that the model using the MECC outperforms those using other copulas.

10.5.1 Analysis of Alternative Models

Let $r_{1,t}$ and $r_{2,t}$ denote the 'growth' and 'value' returns with some conditional joint distribution, F_t, associated with a conditional copula, C_t, and conditional marginals, $G_{1,t}$ and $G_{2,t}$. By the conditional Sklar theorem: $F_{t+1}(X, Y|\mathcal{F}_t) = C_{t+1}(G_{1,t+1}(X|\mathcal{F}_t), G_{2,t+1}(Y|\mathcal{F}_t)|\mathcal{F}_t)$, where $\mathcal{F}_t$ is a set of information available up to t (see Patton, 2004, 2006), the one-period ahead optimal weights $\omega_{t+1}^* = \{\omega_{1,t+1}, \omega_{2,t+1}\}$ can be written as follows:

$$\omega_{t+1}^* = \arg\max_{\omega \in W} E_{\hat{F}_{t+1}}[\mathcal{U}(1 + \omega_1 r_{1,t+1} + \omega_2 r_{2,t+1})]$$

$$= \arg\max_{\omega \in W} \int\int \mathcal{U}(1 + \omega_1 x + \omega_2 y).\hat{g}_{1,t+1}(x).\hat{g}_{2,t+1}(y).\hat{c}_{t+1}(\hat{G}_{1,t+1}(x), \hat{G}_{2,t+1}(y))dxdy,$$

where $\hat{G}_{1,t+1}$ and $\hat{G}_{2,t+1}$ are conditional marginal distribution forecasts, $\hat{g}_{1,t+1}(x)$ and $\hat{g}_{2,t+1}(y)$ are conditional marginal density forecasts, $\hat{c}_{t+1}$ is a conditional copula density forecast, $\mathcal{W}$ is defined as some compact subset of $\mathbb{R}^2$ for unconstrained investors and as the set $\{(\omega_1, \omega_2) \in [0,1]^2 : \omega_1 + \omega_2 \le 1\}$ for short-sales constrained investors, and $\mathcal{U}(x)$ is the CRRA utility function given by

$$\mathcal{U}(x) = \begin{cases} (1 - RRA)^{-1}x^{1-RRA}, & \text{if} \quad RRA \ne 1, \text{ where } RRA \text{ is a degree of risk aversion,} \\ \log(x), & \text{if} \quad RRA = 1. \end{cases}$$

Note that we used the method of Levin (1983) to approximate the double integral in the above expected utility function, instead of the Monte Carlo method. The former method is very efficient because it guarantees that any double integral of bounded and piecewise continuous functions can be effectively approximated by optimal (or asymptotically optimal) quadratures, and that the approximation error is minimal.

Now, we shall proceed to estimate the joint model, $F_{t+1}(X, Y|\mathcal{F}_t)$, by applying the inference function for margins (IFM) method, introduced by Joe and Xu (1996). The IFM method has been used in, for instance, Patton (2004) and Jondeau and Rockinger (2006).

10.5.1.1 Conditional Marginal Distribution   Since the time-varying feature of a conditional marginal distribution can be specified through the dynamics of its conditional moments such as the conditional mean, the conditional variance and the conditional skewness (see, e.g., Patton, 2004 or Jondeau and Rockinger, 2003, among others), it is natural to use a TGARCH model to forecast the conditional marginals. We have implemented some log-likelihood-based model selection tests for the optimal lags of the returns and best predictive instruments (not reported), and ended up with the following TGARCH(1,1) model:

$$r_{i,t} = \alpha_{i,0} + \alpha_{i,1}r_{i,t-1} + \alpha_{i,2}r_{t-1}^f + \alpha_{i,3}DY_{i,t-1} + \alpha_{i,4}PER_{i,t-1} + \alpha_{i,5}TS_{t-1} + \alpha_{i,6}DS_{t-1} + \alpha_{i,7}Cay_{t-1}$$
$$+ \sigma_{i,t}\epsilon_{i,t} \tag{10.24}$$

with

$$\sigma_{i,t}^2 = \alpha_{i,8} + \alpha_{i,9}\sigma_{i,t-1}^2 + \alpha_{i,10}\sigma_{i,t-1}^2\epsilon_{i,t-1}^2 \mathbf{1}(\epsilon_{i,t-1} > 0) + \alpha_{i,11}\sigma_{i,t-1}^2\epsilon_{i,t-1}^2 \mathbf{1}(\epsilon_{i,t-1} < 0) + \alpha_{i,12}r_{t-1}^f$$
$$+ \alpha_{i,13}DY_{i,t-1} + \alpha_{i,14}PER_{i,t-1} + \alpha_{i,15}TS_{t-1} + \alpha_{i,16}DS_{t-1} + \alpha_{i,17}Cay_{t-1}, \tag{10.25}$$

where $i = 1$ (*growth*) or 2 (*value*). The distribution of the error $\epsilon_{i,t}$ is modelled with Hansen (1994)'s skewed t distribution [i.e., $\epsilon_{i,t} \sim G(\epsilon|\kappa_{i,t}, \lambda_{i,t})$, where $\kappa_{i,t} = 2.1 + (Z_{i,t-1}'\gamma_i)^2$ and $\lambda_{i,t} = \Lambda(Z_{i,t-1}'\gamma_i)$ with $Z_{i,t}' = \{r_t^f, DY_{i,t}, PER_{i,t}, TS_t, DS_t, Cay_t\}$ and $\Lambda(x) = (1 - e^{-x})/(1 + e^{-x})]$.

We estimated Equations (10.24) and (10.25) by the method of MLE. Due to the high dimensionality of this problem, we used a fast stochastic search algorithm[8] to find global maximum log-likelihood values. The algorithm consists of four steps: (1) transforming the domains of (multi-)parameters into unit cubes; (2) drawing 5,000 vectors of transformed parameter values from these cubes; (3) ordering the samples descendingly with respect to the values of the objective function, then picking up five samples on the top; and (4) using those five samples as the starting values to run five local maximization algorithms (e.g., quasi-Newton algorithm). The global maximum value is, then, the best local maximum value.

We found significant evidence (not reported) that the parameters of the error distributions, $\kappa_{i,t}$ and $\lambda_{i,t}$, are time-varying in the whole sample period. We also conducted goodness-of-fit tests for our conditional marginal distribution models. These tests are based on the assertion that the transformed random

---

[8]C++ code to implement this method was downloaded from http://www.inf.u-szeged.hu/~csendes /linkek_en.html.

variables $U_t = F_t(X_t|\mathcal{F}_{t-1})$, where F_t is a cumulative distribution, are IID Uniform[0,1] (see Rosenblatt, 1952); thus to test for a correct specification of F_t, we need to test that (1) U_t are Uniform[0,1] and (2) U_t are serially independent. Specifically, we used classical goodness-of-fit tests (i.e., the Cramer–von Mises, Watson, Anderson–Darling and Zhang tests) to test for the uniformity of $U_t = G(\hat{\epsilon}_{i,t}|\kappa_{i,t}, \lambda_{i,t})$, where $\hat{\epsilon}_{i,t}$ are the residuals and the *sup* (Andrews and Ploberger, 1996) tests for the serial correlation of $\hat{\epsilon}_{i,t}$. In addition, to account for time variation in the error distribution, we repeated these tests on 83 subsamples – each containing 50 standardized excess returns (or residuals) – then calculated the mean, the minimum value and the maximum value of the test statistics' values. Table 10.2(a) shows little evidence supporting serial correlation on average, but in a few subsamples. Table 10.2(b) shows that the goodness-of-fit tests, except for Zhang's Z_K and Z_C tests, do not clearly reject the null hypothesis of the uniform distribution on average, but in some subsamples. These results suggest that the skewed t distribution is appropriate for our data.

10.5.1.2 Copula Models The benchmark models are the conditional normal copula, the conditional Clayton copula and the conditional Gumbel copula. These models can be specified by

$$\left(\frac{r_{1,t} - \mu_{1,t}}{\sigma_{1,t}}, \frac{r_{2,t} - \mu_{2,t}}{\sigma_{2,t}}\right) \sim C(G(\epsilon_{1,t}|\kappa_{1,t}, \lambda_{1,t}), G(\epsilon_{2,t}|\kappa_{2,t}, \lambda_{2,t}); \delta_t)$$

with $\delta_t = \Gamma(\beta_0 + \beta_1 r_{t-1}^f + \beta_2 DY_{t-1} + \beta_3 PER_{t-1} + \beta_4 TS_{t-1} + \beta_5 DS_{t-1} + \beta_6 Cay_{t-1})$,

where C denotes the normal, Clayton or Gumbel copula; $\mu_{i,t} = E[r_{i,t}|\mathcal{F}_{t-1}]$, for $i = 1, 2$, denotes the conditional mean of $r_{i,t}$, defined in Equation (10.24); and $\Gamma(x)$ is a function transforming x into a feasible copula parameter.

The *conditional MECC* model is defined in the following way: given the rank correlations between the standardized excess returns $\{\hat{\rho}_S, \hat{v}_1, \hat{v}_2, \hat{\eta}\}$ and a logistic function, $\Lambda(x)$, we specify

$$\left(\frac{r_{1,t} - \mu_{1,t}}{\sigma_{1,t}}, \frac{r_{2,t} - \mu_{2,t}}{\sigma_{2,t}}\right) \sim MECC(G_{1,t}, G_{2,t}; \rho_{S_t}, v_{1,t}, v_{2,t}, \eta_t), \tag{10.26}$$

where

$$\frac{\rho_{S_t}}{\hat{\rho}_S} = \Lambda(\theta_0 + \theta_1 r_{t-1}^f + \theta_2 DY_{t-1} + \theta_3 PER_{t-1} + \theta_4 TS_{t-1} + \theta_5 DS_{t-1} + \theta_6 Cay_{t-1}), \tag{10.27}$$

$$\frac{v_{1,t}}{\hat{v}_1} = \Lambda(\theta_7 + \theta_8 r_{t-1}^f + \theta_9 DY_{t-1} + \theta_{10} PER_{t-1} + \theta_{11} TS_{t-1} + \theta_{12} DS_{t-1} + \theta_{13} Cay_{t-1}), \tag{10.28}$$

$$\frac{v_{2,t}}{\hat{v}_2} = \Lambda(\theta_{14} + \theta_{15} r_{t-1}^f + \theta_{16} DY_{t-1} + \theta_{17} PER_{t-1} + \theta_{18} TS_{t-1} + \theta_{19} DS_{t-1} + \theta_{20} Cay_{t-1}), \tag{10.29}$$

$$\frac{\eta_t}{\hat{\eta}} = \Lambda(\theta_{21} + \theta_{22} r_{t-1}^f + \theta_{23} DY_{t-1} + \theta_{24} PER_{t-1} + \theta_{25} TS_{t-1} + \theta_{26} DS_{t-1} + \theta_{27} Cay_{t-1}). \tag{10.30}$$

Here note that, with an aim in our mind to keep the models parsimonious, we assumed that the parameters of the copulas under our consideration have the same predictive instruments [i.e., DY_t, PER_t (the dividend yield and the price–earnings ratio of Russell 1000), TS_t, DS_t and Cay_t]. In addition, we did not include the dynamics of Blest's measure IV in the model (10.26)–(10.30) because including Blest's measure IV results in a model with higher AIC and BIC (not reported).

We estimated the MECC model (10.26)–(10.30) by using the empirical likelihood (EL) method. This is a commonly used, efficient method when the log-likelihood function has neither a trackable nor a close form (see, e.g., Rockinger and Jondeau, 2002, among many others). (Further details are presented in the appendices.) The other copula models were estimated by the conventional ML technique.

TABLE 10.2(a) Results obtained from the *fluctuation* tests for serial correlation of the transformed residuals: $U_t = F(X_t|F_t)$

	SupLR			ExpLR			Durbin–Watson (DW)			Box–Pierce 1 (BP6)			Box–Pierce 2 (BP12)		
	Mean	Min	Max	Mean	Min	Max	Mean	Min	Max	Mean	Min	Max	Mean	Min	Max
Russell 1000 Growth	4.1623*	0.3423	31.0831	1.6587*	0.0262	14.4156	1.4214*	0.4601	1.9277	12.6193	1.5628	133.272	18.0172	2.2809	174.188
Russell 1000 Value	3.9461*	0.1705	27.196	1.5758*	0.0298	12.4591	1.4161*	0.5914	1.9756	12.9842	0.9722	80.7073	17.6181	2.3360	91.4092

Notes: *Denotes that the test under consideration does not, on average, reject the null with odds of 95%. (See Andrews and Ploberger, 1996 for the critical values of SupLR and ExpLR.)

TABLE 10.2(b) Results obtained from the *fluctuation* goodness-of-fit tests for the uniformity of the transformed residuals: $U_t = F(X_t|F_t)$

	Cramer–von Mises (W^2)			Watson (U^2)			Anderson–Darling (A^2)			Zhang's Z_K			Zhang's Z_A			Zhang's Z_C		
	Mean	Min	Max	Mean	Min	Max	Mean	Min	Max	Mean	Min	Max	Mean	Min	Max	Mean	Min	Max
Russell 1000 Growth	2.3306*	0.0210	3.1265	2.3356*	0.0957	3.1701	11.6335	1.9569	14.9135	19.1422	10.5601	28.0751	−30.5551*	−37.7896	−12.0666	121.6155	76.6576	146.1820
Russell 1000 Value	2.3748*	0.0778	3.1355	2.3901*	0.0751	3.1834	11.7996	1.7357	14.9406	19.4453	9.0409	25.5494	−29.8704*	−39.6002	−20.6265	122.3934	65.3194	145.3900

Notes: *Denotes that the test under consideration does not, on average, reject the null with odds of 95%. The stimulated 5% critical values of W^2, U^2, A^2, Z_K, Z_A and Z_C are 5.461, 4.187, 12.492, 5.25, 1.06 and 34.8, respectively.

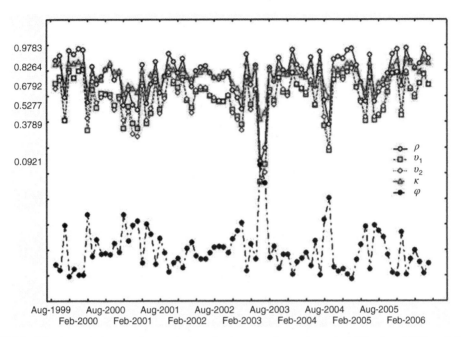

FIGURE 10.5 Moving-window rank correlations in the out-of-sample period (October 1999 to July 2006). ρ is the Spearman's rho, v_1, v_2, κ and φ are, as defined in Section 10.2, the second, third, fourth and fifth rank correlations, respectively. The horizontal axis shows the out-of-sample period, and the vertical axis shows rank correlations.

We then assessed the relative performance of the estimated copula models. Due to time variations in the rank correlations between the returns (Figure 10.5), we allowed for fluctuations in the relative performance of the models by using moving windows to recursively estimate the models. In the sequel, we applied the out-of-sample fluctuation test [based on one-period forecasts of the (empirical) log-likelihoods of the copulas for all the moving windows], proposed by Giacomini and Rossi (2007) and Giacomini and White (2006), to test the null hypothesis that two models perform equally well in the out-of-sample period. The p-values of the test, using the critical values computed by Giacomini and Rossi (2007), are reported in Table 10.3. The null hypothesis is clearly rejected for the following pairs: Clayton vs. Gumbel, Clayton vs. MECC, Gumbel vs. MECC (cf. Figure 10.6). Table 10.4 suggests that, in terms of average maximum ELs, the MECC provides the best performance while the normal copula performs slightly better than the Clayton and Gumbel copulas. These results are also confirmed by the information criteria values reported.

TABLE 10.3 Results of the out-of-sample copula fluctuation test

Model	Average p-value	Minimum p-value	Maximum p-value
Clayton–Gumbel	0.5303	0.0901	0.8889
Clayton–MECC	0.5729	0.0000	1.0000
Gumbel–MECC	0.5684	0.0000	1.0000

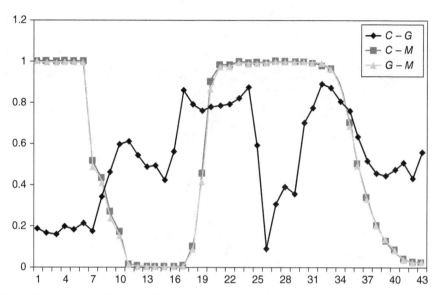

FIGURE 10.6 The *p*-values of the out-of-sample fluctuation test for equal performance of two copulas over time. The horizontal axis shows the orders of out-of-sample data and the vertical axis shows the *p*-values. Let 'C', 'G' and 'M' denote the Clayton copula, the Gumbel copula and the MECC, respectively.

TABLE 10.4 Results of copula specification search using information criteria

Model	Average log-likelihood	Number of parameters	Average AIC	Average cAIC	Average BIC	Average HQIC
Normal	1.8379	7	−6.5136	12.3242	−5.9660	−6.3227
Clayton	1.3092	7	−5.4564	13.3815	−4.9087	−5.2654
Gumbel	1.3586	7	−5.5550	13.2829	−5.0073	−5.3640
MECC	5.7761	28	−9.7143	−261.5523	−11.4527	−9.6692

10.5.2   Relative Performance of Investment Models

In this section, we report the relative performances of eight different asset allocation strategies for four RRA levels, 3, 7, 15 and 25. These strategies are defined as the optimal weights invested in the 'growth' and 'value' indices for each period ahead by (1) using the normal copula – the normal strategy; (2) using the Clayton copula – the Clayton strategy; (3) using the Gumbel copula – the Gumbel strategy; and (4) using the MECC – the MECC strategy. Strategies (5)–(8) are strategies (1)–(4) with short-sales constraints imposed.

Table 10.5 provides descriptive statistics of the continuously compounded portfolio returns computed for the eight above-mentioned strategies. The scenarios turn out differently, depending on whether

TABLE 10.5   Descriptive statistics of realized portfolio returns

	Unconstrained				Short-sales constrained			
	Normal	Clayton	Gumbel	MECC	Normal	Clayton	Gumbel	MECC
				RRA = 3				
Mean	0.9806	0.5646	1.1362	0.8655	1.0078	1.0078	1.0095	1.0077
Std. Dev.	0.3538	2.8754	0.8711	1.4105	0.0393	0.0280	0.0376	0.0477
Sharpe ratio	2.7717	0.1963	1.3044	0.6136	25.6147	35.9540	26.8645	21.1357
Skewness	1.1703	−8.5290	1.6482	−8.3289	−0.1321	1.1445	0.1172	1.4038
Kurtosis	8.2222	75.4105	17.6369	73.6448	0.2316	4.0581	1.1847	5.6840
10% quantile	0.5652	0.4243	0.8247	0.8107	0.9609	0.9893	0.9732	0.9579
90% quantile	1.2675	1.1819	1.6606	1.2372	1.0567	1.0421	1.0626	1.0548
				RRA = 7				
Mean	0.9772	0.9440	1.1070	0.9154	1.0102	1.0078	1.0070	1.0097
Std. Dev.	0.2862	0.3453	0.4926	1.1942	0.0496	0.0355	0.0420	0.0509
Sharpe ratio	3.4139	2.7337	2.2474	0.7666	20.3604	28.4240	23.9917	19.8200
Skewness	−0.4918	−0.5886	3.3726	−7.3603	−0.3709	0.5856	−0.0857	1.7248
Kurtosis	3.0483	2.8632	18.5277	64.0690	0.4386	3.7046	0.2711	7.1301
10% quantile	0.6803	0.5352	0.7202	0.8321	0.9561	0.9807	0.9491	0.9605
90% quantile	1.2205	1.2638	1.3313	1.1283	1.0781	1.0481	1.0662	1.0635
				RRA = 15				
Mean	0.9867	0.9987	1.0182	1.0142	1.0091	1.0094	1.0098	1.0081
Std. Dev.	0.0914	0.1510	0.2261	0.7752	0.0483	0.0416	0.0448	0.0520
Sharpe ratio	10.7918	6.6140	4.5028	1.3083	20.9019	24.2914	22.5284	19.3823
Skewness	−0.3631	−1.6466	0.5243	1.5470	−0.5260	0.1593	−0.2293	1.8270
Kurtosis	1.6121	15.4838	5.0600	26.9495	0.8780	0.1635	1.0685	8.6756
10% quantile	0.8681	0.8918	0.8404	0.8794	0.9540	0.9573	0.9670	0.9533
90% quantile	1.0886	1.1398	1.1534	1.1394	1.0665	1.0667	1.0629	1.0596
				RRA = 25				
Mean	0.9963	0.9886	1.0115	0.9696	1.0109	1.0109	1.0083	1.0060
Std. Dev.	0.0794	0.0752	0.1230	0.5810	0.0431	0.0419	0.0412	0.0513
Sharpe ratio	12.5485	13.1501	8.2236	1.6688	23.4544	24.1502	24.5012	19.6174
Skewness	−2.4794	−0.3464	1.4049	0.0377	−0.4331	−0.1296	−0.3046	1.7097
Kurtosis	12.7335	1.7569	10.3033	12.0053	0.8359	1.0711	1.3174	10.5269
10% quantile	0.9133	0.8951	0.9029	0.7356	0.9671	0.9687	0.9626	0.9466
90% quantile	1.0789	1.0742	1.0799	1.1578	1.0655	1.0613	1.0598	1.0561

the short-sales constraint is imposed. When the RRA level is equal to 3, 7 or 15, the Sharpe ratios based on the normal copula, in the unconstrained case, are highest; and in the short-sales constrained case, the Sharpe ratios based on the Clayton copula are highest. Moreover, the portfolio returns based on the normal copula, in the short-sales constrained case, often have negative skewness and smallest kurtosis. Meanwhile, the portfolio returns based on the MECC with a short-sales constraint always exhibit strong, positive skewness and high, positive kurtosis, suggesting that using the MECC to model AD may potentially help investors with short-sales constraints to avoid negative skewed portfolios.

Tables 10.6 and 10.7 report descriptive statistics of the optimal portfolio weights for four among eight above-mentioned strategies – the normal strategies and the MECC strategies. As expected, an increase in the RRA level (the investor becomes more risk-averse) leads to an increase in the median of the portfolio weights invested in the 'value' index and a decrease in the median of those invested in the 'growth' index – this is especially true for the MECC model. These findings are consistent with the remark of Ibbotson and Riepe (1997) that 'the superior historical performance of value leads us to tilt the equity allocation in that direction for all but the most aggressive investors'. Moreover, while

TABLE 10.6   Descriptive statistics of optimal portfolios (normal copula)

	RRA = 3		RRA = 7		RRA = 15		RRA = 25	
	Growth	Value	Growth	Value	Growth	Value	Growth	Value
Unconstrained								
Mean	0.2969	−1.0153	−0.6238	1.0488	0.3463	1.0581	−0.2063	1.0704
Min	−15.6632	−22.8090	−15.3314	−10.1389	−4.3280	−3.8435	−2.4541	−2.0194
25% quantile	−2.5726	−3.7589	−3.5001	−2.3879	−0.9182	−0.9342	−0.8802	−0.7516
Median	0.7327	−0.2068	−0.9591	1.0881	0.8061	1.6245	−0.6423	1.6719
75% quantile	3.1520	3.0401	3.0608	3.3116	1.0077	2.9448	0.7017	2.8729
Max	16.0126	12.7075	7.2890	31.4231	6.3339	3.7937	2.3882	3.0953
Short-sales constrained								
Mean	0.4714	0.4047	0.4256	0.5035	0.5250	0.4107	0.4708	0.4761
Min	0.0000	0.0000	0.0000	0.0000	0.0000	0.0000	0.0000	0.0017
25% quantile	0.0884	0.0660	0.0341	0.0633	0.0676	0.0495	0.1523	0.1466
Median	0.6595	0.2626	0.4177	0.3040	0.6870	0.4006	0.4300	0.4916
75% quantile	0.7537	0.7364	0.8461	0.8943	0.8732	0.8429	0.7961	0.7501
Max	0.9837	0.9919	0.9742	0.9963	0.9757	0.9562	0.9684	0.9443

TABLE 10.7 Descriptive statistics of optimal portfolios (MECC)

	RRA = 3		RRA = 7		RRA = 15		RRA = 25	
	Growth	Value	Growth	Value	Growth	Value	Growth	Value
			Unconstrained					
Mean	−0.0431	−3.2130	−0.5601	−4.5784	−1.1203	2.0668	1.0984	0.8952
Min	−56.6288	−234.1930	−24.3194	−426.3080	−42.1233	−37.1485	−25.2172	−39.5055
25% quantile	−0.9662	−0.8578	−0.9711	−0.8836	−0.9515	−0.8835	−0.8620	−0.8993
Median	0.0000	0.1789	−0.5256	0.2652	−0.1845	2.3832	0.1948	3.2479
75% quantile	0.9644	0.9176	0.8800	0.9579	0.9070	4.8914	0.9333	5.7697
Max	70.1992	8.5971	27.4618	18.7443	15.8168	28.5662	25.4485	113.9150
			Short-sales constrained					
Mean	0.4176	0.4258	0.4099	0.4821	0.4932	0.4610	1.0984	0.8952
Min	0.0000	0.0000	0.0000	0.0000	0.0000	0.0000	−25.2172	−39.5055
25% quantile	0.0001	0.0227	0.0243	0.0543	0.0367	0.0884	−0.8620	−0.8993
Median	0.2854	0.2958	0.1989	0.4689	0.6620	0.4347	0.1948	1.2479
75% quantile	0.8659	0.8283	0.8885	0.9303	0.8909	0.9023	0.9333	8.7697
Max	0.9987	0.9928	0.9949	0.9975	0.9986	0.9921	25.4485	113.9150

the normal and Gumbel portfolio weights display similar patterns in most periods (cf. Figure 10.8), the MECC portfolio weights are often more extreme and more volatile than the normal portfolio weights (cf. Figure 10.7), suggesting that the MECC may capture hidden AD which the normal or Gumbel copula fails to capture.

We can determine the main causes of the differences between the optimal weights of the MECC strategies and those of the normal strategies by regressing these differences on a constant, two standardized expected excess returns, two skewnesses, two kurtoses and four rank correlations; the regression equation is given by

$$\omega_{i,t}^{MECC} - \omega_{i,t}^{Normal} = \phi_0 + \phi_1 \frac{\mu_{1,t}}{\sigma_{1,t}} + \phi_2 \frac{\mu_{2,t}}{\sigma_{2,t}} + \phi_3 \kappa_{1,t} + \phi_4 \kappa_{2,t} + \phi_5 \lambda_{1,t} + \phi_6 \lambda_{2,t}$$

$$+ \phi_7 \rho_{S_t} + \phi_8 \nu_{1,t} + \phi_9 \nu_{2,t} + \phi_{10} \eta_t. \tag{10.31}$$

Table 10.8 shows that, as we expected from discussions in the Introduction, these differences are considerably sensitive to the rank correlations. In addition, the OLS estimates of the regression coefficients $\hat{\phi}_7, \hat{\phi}_8, \hat{\phi}_9$ and $\hat{\phi}_{10}$ are statistically significant, suggesting that AD, measured through the rank correlations, is the main force underlying the outperformance of the MECC model over the normal model.

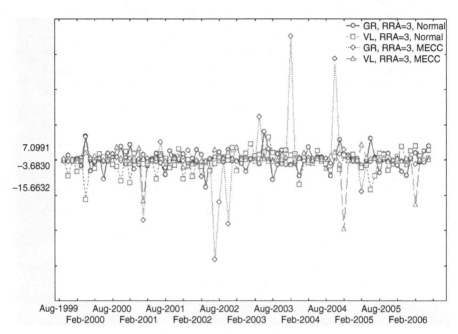

FIGURE 10.7 Optimal *unconstrained* normal and MECC portfolios weights for an investor with degree of relative risk aversion equal to 3 over the out-of-sample period (October 1999 to July 2006). Note that 'GR' stands for the weight put in Russell 1000 Growth and 'VL' stands for the weight put in Russell 1000 Value. The horizontal axis shows the out-of-sample period, and the vertical axis shows optimal portfolio weights.

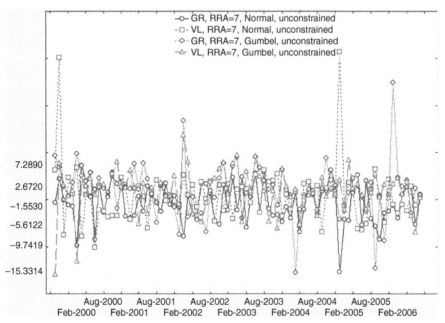

FIGURE 10.8 Optimal *unconstrained* normal and Gumbel portfolio weights for an investor with the degree of relative risk aversion equal to 7 over the out-of-sample period (October 1999 to July 2006). Note that 'GR' stands for the weight put in Russell 1000 Growth and 'VL' stands for the weight put in Russell 1000 Value. The horizontal axis shows the out-of-sample period, and the vertical axis shows optimal portfolio weights.

TABLE 10.8 Explaining optimal portfolio weights

Regressors	MECC weights		MECC - normal weights	
	Russell 1000 Growth	Russell 1000 Value	Russell 1000 Growth	Russell 1000 Value
Intercept	224.6849	−1829.3064	65.9486	−1132.7304
Standardized expected return (*Growth*)	0.0809	−0.0744	0.1139	−0.0367
	(−0.1479)	(−0.1563)	(0.1445)	(0.1562)
Standardized expected return (*Value*)	0.1387	0.0779	0.0398	0.0651
	(−0.1485)	(0.1570)	(0.1452)	(0.1569)
Skewness (*Growth*)	0.0517	−0.0469	0.1484	−0.0549
	(−0.1173)	(0.1241)	(0.1147)	(0.1240)
Degrees-of-freedom (*Growth*)	−0.0450	0.0165	0.0422	0.0114
	(−0.1171)	(0.1238)	(0.1144)	(0.1237)
Skewness (*Value*)	−0.0840	−0.1951	0.0547	−0.1862
	(−0.1375)	(0.1454)	(0.1344)	(0.1453)
Degrees-of-freedom (*Value*)	−0.0544	0.0824	−0.1880	0.0591
	(0.1318)	(0.1394)	(0.1288)	(0.1393)
First-order rank correlation ($\hat{\rho}$)	−25.2139*	24.4696*	−28.1465*	23.3957*
	(9.9650)	(10.5349)	(9.7407)	(10.5289)
Second-order rank correlation ($\hat{v}_1$)	8.8530	−4.0244	11.0091	−3.4447
	(6.3778)	(6.7426)	(6.2343)	(6.7387)
Third-order rank correlation ($\hat{v}_2$)	7.5601*	−9.6911*	8.2349*	−9.3775*
	(3.0741)	(3.2500)	(3.005)	(3.2481)
Fourth-order rank correlation ($\hat{\kappa}$)	8.7421*	−12.2076*	9.9156*	−11.7773*
	(3.7652)	(3.9806)	(3.6805)	(3.9783)
R-squared coefficient	0.6657	0.0678	0.6741	0.0613

Notes: This table reports the regression results of the *unconstrained* optimal portfolio weights (and the differences between those of the MECC and the normal copula) on 11 regressors for the degree of relative risk aversion equal to 7. The standard errors of the estimates of the regression coefficients are reported in parentheses; the estimates that are significantly different from 0 at the 5% critical level are marked with (*).

We also used a bootstrap test (via pairwise comparisons of bootstrap samples) to examine whether the differences in the numerical expected utilities of the eight above-mentioned strategies are statistically significant. Indeed, the normal strategy, in the *unconstrained* case, significantly outperforms both the Clayton and Gumbel ones for three RRA levels, 3, 15 and 25, except for the RRA level 7, where these three strategies perform equally well (cf. Table 10.9). It may well be the case that the standardized

TABLE 10.9   Pairwise comparisons of the models' performance

	RRA							
	3		7		15		25	
	p-Value*	p-Value**	p-Value*	p-Value**	p-Value*	p-Value**	p-Value*	p-Value**
Unconstrained								
Clayton vs. normal	0.0000	1_2	0.1438	0.8561_0	0.0173	0.9826_2	0.0296	0.9703_2
Gumbel vs. normal	0.0000	1_2	0.1152	0.8847_0	0.0222	0.9777_2	0.0650	0.9349_2
MECC vs. normal	1_1	0.0000	1_1	0.0000	1_1	0.0000	1_1	0.0000
Gumbel vs. Clayton	0.1542	0.8457_0	0.6789_0	0.3210	0.7445_0	0.2554	0.7347_0	0.2652
MECC vs. Clayton	1_1	0.0000	1_1	0.0000	1_1	0.0000	1_1	0.0000
MECC vs. Gumbel	1_1	0.0000	1_1	0.0000	1_1	0.0000	1_1	0.0000
Short-sales constrained								
Clayton vs. normal	0.0000	1_2	0.0104	0.9895_2	0.0008	0.9992_2	0.0108	0.9891_2
Gumbel vs. normal	0.0360	0.963996_2	0.0036	0.9964_2	0.0015	0.9985_2	0.0281	0.9718_2
MECC vs. normal	0.9763_1	0.0236	1_1	0.0000	1_1	0.0000	1_1	0.0000
Gumbel vs. Clayton	1_1	0.0000	0.9118_1	0.0881	0.9353_1	0.0646	0.8834_0	0.1165
MECC vs. Clayton	0.9843_1	0.0156	1_1	0.0000	1_1	0.0000	1_1	0.0000
MECC vs. Gumbel	0.9822_1	0.0177	1_1	0.0000	1_1	0.0000	1_1	0.0000

Notes: This table presents the results from pairwise comparisons of the optimal portfolios based on the normal copula, the Clayton copula, the Gumbel copula and the MECC. Let the performance measure of portfolio i be μ_i. The *p*-value* denotes the bootstrapping probability that $\mu_i - \mu_j$ is greater than zero; the *p*-value** denotes the bootstrapping probability that $\mu_i - \mu_j$ is less than zero. The bootstrapping t tests were conducted at the 10% significance level. Subscript '0' indicates that the test was inconclusive; subscript '1' indicates that the first model outperforms the second one; subscript '2' indicates that the second model outperforms the first one. (The performance measure that we have used is the sample mean of realized utilities.)

TABLE 10.10 Results obtained from White's reality check

	RRA			
	3	7	15	25
Unconstrained				
Bootstrapping reality				
check *p*-value	0.09161	0.09671	0.09651	0.95720
Naïve *p*-value	0.09161	0.09671	0.09651	0.25883
Short-sales constrained				
Bootstrapping reality				
check *p*-value	0.09821	0.96740	0.97870	0.96260
Naïve *p*-value	0.09821	0.26353	0.11841	0.25933

Notes: The 'Bootstrapping reality check *p*-value' is the bootstrapping *p*-value corresponding to the best model found. The 'Naïve *p*-value' is the bootstrapping reality check *p*-value computed by treating the best model as if it were the only model considered.

returns are asymmetrically dependent in a complex way which is not sufficiently captured by the normal, Gumbel or Clayton copula; in other words, these copulas may be misspecified, and the normal strategy is better than the other two. In addition, in the *constrained* case, while the Gumbel strategy significantly outperforms the Clayton strategy for three RRA levels, 3, 7 and 15, the Clayton and Gumbel strategies perform equally well for all the RRA levels. Nevertheless, the MECC strategy always outperforms the other strategies, and the degree of outperformance is rather strong in the unconstrained case.

To compare all the models jointly, we applied the reality check test of White (2000). The null hypothesis is that the benchmark model performs as well as the best competing model. We used the normal copula as a benchmark model and rejected the null hypothesis when the *p*-value is less than 10%. We found that, without short-sales constraints, the null hypothesis is always rejected for all RRA levels except 25 (cf. Table 10.10). Nevertheless, with short-sales constraints, the normal model may perform as well as the best competing model.

10.6 CONCLUSION

In this chapter, we have made two contributions to the growing literature of entropy and copulas. First, we provided an analytical approach to recover the RE measure of dependence from limited information by building the most entropic copula (MEC). Among the MECs, there exists a canonical form called the most entropic canonical copula (MECC). Second, we showed that our approach and the minimum KLCE approach are dual, that is, the minimum KLCE joint distributions, obtained by minimizing the KLCE subject to constraints on joint moments and marginal distributions, can be constructed from a MECC and arbitrary sets of marginals.

We have illustrated the practicability of our approach by considering a 'style investing' problem for an investor with the CRRA utility allocating his/her wealth between the 'growth' and 'value' indices. The main finding is that, using the skewed-*t* distributions (to capture time-varying skewnesses and kurtoses), the MECC model significantly outperforms the normal copula model in terms of investment gains, and the normal copula model may outperform the Clayton or Gumbel copula model in certain cases. The most economically and statistically significant gains from using the MECC over the other copulas are brought about by the unconstrained portfolios.

We conclude this chapter with a thoughtful remark: since outliers are an ill-defined, albeit important concept without clear boundaries, the improved immunity to outliers offered by robust techniques is usually obtained at the expense of a considerable increase in computation. Admittedly, given some considerable merits the method of MEC, which is based on the premise that rank correlations are resistant against noise and outliers, is unfortunately not an exception. Hence, future researches should focus on computationally efficient, nonparametric approximators of the MECC. We believe that this is an absolutely feasible task.

REFERENCES

Abramowitz, M. and Stegun, I.A. (1972). *Handbook of Mathematical Functions*. Dover Publications, New York.

Ait-Sahalia, Y. and Brandt, M.W. (2001). Variable selection for portfolio choice. *Journal of Finance*, 56, 1297–1355.

Andrews, D.W.K. and Ploberger, W. (1996). Testing for serial correlation against an ARMA(1,1) process. *Journal of the American Statistical Association*, 91, 1331–1342.

Ang, A. and Chen, J. (2002). Asymmetric correlations of equity portfolios. *Journal of Financial Economics*, 63, 443–494.

Barberis, N. and Shleifer, A. (2003). Style investing. *Journal of Financial Economics*, 68, 161–199.

Barberis, N., Shleifer, A. and Wurgler, J. (2005). Comovement. *Journal of Financial Economics*, 75, 283–317.

Basu, S. (1977). Investment performance of common stocks in relation to their price–earnings ratios: a test of the efficient market hypothesis. *Journal of Finance*, 3, 663–682.

Beliakov, G. (2006). Interpolation of Lipschitz functions. *Journal of Computational and Applied Mathematics*, 196, 20–44.

Blest, D.C. (2000). Rank correlation – an alternative measure. *Australia & New Zealand Journal of Statistics*, 42(1), 101–111.

Brandt, M.W. (2004). Portfolio choice problem, in Y. Ait-Sahalia and L.P. Hansen (eds), *Handbook of Financial Econometrics*. Elsevier Science, Amsterdam.

Campbell, J.Y. and Shiller, R.J. (1988). The dividend–price ratio and expectations of future dividends and discount factors. *Review of Financial Studies*, 1, 195–228.

Campbell, J.Y., Polk, C. and Vuolteenaho, T. (2005). Growth or glamour? Fundamentals and systematic risk in stock returns. NBER Working Paper 11389.

Chen, Y.-T. (2007). Moment-based copula tests for financial returns. *Journal of Business & Economic Statistics*, 25, 377–397.

Cherubini, U., Luciano, E. and Vecchiato, W. (2004). *Copula Methods in Finance*. John Wiley & Sons, London.

Csendes, T. (1988). Nonlinear parameter estimation by global optimization – efficiency and reliability. *Acta Cybernetica*, 8, 361–370.

Damodaran, A. (2004). *Investment Fables: Exposing the Myths of "Can't Miss" Investment Strategies*. FT Press, London.

DeMiguel, V., Garlappi, L. and Uppal, R. (2009). Optimal versus naive diversification: how inefficient is the 1/n portfolio strategy? *Review of Financial Studies*, 22(5), 1915–1953.

Fama, E. (1981). Stock returns, real activity, inflation, and money. *American Economic Review*, 71, 545–565.

Fama, E.F. and French, K.R. (1988). Dividend yields and expected stock returns. *Journal of Financial Economics*, 22, 3–25.

Fama, E.F. and French, K.R. (1998). Value versus growth: The international evidence. *Journal of Finance*, LIII(6), 1975–1999.

Fermanian, J.-D. (2005). Goodness-of-fit tests for copulas. *Journal of Multivariate Analysis*, 95, 119–152.

Genest, C. and MacKay, J. (1986). The joy of copulas: bivariate distributions with uniform marginal. *The American Statistician*, 40(4), 280–283.

Genest, C. and Plante, J.-F. (2003). On Blest's measure of rank correlation. *Canadian Journal of Statistics*, 31, 1–18.

Giacomini, R. and White, H. (2006). Tests of conditional predictive ability. *Econometrica*, 74, 1545–1578.

Giacomini, R. and Rossi, B. (2007). Model selection and forecast comparison in unstable environment. Working paper.

Gideon, R.A. and Hollister, R.A. (1987). A rank correlation coefficient resistant to outliers. *Journal of the American Statistical Association*, 82(398), 656–666.

Golan, A. (2002). Information and entropy econometrics: Editor's view. *Journal of Econometrics*, 107, 1–15.

Golan, A. (2007). Information and entropy econometrics – volume overview and synthesis. *Journal of Econometrics*, 138, 379–387.

Hajek, J. and Sidak, Z. (1967). *Theory of Rank Tests*. Academic Press, New York.

Hang, R.K. (1993). Maximum entropy estimation of density and regression functions. *Journal of Econometrics*, 56, 397–400.

Hansen, B.E. (1994). Autoregressive conditional density estimation. *International Economic Review*, 35, 705–729.

Hong, Y., Tu, J. and Zhou, G. (2007). Asymmetries in stock returns: statistical tests and economic evaluation. *Review of Financial Studies*, 20, 1547–1581.

Ibbotson, R.G. and Riepe, M.W. (1997). Growth vs. value investing and the winner is… *Journal of Financial Planning*, June, 64–71.

Ioffe, A.D. and Tihomirov, V.M. (1979). *Theory of Extremal Problems*. Studies in Mathematics and its Applications, Vol. 6. North Holland, Amsterdam.

Joe, H. (1989a). Estimation of entropy and other functionals of a multivariate density. *Annals of the Institute of Statistical Mathematics*, 41, 683–697.

Joe, H. (1989b). Relative entropy measures of multivariate dependence. *Journal of the American Statistical Association*, 84(405), 157–164.

Joe, H. and Xu, J.J. (1996). The estimation method of inference functions for margins for multivariate models. Working paper, UBC.

Jondeau, E. and Rockinger, M. (2003). Conditional volatility, skewness, and kurtosis: existence, persistence and comovement. *Journal of Economic Dynamics and Control*, 27, 1699–1737.

Jondeau, E. and Rockinger, M. (2006). The copula-GARCH models of conditional dependencies: an international stock market application. *Journal of International Money and Finance*, 25, 827–853.

Kutoyants, Y.A. (2004). *Statistical Inference for Ergodic Diffusion Processes*. Springer, Berlin.

Lettau, M. and Ludvigson, S. (2001). Consumption, aggregate wealth, and expected stock returns. *Journal of Finance*, LVI(3), 815–849.

Levin, M. (1983). On the approximate calculation of double integrals. *Mathematics of Computation*, 40, 273–282.

Longin, F. and Solnik, B. (2001). Extreme correlation of international equity markets. *Journal of Finance*, 56, 649–676.

Maasoumi, E. and Racine, J. (2002). Entropy and predictability of stock market returns. *Journal of Econometrics*, 107, 291–312.

Miller, D.J. and Liu, W. (2002). On the recovery of joint distributions from limited information. *Journal of Econometrics*, 107, 259–274.

Nelsen, R.B. (1998). *An Introduction to Copulas*. Springer, Berlin.

Patton, A.J. (2004). On the out-of-sample importance of skewness and asymmetric dependence for asset allocation. *Journal of Financial Econometrics*, 2(1), 130–168.

Patton, A.J. (2006). Modelling asymmetric exchange rate dependence. *International Economic Review*, 47(2), 527–555.

Petkova, R. and Zhang, L. (2005). Is value riskier than growth. *Journal of Financial Economics*, 78, 187–202.

Poon, S.-H., Jondeau, E. and Rockinger, M. (2007). *Financial Modelling under Non-Gaussian Distributions*. Springer, London.

Puri, M.L., Sen, P.K. and Gokhale, D.V. (1970). On a class of rank order tests for independence in multivariate distributions. *Sankhya, Series A*, 32, 271–298.

Robinson, P.M. (1991). Consistent nonparametric entropy-based testing. *Review of Economic Studies*, 58, 437–453.

Rockinger, M. and Jondeau, E. (2002). Entropy densities with an application to autoregressive conditional skewness and kurtosis. *Journal of Econometrics*, 106, 119–142.

Rosenblatt, M. (1952). Remarks on a multivariate transformation. *Annals of Mathematical Statistics*, 23, 470–472.

Sancetta, A. and Satchell, S. (2004). The Bernstein copula and its applications to modeling and approximation of multivariate distributions. *Econometric Theory*, 20, 535–562.

Scaillet, O. (2007). Kernel-based goodness-of-fit tests for copulas with fixed smoothing parameters. *Journal of Multivariate Analysis*, 98, 533–543.

Shannon, C.E. (1948). The mathematical theory of communication. *Bell System Technical Journal*, Jul/Oct, 3–91.

Shiryaev, A.N. (1995). *Probability*, 2nd edn. Graduate Text in Mathematics, Vol. 952. Springer, Berlin.

Skaug, H.J. and Tjøstheim, D. (1996) Measures of distance between densities with application to testing for serial independence, in P. Robinson and M. Rosenblatt (eds), *Time Series Analysis in Memory of E.J. Hannan*. Springer, New York, pp. 363–377.

Sklar, A. (1959). Fonctions de répartition *n* dimensions et leurs marges. *Publications de l'Institut Statistique de l'Université de Paris*, 8, 229–231.

White, H. (2000). A reality check for data snooping. *Econometrica*, 68, 1097–1126.

Wu, X. (2003). Calculation of maximum entropy densities with application to income distribution. *Journal of Econometrics*, 115, 347–354.

Wu, X. and Stengos, T. (2005). Partially adaptive estimation via the maximum entropy densities. *Econometrics Journal*, 8, 352–366.

Wu, X. and Perloff, J.M. (2007). GMM estimation of a maximum entropy distribution with interval data. *Journal of Econometrics*, 138, 532–546.

Zellner, A. and Highfield, R.A. (1988). Calculation of maximum entropy distributions and approximation of marginal posterior distributions. *Journal of Econometrics*, 37, 195–209.

Zong, Z. (2006). *Information-Theoretic Methods for Estimating Complicated Probability Distributions*. Elsevier, Amsterdam.

Basic Results

Definition 10.A.1 (Adapted and modified from Nelsen, 1998, p. 10). *A two-dimensional copula,* $C(u, v)$, *is a real function defined on the unit square* $[0, 1]^2$:

$$C : [0, 1]^2 \implies [0, 1]$$

such that

1. $C(u, 0) = C(0, v) = 0$,
2. $C(u, 1) = u$ and $C(1, v) = v$ for every (u, v) of $[0, 1]^2$, and
3. C is 2-increasing [i.e., $C(u_2, v_2) - C(u_1, v_2) - C(u_2, v_1) + C(u_1, v_1) \geq 0$ for every rectangle $[u_1, u_2] \times [v_1, v_2]$, where $u_1 \leq u_2$ and $v_1 \leq v_2$, whose vertices lie in $[0, 1]^2$.]

Note that requirement (3) in the above definition purports to guarantee that copulas fall within the Fréchet bounds (cf. Cherubini, et al., Theorem 2.4).

Definition 10.A.2 (Adapted and modified from Nelsen, 1998, Chapter 5). *Let* τ *denote the difference between the probabilities of concordance and discordance of* (X_1, Y_1) *and* (X_2, Y_2) *as follows:*

$$\tau = P\{(X_1 - X_2)(Y_1 - Y_2) > 0\} - P\{(X_1 - X_2)(Y_1 - Y_2) < 0\}, \tag{10.A.1}$$

where (X_1, Y_1) *and* (X_2, Y_2) *are independent vectors of continuous random variables with the joint distributions* $F_1(X, Y)$ *and* $F_2(X, Y)$, *respectively, which have common marginals,* $G_1(X)$ *and* $G_2(Y)$. *When* $F_1 = F_2$, τ *is Kendall's tau,* τ_K. *Other measures of association such as Spearman's rho and Gini's gamma can be defined immediately.*

The copula representations of Kendall's tau, Spearman's rho and Gini's gamma are given in Theorem 10.A.1.

Theorem 10.A.1 (Nelsen, 1998, Chapter 5) *Let* C_1 *and* C_2 *denote copulas such that* $F_1(X, Y) = C_1(G_1(X), G_2(Y))$ *and* $F_2(X, Y) = C_2(G_1(X), G_2(Y))$, *then*

$$\tau = Q(C_1, C_2) = 4 \int_{[0,1]^2} C_2(u, v) dC_1(u, v) - 1. \tag{10.A.2}$$

For instance, if $C_2(u, v) = uv$, *then* τ *is Spearman's rho,* ρ_S; *if* $C_2(u, v) = 2(|u + v - 1| - |u - v|)$, *then* τ *is Gini's gamma; and if* $C_1(u, v) = C_2(u, v)$, *then* τ *is* τ_K.

APPROXIMATION OF POTENTIAL FUNCTIONS

We now present a Gaussian–Legendre quadrature method to approximate the potential function (10.15) for the MECC. (Note that the potential function (10.20) can be approximated by the same method presented here.) Using affine transformations, $x_1(u) : [0, 1] \to [-1, 1]$ with $x_1 = 2u - 1$ and $x_2(v) : [0, 1] \to [-1, 1]$ with $x_2 = 2v - 1$, Equation (10.15) can be rewritten as follows:

$$
\begin{aligned}
Q_n(\Lambda, \widehat{\Theta}) &= \frac{1}{4} \int_{[-1,1]^2} \exp \left\{ \sum_{k=0}^{2^n-1} \left[\lambda_k \left(\Phi(k - 2^{n-1}(x_1 + 1)) + \Phi(2^{n-1}(x_1 + 1) - k - 1) - 1 + 2^{-n} \right) \right. \right. \\
&\quad \left. + \gamma_k \left(\Phi(k - 2^{n-1}(x_2 + 1)) + \Phi(2^{n-1}(x_2 + 1) - k - 1) - 1 + 2^{-n} \right) \right] \\
&\quad \left. - \lambda_{2^n} \left(h \left(\frac{x_1 + 1}{2}, \frac{x_2 + 1}{2} \right) - \widehat{\Theta} \right) \right\} dx_1 dx_2 \\
&= \frac{1}{4} \int_{[-1,1]^2} \exp\{-\Lambda' \Psi(X)\} dX,
\end{aligned}
\tag{10.B.1}
$$

where $X = \{x_1, x_2\}$, $\Lambda' = \{\lambda_0, \gamma_0, \ldots, \lambda_k, \gamma_k, \ldots, \lambda_{2^n-1}, \gamma_{2^n-1}, \lambda_{2^n}\}$ and $\Psi(X)$ has an obvious meaning.

The function $\exp\{-\Lambda'\Psi(X)\}$ can be expanded into a series of orthogonal Legendre polynomials, that is,

$$
\exp\{-\Lambda'\Psi(X)\} = \sum_{n=0}^{\infty} \sum_{m=0}^{\infty} a_{nm} P_{nm}(X),
\tag{10.B.2}
$$

where $P_{nm}(X) = P_n(x_1)P_m(x_2)$ are products of two Legendre orthogonal polynomials (see, e.g., Abramowitz and Stegun, 1972 for further details of the Legendre polynomials),

$$
a_{nm} = \frac{(2n + 1)(2m + 1)}{4} \int_{[-1,1]^2} \exp\{-\Lambda'\Psi(X)\} P_{nm}(X) dX
$$

and

$$
a_{00} = \frac{1}{4} \int_{[-1,1]^2} \exp\{-\Lambda'\Psi(X)\} dX.
$$

Now, let $X_{i,j} = (x_{1i}, x_{2j})$, $\forall i = 1, \ldots, N$ and $j = 1, \ldots, M$, be the roots of the polynomials $P_N(x_1) = 0$ and $P_M(x_2) = 0$, respectively – $X_{i,j}$ are also called the abscissae of the Legendre polynomials – then, choose weights, ω_{ij}, satisfying the following $M \times N$ relations:

$$
\begin{cases}
\sum_{i=1}^{N} \sum_{j=1}^{M} \omega_{ij} P_{00}(X_{i,j}) = \sum_{1}^{N} \sum_{1}^{M} \omega_{ij} = 1, \\[2mm]
\sum_{1}^{N} \sum_{1}^{M} \omega_{ij} P_{kh}(X_{i,j}) = 0, \quad \omega_{ij} \geq 0,
\end{cases}
\tag{10.B.3}
$$

where $(k, h) \in (1, \ldots, N) \otimes (1, \ldots, M)$. We obtain:

$$
\sum_{i=1}^{N} \sum_{j=1}^{M} \omega_{ij} \exp\{-\Lambda'\Psi(X_{ij})\} = \sum_{n=0}^{\infty} \sum_{m=0}^{\infty} a_{nm} \sum_{i=1}^{N} \sum_{j=1}^{M} \omega_{ij} P_{nm}(X_{ij})
$$

$$
= a_{00} + \sum_{n=N+1}^{\infty} \sum_{m=M+1}^{\infty} a_{nm} \sum_{i=1}^{N} \sum_{j=1}^{M} \omega_{ij} P_{nm}(X_{ij}).
\tag{10.B.4}
$$

Hence,

$$
a_{00} = Q_n(\Lambda, \hat{\Theta}) = \sum_{i=1}^{N} \sum_{j=1}^{M} \omega_{ij} \exp\{-\Lambda'\Psi(X_{ij})\} - \sum_{n=N+1}^{\infty} \sum_{m=M+1}^{\infty} a_{nm} \sum_{i=1}^{N} \sum_{j=1}^{M} \omega_{ij} P_{nm}(X_{ij})
$$

$$
= \underbrace{\sum_{i=1}^{N} \sum_{j=1}^{M} \omega_{ij} \exp\{-\Lambda'\Psi(X_{ij})\}}_{\text{Approximation}} + R_{NM},
\tag{10.B.5}
$$

where $R_{NM} = -\sum_{n=N+1}^{\infty} \sum_{m=M+1}^{\infty} a_{nm} \sum_{i=1}^{N} \sum_{j=1}^{M} \omega_{ij} P_{nm}(X_{ij})$ is an error term and (M, N) are large enough.

To compute the MECC, we used a stochastic search algorithm to minimize Equation (10.B.5) with $M = N = 30$.

In our proofs, we will use the following lemmas:

Lemma 10.C.1 *Let $\Omega = [0, 1]$, let P denote the Lebesgue measure and let $f(x) \in L^1(\Omega)$. Put*

$$f_n(x) = 2^n \int_{[k2^{-n}, (k+1)2^{-n}]} f(y)dy \text{ for some } x \in [k2^{-n}, (k+1)2^{-n}), \tag{10.C.1}$$

where $\{k2^{-n}\}$ is a compact, dense dyadic sequence in Ω. [Note that a sequence is defined to be dense in an interval if, for every point in the interval, there exists a point (in the sequence) which is arbitrarily close to it.] Then, $f_n(x) \xrightarrow{P\text{- }as} f(x)$. (See Shiryaev, 1995, p. 515.)

Lemma 10.C.2 (DuBois–Reymond's lemma) *Let $b(t)$ denote a continuous on $[t_0, t_1]$. Assuming that the following equality:*

$$\int_{t_0}^{t_1} b(t)v(t)dt = 0 \tag{10.C.2}$$

holds for any continuous function, $v(t)$, with $\int_{t_0}^{t_1} v(t)dt = 0$, then $b(t)$ must be a constant. Conversely, if $b(t)$ is a constant, then $\int_{t_0}^{t_1} b(t)v(t)dt = 0$. (See Ioffe and Tihomirov, 1979, p. 400.)

Lemma 10.C.3 *An indicator function, $1_{y>x}(y)$, can be approximated by a continuous function, $\Phi_N(y, x)$, given by*

$$\Phi_N(y, x) = \frac{N}{2\pi} \int_{-\infty}^{y} \exp\{-(v - x)^2 N^2/2\}dv, \tag{10.C.3}$$

which has the following properties:

$$\lim_{N \to \infty} \Phi_N(y, x) \Longrightarrow 1_{y>x}(y)$$

and

$$\lim_{N \to \infty} \frac{\partial \Phi_N(y, x)}{\partial y} \Longrightarrow \delta(y - x),$$

where $\delta(\cdot)$ is Dirac's delta function. (See Kutoyants, 2004, p. 30.)

Proof of Theorem 10.1: Since Equations (10.5) and (10.6) are continuums of constraints with varying end-points, we need to replace these continuums with sets of definite integrals:

$$\int_{[a,b]}\int_{[0,1]} c(u,v)dudv = \int_{[0,1]}\int_{[a,b]} c(u,v)dudv = b - a, \tag{10.C.4}$$

where a and b are arbitrary numbers in $[0,1]$. Using a dense dyadic sequence in $[0,1]$, Equation (10.C.4) can be approximated by

$$\sum_{k=k_1}^{k=k_2}\int_{[k2^{-n},(k+1)2^{-n}]}\int_{[0,1]} c(u,v)dudv = \sum_{k=k_1}^{k=k_2}\int_{[0,1]}\int_{[k2^{-n},(k+1)2^{-n}]} c(u,v)dudv = \frac{k_2 - k_1}{2^n},$$

where k_1 and k_2 are chosen such that $|a - k_1 2^{-n}| \leq \epsilon$ and $|b - k_2 2^{-n}| \leq \epsilon$, where ϵ is small enough. Hence, Equation (10.C.4) is equivalent to

$$\int_{[k2^{-n},(k+1)2^{-n}]}\int_{[0,1]} c(u,v)dudv = \int_{[0,1]}\int_{[k2^{-n},(k+1)2^{-n}]} c(u,v)dudv = \frac{1}{2^n}$$

$$\forall k = 0, 1, 2, \dots, (2^n - 1), \text{ and } n \text{ is large enough.} \tag{10.C.5}$$

The Lagrangian function of Problem A can be formulated as follows:

$$\mathcal{L}(c(u,v),\Lambda) = -\int_{[0,1]^2} c(u,v)\log c(u,v)dudv - \lambda_{-1}\left[\int_{[0,1]^2} c(u,v)dudv - 1\right]$$

$$- \sum_{k=0}^{2^n-1}\left\{\lambda_k\int_{[k2^{-n},(k+1)2^{-n}]}\int_{[0,1]}[c(u,v) - 2^{-n}] + \gamma_k\int_{[0,1]}\int_{[k2^{-n},(k+1)2^{-n}]}[c(u,v) - 2^{-n}]\right\}$$

$$- \lambda_{2^n}\int_{[0,1]^2}(h(u,v) - \hat{\Theta})c(u,v)dudv$$

$$= -\int_{[0,1]^2}\left\{c(u,v)\log c(u,v) + \lambda_{-1}[c(u,v) - 1]\right.$$

$$+ \sum_{k=0}^{2^n-1}\left(\lambda_k\mathbf{1}_{[k2^{-n},(k+1)2^{-n}]}(u) + \gamma_k\mathbf{1}_{[k2^{-n},(k+1)2^{-n}]}(v)\right)[c(u,v) - 2^{-n}]$$

$$\left. + \lambda_{2^n}(h(u,v) - \hat{\Theta})c(u,v)\right\} dudv. \tag{10.C.6}$$

Taking the first derivative of $\mathcal{L}(c(u,v),\Lambda)$ with respect to $c(u,v)$ leads to

$$\int_{[0,1]^2}\left\{\log c(u,v) + (1 + \lambda_{-1}) + \sum_{k=0}^{2^n-1}\left[\lambda_k\mathbf{1}_{[k2^{-n},(k+1)2^{-n}]}(u)\right.\right.$$

$$\left.\left. + \gamma_k\mathbf{1}_{[k2^{-n},(k+1)2^{-n}]}(v)\right] + \lambda_{2^n}(h(u,v) - \hat{\Theta})\right\} dudv = 0. \tag{10.C.7}$$

Applying Lemma 10.C.2 to the function

$$b(u,v) = \frac{\log c(u,v) + (1 + \lambda_{-1}) + \sum_{k=0}^{2^n-1}\left[\lambda_k\mathbf{1}_{[k2^{-n},(k+1)2^{-n}]}(u) + \gamma_k\mathbf{1}_{[k2^{-n},(k+1)2^{-n}]}(v)\right] + \lambda_{2^n}(h(u,v) - \hat{\Theta})}{\tilde{c}(u,v) - 1}, \tag{10.C.8}$$

where $\tilde{c}(u, v)$ is an arbitrary copula density such that $\int_{[0,1]^2} (\tilde{c}(u, v) - 1) du dv = 0$, we obtain the following representation:

$$\hat{c}(u, v) = \lim_{n \to \infty} \hat{c}_n(u, v),$$

where

$$\hat{c}_n(u, v) = \exp\left\{-(1 + \lambda_{-1} - b_0) - \sum_{k=0}^{2^n-1} \left[\lambda_k \mathbf{1}_{[k2^{-n},(k+1)2^{-n}]}(u) + \gamma_k \mathbf{1}_{[k2^{-n},(k+1)2^{-n}]}(v)\right]\right.$$
$$\left. - \lambda_{2^n}(h(u, v) - \hat{\Theta}) - b_0\tilde{c}(u, v)\right\}, \tag{10.C.9}$$

and b_0 is a generic constant.

Substituting Equation (10.C.9) into Equation (10.4), the leading term, $1 + \lambda_{-1} - b_0$, is cancelled out, then we obtain:

$$\hat{c}_n(u, v) = \frac{\mathcal{E}_n(u, v)}{\int_{[0,1]^2} \mathcal{E}_n(u, v) du dv}, \tag{10.C.10}$$

where

$$\mathcal{E}_n(u, v) = \exp\left\{-\sum_{k=0}^{2^n-1} \left[\hat{\lambda}_k \mathbf{1}_{[k2^{-n},(k+1)2^{-n}]}(u) + \hat{\gamma}_k \mathbf{1}_{[k2^{-n},(k+1)2^{-n}]}(v)\right] - \hat{\lambda}_{2^n}(h(u, v) - \hat{\Theta}) - b_0\tilde{c}(u, v)\right\}.$$

The Lagrangian multipliers $\hat{\Lambda} = \{\{\hat{\lambda}_k\}_{k=0}^{2^n}, \{\hat{\gamma}_k\}_{k=0}^{2^n-1}\}$ can be solved out by substituting Equation (10.C.10) into Equations (10.5), (10.6) and (10.7), which leads to the following system of equations:

$$\begin{cases} \dfrac{1}{\int_{[0,1]^2} \mathcal{E}_n(u, v) du dv} \int_{[0,1]^2} \mathbf{1}_{[k2^{-n},(k+1)2^{-n}]}(u) \mathcal{E}_n(u, v) du dv = 2^{-n}, \\[2mm] \dfrac{1}{\int_{[0,1]^2} \mathcal{E}_n(u, v) du dv} \int_{[0,1]^2} \mathbf{1}_{[k2^{-n},(k+1)2^{-n}]}(v) \mathcal{E}_n(u, v) du dv = 2^{-n}, \\[2mm] \dfrac{1}{\int_{[0,1]^2} \mathcal{E}_n(u, v) du dv} \int_{[0,1]^2} (h(u, v) - \hat{\Theta}) \mathcal{E}_n(u, v) du dv = 0, \end{cases} \tag{10.C.11}$$

$\forall k = 0, \ldots, (2^n - 1)$.

Since Equation (10.C.10) can be rewritten as

$$\hat{c}_n(u, v) = \frac{-\sum_{k=0}^{2^n-1}(\hat{\lambda}_k 2^{-n} + \hat{\gamma}_k 2^{-n})}{\int_{[0,1]^2} \mathcal{E}_n(u, v) du dv} \exp\left\{-\sum_{k=0}^{2^n-1} \left[\hat{\lambda}_k(\mathbf{1}_{[k2^{-n},(k+1)2^{-n}]}(u) - 2^{-n})\right.\right.$$
$$\left.\left. + \hat{\gamma}_k(\mathbf{1}_{[k2^{-n},(k+1)2^{-n}]}(v) - 2^{-n})\right] - \hat{\lambda}_{2^n}(h(u, v) - \hat{\Theta}) - b_0\tilde{c}(u, v)\right\},$$

we can define the potential function as follows:

$$Q_n(\Lambda, \widehat{\Theta}) = \int_{[0,1]^2} \exp\left\{ - \sum_{k=0}^{2^n-1} \left[\lambda_k (1_{[k2^{-n},(k+1)2^{-n}]}(u) - 2^{-n}) \right. \right.$$

$$\left. \left. + \gamma_k (1_{[k2^{-n},(k+1)2^{-n}]}(v) - 2^{-n}) \right] - \lambda_{2^n}(h(u,v) - \widehat{\Theta}) - b_0 \tilde{c}(u,v) \right\} dudv.$$

Then, Equation (10.C.11) is equivalent to the following system of equations:

$$\begin{cases} \dfrac{\partial}{\partial \lambda_k} Q_n(\Lambda, \widehat{\Theta}) = 0, \\[2mm] \dfrac{\partial}{\partial \gamma_k} Q_n(\Lambda, \widehat{\Theta}) = 0, \\[2mm] \dfrac{\partial}{\partial \lambda_{2^n}} Q_n(\Lambda, \widehat{\Theta}) = 0, \end{cases} \tag{10.C.12}$$

$\forall\, k = 0, \ldots, (2^n - 1)$. Note that the second-order derivative of $Q_n(\Lambda, \widehat{\Theta})$ is the covariance matrix of $\left\{ 1_{[k2^{-n},(k+1)2^{-n}]}(u), 1_{[k2^{-n},(k+1)2^{-n}]}(v), h(u,v) - \widehat{\Theta} \right\}_{k=0}^{2^n-1}$, thus positive definite, and that the solutions to Equation (10.C.12) are the minimum values of $Q_n(\Lambda, \widehat{\Theta})$, which depend on $\widehat{\Theta}$, b_0 and $\tilde{c}(u,v)$.

Since the potential function $Q_n(\Lambda, \widehat{\Theta})$ and the MEC (10.C.10) are discontinuous, following common practice, they need to be smoothed out. We can obtain their smoothings by using a continuous approximation to the indicator function, $\sum_{k=0}^{2^n-1} \lambda_k 1_{[k2^{-n},(k+1)2^{-n}]}(u)$, for a sufficiently large n. An application of Lemma 10.C.3 yields

$$1_{[k2^{-n},(k+1)2^{-n}]}(u) = 1 - 1_{[u<k2^{-n}]} - 1_{[u>(k+1)2^{-n}]}$$

$$= 1 - \lim_{N\to\infty} \frac{N}{\sqrt{2\phi}} \int_{-\infty}^{k2^{-n}} \exp\{-(x-u)^2 N^2/2\} dx$$

$$- \lim_{N\to\infty} \frac{N}{\sqrt{2\pi}} \int_{-\infty}^{-(k+1)2^{-n}} \exp\{-(x+u)^2 N^2/2\} dx$$

$$= 1 - \lim_{N\to\infty} \Phi[N(k2^{-n} - u)] - \lim_{N\to\infty} \Phi[-N((k+1)2^{-n} - u)].$$

Setting $N = 2^n$, using Lemma 10.C.1 and the same arguments as in the previous part, we obtain:

$$\lim_{n\to\infty} Q_n(\Lambda, \widehat{\Theta}) = \lim_{n\to\infty} \int_{[0,1]^2} \exp\left\{ \sum_{k=0}^{2^n-1} \left[\lambda_k(\Phi(k - 2^n u) + \Phi(2^n u - k - 1) - 1 + 2^{-n}) \right. \right.$$

$$\left. + \gamma_k(\Phi(k - 2^n v) + \Phi(2^n v - k - 1) - 1 + 2^{-n}) \right]$$

$$\left. - \lambda_{2^n}(h(u,v) - \widehat{\Theta}) - b_0 \tilde{c}(u,v) \right\} dudv, \tag{10.C.13}$$

$$\lim_{n\to\infty} \mathcal{E}_n(\widehat{\Lambda}, \widehat{\Theta}) = \lim_{n\to\infty} \exp\left\{ \sum_{k=0}^{2^n-1} \left[\widehat{\lambda}_k(\Phi(k - 2^n u) + \Phi(2^n u - k - 1)) \right. \right.$$

$$\left. + \widehat{\gamma}_k(\Phi(k - 2^n v) + \Phi(2^n v - k - 1)) \right]$$

$$\left. - \widehat{\lambda}_{2^n}(h(u,v) - \widehat{\Theta}) - b_0 \tilde{c}(u,v) \right\}, \tag{10.C.14}$$

where $\widehat{\Lambda}$ are the minimum values of Equation (10.C.13). Particularly, $\hat{c}_n(u,v)$ can be symmetrized by letting $\lambda_k = \gamma_k \forall k = 0, \ldots, (2^n - 1)$, and letting $h(u,v)$ be a symmetric function.

Finally, to complete this proof, we still need to prove that the MEC approximator, $\widehat{C}_n(u,v) = \int_0^u \int_0^v \hat{c}_n(u,v) du\, dv$, is *2-increasing* (cf. Definition 10.A.1). Let $[u_1, u_1 + \Delta] \times [v_1, v_1 + \Delta]$ denote a rectangle in $[0,1]^2$. We immediately establish that, since $\hat{c}_n(u,v)$ is a [positive] exponential function, the mass of the rectangle, $\widehat{C}_n(u_1 + \Delta, v_1 + \Delta) - \widehat{C}_n(u_1 + \Delta, v_1) - \widehat{C}_n(u_1, v_1 + \Delta) + \widehat{C}_n(u_1, v_1) = \int_{u_1}^{u_1+\Delta} \int_{v_1}^{v_1+\Delta} \hat{c}_n(u,v) du\, dv$, is thus non-negative. Now, we can obtain the MECs by letting n become sufficiently large. ∎

Proof of Theorem 10.2: In view of AS1 and AS2, for $\Theta^* \in \mathcal{M}$, $Q_n(\Lambda, \Theta^*)$ has a unique finite supremum, Λ^*, and $Prob\{\widehat{\Lambda}_T \in \partial\mathcal{N}\} \to 0$. Let Λ^0 denote the unique supremum of $Q_n(\Lambda, \Theta^0)$. In view of AS3, $\widehat{\Theta}_T \xrightarrow{p} \Theta^0$ implies $\widehat{\Lambda}_T \xrightarrow{p} \Lambda^0$.

An application of the mean-value theorem yields

$$\nabla Q_n(\widehat{\Lambda}_T, \Theta^0) = \nabla Q_n(\Lambda^0, \Theta^0) + \mathcal{H}_{1,n}(\widehat{\Lambda}_T^*, \Theta^0)(\widehat{\Lambda}_T - \Lambda^0),$$

where $\min(\widehat{\Lambda}_T, \Lambda^0) < \widehat{\Lambda}_T^* < \max(\widehat{\Lambda}_T, \Lambda^0)$. Thus, we have

$$\widehat{\Lambda}_T - \Lambda^0 = \mathcal{H}_{1,n}^{-1}(\widehat{\Lambda}_T^*, \Theta^0)\nabla Q_n(\widehat{\Lambda}_T, \Theta^0).$$

Another application of the mean-value theorem yields

$$\nabla Q_n(\widehat{\Lambda}_T, \widehat{\Theta}_T) = \nabla Q_n(\widehat{\Lambda}_T, \Theta^0) + \mathcal{H}_{2,n}(\widehat{\Lambda}_T, \widehat{\Theta}_T^*)(\widehat{\Theta}_T - \Theta^0),$$

where $\min(\widehat{\Theta}_T, \Theta^0) < \widehat{\Theta}_T^* < \max(\widehat{\Theta}_T, \Theta^0)$. Thus, we obtain

$$T^{1/2}(\widehat{\Lambda}_T - \Lambda^0) = -T^{1/2}\mathcal{H}_{1,n}^{-1}(\widehat{\Lambda}_T^*, \Theta^0)\mathcal{H}_{2,n}(\widehat{\Lambda}_T, \widehat{\Theta}_T^*)(\widehat{\Theta}_T - \Theta^0).$$

Since $\widehat{\Theta}_T \xrightarrow{p} \Theta^0$ implies $\widehat{\Lambda}_T \xrightarrow{p} \Lambda^0$, the continuous mapping theorem yields

$$\mathcal{H}_{1,n}(\widehat{\Lambda}_T^*, \Theta^0) \xrightarrow{p} \mathcal{H}_{1,n}(\Lambda^0, \Theta^0),$$

$$\mathcal{H}_{2,n}(\widehat{\Lambda}_T, \widehat{\Theta}_T^*) \xrightarrow{p} \mathcal{H}_{2,n}(\Lambda^0, \Theta^0).$$

Since the first-order derivative of the potential function with respect to Λ^0 and Θ^0 is a diagonal matrix [i.e., $\mathcal{H}_{2,n}(\Lambda^0, \Theta^0) = I$, where I denotes a $\dim(\Lambda^0) \times \dim(\Theta^0)$ diagonal matrix], by Slutsky's theorem and AS4, we obtain:

$$T^{1/2}(\widehat{\Lambda}_T - \Lambda^0) \xrightarrow{d} N(0, \mathcal{H}_{1,n}^{-1}(\Lambda^0, \Theta^0)I\Psi I'\mathcal{H}_{1,n}^{-1'}(\Lambda^0, \Theta^0)).$$ ∎

ESTIMATION OF THE DYNAMIC MECC MODEL

In this section, we briefly present a numerical method based on empirical likelihoods to estimate the dynamic MECC model specified in Equations (10.26)–(10.30). Basically, we need to estimate the set of parameters $\Xi = \{\theta_0, \ldots, \theta_{27}\}$. Let $\hat{\Xi}$ denote an estimate of Ξ, then our estimation procedure comprises the two steps described below.

Step 1: Let $MECC - likelihood(\Xi)$ denote the empirical log-likelihood function of Ξ, which can be computed in two substeps:

  (a) Given a value, Ξ, in view of Equations (10.27)–(10.30), we can compute measures of association, $\{\rho_{S_t}, \nu_{1,t}, \nu_{2,t}, \eta_t\}_{t=1}^{T}$.

  (b) Given these measures of association, compute the time-varying parameters of the MECC $(\Lambda_t, \forall t = 1, \ldots, T)$ by using the stochastic optimization algorithm to optimize the potential functions defined in Corollary 10.2. Hence, we can immediately obtain the empirical log-likelihood function: $MECC - likelihood(\Xi) = \frac{1}{T}\sum_{t=1}^{T}\log c(\hat{G}_{1,t}, \hat{G}_{2,t}, \Lambda_t)$, where $c(u, v, \Lambda)$ is the MECC density.

Step 2: In the sequel, use the stochastic optimization algorithm to find a global maximum value, $\hat{\Xi}$, for $MECC - likelihood(\Xi)$. This step requires the algorithm to go back to **Step 1** to recursively compute the MECC for each Ξ until a global maximum point is reached.

In order to reduce the computational time of finding the global maximum value of $MECC - likelihood(\Xi)$, we computed Λ_t, for $t = 1, \ldots, T$, in **Step 1**(b) by using an efficient interpolation method proposed by Beliakov (2006). This method requires constructing a common efficient interpolant, $g(\rho_{S_t}, \nu_{1,t}, \nu_{2,t}, \eta_t)$, which approximates the mapping, $\Lambda_t = f(\rho_{S_t}, \nu_{1,t}, \nu_{2,t}, \eta_t)$, from the domains of ρ_S, ν_1, ν_2 and η to the domains of Λ; and it is assumed that this mapping satisfies the following Lipschitz condition with a Lipschitz constant, M:

$$|f(x) - f(z)| \leq Md(x, z)$$

for all x and z, where $d(x, z)$ is a distance function. Assume that the mapping $f(x)$ exists, then $g(x)$ provides the best uniform approximation to $f(x)$ in the worst-case scenario – that is, $g(x)$ minimizes the maximum possible error given by

$$\max_{f} \max_{x \in X} |f(x) - g(x)|, \text{ where } X \text{ is the domain of } x.$$

In our empirical application, to construct $g(x)$, we first draw 50,000 sample values of measures of association, $\{\rho_{S_i}, v_{1,i}, v_{2,i}, \eta_i\}_{i=1}^{50,000}$, from their domains, then compute the corresponding values of the MECC parameters, $\{\Lambda_i\}_{i=1}^{50,000}$, by minimizing the potential functions. Next, given this sample of scattered data, $\{\rho_{S_i}, v_{1,i}, v_{2,i}, \eta_i, \Lambda_i\}_{i=1}^{50,000}$, we used the C++ interface developed by Beliakov (2006) to find $g(x)$. Thereby, we could substantially reduce our computational time by avoiding a rather time-consuming task of finding global optimal values (**Step 1**(b)) because the efficient interpolant $g(x)$ facilitates prompt computations of Λ from $\{\rho_S, v_1, v_2, \eta\}$.

Canonical Vine Copulas in the Context of Modern Portfolio Management: Are They Worth It?

Rand Kwong Yew Low[a]**, Jamie Alcock**[b,c]**, Robert Faff**[a]
and Timothy Brailsford[d]

[a]UQ Business School, University of Queensland
[b]School of Mathematics and Physics, University of Queensland
[c]Department of Land Economy, University of Cambridge
[d]Bond University

Abstract

In the context of managing downside correlations, we examine the use of multi-dimensional elliptical and asymmetric copula models to forecast returns for portfolios with 3–12 constituents. Our analysis assumes that investors have no short-sales constraints and a utility function characterized by the minimization of Conditional Value-at-Risk (CVaR). We examine the efficient frontiers produced by each model and focus on comparing two methods for incorporating scalable asymmetric dependence (AD) structures across asset returns using the Archimedean Clayton copula in an out-of-sample, long-run multi-period setting. For portfolios of higher dimensions, we find that modelling asymmetries within the marginals and the dependence structure with the Clayton canonical vine copula (CVC) consistently produces the highest-ranked outcomes across a range of statistical and economic metrics when compared to other models incorporating elliptical or symmetric dependence structures. Accordingly, we conclude that CVC copulas are 'worth it' when managing larger portfolios.

11.1   INTRODUCTION

Equity returns suffer from increased correlations during bear markets (Longin and Solnik, 1995, 2001; Ang and Chen, 2002). This characteristic, known as asymmetric or lower-tail dependence, violates the assumption of elliptical dependence that is the basis of modern portfolio theory and mean-variance analysis (Markowitz, 1952; Ingersoll, 1987). While forecasting models incorporating asymmetric dependence (AD) produce significant gains for the investor with no short-sales constraints, they have been limited to bivariate or trivariate settings using standard Archimedean copulas (Patton, 2004; Ba, 2011; Garcia and Tsafack, 2011). More advanced flexible multivariate copulas ('vine copulas') introduced by Aas *et al.* (2009) present an important opportunity for extending this literature further. Specifically, there are several interesting questions in the context of modern portfolio management. Does the more advanced Clayton canonical vine copula (CVC) produce economic and statistical outcomes superior to those of the Clayton standard copula (SC) in out-of-sample tests? Does the Clayton CVC exhibit superiority above some threshold size of portfolio? Does a more advanced model of the dependence structure produce outcomes superior to those of multi-variate normality?

We answer these questions using an out-of-sample, long-run, multi-period investor horizon setting with portfolios comprising up to 12 US industry indices in a tactical asset allocation exercise. It is worth noting that our chosen focus on indices as 'assets' delivers an important experimental advantage: collectively, the full set of 12 indices constitutes the entire US market index. Thus, due to a binding dimensionality constraint, by employing indices as the basic constituents of the portfolios, our analysis is far more comprehensive than the alternative approach of using individual stocks. Moreover, as each index consists of hundreds of stocks, our investigation effectively involves highly diversified portfolios that exhibit low levels of idiosyncratic risk compared to other applications that form portfolios of individual stocks. Asymmetric dependence is evident regardless of whether an investor has a large number of US stocks within an equity investment portfolio (Ang and Chen, 2002) or is internationally diversified (Longin and Solnik, 1995, 2001). Furthermore, Aggarwal and Aggarwal (1993) show that with 25 securities in a naive portfolio, the degree of negative skewness within the portfolio increases significantly and similar evidence is shown by Simkowitz and Beedles (1978) and Cromwell et al. (2000). Therefore, although diversification is prudent financial investment advice for 'normal' times, it becomes questionable when all stocks in the portfolio fall in times of market stress. Moreover, due to AD and negative skewness, the positive effects of diversification are greatly diminished when they are needed most (Chua et al., 2009). Thus, explicitly managing AD could be very worthwhile as investors might require additional compensation for undertaking downside risk (Ang et al., 2006), negative skewness (Simkowitz and Beedles, 1978; Cromwell et al., 2000) and have a preference for positively skewed portfolios (Arditti, 1967).

Our work is most relevant to Patton (2004) and Hatherley and Alcock (2007), who conduct studies upon portfolios of two and three assets respectively over investment horizons of less than a decade. Patton (2004) investigates whether asymmetries are predictable out-of-sample and portfolio decisions are improved by forecasting these asymmetries, as opposed to ignoring them over a single-period investment horizon. He shows that investors with no short-sales constraints (i.e., portfolio weights are allowed to be negative) experience economic gains. Hatherley and Alcock (2007) report that managing AD, using a Clayton standard copula (SC) against the benchmark multivariate normal probability model, results in reduced downside exposure. Patton (2009) states that the obvious and perhaps most difficult avenue for future research is the extension of copula-based multivariate time-series models to high dimensions. Such a breakthrough came with the CVC technology developed by Aas et al. (2009). The CVC consists of building blocks of pair copula and with a multitude of bivariate copulas from which to choose from, it is now possible to flexibly model the dependence structure for a multivariate joint distribution.

The novelty of our contribution lies in the non-trivial extension of this literature by incorporating methods that allow for higher scalability for capturing AD, with larger data sets over a multi-period investment horizon spanning several decades. Moreover, we apply a broad range of metrics to further investigate economic and statistical performance. We demonstrate how to meaningfully capture AD for higher portfolio dimensions by using the CVC model and mathematically expanding the SC.[1] A multi-period long-term investment horizon study is necessary, as Barberis (2000) finds that multi-period decisions are substantially different from single-period decisions due to hedging demands if investment opportunities are time-varying (Merton, 1971). As investors might have different risk preferences, testing portfolio management strategies should include the application of a variety of risk-adjusted measures that incorporate downside risk and robustness against non-linear payoffs. Using an array of metrics to gauge portfolio performance is important as the presence of

---

[1]A detailed introduction to copula theory can be found in Joe (1997) and Nelsen (2006). Other resources for vine copula theory can be found in Aas et al. (2009) and Kurowicka and Joe (2011).

distributional asymmetries within asset returns can impact investors' portfolio choices (Harvey and Siddique, 2000; Longin and Solnik, 2001; Harvey *et al.*, 2010). More specifically, our work manages AD by using the Clayton CVC that models AD of a portfolio of N assets with $N(N-1)/2$ parameters compared to the Clayton SC that employs just one parameter. Thus, the Clayton CVC, with its higher degree of parameterization, is capable of leading to superior forecasts of equity returns and improved portfolio management decisions. However, much of the forecasting literature indicates that more complicated models often provide poorer forecasts than simple and misspecified models (Swanson and White, 1997; Stock and Watson, 1999). Kritzman *et al.* (2010) state that practitioners often use simpler models to discriminate amongst investment opportunities, as complex econometric models can suffer from issues such as data mining, poor performance out-of-sample and failure to produce meaningful profitability in a portfolio management context.

Given this background, our work leads to a deeper understanding of whether the increase in parameterization of an asset portfolio leads to both statistical and economically significant benefits. From a modelling viewpoint, the lower the dimensionality of a model, the higher the reliability of the parameters (Ané and Kharoubi, 2003). Furthermore, the main feature of the CVC compared to the SC is its mathematical scalability for portfolios of high dimensions. Thus, we seek insights into the portfolio size over which the model exhibits superiority. Furthermore, we assess whether the modelling of the dependence structure or the modelling of the marginals has the greater impact on a portfolio. This allows practitioners to understand the areas of a probability model that need to be analysed further. We also demonstrate a method for building the CVC based on the sums of correlations of assets within the portfolio.

Our results show that for portfolios of 10 constituents and above, our most advanced model that captures asymmetries within the marginals and the dependence structure using the Clayton CVC consistently produces highly ranked outcomes across a range of statistical and economic performance metrics. Economic gains only exist for non-short-sales-constrained portfolios such as those used by hedge funds. In addition, it produces a returns distribution that exhibits significant positive skewness from a portfolio comprising industry indices that together represent the US market index. This is notable as US industry indices exhibit high levels of negative skewness. Our findings indicate that asymmetries should be incorporated in the modelling of both the marginals and the dependence structure and we find that modelling of asymmetries within the dependence structure has a greater impact than modelling of the marginals for portfolios of higher dimensions.

The chapter is organized as follows. Section 11.2 describes the data set. Section 11.3 details the methods used in modelling of the dependence structure and marginals, and the selection of the investor's utility function for portfolio optimization. Section 11.4 presents and discusses the empirical results of our study and we conclude in Section 11.5.

11.2 DATA

Our data set consists of US monthly returns on 12 indices, constituting the full US market (data sourced from Ken French's website).[2] The indices are manufacturing (Manuf), other, money, chemicals (Chems), consumer non-durables (NoDur), retail (Shops), consumer durables (Durbl), business equipment (BusEq), healthcare (Hlth), telecommunications (Telcm), utilities (Util) and energy (Enrgy). Similar to DeMiguel *et al.* (2009), we calculate arithmetic returns in excess of the US 1-month T-bill.

---

[2]The US market index is the value-weighted return on all NYSE, AMEX and NASDAQ stocks from CRSP. Industry indices are value-weighted returns formed by assigning each NYSE, AMEX and NASDAQ stock from CRSP to an industry portfolio according to its 4-digit SIC code.

TABLE 11.1 Input data descriptive statistics

Industry index	Mean	Std. deviation	Skewness	Kurtosis	Min	Max	Jarque–Bera
Manuf	0.55	0.054	−0.525	5.73	−29.15	21.55	203.12*
Other	0.39	0.056	−0.507	5.02	−29.92	18.80	121.71*
Money	0.51	0.055	−0.376	4.75	−22.40	20.51	87.43*
Chems	0.48	0.047	−0.240	5.16	−25.18	19.68	115.97*
NoDur	0.63	0.044	−0.296	5.08	−21.63	18.15	110.61*
Shops	0.57	0.053	−0.269	5.31	−28.91	25.22	133.19*
Durbl	0.42	0.063	0.146	8.31	−32.97	42.91	672.91*
BusEq	0.53	0.067	−0.213	4.14	−26.59	20.02	35.28*
Hlth	0.59	0.050	0.057	5.44	−21.07	29.07	142.20*
Telcm	0.39	0.047	−0.122	4.31	−15.97	21.98	42.10*
Util	0.37	0.041	−0.077	4.04	−12.94	18.22	26.00*
Enrgy	0.66	0.054	−0.001	4.47	−19.10	23.33	50.88*

This table presents the descriptive statistics for excess monthly returns (relative to the 1-month T-bill) of 12 US industry indices (sourced from Ken French's website). The full sample runs from July 1963 to December 2010, yielding 570 observations. The indices are manufacturing (Manuf), other, money, chemicals (Chems), consumer non-durables (NoDur), retail (Shops), consumer durables (Durbl), business equipment (BusEq), healthcare (Hlth), telecommunications (Telcm), utilities (Util) and energy (Enrgy). The mean, minimum and maximum are presented as percentages. Jarque–Bera tests the normality of the unconditional distribution of returns.
*Statistical significance at the 1% level.

The sample period extends from July 1963 to December 2010, yielding 570 observations in total. The first 120 observations are reserved for the parameterization process for our portfolio management strategy, while the out-of-sample period consists of 450 months from July 1973 to December 2010.

We implement our strategies in portfolios of 3, 6, 9, 10, 11 and 12 constituents, as shown in Table 11.1. All indices exhibit excess kurtosis and reject the null hypotheses for the Jarque–Bera test of normality at the 1% level. All indices exhibit negative skewness except for Durbl and Hlth. Durbl exhibits the minimum (−32.97%) and maximum (42.91%) return for our sample. We report sample correlations in Table 11.2. The highest correlation occurs between Manuf and Other (0.92), while the lowest correlation occurs between Util and BusEq (0.31).

The vine copula model by Aas *et al.* (2009) is a scalable methodology that can allow for large portfolios of assets but the user is constrained by the computational resources available. Our work involves the construction of investment portfolios consisting of indices as opposed to individual stocks. Modern portfolio theory suggests that such portfolios are more likely to exhibit elliptical dependence than are individual stocks. Thus, our analysis is biased against our empirical tests of portfolio optimization based on returns forecasts incorporating AD. Furthermore, by using indices we minimize other drawbacks that would occur with individual stocks – issues of size bias, selection bias, short-sales restrictions, idiosyncratic risk, higher transaction costs and illiquidity.

TABLE 11.2   Unconditional sample correlations

	Manuf	Other	Money	Chems	NoDur	Shops	Durbl	BusEq	Hlth	Telcm	Util	Enrgy
Manuf	1.00											
Other	0.92	1.00										
Money	0.81	0.83	1.00									
Chems	0.87	0.82	0.77	1.00								
NoDur	0.79	0.79	0.81	0.82	1.00							
Shops	0.82	0.83	0.79	0.77	0.83	1.00						
Durbl	0.85	0.79	0.74	0.74	0.68	0.76	1.00					
BusEq	0.79	0.78	0.63	0.64	0.59	0.71	0.68	1.00				
Hlth	0.67	0.69	0.68	0.72	0.77	0.67	0.52	0.61	1.00			
Telcm	0.63	0.63	0.64	0.55	0.60	0.62	0.59	0.61	0.52	1.00		
Util	0.53	0.53	0.60	0.53	0.61	0.46	0.45	0.31	0.47	0.50	1.00	
Enrgy	0.61	0.58	0.53	0.58	0.49	0.43	0.46	0.44	0.43	0.40	0.58	1.00

This table presents sample unconditional Pearson's correlations between monthly index returns for 12 US industries over the full sample period, July 1963 to December 2010. The indices are manufacturing (Manuf), other, money, chemicals (Chems), consumer non-durables (NoDur), retail (Shops), consumer durables (Durbl), business equipment (BusEq), healthcare (Hlth), telecommunications (Telcm), utilities (Util) and energy (Enrgy).

11.3   RESEARCH METHOD

Portfolio management is a two-stage process of (1) forecasting asset returns and (2) allocating weights to each asset within the portfolio (Markowitz, 1952). The portfolio weights are calculated based on optimizing an investor's utility function for the portfolio asset returns forecasts. Intuitively, our research method follows the typical scenario faced by a portfolio manager in an investment fund. As new information arrives for each asset at month t, the portfolio manager has to make a forecast of asset returns for the next month $t + 1$. Based on the forecast of asset returns, the manager rebalances the weights to construct a portfolio that achieves the desired investment objective. The objective might be to achieve maximum utility based on the investor's utility function or for the portfolio to maintain a fixed level of risk.

In the first stage of forecasting returns, similar to DeMiguel *et al.* (2009) we use a 'rolling-window' approach. Each month t, starting from $t = W + 1$, uses the data within the previous W months (sample window = 120 months) to parameterize the multivariate probability distribution (detailed in Section 11.3.1) and using Monte Carlo simulation[3] methods, 10,000 returns are produced using the Clayton Archimedean copula for each asset. These simulated data are used as a returns forecast. In the second stage, using these simulated data, we optimize a utility function defined by the minimization of

---

[3] We use the conditional sampling method for the SC as detailed in Cherubini *et al.* (2004, p. 183). For the CVC, we use the Monte Carlo simulation algorithm detailed by Aas *et al.* (2009).

Conditional Value-at-Risk (CVaR) (detailed in Section 11.3.2) to calculate the 'ideal' weights for the portfolio management strategy and apply it to each out-of-sample window month, $t + 1$. Therefore, the calculated target weights are continually updated in each time period as they are dependent upon maximizing the investor's utility function based on the asset returns forecast.

11.3.1 Multivariate Probability Modelling

The cumulative distribution function (cdf) of a random vector can be expressed in terms of its component marginal distribution functions and a copula that describes the dependence structure between these components (Sklar, 1973). The copula approach is designed to use subjective judgement about marginal distributions, leaving all information relating to the dependence structure (as represented by the copula function) to be estimated separately. Thus, copulas allow the creation of multivariate distributions that have the flexibility required of risk management models and overcome the limitations of traditional multivariate models.

A copula function $C(u_1, u_2, \dots, u_n)$ is defined as a cdf for a multivariate vector with support in $[0,1]^n$ and uniform marginals. The copula function is defined as:

$$C(u_1, u_2, \dots, u_n) = P(U_1 \leqslant u_1, \dots, U_n \leqslant u_n), \tag{11.1}$$

where $(U_1, U_2, \dots, U_n)$ is the corresponding multivariate vector. Arbitrary marginal distribution functions may be selected such that by using the transformations $U_i = F_i(X_i)$, Equation (11.2) defines a new multi-variate distribution evaluated by $x_1, x_2, \dots, x_n$ with marginals F_i, where $i = 1, 2, \dots, n$. The copula function is defined in terms of cumulative distributive functions as shown:

$$F(x_1, x_2, \dots, x_n) = C\left[F_1(x_1), F_2(x_2), \dots, F_n(x_n)\right]. \tag{11.2}$$

Sklar (1973) shows the converse of Equation (11.2), where any multivariate distribution F can be written in terms of its marginals using a copula representation. It is possible to represent the density of the copula if we assume F_i and C to be differentiable. The joint density function $f(x_1, x_2, \dots, x_n)$ is defined as:

$$f(x_1, x_2, \dots, x_n) = f_1(x_1) \times f_2(x_2) \times \cdots \times f_n(x_n) \times c\left[F_1(x_1), F_2(x_2), \dots, F_n(x_n)\right], \tag{11.3}$$

where the density of F_i is given by $f_i(x_i)$ and the density of the copula is given by:

$$c(u_1, u_2, \dots, u_n) = \frac{\partial^n C(u_1, u_2, \dots, u_n)}{\partial u_1 \partial u_2 \dots \partial u_n}. \tag{11.4}$$

As can be seen from Equation (11.3), under appropriate conditions, the joint density can be written as a product of the marginal densities and the copula density, as opposed to the traditional modelling approaches where the joint density is decomposed into a product of marginal and conditional densities. The dependence structure among the X_i's is captured by the density $C(u_1, u_2, \dots, u_n)$ while the f_i's capture the behaviour of the marginals. The copula is chosen to select the dependence between asset returns and is able to account for asymmetric and symmetric correlation structures depending upon the copula chosen.

11.3.1.1 Clayton Archimedean Copula

Archimedean copulas are commonly used due to their flexibility and usefulness in modelling complex dependence structures from a generator function as shown in Equation (11.5)

$$C(u_1, u_2, \dots, u_n) = G^{-1}\left[G(u_1) + G(u_2) + \cdots + G(u_n)\right]. \tag{11.5}$$

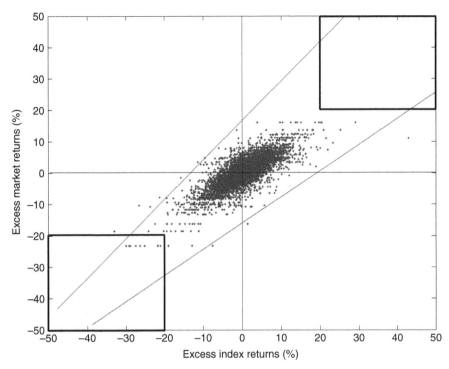

FIGURE 11.1 Empirical relation between the US market and industry indices. This figure plots monthly excess returns for the US market vs. 12 constituent industry indices from July 1963 to December 2010 (in excess of the US 1-month T-bill). The boxed regions highlight threshold return values above +20% and below −20% for the industry indices and the US market.

We use the Clayton copula due to its ability to parameterize lower-tail dependence across asset returns. Figure 11.1 is a plot of US monthly market returns against 12 counterpart US industry index returns from July 1963 to December 2010 (in excess of the 1-month T-bill rate). The 'fan-shape' behaviour exhibited by the index and market returns is indicative of an asymmetric (lower-tail) dependence structure. The boxed regions in Figure 11.1 show that the correlations between the aggregate US market and its constituent indices are higher (lower) when returns are below (above) the market monthly threshold return of −20% (+20%), as the density of points on the downside is greater than that on the upside (indeed the upside box is totally vacant). This pattern corroborates other studies (e.g., Longin and Solnik, 1995; Ang and Chen, 2002; Patton, 2004) that describe these conditional correlations as 'exceedance correlations'. Our application of the Clayton copula is such that lower-tail dependence across equity returns is accommodated but not imposed. By focusing on managing the scenario of lower-tail dependence, we seek to design a portfolio management strategy capable of providing reliably good performance during times of market stress (Chua *et al.*, 2009).

Figure 11.2 shows a variety of dependence structures for the bivariate case. If the Clayton copula or the Pearson's correlation parameters are close to zero, the dependence structure is circular as shown in Figure 11.2(a). Elliptical (Figure 11.2b) and asymmetric (Figure 11.2c) dependence structures are accommodated but not imposed by the covariance matrix and Clayton copula, respectively. It can be seen that the Clayton copula, with its ability to parameterize lower-tail dependence, is a more appealing model of actual returns in the long run when compared to the assumptions of Mean–Variance Portfolio Theory (MVPT), where asset returns are assumed to have elliptical dependence as shown in Figure 11.2(b).

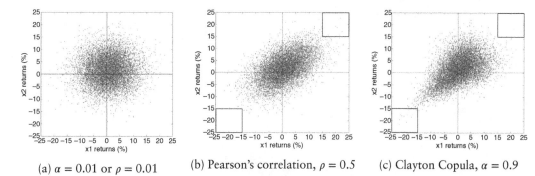

(a) $\alpha = 0.01$ or $\rho = 0.01$ (b) Pearson's correlation, $\rho = 0.5$ (c) Clayton Copula, $\alpha = 0.9$

FIGURE 11.2   Plots illustrating alternative dependence structures. This figure shows a variety of dependence structures for the bivariate case of x_1 and x_2 asset returns. (a) The circular dependence structure when the Pearson's correlation and Clayton copula parameters are close to zero. (b) The elliptical dependence structure produced for a correlation parameter of 0.5. (c) The asymmetric (lower-tail) dependence structure produced for a Clayton copula parameter of 0.9.

Substituting the Clayton copula generator function into Equation (11.5) and using Equation (11.4), for illustrative purposes, we can generate a Clayton SC probability distribution function (pdf) for six assets as shown:

$$c_{123456} = C_\alpha(u_1, u_2, \ldots, u_6)$$

$$= (u_1^{-\alpha} + u_2^{-\alpha} + u_3^{-\alpha} + u_4^{-\alpha} + u_5^{-\alpha} + u_6^{-\alpha} - 5)^{\frac{1}{\alpha}+6}. \tag{11.6}$$

Thus, lower-tail dependence across six assets is characterized by a single parameter α. This results in a multivariate probability distribution of the form given by Equation (11.7), where f_n denotes the marginal pdf and c_n is the copula pdf:

$$f_{12345} = f_1 \cdot f_2 \cdot f_3 \cdot f_4 \cdot f_5 \cdot f_6 \cdot c_{123456}. \tag{11.7}$$

11.3.1.2   Canonical Vine Copula   Conventionally, a copula model is limited to a 1-parameter or 2-parameter specification of the dependence structure, which represents a potentially severe empirical constraint. Clearly, when modelling the joint distribution of multiple assets, such limited parameter models are unlikely to adequately capture the dependence structure. Moreover, the Gaussian copula lacks tail dependence and even though the multivariate Student t copula is able to generate different tail dependence[4] for each pair of variables, it imposes the same upper and lower-tail dependence across all pairs. These limitations are overcome by the canonical vine model by building bivariate copulas of conditional distributions.

Canonical vine copulas are flexible multivariate copulas that are generated via hierarchical construction and can be decomposed into a cascade of bivariate copulas. The principle is to model dependence using simple local building blocks (pair-copulas) based on conditional independence. A joint probability density function of n variables $u_1, u_2, \ldots, u_n$ can be decomposed without loss of generality by iteratively conditioning as shown in Equation (11.8):

$$f(u_1, u_2, \ldots, u_n) = f(u_1) \cdot f(u_2|u_1) \cdot f(u_3|u_1, u_2) \ldots f(u_n|u_1, \ldots, u_{n-1}). \tag{11.8}$$

---

[4]Tail dependence for a multivariate Student t copula is a function of the correlation and degrees of freedom.

Each of the terms in this product can be decomposed further using conditional copulas. For example, the first conditional density can be decomposed into the copula function c_{12} (the copula linking u_1 and u_2) multiplied by the density of u_2 as shown in Equation (11.9), where $F_i(\cdot)$ is the cdf of u_i:

$$f(u_2|u_1) = c_{12}\left[F_1(u_1), F_2(u_2)\right] f_2(u_2). \tag{11.9}$$

Thus, the joint density of the three-dimensional case can be represented by a function of the bivariate conditional copulas and the marginal densities:

$$f(u_1, u_2, u_3) = c_{23|1}(F_{2|1}(u_2|u_1), F_{3|1}(u_3|u_1))c_{12}(F_1(u_1), F_2(u_2))$$
$$c_{13}(F_1(u_1), F_3(u_3))f_1(u_1)f_2(u_2)f_3(u_3). \tag{11.10}$$

Joe (1997) proves that conditional distribution functions may be solved using Equation (11.11):

$$F(u|v) = \frac{\partial C_{u,v_j|v_{-j}}(F(u|v_{-j}), F(v_j|v_{-j}))}{\partial F(v_j|v_{-j})}, \tag{11.11}$$

where v_{-j} is the vector v that excludes the component v_j.

While other vine specifications exist, such as the D-vine case (Aas *et al.*, 2009), we select the canonical vine alternative due to the efficiency of its hierarchical structure. If key variables that govern the interactions in the data set can be identified during the modelling process, it is possible to locate these variables towards the root of the canonical vine. Thus, we are able to build the canonical vine by ordering assets closer to the root of the structure by their degree of correlation with other assets within the portfolio.

If the Clayton CVC is implemented, the dependence structure of a portfolio of six assets would be parameterized with 15 pairwise copula parameters.[5] As a result, the multivariate probability distribution for the six-asset case is as shown in Equation (11.12), where f_n denotes the marginals pdf and c_n denotes the pairwise copula pdfs:

$$f_{123456} = f_1 \cdot f_2 \cdot f_3 \cdot f_4 \cdot f_5 \cdot f_6 \cdot c_{12} \cdot c_{13} \cdot c_{14} \cdot c_{15} \cdot c_{16} \cdot c_{23|1} \cdot c_{24|1}$$
$$\cdot c_{25|1} \cdot c_{26|1} \cdot c_{34|12} \cdot c_{35|12} \cdot c_{36|12} \cdot c_{45|123} \cdot c_{46|123} \cdot c_{56|1234}. \tag{11.12}$$

11.3.1.3 Marginals Modelling We model the marginals using two alternative methods. First, to establish a baseline, we assume that they adhere to a normal distribution. However, assumptions of normality within the marginals can lead to the copula model capturing asymmetries within the marginals. Thus, for further comparison between the standard copula and the vine copula model, the marginal distributions are also modelled using the univariate skewed Student t (Skew-T) setup of Hansen (1994) with constant unconditional mean and variance:[6]

$$y_{i,t} = c_{i,t} + \sqrt{h_{i,t}} \cdot z_{i,t}, \text{ for } i = 1, \dots, n, \tag{11.13}$$

---

[5]The number of parameters required to parameterize a dependence structure using a canonical vine model given a k-parameter copula is given by $k \sum_{i=1}^{N-1} i$, where N is the number of assets.
[6]Although return variance is known to be heteroscedastic, our study makes the simplifying assumption of homoscedasticity. This allows us to focus upon performance improvements by incorporating asymmetries into the dependence structure and marginal distribution, as these are identified to have a greater impact on the portfolio selection process (Scott and Horvath, 1980; Kane, 1982; Peiro, 1999; Harvey *et al.*, 2010). In untabulated analysis, when we incorporate asymmetric volatility in the marginals, using the GARCH-GJR model (Glosten *et al.*, 1993), we find no qualitative difference in results. Details (available from the authors upon request) are suppressed to conserve space.

$$h_{i,t} = \omega_i, \tag{11.14}$$

$$z_{i,t} \sim \text{skewed Student } t(v_i, \lambda_i), \tag{11.15}$$

where the skewed Student t density is given by

$$g(z|v, \lambda) = \begin{cases} bc\left(1 + \frac{1}{v-2}\left(\frac{bz+a}{1-\lambda}\right)^2\right)^{-(v+1)/2} & z < -a/b, \\ bc\left(1 + \frac{1}{v-2}\left(\frac{bz+a}{1+\lambda}\right)^2\right)^{-(v+1)/2} & z \geq -a/b. \end{cases} \tag{11.16}$$

The constants a, b and c are defined as

$$a = 4\lambda c\left(\frac{v-2}{v-1}\right), b^2 = 1 + 3\lambda^2 - a^2, c = \frac{\Gamma\left(\frac{v+1}{2}\right)}{\sqrt{\pi(v-2)}\Gamma\left(\frac{v}{2}\right)}. \tag{11.17}$$

Using a skewed marginal distribution gives greater confidence that any asymmetry found in the dependence structure truly reflects dependence and cannot be attributed to poor modelling of the marginals. During bear markets we are likely to observe a higher incidence of large negative returns than of large positive returns (of similar magnitude) in a booming market. Thus, we expect this observation to be captured by a negative λ (indicating a left-skewed density).

11.3.1.4 Portfolio Parameterization Process Given that the Clayton SC parameterizes lower-tail dependence with a single parameter, the order of the assets entering the portfolio has no impact on the modelling process. In contrast, the hierarchical structure of the CVC means that the ordering is important. Accordingly, we design the canonical vine structure by placing assets that have the highest degree of linear correlation with all the other assets in the sample window at the 'root' of the structure. This is achieved by calculating and summing the Pearson's correlations between all assets during the sample window. More formally, we define the correlation metric in Equation (11.18):

$$\Theta_y = \sum_{x=1}^{N} \theta_{xy}, \text{ where } x, y \in N. \tag{11.18}$$

θ_{xy} is an $N \times N$ matrix of the Pearson's correlation parameter of the monthly returns between each pair of assets x and y that are both part of our portfolio of N assets. Θ_y is an $N \times 1$ matrix where each element is the sum of the Pearson's correlation parameter of y with all other assets x. The largest value in Θ_y has the highest absolute linear correlation with all other assets within the portfolio during the sample window and is placed at the root of the hierarchical structure of the canonical vine.

In our application of the model, we use maximum likelihood estimation. Due to the large number of parameters that need to be incorporated in our model, numerical maximization of the likelihood function is difficult and requires substantial computer resources. For example, for each of the 450 out-of-sample time periods, a portfolio of 12 assets modelled using the Clayton CVC with univariate skewed Student t marginals requires an estimate of 114 parameters.[7] We use the inference for margins (IFM) (Joe, 1997) method that is a 2-step parametric estimation procedure where the copula and marginal distribution parameters are estimated separately.

---

[7]For the 12-asset case, a Clayton CVC requires an estimate of 66 pairwise correlation parameters. Each of the Skew-T marginal distributions require an estimate of four parameters, namely, the unconditional mean, unconditional variance, skewness and degrees of freedom.

11.3.2   Optimization of the Investor's Utility Function

Given that our focus is on lower-tail dependence, it makes sense to select an optimization strategy that has a meaningful downside risk emphasis. Accordingly, we choose to minimize CVaR in preference to Value-at-Risk (VaR), as the former metric is considered to be a coherent risk measure (Uryasev, 2000). It is suitable for an investor who is focused on minimizing downside risk and is indifferent (or might even prefer) upside variance. Furthermore, it generates an efficient frontier that incorporates non-normality. Thus, if asset returns exhibit lower-tail dependence, more emphasis will be placed on reducing this risk in comparison to MVPT portfolios that assume quadratic utility and ignore all higher moments of the returns distribution. Optimizing portfolios to reduce CVaR is a linear programming exercise and leads to lower values of VaR. Rockafellar and Uryasev (2000) present CVaR in integral form as shown below:

$$\phi_\beta(\mathbf{w}) = \frac{1}{1-\beta} \int_{f(\mathbf{w},\mathbf{r}) \geq \alpha_\beta(\mathbf{w})} f(\mathbf{w},\mathbf{r})p(\mathbf{r})d\mathbf{r}, \tag{11.19}$$

where a loss function is presented by $f(\mathbf{w}, \mathbf{r})$ and the probability that $\mathbf{r}$ occurs is $p(\mathbf{r})$. In addition, they show that, when Monte Carlo integration is used, Equation (11.20) is a suitable approximation to minimize CVaR for a given level of return:

$$\min_{(\mathbf{w},\alpha)} F_\alpha(\mathbf{w}, \beta) = \alpha + \frac{1}{q(1-\beta)} \sum_{k=1}^{q} [-\mathbf{w}^T\mathbf{r}_k - \alpha]^+, \tag{11.20}$$

where

$$\mu(\mathbf{w}) \leq -R, \tag{11.21}$$

$$w^T \mathbf{1} = 1, \tag{11.22}$$

q represents the number of samples generated by Monte Carlo simulation, α represents VaR and $\mathbf{1}$ is a vector of ones. β represents the threshold value usually set at 0.99 or 0.95 and $\mathbf{r}_k$ is the kth vector of simulated returns. The vector of portfolio weights, $\mathbf{w}$, is extracted from the optimization procedure to generate the portfolio that minimizes CVaR for a given R. As we consider the investor who is averse to extreme downside losses, we set β to 0.99 – analogous to an investor who wishes to minimize losses at the 1% level of CVaR, similar to Basel (2004) requirements.

11.4   RESULTS

We investigate the applicability of the different multivariate probability models in the context of investors who wish to minimize the event of extreme losses within their portfolio. First, we perform an in-sample study to observe the efficient frontiers produced from a range of probability models and also from historical data of index excess returns for portfolios of different sizes. We perform this analysis to observe which probability model produces an efficient frontier closest to that of historical returns. Second, we perform a multi-period, long-term, out-of-sample study which uses the probability models as returns forecasts and optimize our portfolios to minimize CVaR. We use a wide range of statistical and economic metrics, including VaR backtests, to assess the superiority of each model in an out-of-sample portfolio management context.

11.4.1   Efficient Frontiers, E (R) vs. CVaR

Figure 11.3 shows the efficient frontiers produced when we apply simulated returns data generated from several multivariate probability models, and historical excess returns data, over the entire sample

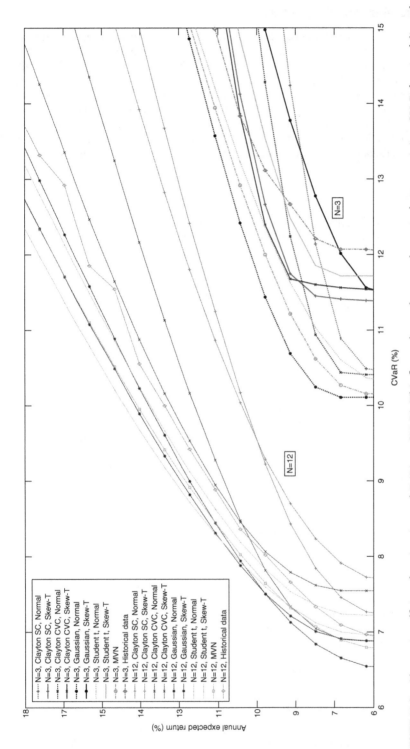

FIGURE 11.3 Alternative efficient frontiers (annual $E(R)$ vs. CVaR). This figure shows the annual expected returns against CVaR for portfolios of 3 and 12 assets. Nine alternative strategies are implemented for each portfolio using the full sample from July 1963 to December 2010. Clayton SC and Clayton CVC models allow for asymmetric dependence. Models that allow for elliptical dependence structures are the Gaussian, Student t copulas and MVN models. The Skew-T model allows for asymmetries within the marginals while the Normal model does not.

period from June 1963 to December 2010 without constraining short-sales. Annual expected returns are plotted against CVaR as a measure of risk. We use an in-sample analysis to investigate which multivariate probability model produces an efficient frontier closest to that of the historical data of excess index returns.

The copulas used are (1) Clayton SC; (2) Clayton CVC; (3) Student *t*; and (4) Gaussian. The marginals are either modelled as a normal (Normal) or with unconditional mean and variance and incorporating skewness and kurtosis using the model of Hansen (1994) within the resulting error distribution (Skew-T). The multivariate normal (MVN) model is included as a benchmark to indicate the resulting efficient frontier based on the assumptions of MVPT, where the marginals are normal and the elliptical dependence structure is defined by the covariance matrix.

For the three-asset case, we find clustering of efficient frontiers largely based on whether the marginals are normal or Skew-T. Models with normal marginals underestimate risk relative to the Skew-T. Furthermore, elliptical dependence models with normal marginals generate efficient frontiers that cluster together (e.g., MVN, Student *t* Normal, Gaussian Normal) and tend to underestimate risk relative to the models incorporating asymmetries either in the dependence structure or in the marginals. However, when elliptical dependence structures are modelled with Skew-T marginals (e.g., Student *t* Skew-T, Gaussian Skew-T), the efficient frontier changes considerably. These findings are consistent with the intuition that in the case of modelling small portfolios, modelling of the marginals will have a greater effect on the portfolio than the dependence structure. When Skew-T marginals are used, only asymmetries within the dependence structure need to be modelled by the copula and in the case of a small portfolio, there are no significant improvements to be gained by using the CVC. The efficient frontier produced by using historical returns is closer to the models that incorporate asymmetries within the marginals with the Skew-T.

For the 12-asset case, models incorporating elliptical dependence structures cluster together (e.g., MVN, Gaussian, Student *t*) even though Skew-T marginals are used. Visibly different efficient frontiers are present for the Clayton CVC and SC, even when Skew-T or normal marginals are used. Elliptical dependence structures generally underestimate the level of risk compared to AD structures. For elliptical dependence models, normal marginals underestimate the level of risk relative to Skew-T marginals. In an opposing fashion, for AD models, normal marginals produce efficient frontiers that overestimate the level of risk relative to Skew-T marginals. As the mathematical model that generates an efficient frontier closest to that produced by historical returns data is the most suitable in a portfolio and risk management context, this is indicative that the Clayton CVC model with Skew-T marginals provides the closest fit in the 12-asset case.

Similar to modern portfolio theory for large portfolios, modelling of asymmetry within the dependence structure has a much greater impact on the efficient frontier than just incorporating it in the modelling of the marginals. The diversification effect is visible as the efficient frontier for 12 assets dominates each three-asset counterpart, irrespective of the model being used. The efficient frontiers produced by historical returns for portfolios of 12 and 3 assets are closest to models that allow for asymmetries in the dependence structure and marginals. Therefore, from an in-sample perspective, multivariate probability models that do not incorporate these asymmetries can produce less reliable forecasts.

11.4.2 Out-of-Sample Portfolio Performance

We study the use of multivariate probability models incorporating asymmetries within the dependence structure or marginals in portfolio asset returns forecasts. We then optimize our portfolios to minimize CVaR. This out-of-sample analysis is performed in a long-run, multi-period investor horizon from June 1973 to December 2010. We investigate the Clayton SC with normal marginals (SC-N), Clayton CVC with normal marginals (CVC-N), Clayton SC with Skew-T marginals (SC-S) and Clayton CVC with Skew-T marginals (CVC-S). We explore their performance out-of-sample in relation to each other and against the benchmark of the MVN probability model. As the SC-N, CVC-N, SC-S and CVC-S models have in common the incorporation of returns asymmetry in some form, we will refer to them collectively as asymmetric returns (AR) models. As before, all portfolio strategies are not short-sales constrained.

11.4.2.1 Descriptive Statistics of Portfolio Strategies Table 11.3 shows the descriptive statistics of the returns distribution for each of the five portfolio strategies; we report mean, standard deviation, skewness, kurtosis, minimum value, maximum value and maximum drawdown. Maximum drawdown is the largest peak-to-trough percentage drop in returns during the investment period. As the size of the portfolio increases, across all portfolio strategies, the mean tends to improve (the one contrary case is SC-N) and the standard deviation decreases. This supports the maxim that increasing the number of assets in an investment portfolio achieves diversification benefits.

SC-N produces the highest mean when there are three assets. The most advanced model, CVC-S, produces the highest mean for 6, 10, 11 and 12 assets, while CVC-N produces the highest mean for the nine-assets case. These results are indicative that models that account for asymmetry in some way outperform the benchmark model (MVN) in terms of a higher mean value. Notably, the mean for SC-N underperforms the MVN benchmark beyond three assets, suggesting that the covariance matrix is able to capture the dependence model in a superior fashion. As the number of assets within the portfolio increases, the SC parameter asymptotes towards zero and is unable to capture AD sufficiently. The CVC models (CVC-N and CVC-S) are not restricted in this fashion mathematically and produce higher means than SC-N for portfolios of six assets and above. Similarly, the SC-S produces higher means than the SC-N as the former captures asymmetries within the marginals whereas the SC-N does not.

MVN exhibits the lowest standard deviation for portfolios comprising six assets and above. SC models exhibit higher standard deviation than the CVC models for all portfolio sizes. However, the higher standard deviations exhibited by the AR models could be indicative of a larger upside variance that is desirable for loss-averse investors. Therefore, we explore the performance of the strategies in relation to a range of downside risk measures in Section 11.4.2.2. For portfolios exceeding nine assets, CVC-S consistently produces highly positively skewed returns – a desirable attribute, especially given that (a) the constituent indices in our data set largely exhibit negative skewness and (b) investors are likely to prefer positively skewed portfolios. In addition, CVC-S also exhibits the lowest maximum drawdown for portfolios of 10 assets and above. For any given portfolio size, a strategy that incorporates asymmetry in some form exhibits returns with a much higher level of skewness and kurtosis compared to the benchmark model (MVN). Analysis of the minimum and maximum returns shows that the high levels of kurtosis are largely attributed to the exposure of the SC and CVC to large maximum returns. Finally, we observe that CVC-S produces the highest mean, skewness (second highest for portfolio size 12) and lowest maximum drawdown for portfolios of 10 assets and above.

11.4.2.2 Risk-Adjusted Performance Table 11.4 reports a range of risk-adjusted measures used to assess the out-of-sample performance of each portfolio management strategy. The Sharpe ratio penalizes the entire standard deviation of portfolio returns, whereas the Sortino ratio penalizes only downside standard deviation. The Omega ratio is a practical measure that makes no assumptions regarding investor risk preferences or utility functions, except that investors prefer more to less. The MPPM is a portfolio ranking metric developed by Goetzmann *et al.* (2007) for robustness against non-linear payoffs from managed portfolios.[8] The Mean/CVaR and Mean/VaR metrics measure portfolio performance relative to extreme downside risk exposure at the 1% level. The best performing strategies exhibit the highest values for each measure.

---

[8] Goetzmann *et al.* (2007) test seven alternative measures of portfolio performance and assess their vulnerability to manipulation with a number of simple dynamic strategies. As recommended by Goetzmann *et al.* (2007), we use a relative risk aversion parameter of 3.

TABLE 11.3 Out-of-sample copula-based portfolio strategy descriptive statistics

Metric	Method	Portfolio size, N					
		3	6	9	10	11	12
Mean	SC-N	0.57	−0.01	0.20	0.14	0.04	0.29
	CVC-N	0.35	0.23	0.49	0.36	0.26	0.42
	SC-S	0.33	0.06	0.09	0.32	0.10	0.48
	CVC-S	0.22	0.26	0.35	0.41	0.41	0.52
	MVN	0.53	0.20	0.38	0.27	0.23	0.42
Std. dev.	SC-N	0.090	0.079	0.068	0.067	0.063	0.061
	CVC-N	0.085	0.066	0.068	0.063	0.059	0.055
	SC-S	0.088	0.074	0.068	0.067	0.062	0.061
	CVC-S	0.083	0.068	0.065	0.061	0.060	0.055
	MVN	0.086	0.057	0.058	0.054	0.053	0.050
Skewness	SC-N	−0.30	1.55	0.86	0.93	0.86	1.42
	CVC-N	−0.49	−0.67	1.08	0.67	0.83	1.02
	SC-S	−0.31	−0.74	0.73	1.05	0.73	1.09
	CVC-S	−0.59	−0.75	0.76	1.11	1.52	1.20
	MVN	−0.34	−0.43	0.61	0.38	0.66	0.30
Kurtosis	SC-N	8.62	27.34	11.77	12.67	13.63	17.51
	CVC-N	7.17	5.55	13.48	12.13	17.12	15.32
	SC-S	6.67	8.14	13.37	14.68	10.91	14.41
	CVC-S	5.96	6.80	13.69	17.46	23.59	17.85
	MVN	8.62	5.05	9.95	8.32	11.00	8.57
Min	SC-N	−47.55	−33.79	−22.29	−25.42	−23.78	−22.00
	CVC-N	−47.55	−26.54	−23.60	−23.22	−29.26	−21.03
	SC-S	−41.73	−37.74	−26.23	−27.46	−23.62	−24.49
	CVC-S	−41.53	−31.14	−28.79	−23.45	−22.71	−20.83
	MVN	−47.55	−22.41	−20.80	−18.48	−17.72	−17.74
Max	SC-N	50.78	80.26	52.22	51.80	49.92	54.41
	CVC-N	35.34	25.08	54.28	48.76	51.32	46.81
	SC-S	41.99	34.08	55.32	55.00	45.93	52.27
	CVC-S	31.17	31.46	53.94	54.74	59.33	50.05
	MVN	42.68	21.84	41.64	36.77	41.05	35.23
Max. drawdown	SC-N	94.15	98.30	94.37	94.24	93.47	77.78
	CVC-N	91.15	96.61	88.49	91.25	90.65	75.05
	SC-S	87.95	96.99	93.88	87.13	91.58	68.01
	CVC-S	96.10	94.54	88.91	81.40	85.63	65.65
	MVN	91.80	93.72	86.09	87.05	87.68	70.49

This table reports a statistical overview of the returns distributions generated by each portfolio strategy out-of-sample. The mean, minimum, maximum and maximum drawdown are presented as percentages. SC-N is the Clayton standard copula (SC) with normal marginals, CVC-N is the Clayton canonical vine copula (CVC) with normal marginals, SC-S is the Clayton SC with Skew-T marginals, CVC-S is the Clayton CVC with Skew-T marginals and MVN is the multivariate normal model (benchmark case).

TABLE 11.4   Out-of-sample risk-adjusted performance of copula-based portfolio strategies

Risk-adjusted metric	Method	Portfolio size, N					
		3	6	9	10	11	12
Sharpe ratio	SC-N	0.064	−0.001	0.030	0.020	0.007	0.048
	CVC-N	0.041	0.035	0.073	0.057	0.045	0.076
	SC-S	0.037	0.008	0.014	0.048	0.016	0.079
	CVC-S	0.027	0.038	0.054	0.067	0.068	0.094
	MVN	0.061	0.035	0.066	0.050	0.043	0.084
Sortino ratio	SC-N	0.091	−0.002	0.044	0.030	0.009	0.075
	CVC-N	0.057	0.046	0.113	0.085	0.066	0.117
	SC-S	0.052	0.010	0.019	0.073	0.023	0.123
	CVC-S	0.037	0.051	0.080	0.101	0.103	0.146
	MVN	0.088	0.048	0.100	0.074	0.064	0.124
Omega ratio	SC-N	1.201	0.996	1.090	1.061	1.019	1.148
	CVC-N	1.122	1.100	1.238	1.181	1.142	1.248
	SC-S	1.109	1.023	1.040	1.154	1.046	1.248
	CVC-S	1.076	1.115	1.166	1.211	1.223	1.306
	MVN	1.194	1.099	1.202	1.148	1.127	1.254
MPPM	SC-N	−0.037	−0.075	−0.030	−0.037	−0.042	−0.007
	CVC-N	−0.054	−0.028	0.006	−0.003	−0.010	0.015
	SC-S	−0.060	−0.066	−0.044	−0.014	−0.034	0.014
	CVC-S	−0.064	−0.028	−0.008	0.006	0.007	0.027
	MVN	−0.034	−0.016	0.006	−0.002	−0.006	0.020
Mean/VaR 1%	SC-N	2.31	−0.04	1.04	0.73	0.21	2.21
	CVC-N	1.41	0.97	2.61	1.87	1.50	2.71
	SC-S	1.29	0.21	0.46	1.74	0.62	3.24
	CVC-S	0.86	1.05	1.83	2.54	2.25	3.81
	MVN	2.25	1.20	2.57	2.02	1.74	3.23
Mean/CVaR 1%	SC-N	1.63	−0.04	0.97	0.62	0.19	1.63
	CVC-N	1.07	0.92	2.45	1.72	1.24	2.32
	SC-S	0.99	0.18	0.40	1.48	0.51	2.70
	CVC-S	0.70	0.97	1.64	2.15	1.99	3.04
	MVN	1.52	1.00	2.13	1.66	1.43	2.68

This table reports a range of risk-adjusted measures for the portfolio management strategies out-of-sample. The Sharpe (Sortino) ratio is the ratio of mean excess return to the total standard deviation (lower partial moment) of the portfolio. The Omega ratio is a probability weighted ratio of gains to losses relative to a threshold value of 0%. The Manipulation Proof Performance Measure (MPPM) is a metric that is robust against portfolios with non-linear payoffs. Mean/VaR and Mean/CVaR capture portfolio performance relative to extreme downside risk at the 1% level. SC-N is the Clayton standard copula (SC) with normal marginals, CVC-N is the Clayton canonical vine copula (CVC) with normal marginals, SC-S is the Clayton SC with Skew-T marginals, CVC-S is the Clayton CVC with Skew-T marginals and MVN is the multivariate normal model (benchmark case).

Across all portfolio sizes, at least one of the AR models outperform the MVN benchmark for the Sharpe, Sortino and Omega metrics. For the MPPM metric, this result holds true for portfolios of nine assets and above. This is also generally the case for Mean/VaR and Mean/CVaR, except for a portfolio of six assets where MVN produces the highest value. Thus, based on our analysis, models incorporating return asymmetries in some form outperform the MVN benchmark.

Across the Sharpe, Sortino and Omega ratios, it is observed that as the portfolio increases in size, so does the level of complexity required in the model to produce the highest ranked outcome. For portfolio sizes above three assets, the CVC model outperforms its counterpart SC model across the Sharpe, Sortino and Omega ratios. While SC-N excels in our smallest portfolio setting, it performs very poorly across all metrics for portfolios of six assets and above. This finding suggests that the Clayton SC is too simplistic and is unable to meaningfully capture AD. CVC-S excels in large portfolios of 10 assets and above and performs poorly for small portfolios of three assets. This contrast is potentially due to the fact that there is little or no benefit to be gained by using a complex model of the dependence structure and marginals for simpler, smaller portfolios. In such cases, using advanced models induces estimation error which swamps any benefits from the modelling, resulting in poor portfolio decisions.

For the MPPM, Mean/VaR and Mean/CVaR metrics, CVC-S consistently produces the highest ranked outcomes for portfolios of 10 assets and above. The latter two are indicative that this CVC method is able to produce a higher return without a substantial increase in downside exposure. At less than 10 assets, MVN produces the highest ranked MPPM values but some of these values are negative due to non-linear payoffs.

Generally, these results support the view that increases in model complexity and parameterization for small portfolios have little or even negative benefits due to noise-prone estimation. At 10 assets and above, CVC-S consistently achieves the highest rank across all portfolio metrics. As the number of assets within the portfolio increases, the greater degree of parameterization in the modelling process of CVC-S produces various out-of-sample benefits including improved risk-adjusted returns and performance benefits robust against non-linear payoffs.

11.4.2.3 Portfolio Re-balancing Analysis Our investigation re-calculates the desired target weights every month and the portfolio is re-balanced accordingly. In such a multi-period setting, adjustments to portfolio weights are due to the volatility of out-of-sample asset returns and changes in investment decisions. Since we use the same out-of-sample data for each portfolio size, the adjustments to portfolio weights capture the varying changes in investment decisions made by each portfolio strategy. Large portfolio adjustments due to re-balancing are undesirable for two reasons. First, they are difficult to implement and can undermine the feasibility of a portfolio strategy. Second, other things equal, a superior strategy should require smaller adjustments to asset weights rather than large volatile changes each period.

Table 11.5 shows the variance, maximum positive and maximum negative portfolio asset weight adjustments required to rebalance to the desired target weight for each strategy. For example, in portfolios of 11 assets, the CVC-S model produces a maximum positive target weight adjustment of 4.23 (i.e., the weight of one portfolio asset moves from −1.50 to 2.73) and a maximum negative target weight adjustment of −1.77 (i.e., the weight of one portfolio asset moves from 1.23 to −0.54). For portfolios of 10 assets and above, CVC models generally exhibit lower variance in weight adjustments compared to SC models. At nine assets and above, the MVN benchmark has the highest variance in portfolio weight adjustments. This higher variance is undesirable in practice and might lead to higher turnover. Also, the magnitude of MVN's negative portfolio weight adjustment is much larger relative to the other strategies. This suggests that MVN might require more downward adjustments than other approaches. Finally, we observe that the degree of variance and the maximum positive or negative adjustment in portfolio weights required to execute each strategy tends to decrease as the size of the portfolio increases.

TABLE 11.5 Portfolio re-balancing analysis across out-of-sample copula-based portfolio strategies

Metric	Method	Portfolio size, N					
		3	6	9	10	11	12
Variance	SC-N	112.62	15.07	0.57	0.23	0.16	0.03
	CVC-N	116.74	9.15	0.84	0.15	0.14	0.03
	SC-S	108.25	8.33	0.66	0.18	0.10	0.04
	CVC-S	107.50	16.58	0.71	0.17	0.12	0.04
	MVN	113.12	10.55	1.49	0.23	0.23	0.07
Maximum positive	SC-N	7.92	8.59	5.18	5.11	6.26	3.06
adjustment	CVC-N	8.51	6.76	5.32	4.09	3.64	3.24
	SC-S	7.93	8.14	5.30	4.74	4.00	3.39
	CVC-S	7.09	6.56	5.29	4.28	4.23	3.48
	MVN	7.92	6.35	6.04	3.28	4.05	3.03
Maximum negative	SC-N	−8.57	−7.17	−2.70	−2.18	−1.86	−0.86
adjustment	CVC-N	−9.24	−6.45	−2.74	−2.20	−1.70	−1.46
	SC-S	−8.49	−4.68	−2.59	−1.82	−1.89	−1.33
	CVC-S	−7.60	−6.40	−2.50	−1.87	−1.77	−1.50
	MVN	−8.57	−6.44	−5.06	−3.19	−3.12	−2.72

This table shows the variance, maximum positive and maximum negative asset re-balancing adjustments for each portfolio strategy out-of-sample. SC-N is the Clayton standard copula (SC) with normal marginals, CVC-N is the Clayton canonical vine copula (CVC) with normal marginals, SC-S is the Clayton SC with Skew-T marginals, CVC-S is the Clayton CVC with Skew-T marginals and MVN is the multivariate normal model (benchmark case).

11.4.2.4 Economic Performance Table 11.6 reports three alternative economic metrics across the portfolio management strategies. Specifically, we model terminal wealth by hypothetically investing $100 at the start of the out-of-sample periods for each portfolio management strategy. To gauge the feasibility of implementing each strategy, we also calculate the average turnover requirement and the effect of transaction costs on each portfolio. The average turnover is calculated as the average sum of the absolute value of the trades across the N available assets following DeMiguel *et al.* (2009):

$$\text{Average turnover} = \frac{1}{T-M} \sum_{t=1}^{T-M} \sum_{j=1}^{N} \left(|w_{k,j,t+1} - w_{k,j,t+}| \right), \tag{11.23}$$

where N is the total number of assets in the portfolio, T is the total length of the time series, M is the sample period used to parameterize the forecast models, $w_{k,j,t+1}$ is the desired target portfolio weight for asset j at time $t + 1$ using strategy k and $w_{k,j,t+}$ is the counterpart portfolio weight before re-balancing. Similar to DeMiguel *et al.* (2009), we apply proportional transaction costs of 1 basis point per transaction [as assumed in Balduzzi and Lynch (1999) based on studies of transaction costs by Fleming *et al.* (1995) for trades on futures contracts on the S&P 500 index].

For portfolios of 10 assets and above, CVC-S produces the largest terminal wealth – regardless of whether transaction costs are included or not. Even though CVC-S's re-balancing decisions require higher turnover compared to the other strategies, the higher costs are still outweighed by the greater economic benefits. SC-S is the second best performing strategy irrespective of transaction costs and exhibits much lower turnover requirements compared to CVC-S. While SC-N performs well for small

TABLE 11.6 Economic measures of out-of-sample performance of copula-based portfolio strategies

Economic metric	Method	Portfolio size, N					
		3	6	9	10	11	12
Terminal wealth exc.	SC-N	199.18	24.03	90.08	67.52	49.51	167.96
transaction costs	CVC-N	86.36	101.54	336.93	210.54	151.43	338.45
	SC-S	72.60	34.86	54.14	159.50	65.99	385.11
	CVC-S	53.41	109.90	190.00	276.84	283.71	524.93
	MVN	187.41	117.00	266.36	177.73	150.56	376.20
Average turnover	SC-N	2.15	2.32	1.75	1.30	1.43	1.21
	CVC-N	2.12	2.29	1.83	1.46	1.65	1.50
	SC-S	2.47	2.43	2.20	1.55	1.61	1.32
	CVC-S	2.43	2.65	2.26	1.86	1.75	1.65
	MVN	1.62	1.87	1.87	1.58	1.77	1.61
Terminal wealth inc.	SC-N	180.77	21.65	83.26	63.67	46.43	159.06
transaction costs	CVC-N	78.50	91.60	310.26	197.12	140.62	316.36
	SC-S	64.97	31.25	49.04	148.77	61.37	362.88
	CVC-S	47.88	97.55	171.61	254.64	262.17	487.34
	MVN	174.24	107.53	244.87	165.55	139.01	349.98

This table shows the hypothetical terminal wealth generated by each portfolio management strategy. Terminal wealth is modelled as the final portfolio value (either excluding or including transaction costs) assuming an initial investment of $100 at the start of the out-of-sample period for each strategy. The turnover required to implement each strategy is also reported and can be interpreted as the average percentage of portfolio wealth traded in each period. The final portfolio value including transaction costs assumes transaction costs of 1 bps per transaction. SC-N is the Clayton standard copula (SC) with normal marginals, CVC-N is the Clayton canonical vine copula (CVC) with normal marginals, SC-S is the Clayton SC with Skew-T marginals, CVC-S is the Clayton CVC with Skew-T marginals and MVN is the multivariate normal model (benchmark case).

portfolios of three assets, at six assets and above, it exhibits the lowest final portfolio values and has the lowest turnover requirements in portfolios of nine assets and above. For portfolios of six assets and above, CVC-N and CVC-S outperform SC-N and SC-S, respectively. This shows that the higher degree of parameterization of CVC models leads to performance benefits above the simpler SC model for larger portfolios.

11.4.2.5 Value-at-Risk (VaR) Backtests Table 11.7 shows the performance of our portfolio management strategies using a range of VaR backtests at the 1% level, similar to Basel (2004) requirements. During each out-of-sample period, a VaR violation is recorded when the portfolio strategy return is less than the 1% VaR value of the total forecast return series for all constituent assets within the portfolio (Christoffersen, 2012). The Percentage of Failure Likelihood Ratio (PoFLR) and Conditional Coverage Likelihood Ratio (CCLR) are test statistics designed by Kupiec (1995) and Christoffersen (2012), respectively. The PoFLR focuses on the property of unconditional coverage whereas the CCLR incorporates both unconditional coverage and independence testing. Intuitively, tests of unconditional coverage indicate the magnitude of the difference between the actual and promised percentage of VaR violations in a risk management model and independence testing indicates the existence of serial VaR violations in a row. Large PoFLR and CCLR values are indicative that the proposed risk or portfolio management strategy systematically understates or overstates the portfolio's underlying level of risk. Therefore, a

TABLE 11.7 Value-at-Risk (VaR) backtests across copula-based portfolio strategies

VaR backtest metric	Method	Portfolio size, N					
		3	6	9	10	11	12
Percentage of failure likelihood ratio	SC-N	42.22	45.70	15.37	15.37	12.98	5.04
		(0.00)	(0.00)	(0.00)	(0.00)	(0.00)	(0.02)
	CVC-N	42.22	32.32	12.98	8.67	5.04	3.52
		(0.00)	(0.00)	(0.00)	(0.00)	(0.02)	(0.06)
	SC-S	42.22	32.32	10.75	10.75	5.04	1.20
		(0.00)	(0.00)	(0.00)	(0.00)	(0.02)	(0.27)
	CVC-S	38.82	20.54	5.04	3.52	2.23	0.46
		(0.00)	(0.00)	(0.02)	(0.06)	(0.14)	(0.50)
	MVN	29.21	15.37	2.23	2.23	3.52	2.23
		(0.00)	(0.00)	(0.14)	(0.14)	(0.06)	(0.14)
Conditional coverage likelihood ratio	SC-N	44.15	64.67	15.37	22.04	12.98	5.04
		(0.00)	(0.00)	(0.00)	(0.00)	(0.00)	(0.08)
	CVC-N	46.58	51.91	13.56	13.14	5.04	10.32
		(0.00)	(0.00)	(0.00)	(0.00)	(0.08)	(0.01)
	SC-S	46.58	35.41	10.75	10.75	5.04	1.20
		(0.00)	(0.00)	(0.00)	(0.00)	(0.08)	(0.55)
	CVC-S	39.36	22.60	5.04	3.52	2.23	0.46
		(0.00)	(0.00)	(0.08)	(0.17)	(0.33)	(0.80)
	MVN	32.77	22.04	10.05	10.05	10.32	10.05
		(0.00)	(0.00)	(0.01)	(0.01)	(0.01)	(0.01)
Traffic light classification	SC-N	Red	Red	Red	Red	Red	Yellow
	CVC-N	Red	Red	Red	Yellow	Yellow	Yellow
	SC-S	Red	Red	Red	Red	Yellow	Yellow
	CVC-S	Red	Red	Yellow	Yellow	Yellow	Green
	MVN	Red	Red	Yellow	Yellow	Yellow	Yellow

This table reports VaR backtests performed at the 1% level. The percentage of failure likelihood ratio (Kupiec, 1995) measures only unconditional coverage. The conditional coverage test (Christoffersen, 2012) is a simultaneous test of both the unconditional coverage and the independence properties of VaR violations. The traffic light approach is taken from the Basel II regulatory framework, where models are categorized as 'Red': unacceptable, 'Yellow': uncertain and 'Green': acceptable. SC-N is the Clayton standard copula (SC) with normal marginals, CVC-N is the Clayton canonical vine copula (CVC) with normal marginals, SC-S is the Clayton SC with Skew-T marginals, CVC-S is the Clayton CVC with Skew-T marginals and MVN is the multivariate normal model (benchmark case).

superior strategy results in a test statistic closest to zero. Following Christoffersen (2012), we report the p-values for these test statistics where the null hypothesis is that the portfolio/risk management model is correct on average.

Generally, we find that CVC-S and MVN are the best performing models across all portfolio sizes and that there is a large improvement when there are nine assets or more. At 12 assets, CVC-S shows a substantial performance improvement for PoFLR compared to MVN. For portfolios less than 12 assets, the PoFLR test statistic indicates similar performance between CVC-S and MVN. However, when we account for the independence property of VaR backtests using CCLR, CVC-S exhibits superior performance compared to MVN. We also observe that when the independence property is accounted for in the testing, the performance of MVN deteriorates across all portfolio sizes. For each of the other portfolio strategies that incorporate returns asymmetry in some form, we do not always observe an increase in the CCLR test statistic. In fact, for CVC-S, incorporation of independence testing has only a negligible impact, particularly in portfolios above six assets. Therefore, incorporation of return asymmetry in forecasting improves the independence property as the likelihood of having a sequence of VaR violations is reduced.

Based on a 10%[9] significance level for the PoFLR test statistic, CVC-S (MVN) is acceptable for portfolios of 11 and 12 assets (9, 10 and 12 assets). Based on the same statistic, SC-S is also acceptable for portfolios of 12 assets. However, applying the same significance level to the CCLR statistic (notably a stricter test), CVC-S is an acceptable model for portfolios of 10 assets and above, while MVN is now rejected across all portfolio sizes. SC-S remains acceptable using the CCLR test statistic for a portfolio of 12 assets.

As a third form of analysis we apply the 'traffic light' approach, taken from Basel (2004), in which risk management models are classified into three categories depending on the number of VaR violations. For our scenario of 450 out-of-sample periods, models with 13 or more VaR violations are within the 'Red' category. Models within the 'Green' category have less than 6 violations, those within the 'Yellow' category have between 6 and 12 violations. We find that all strategies perform poorly for portfolios of three and six assets. However, CVC-S and MVN improve dramatically for portfolio sizes of nine and above. CVC-S is the only strategy that achieves a 'Green' zone classification for the 12-asset portfolio.

Generally, for portfolios of three and six assets, the multivariate probability models do not perform well when VaR backtests are considered. However, our results continue to support the view that for portfolios of 10 assets and above, the CVC-S strategy improves portfolio decisions as there is reduced frequency and increased independence of VaR violations. This conclusion comes from the CCLR and the Basel (2004) traffic light tests.

11.4.2.6   Further Analysis of Time-Series Performance   Figure 11.4 shows the accumulation of wealth for all the strategies when the portfolio contains either 3 or 12 assets. In Figure 11.4(a), analysing portfolios of three assets, from 1973 to 1990, the portfolio management strategies perform similarly. Beyond 1991, simple portfolio strategies such as SC-N and MVN start to outperform the other models. MVN tends to outperform SC-N from 1993 onwards but experiences large losses in 2007. SC-N experiences lower losses and is able to recover its portfolio value from 2008 to 2010 to outperform MVN. Based on this analysis, for small portfolios the Clayton SC captures lower-tail dependence adequately and implementing the more complicated Clayton CVC is unnecessary.

We see in Figure 11.4(b) analysing portfolios of 12 assets, from 1973 to 1987, that all portfolio strategies perform similarly. From 1987 onwards, CVC-S begins to exhibit economic superiority by producing returns above those of other models. From 1993 onwards, CVC-N also begins to exhibit relative superiority over the other models (except for CVC-S). This figure shows that controlling for lower-tail dependence using the Clayton CVC and asymmetries within the marginals, the portfolio has the ability to insulate downside risk and, to some extent, protect the value of the portfolio with little loss to upside return. Within our data set after 1987, all indices exhibit high levels of negative skewness, whereas before 1987, about half the indices exhibit positive skewness. Thus, the use of CVC-S results in improved portfolio management when negative skewness is prominent. SC-N performs poorly for large portfolios as the single AD parameter in the Clayton SC asymptotes towards zero due to the size of the portfolio. However, as CVC-N captures asymmetries within the marginals it is less affected by the dilution of the AD parameter for large portfolios.

---

[9]Christoffersen (2012) recommends the use of a 10% significance level for practical risk management purposes because Type II errors (i.e., a failure to reject an incorrect model) can be very costly.

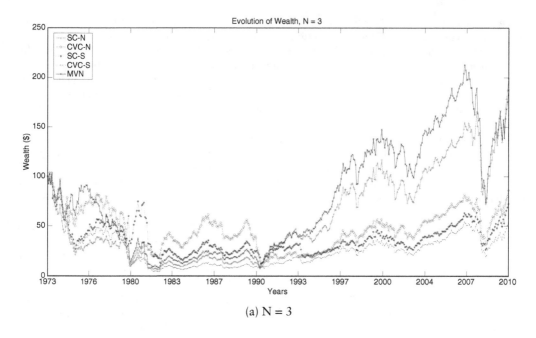

(a) N = 3

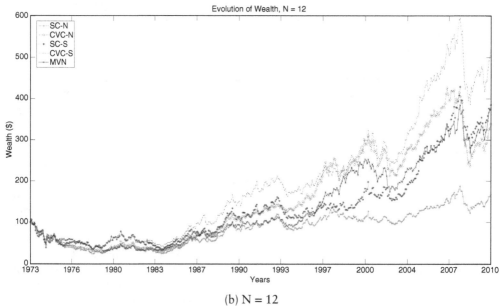

(b) N = 12

FIGURE 11.4   Pattern of wealth accumulation for out-of-sample copula-based portfolio strategies. This figure shows the accumulation of wealth from an initial hypothetical investment of $100 in each portfolio strategy at the start of the out-of-sample period for 3-asset and 12-asset portfolios. SC-N is the Clayton standard copula (SC) with normal marginals, CVC-N is the Clayton canonical vine copula (CVC) with normal marginals, SC-S is the Clayton SC with Skew-T marginals, CVC-S is the Clayton CVC with Skew-T marginals and MVN is the multivariate normal model (benchmark case).

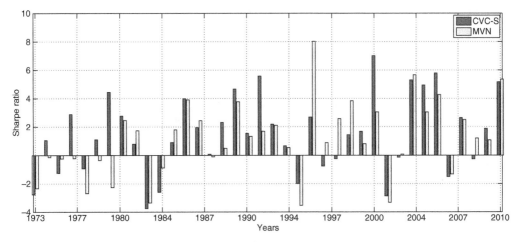

(a) Annual Sharpe ratio

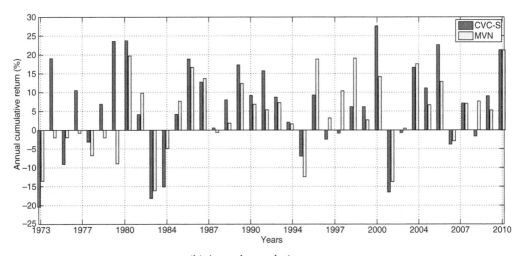

(b) Annual cumulative return

FIGURE 11.5 Annual Sharpe ratio and cumulative return, out-of-sample, for CVC-S vs. MVN models. This figure shows annual comparisons between the Sharpe ratio and annual cumulative returns between the CVC-S and MVN models. CVC-S is the Clayton canonical vine copula (CVC) with Skew-T marginals and MVN is the multivariate normal model (benchmark case).

Figure 11.5 shows the annual Sharpe ratios and cumulative annual returns for each year out-of-sample, focusing on CVC-S and MVN for portfolios of 12 assets. We can see that CVC-S often produces Sharpe ratios and upside gains greater than that of MVN. Notably, during the years 2000 onwards, compared to MVN, CVC-S mainly produces larger or similar Sharpe ratios and annual cumulative returns.

Figure 11.6 shows the difference in (hypothetical) end-of-year portfolio values between CVC-S and MVN (based on a hypothetical investment of $100 in each strategy at the beginning of each year).

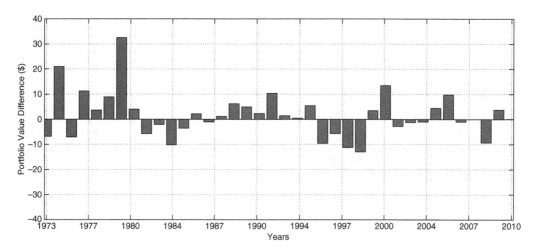

FIGURE 11.6 Difference in end-of-year portfolio value, out-of-sample, for CVC-S vs. MVN models. This figure shows the difference in end-of-year portfolio values between CVC-S and MVN annually. The end-of-year portfolio value of MVN is subtracted from CVC-S, based on a hypothetical investment of $100 in each strategy at the beginning of each year. CVC-S is the Clayton canonical vine copula (CVC) with Skew-T marginals and MVN is the multivariate normal model (benchmark case).

The difference in values at the end of each year is obtained by subtracting the portfolio value of MVN from CVC-S. Generally, we can see that CVC-S produces greater economic returns than MVN overall. Moreover, a majority of years favour the CVC-S strategy and the magnitude of the value difference tends to be higher in years when CVC-S outperforms MVN.

Table 11.8 shows the average annual differential across three alternative portfolio metrics for CVC-S minus MVN for the 'Whole', 'Crisis' and 'Normal' periods within the out-of-sample study. The 'Whole' period denotes the entire out-of-sample period, 1973 to 2010. The 'Crisis' years are identified as the bottom quintile of US market index monthly returns – that is, the 8 years that exhibit the largest frequency of the worst performing months.[10] The 'Normal' period consists of the remaining 29 years.

TABLE 11.8   Average annual out-of-sample performance differential between CVC-S vs. MVN models

Metric	Whole	Normal	Crisis
Sharpe ratio	0.33	0.27	0.56
Sortino ratio	0.63	0.49	1.14
Portfolio value	1.59	0.91	4.11

This table shows the average annual differential between CVC-S and MVN (i.e., CVC-S minus MVN) for the Sharpe ratio, Sortino ratio and end-of-year portfolio values generated annually by hypothetically investing $100 at the start of each year. 'Whole' denotes all years in the out-of-sample data set from 1973 to 2010. 'Crisis' denotes the annual subperiods constituting the bottom quintile of US stock market returns (i.e., the 8 worst performing years out of the entire 37-year out-of-sample period) and 'Normal' denotes the remaining annual subperiods in the out-of-sample data set. CVC-S is the Clayton canonical vine copula (CVC) with Skew-T marginals and MVN is the multivariate normal model (benchmark case).

---

[10]The 8 'Crisis' years identified are 1974, 1975, 1979, 1981, 1982, 1987, 1990 and 2008.

Across the entire out-of-sample period, on an average annual basis, CVC-S outperforms MVN by 0.33 when applying the Sharpe ratio. Given a focus on downside risk, the Sortino ratio indicates that CVC-S delivers a substantial performance advantage over MVN: the differential is 0.63. To complete the overall comparison, on average, CVC-S results in a higher dollar value of $1.59 per year based on hypothetically investing $100 at the start of each year.

Asymmetric dependence or excessive downside correlation across equity returns is more prevalent during bear markets or 'Crisis' periods. Thus intuitively, during such periods a strategy that explicitly manages AD should exhibit superior performance compared to strategies that do not. Interestingly, while we find that CVC-S exhibits superior performance during both 'Crisis' and 'Normal' periods, the superiority is greater during the 'Crisis' period. Specifically, during this part of our sample the Sharpe ratio of CVC-S is larger than MVN by a magnitude of 0.56, compared to 0.27 during the 'Normal' period. This effect is even more pronounced when we focus on downside risk: the difference in the Sortino ratio is 1.14 in favour of the copula-based strategy during 'Crisis' years and this differential is more than twice the value observed during 'Normal' years. Finally, when we focus on the average end-of-year portfolio value differences, CVC-S has a higher value of $4.11 during the 'Crisis' period compared to a smaller superiority of $0.91 during 'Normal' years (relative to $100 hypothetical investments occurring at the beginning of each year).

These results show further evidence that CVC-S, the strategy that incorporates AD using the Clayton CVC and skewness within the marginals, is able to produce superior forecasts of equity returns compared to competing models, leading to improved portfolio allocation decisions and enhanced performance.

11.5   CONCLUSION

In this study, we investigate whether using asymmetric copula models to forecast returns for portfolios ranging from 3 to 12 assets can produce superior investment performance compared to traditional models. We examine the efficient frontiers produced by each model and focus on comparing two methods for incorporating scalable AD structures across asset returns using the Archimedean Clayton copula in an out-of-sample, long-run multi-period investment. As traditional MVPT does not account for asymmetry in returns distributions, it is quite plausible that there is a need for more advanced portfolio management strategies that incorporate asymmetries within the forecasting process and during the optimization of the investor's utility function.

We find evidence that for portfolios of 10 assets and above, the Clayton CVC outperforms the Clayton standard copula (SC) across a broad range of metrics over a long-run, multi-period horizon. The most advanced model we implement, in which asymmetries within the dependence structure and marginals are modelled using the Clayton CVC and skewed Student t of Hansen (1994) (CVC-S), consistently produces statistical and economically significant gains superior to the other models tested, including the multivariate normal (MVN) model. Despite the strategy having high turnover requirements, even when transaction costs are incorporated, there are greater economic benefits relative to the other strategies. CVC-S also exhibits the best performance when a series of VaR backtests are applied to larger portfolios. Furthermore, it is able to consistently generate strong positively skewed returns for larger portfolios – a portfolio characteristic that is highly attractive to most rational investors. While the superiority of the CVC-S strategy over the traditional symmetric MVPT approach is generally seen across our sample, it is strongest during 'Crisis' years. This finding suggests that the CVC-S approach successfully manages AD compared to the other models tested.

In addition, our analysis shows that as the number of assets increases within the portfolio, modelling of the dependence structure across the assets has a greater impact. For smaller portfolios, modelling the asymmetry within the marginals themselves plays a more crucial role. The Clayton CVC produces superior statistical and economic outcomes compared to the Clayton SC for portfolios of six assets and above. Accordingly, we conclude that CVC copulas are 'worth it' when managing portfolios of high dimensions due to their ability to better capture asymmetries within the dependence structure than either the SC copula or multivariate normality models.

REFERENCES

Aas, K., Czado, C., Frigessi, A. and Bakken, H. (2009). Pair-copula constructions of multiple dependence. *Insurance: Mathematics and Economics*, 44(2), 182–198.

Aggarwal, R. and Aggarwal, R. (1993). Security return distributions and market structure: evidence from the NYSE/AMEX and the NASDAQ markets. *Journal of Financial Research*, 16(3), 209–220.

Ané, T. and Kharoubi, C. (2003). Dependence structure and risk measure. *Journal of Business*, 76(3), 411–438.

Ang, A. and Chen, J. (2002). Asymmetric correlations of equity portfolios. *Journal of Financial Economics*, 63(3), 443–494.

Ang, A., Chen, J. and Xing, Y. (2006). Downside risk. *Review of Financial Studies*, 19(4), 1191–1239.

Arditti, F.D. (1967). Risk and the required return on equity. *Journal of Finance*, 22(1), 19–36.

Ba, C. (2011). Recovering copulas from limited information and an application to asset allocation. *Journal of Banking & Finance*, 35(7), 1824–1842.

Balduzzi, P. and Lynch, A.W. (1999). Transaction costs and predictability: some utility cost calculations. *Journal of Financial Economics*, 52(1), 47–78.

Barberis, N. (2000). Investing for the long run when returns are predictable. *Journal of Finance*, 55(1), 225–264.

Basel II (2004). International convergence of capital measurement and capital standards. Basel Committee on Banking Supervision, June.

Cherubini, U., Luciano, E., Vecchiato, W. and Cherubini, G. (2004). *Copula Methods in Finance*. John Wiley & Sons, Chichester.

Christoffersen, P. (2012). *Elements of Financial Risk Management*, 2nd edn. Academic Press, New York.

Chua, D.B., Kritzman, M. and Page, S. (2009). The myth of diversification. *Journal of Portfolio Management*, 36(1), 26–35.

Cromwell, N.O., Taylor, W.R.L. and Yoder, J.A. (2000). Diversification across mutual funds in a three-moment world. *Applied Economics Letters*, 7(4), 243–245.

DeMiguel, V., Garlappi, L. and Uppal, R. (2009). Optimal versus naive diversification: how inefficient is the 1/N portfolio strategy? *Review of Financial Studies*, 22(5), 1915–1953.

Fleming, J., Ostdiek, B. and Whaley, R. (1995). Predicting stock market volatility: a new measure. *Journal of Futures Markets*, 3(15), 265–302.

Garcia, R. and Tsafack, G. (2011). Dependence structure and extreme comovements in international equity and bond markets. *Journal of Banking & Finance*, 35(8), 1954–1970.

Glosten, L.R., Jagannathan, R. and Runkle, D.E. (1993). On the relation between the expected value and the volatility of the nominal excess return on stocks. *Journal of Finance*, 48(5), 1779–1801.

Goetzmann, W., Goetzmann, J., Ingersoll, J. and Welch, I. (2007). Portfolio performance manipulation and manipulation-proof performance measures. *Review of Financial Studies*, 20(5), 1503–1546.

Hansen, B.E. (1994). Autoregressive conditional density estimation. *International Economic Review*, 35(3), 705–730.

Harvey, C.R. and Siddique, A. (2000). Conditional skewness in asset pricing tests. *Journal of Finance*, 55(3), 1263–1295.

Harvey, C.R., Liechty, J.C., Liechty, M.W. and Müller, P. (2010). Portfolio selection with higher moments. *Quantitative Finance*, 10(5), 469–485.

Hatherley, A. and Alcock, J. (2007). Portfolio construction incorporating asymmetric dependence structures: a user's guide. *Accounting and Finance*, 47(3), 447–472.

Ingersoll, J.E. (1987). *Theory of Financial Decision Making*. Rowman & Littlefield, Lanham, MD.

Joe, H. (1997). Multivariate Models and Dependence Concepts. Chapman & Hall, London.

Kane, A. (1982). Skewness preference and portfolio choice. *Journal of Financial and Quantitative Analysis*, 17(1), 15–25.

Kritzman, M., Page, S. and Turkington, D. (2010). In defense of optimization: the fallacy of 1/N. *Financial Analysts Journal*, 66(2), 1–9.

Kupiec, P. (1995). Techniques for verifying the accuracy of risk measurement models. *Journal of Derivatives*, 3, 73–84.

Kurowicka, D. and Joe, H. (2011). *Dependence Modelling: Vine Copula Handbook*. World Scientific, London.

Longin, F. and Solnik, B. (1995). Is the correlation in international equity returns constant: 1960–1990? *Journal of International Money and Finance*, 14(1), 3–26.

Longin, F. and Solnik, B. (2001). Extreme correlation of international equity markets. *Journal of Finance*, 56(2), 649–676.

Markowitz, H. (1952). Portfolio selection. *Journal of Finance*, 7(1), 77–91.

Merton, R.C. (1971). Optimum consumption and portfolio rules in a continuous-time model. *Journal of Economic Theory*, 3(3), 373–413.

Nelsen, R.B. (2006). *An Introduction to Copulas*. Springer, Berlin.

Patton, A.J. (2004). On the out-of-sample importance of skewness and asymmetric dependence for asset allocation. *Journal of Financial Econometrics*, 2(1), 130–168.

Patton, A.J. (2009). Copula based models for financial time series. *Handbook of Financial Time Series*, pp. 767–785.

Peiro, A. (1999). Skewness in financial returns. *Journal of Banking & Finance*, 23(6), 847–862.

Rockafellar, R.T. and Uryasev, S. (2000). Optimization of conditional value-at-risk. *Journal of Risk*, 2, 493–517.

Scott, R.C. and Horvath, P.A. (1980). On the direction of preference for moments of higher order than the variance. *Journal of Finance*, 35(4), 915–919.

Simkowitz, M.A. and Beedles, W.L. (1978). Diversification in a three-moment world. *Journal of Financial and Quantitative Analysis*, 13(05), 927–941.

Sklar, A. (1973). Random variables: joint distribution functions and copulas. *Kybernetika*, 9(6), 449–460.

Stock, J.H. and Watson, M.W. (1999). *Forecasting Inflation*. National Bureau of Economic Research, Cambridge, MA.

Swanson, N. and White, H. (1997). A model selection approach to real-time macroeconomic forecasting using linear models and artificial neural networks. *Review of Economics and Statistics*, 79(4), 540–550.

Uryasev, S. (2000). Conditional value-at-risk: optimization algorithms and applications. *Financial Engineering News*, 2(3).

Index